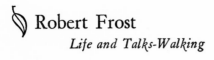

Robert Frost
Life and Talks-Walking

Robert Frost

Life and Talks-Walking

By Louis Mertins

University of Oklahoma Press : Norman

BY LOUIS MERTINS

Books of Verse
> *The Wishing Gate* (Chicago, 1919)
> *The Sumac Trail* (Chicago, 1919)
> *The Covered Wagon* (Chicago, 1921)
> *The Mail Cart Man* (Chicago, 1921)
> *Tales of Kettle's Shop* (Chicago, 1923)
> *A Voice Crying in the Wilderness* (Chicago, 1923)
> *The Baratarians* (Chicago, 1924)

Others
> *This Way Out* (New York, 1936)
> *Blue River Baptist Association Missouri,* Part I (Kansas City, Mo., 1947)
> *The Intervals of Robert Frost* (Berkeley, 1947)
> *Robert Frost: Life and Talks-Walking* (Norman, 1965)

This book is printed on paper designed for an effective life
of at least three hundred years and bearing the watermark
of the University of Oklahoma Press.

Library of Congress Catalog Card Number: 65-11238

Copyright 1965 by the University of Oklahoma Press, Publishing Division of the University. Composed and printed at Norman, Oklahoma, U.S.A., by the University of Oklahoma Press. First edition.

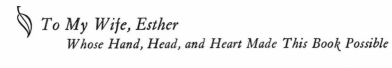 *To My Wife, Esther*
Whose Hand, Head, and Heart Made This Book Possible

Preface

FATE WAS WITH ME in 1932 when, as a perennial collector of literary matter in the field of writing, I sent a poem from my Long Beach, California, home to one of America's great poets, Robert Frost, in New England, for his autograph. To my surprise, the signed poem was returned to me from Monrovia, California—just thirty miles away. Temporarily the poet was residing in Monrovia, where he had come to be with his son, whose wife was seriously ill. When I called upon him, an immediate kinship developed, to be followed unfailingly through letters and conversations to within a few weeks of his passing.

During the frequent visits to his home in Monrovia, Frost revealed much of himself. This information was carefully kept in a diary. In the thirty years that followed, the conversations were continued in Boston, Hanover, Ripton, Amherst, and in California, when he was a family member in our home. As time passed, it seemed that this biographical material would have interest to many and should be preserved. To add local color, my wife and I visited all of his places of residence in the New England states, in England, and in San Francisco.

Frost loved to talk, and he loved to walk—and he was always happy when he could combine the two. He often mentioned the term "talks-walking" which he indicated he would like to use as the title of one of his books. Those who knew and understood the poet will agree that his "talks-walking" with those he called his friends stand alongside the recorded conversations between Plato and Aristotle. Frost was one of the greatest conversationalists of the twentieth century, as Aristotle was of the Golden Age of Greek culture. If some of the conversations of the poet have the aroma of gall and bitterness, such aroma should be taken lightly. His bark was always more dangerous than his bite. His scholarship was high. He was a perfectionist in his conversation as well as in his poetry and his prose. Frost was a lover of the woods and of the hills, and his best conversations were concerned with such, as was his poetry.

The material in this book is gleaned to a great extent from our "talks-walking." Because much of its content is personal and intimate in nature, it was agreed with him that it should not be published until after his death.

My thanks go to all my friends across the nation, who knowing of my interest in Frost have kept a steady stream of Frostana coming to my home. The list is too long to be recorded here, but my gratitude to all who helped me is not lessened. I wish to recognize especially Blanche Rankin Eastman, Frost's childhood nurse, for her information about the early years of his life; James Sloan, for his photograph of Robert Frost; Sylvia Clark for insights into the Derry interval; Dorothy Canfield Fisher, his neighbor in Vermont; Charles R. Green, of the Jones Library at Amherst; Norman Tiptaft, of Birmingham, England, for a trip through the West Midlands and to the Reverend J. E. Gethyn-Jones, of Dymock, who conducted us to Little Iddens and the homes of Frost's English friends and provided photographs; John Haines, who wrote long letters about Frost's stay in England; Wilbert Snow, Sidney Cox, Ray Nash, and other associates in New England; Lawrance Thompson and William Meredith, who traveled with Frost; Earl Cranston, who had an adjoining office at Dartmouth; Bruce McDaniel, who collected material on the Israel visit; Elmer Kingham, for his copies of the photographs; Eleanor Meyering, for the final typing of the manuscript; and my wife, to whom I dedicate this volume because of her devotion to every phase of its development.

LOUIS MERTINS

Redlands, California
April 15, 1965

Contents

 Illustrations

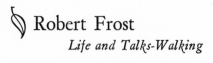 Robert Frost
Life and Talks-Walking

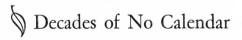 Decades of No Calendar

I. Pan with Us

My famous friend was dead.

I call him friend, for so he had set himself down on paper many times, in that bold but infinitely graceful handwriting, which once seen could never be forgotten.

Now his hand would write no more. Never again would we hold brotherly speech. His magnificent voice was silent, his warm heart stilled.

I fell to thinking of his long life so well spent, and the many times our lines had been cast together. I somehow could not believe him gone. Surely that vibrant personality could never die! It would continue to haunt old familiar places. It would live in the hearts of generations yet unborn, as long as men continued to love the land and the trees and to turn with affection toward bucolic things.

In an age when the classics were familiar, Robert would have been likened to Pan. He was of the very essence of the Arcadian deity—Pan truly with us, everywhere and forever. He recognized this while denying it. "I am not fey," he protested. Yet I never talked with him without my heart likening him to the god of the woods and the fields, remembering those lines he wrote in his youth, how "Pan came out of the woods," and

> . . . *stood in the zephyr, pipes in hand,*
> *On a height of naked pasture land;*

Lover of trees, lover of the land—Pan he is and will be, Pan smelling of the woods and the meadows, always a little earth upon his feet, and the dust of another world upon his head. Were there not hoofs under those leathern shoes—a mischief of woods and winds in his voice—a gleaming of the sun and stars in his eyes? If he were other than Pan, whence his knowledge, unfailing, of all the flora and the fauna of his native heath? If not Pan, how could he have known wind and weather, star and season, ice and fire?

That impish life of his had a beginning, which beginning was far away from the terrain with which he became so intimately associated in life. How we of the West sought to steal him away from New England! "I am a bridge-pier in the middle of the river," he admonished.

He was ours by right of birth; he belonged to Massachusetts by right of repatriation, to New Hampshire and Vermont from choice. There were older ties than umbilical geography. He would not be tempted westward. His roots were set in the hard, stony soil of New England where he must plow between the rocks he couldn't move.

And there were other and older roots, more ancient planting than California or New England. There may have been three hundred years of the latter, a meager decade of the former; but there was something beyond—a further range—something far back in another land, in another time. Only the *Domesday Book* stood a barrier between.

 Decade One

II. ONCE BY THE PACIFIC

RAIN, WIND, AND SEA!

It was just such an angry swell, on just such a wild day that Robert Frost remembered from the long years before. Five of us sat in a window facing the sea and the breakers at Cliff House—four of us wondering. Would the poet break the silence of threescore years and ten? Would he rend the veil which the years of New England expatriation had woven about the San Francisco boyhood of a California native?

The year was 1947, the month March. The four of us were trying sympathetic magic on him, taking him over the old haunts he had frequented as a lad—hoping the magic would work its charm. Over the roar of the breakers which dashed across the ancient monoliths we heard the cry of the seals and attempted to make them out on top of the black rocks.

"That's it," the poet exclaimed, coming out with one of his infrequent smiles, reserved for special occasions—and special people. "That's the barking of the seals I have carried in my memory all these years. The sea, the seals, the wind, the rain. They have come back to me nights when I was thousands of miles from here. I have thought it might have been a freak of the imagination. But there is the sound—the same sound of their cries I have remembered and recalled innumerable times."

The magic charm was working. Would he continue to think aloud for us?

In a moment, as if in answer to our unspoken question, he began again in a voice so low we had to strain to catch the words above the storm.

It was a very long time ago that it happened. It was before Coney Island had come in to spoil the beach here at the Cliff House. I was very small and very impressionable—a child full of imagination and phobias. I watched the big waves coming in, blown by the wind. I recall that I was playing on the sand with a long black seaweed, using it for a whip. The sky must have clouded up, and night begun to come on. The sea seemed to rise up and threaten me. I got scared, imagining that my mother and father, who were somewhere about, had gone away and left me by myself in danger of my life. I was all alone with the ocean water rising higher and higher. I was fascinated and terrorized watching the sea; for it came to me that we were all doomed to be engulfed and swept away. Long years after I remembered the occasion vividly, the feeling which overwhelmed me, and wrote my poem "Once by the Pacific."

There was the sea and the seal rocks and the dashing waves and the lowering sky—and here sat the little boy, grown a man, telling us all about it. Behind the spray-drenched window, the storm again threatening, the poet began those lines. That fine voice, elemental as the wind and wave, the spray and spume, was all mixed up with the storm. As he said the poem, the terror he had experienced and carried through the years almost overcame his listeners.

> *The shattered water made a misty din,*
> *Great waves looked over others coming in.*

I fancy there were four men more deeply moved that afternoon as they listened to Robert Frost saying those lines than they would willingly have admitted. To me, at least, his voice (obbligato to the storm, the wind, the sea) was a symbol of the poet's boyhood. I saw in it the picture of a drunken, irresponsible father, all the uncertainty of the life in the Frost household which had made Robert's childhood a nightmare. These things were reproduced in the picture of a small boy terrorized by the sea.

William Prescott Frost, Jr., and Belle Moodie paused long enough in their gypsying from house to hotel for their first child to be born on Friday, March 26, 1875.[1] They called him, after the boyhood idol of a "Copperhead" New England father, Robert Lee Frost. Never was the old adage about Friday's child being "loving and giving" better borne out. So, at 1630 Sacramento Street, San Francisco, in the turbulent epoch of gold, was born a great poet.

On the day of our sympathetic magic experiment in 1947, standing in the three-step stairway leading up to the house on the plot of ground on which once stood the poet's birthplace, his stubborn white hair blowing in the wind, his elfish face gleaming in good humor, Robert Frost talked.

I don't know how many houses my parents occupied during the twelve years they lived in San Francisco. My mother hated cooking and was a poor hand at it. She despised the drudgery of housekeeping and liked boarding in hotels. The company, the conversation of family hotels was to her liking. So, to please her, my father would move into one and stay till he got bored stiff with the same old banal talk on the same old themes, by the same dull boarders, every meal, every day, day after day, week after week. Then he'd put his foot down and we'd move into a house some place. After a time my mother would rebel and we'd find ourselves back in a hotel. I can remember six places where we lived, which makes one a year for all my remembering years.[2] I'm told we lived awhile at the Connonade. I recall very distinctly the Abbottsford house. It was run by a Scot, and came to be known as Brogan's Folly. While we lived there General Rosecrans was also a guest there. Then the Grace Terrace house, and twice at the Leavenworth house. But wherever we lived there was good

[1] Blanche Rankin Eastman, his childhood nurse, in 1947, and again in 1948, declared his birthday to be in 1874. Frost always gave 1875 in his autobiographical notices. The San Francisco newspapers for the months of March and April give no notice of a child born to the Frosts in either 1874 or 1875.

[2] Homes and occupations of W. P. Frost, Jr., in San Francisco: 1874, dwelling, 14 Eddy; 1875, reporter *Bulletin,* 1630 Sacramento; 1876, city editor, *Evening Post,* residence 502 Montgomery (address of *Post*); 1876–77, local editor *Post,* residence, 1630 Sacramento; 1877–78, journalist *Post;* 1878, local editor *Post,* residence Connonade hotel; 1879, journalist *Post,* residence 502 Montgomery; 1880, local editor *Post,* residence 3 Grace Terrace; 1881–82, business manager *Post,* residence Abbottsford house; 1882–83, journalist *Post,* Abbottsford house; 1883–85, journalist *Post,* 1404 Leavenworth.

·7

and proper food for us kids—green food and fresh milk. This much for California. We had very little bean porridge, hot or cold.

Our choice of a house was always made with an eye to transportation to and from downtown. We simply had to live on or near a cable-car line. The house where we stayed the longest was on Leavenworth. It was convenient to a cable line, and was handy, likewise, to the First Church of the New Jerusalem which was about a mile way. My mother had recently become a communicant of the Swedenborgian faith. Just a block down the street at 1506 Leavenworth lived the pastor, John Doughty. I remember Doughty's house and garden. I remember being in his Sunday school. If I am not mistaken the Indians had done something to his scalp when he was crossing the plains. He was a grave-looking man with a long beard and heavy cane.

Yes, I went to Sunday school all right, and stayed for church—or was it the other way around? I remember a fellow named Sanders—G. H. Sanders, I think. He led the singing. He was very impressive with his curly black beard, lining out the hymns. He was a man at that time about forty-five years of age. There were others, too, whom I recall. The librarian's name was Boynton, and he had charge of the long rows of books by Emanuel Swedenborg: *Heaven and Hell,* the *True Christian Religion,* and all the rest of that dreary, deadly stuff, as well as the books of the church library written by less sacrosanct authors. I can still see those long rows of heavy volumes by Swedenborg standing on the shelves, waiting for the theologically-minded to take them home and read them. Then I remember Pace, Hosmer, and Miller, though for what reason I have no idea.

Religion, I suppose, played quite a major role in my upbringing. You see my mother was a very religious woman.[3] She took church-going quite seriously. Born a Covenanting Presbyterian, she had me baptized first in that faith when I was very small. Then she switched to the Unitarians. Whether I was again baptized by them I have no way of knowing, though probably not. Finally she evolved into the Swedenborgian church, and I was again baptized, maybe twice, in the New Jerusalem faith. So I am sure I was twice, maybe three times, baptized before they were satisfied with it. I don't know how much John Doughty had to do with my mother's going into the First New Jerusalem church, but she was a great believer in him. All this baptizing and church and Sunday school going may have had a

[3] Mrs. Eastman had no memory of Belle Moodie being unduly religious.

bad effect on me. I did so much of it when young that I never felt any
call to continue it later in life.

However, I am inclined to think that the counteracting influence on me
was that of my father, who in religious matters was the exact opposite of
my mother. There was nothing she could have wished more than to make
a Christian out of him. While occasionally he would break down and go
to church and "get" religion, it never lasted. He was a born back-slider,
and was soon back in his old cussin' ways. The memory of New England
and all the stuffy blue-noses and their formal religion was with him, and
he associated the two together. The ugly Gothic building of the Sweden-
borgians to which he was now and then cajoled into going (it was located
as I remember on O'Farrell, between Mason and Taylor streets) took his
mind back to Boston, the national capital of Swedenborgianism.

Strict as she was, my mother was no prohibitionist, though she was
always getting my father to take the pledge. We always, in the San Francisco days, had a bottle of whisky in the house, but she hated and dreaded
what it did to my father. He had another failing that hurt her even worse.
She was a firm commandment-keeper and held to that one about taking
the name of the Lord your God in vain. Certainly she was provoked by
my father, who was always breaking her heart with his voluble profanity.
He had a genius for it, surpassing most others in a city famous for its eloquent cussers. He was a regular "bicycling Jesus" swearer. He could go
on for five minutes and not repeat a single oath.

He might have added unspoken, his own lines so appropos:

> *I own I never really warmed*
> *To the reformer or reformed.*

John Doughty often quoted poetry in his sermons and lectures at the
New Jerusalem church. One day he read moving lines calculated to stir
the imagination of an impressionable boy.

> *Spring came at last, with his vernal train*
> *Of balmy breezes and rainbow showers;*
> *And the sun upsprung in the sky again,*
> *And looked upon earth which so long had lain*
> *Denuded of verdure and flowers;*
> *And he said, O earth! be clothed once more—*

O flowers! your bridal colors don,
And lo, as he spake, from shore to shore,
The earth was mantled in robes of green,
And blossoms of every hue were seen,
Called forth by the voice of the sun.

We may look here for a part of that cloud out of which the poetry of Robert Frost was conceived, when in the coming years he wrote

Pan came out of the woods one day,
And stood in the sun and looked his fill
At wooded valley and wooded hill.

Was not the amazing memory of the young man unconsciously recovering out of the past that which the little boy had heard? Spirit and form are identical.

The Frost houses all seemed to have been located in a hollow. The home on Leavenworth, the poet's favorite, occupied no eminence. It stood on a slope, and being placed on the east side of the street, it at least got the afternoon sun. Above on the top of the hill was a community ball field which was high enough to overlook Nob Hill. On this notable day of sympathetic magic Frost stood on this hill and waved his hand. Memory again.

Here where all these houses stand now—all built after 1906—in my boyhood days was a great open space covered with weeds. It was the neighborhood playground. Here we played town-ball games, here we played all the other rowdy games boys know.

It was here that I challenged a boy bigger than myself to an endurance race. I suppose it was about the time my father was doing the same sort of thing, and I had been bragging. Our race was not patterned after his walkathon. It was a running race, the winner to be the one who held out the longest, the course being round and round this field. I had never understood why we didn't do a bit of cheating, cutting corners, and so saving energy, and making it appear on the surface as all right. There was no reason we couldn't as the runner was out of sight much of the time. It was a wild undertaking and we ran like demons, keeping it up till we were completely exhausted. The race, I recall, put me to bed.

Probably it was just before, maybe just after, that I boasted (still remembering my father and how brave and strong and enduring he was) that I could lick any two boys the size of one I named. The kids went out and brought in two boys. They didn't wait for me to jump 'em, but they jumped me first. I grabbed one around the neck and tried to gouge his eyes out. The other danced round and round, and when he had a chance would rush in and scratch me. I was pretty well all in when we were separated, and I had to be taken home. Apparently nobody won the fight. My mother sent for a doctor who fixed up my scratches and gouged eyes. I suppose I was a little devil.

You see I wanted to be like my father, who was always challenging somebody to some sort of trial by ordeal, or something. He wouldn't admit he was sick. He really had a bad case of tuberculosis, and, as my Aunt Blanche Eastman, who lived with us then, and took care of us kids, said, I was always a weakly child, never very strong. Probably I had a touch of it myself, only they didn't have X ray then. If they had they probably would have found patches on my lungs. I knew how bravely my father was fighting the disease, how he took long walks and swam great distances, sticking out his chin for all comers.

I take it this explains why, as a kid, I would always bring up as a real fighter—able to give and take. I have a lot of memories of such. At Nicasio one vacation we stayed with a man named MacKenzie. I played croquet with his daughter, who was about my own age. One day we got into an argument and before I knew it she had whacked me over the head with a mallet. Didn't put me out, but raised a lump big as a hen-egg. I never let on. I was afraid my father would make fun of me and call me a sissy.

We went oftener to near-by Sausalito than to any other resort for our vacations, so I have many more memories of this place than of any of the others. I never knew why my father wanted me to always be in a fight—unless to make me rugged. I have a memory of walking on the Sausalito beach with my father and four other men. One of these was a fellow named O'Donnell, my father's friend. O'Donnell had a son about my age, but not my friend. We fought on the beach like prize fighters. They'd put gloves on us and egg us on, and we'd pummel one another till we cried. I wanted to please my father—nothing else much mattered.

He was my idol, my ideal. Being sick a great deal, he did all that was humanly possible to make himself strong and well—all except to live a normal, temperate life. He was forever exhausting himself with one form of violent physical exercise or another. He even challenged the champion

· II

walker, Dan O'Leary, and they competed in a six-day walking race. My father really won, and O'Leary admitted it to him in private. But an amateur had no standing, and so couldn't claim to defeat the champ. The papers were full of it all the time. You see, to be a man I felt that I had to do all these things, too. This kept me in a fight with somebody all the time.[4]

Then there was school, of which Robert admitted he saw very little in San Francisco. He recounted his almost negligible experience with schools and teachers, being egged on by the recurring fear he had experienced at Cliff House.

It certainly was not physical fear that I had as a boy. Nor have I ever made up my mind whether all my dread of being left someplace and not picked up at the proper time, or my adult anxiety about missing a train, or being late to a lecture or something, came from the incident on the beach at the Cliff House, or the time I went to Mme Zitska's School. This was a private school not many blocks from our house, and my mother thought it a good idea for me to go. The kids were all picked up in a horse-drawn bus. When night came the driver couldn't find our house, and we rode around a long while looking for it. I was badly frightened, thinking I would never see home again. So next morning I refused to go, and my private-school days were over.

I had one teacher I remember very well. She was a Miss Fisher and taught in the public school on Washington. Whenever I went to school it was mostly to her. I remember she punished me when she caught me crawling along on the floor and stealing valentines from the desks of the girls. Some older boys probably put me up to it, though I wasn't too hard to persuade, likely.

I have always come by schools and colleges naturally. My father was graduated from Harvard with honors. He won the Bowdoin prize. He wore a Phi Beta Kappa key. It was teaching that brought my parents together. When he finished school my father's one thought was to get as far away from Massachusetts as possible, so he started west. His first stop was to earn some money by teaching in an academy in Lewistown, Pennsylvania. He wanted to escape the domination of my grandparents, escape

[4] Mrs. Eastman did not remember Robert's fights, which may be explained by the fact that she married and removed to Napa while he was very small.

from slavery. Grandfather was a pro-Confederacy New Englander in Civil War days. He and my father were always in trouble over the draft. Cotton was king in Lawrence as well as New Orleans, for the little spools in the mills along the Merrimack all would have been idle with no threads to pull them but for cotton. I suppose they talked too much. I know they wanted the South to win against the North. That was how I got my name.

My mother left Edinburgh for Columbus, Ohio, where she had kinfolks, about the time my father was ready to leave Lawrence. She came of the Orkney Island Moodies. She landed at the mouth of the Delaware River and the ship kept right on up the stream into the Schuylkill, past Reading, Pottsville, Pottstown, Norristown. There is a tradition in the family of my mother just from Scotland sitting alone on the deck as the boat nosed through the peach country, while the people on shore tossed lovely ripe peaches to those on shipboard. My mother, as the story goes, got a peach and sat quietly looking at it as it lay in her lap. When somebody asked why she didn't eat it, she replied, "Oh, it's too bonnie to eat," which would be very like her.

By a strange fate my father and mother landed jobs in the same academy at Lewistown, Pennsylvania. They were married soon, and my father came on to California to get located in newspaper work, writing. Next year, after he got a job on the paper and was settled, she followed. The year after I came along.

In spite of all this educational background I hated school and wouldn't go if I could play off sick, or get up some other excuse. So I was mighty glad when, in the Cleveland campaign, my father took me out of school to make me copy boy on the San Francisco *Post,* of which he was editor, political editor. Schools in San Francisco made little impression on me. I do remember that I always had to have my little sister Jeanie tagging along with me when she got big enough for school. That is a burden no small boy hankers to bear.

There were other, and not too good, influences exerted on me. My idol among the equivalent of the Dead End kids of that day was a gang-leader in our community, a fellow named Balso, bad fellow. Later he was to serve time in San Quentin. I must say he already had a good start when I first knew him, and followed him around, and worshipped him as a first-class crook to be emulated, followed. At fifteen he was smoking opium. He stayed my ideal, and I was all set for a life of crime until, before a great while, the police picked him up for some petty theft and hauled him off to jail. That ended it. I reasoned that he must have been a very sorry success, and that maybe the dividends of crime were not what they had been touted. My idol had been smashed.

Balso was ring-leader in a pig-stealing escapade we got into. We all went swimming on the north shore and got tar all over our bodies. We really had a terrible time trying to get it off. To wind up the day we swiped a pig from some Irishman's sty and sold it for ninety cents. My part of the swag was fifteen cents, one of the very few profits I ever made out of crime—unless farming and writing poetry are crimes.

When I was a youngster my father was very strict about my staying in nights. He never minded my robbing and tearing around day times, but nights I had to be home in bed. Lying there in the darkness, not able to get to sleep, like a tom cat itching to be out in the night tom-catting around, I could hear the kids out doors playing, and yelling, and I'd grit my teeth and want to be out. They would play a game I never got to play because of this strict night rule—"Tally-ho." Lying there I'd listen to 'em. They'd come right up and even get into your cellar, calling "Tally-ho!"

I was always inquisitive and wanted to see what made the wheels go round. San Francisco in those days was a town full of gamblers, crooked politicians, sportsmen, and whores. I walked alone one day clear through whore town, when I was about ten, just to see what it was like. My father probably could have told me a lot more about it than I could see. I had not yet learned how poets like François Villon put that sort of thing into verse. There were never any Blanches, Jehannetons, or Guillemethes known to me. My whore house education was always a surface one only.

When we lived at No. 3 Grace Terrace, my father used to send me for cigarettes several blocks away. I'd walk down the hill past St. Mary's church. I have another, and very unpleasant memory of the Grace Terrace house. The landlady had a very mean son whom she would whip unmercifully. I can remember him lying on the floor screaming while she beat him with a black-snake whip. I haven't heard of anybody beating their children that way in a generation. My memory of a happy childhood is of the kindness and gentleness of both my parents. We were never punished by whipping. There were ways.

At night, in his boyhood, Frost never tired of looking on the lights as they came on all over the city. In every direction he could watch the busy lamplighters at their evening task. Constellations formed by gas jets matched the dimmer ones in the sky—of which he was later to write as he looked "up at the constellations by chance." Now and then, though more rarely, forest fires on Mount Tamalpais held him in thrall.

On special days he visited the zoo at Woodward's Gardens, where he was entranced by the pelicans and pink-billed swans and by the brook, diverted from Harmen tract and MacClane's lane and made to flow through the park. Memories of Woodward's Gardens came to flower in future days when he wrote the poem of that name. What nine-year-old boy "presuming on his intellect" could resist scorching the noses of the monkeys with his burning-glass? It must have been a very vivid memory which young Robert had of the theft of his glass at the hands of the tiny simians, "arms laced together at the bars," ending with a "sudden flash of arm, a snatch, and the glass was the monkey's, not the boy's." Standing open-mouthed before the cage, not without a chuckle, despite his loss, he watched as they "bit the glass and listened for the flavor." "It's knowing what to do with things that counts," was his sage conclusion, showing a philosophy far out of reach of an adolescent boy.

Often he would climb the hills accompanied by his little terrier. He would stand for hours looking on the waters of the Golden Gate, watching the water turn from drab to bright blue, then again to green and mottled gray, at sunset to flaming crimson and cerise. Some days there would creep wispy wraiths of fog through the Golden Gate. Or now and then clouds would form about the base of mighty Tamalpais. It was in those years, with dust always blowing about the town that he was

> *One of the children told*
> *Some of the blowing dust was gold.*

Memories of the house on Leavenworth Street stayed green to the end. It was here in the backyard that he decided to become a farmer. Here he raised a vegetable garden and kept chickens at the same time—the work of a genius! Out of this experience came his lifelong feel for the soil.

In the Frost home, life was a serious matter. Many a house had been made livable by singing. It was common in that generation for parents and children to gather round the parlor organ and sing hymns and ballads. Not so here. There was no singing in this San Francisco household. Neither parents nor children, so far as anybody's memory went, made music a part of living.

Odd things were always happening. There is the impossible story of Horace Fletcher and the little ivory man and puzzle. Frost tells it, exhibiting the little recovered puzzle.

There was a man named Horace Fletcher in San Francisco. He had lived in Lawrence, Massachusetts, where he was born, but ran away from home and school as a boy, to follow the sea. After spending almost a generation at sea, and becoming master of his own craft, he put into port at San Francisco, sick of sailing. With a cargo of gimcracks and gewgaws on board, collected mainly from India, China, and Japan, he started an antique shop down on the water front.

Being from the same town, he and my father soon became fast friends, and many times I went down to the shop with my father. One day Fletcher gave me a little ivory man and a little ivory double jig-saw puzzle that fitted together after much contriving. Somewhere in the United States I lost those two boyhood prizes. I hunted for sixty years before I found the puzzle. (Now I have ways of knowing it to be the one I lost—good reasons!) Found it in an antique shop in Key West, Florida. I'm still looking for my little ivory man. Somewhere, somehow, someday I know I'll find it, if I live.

This fellow Fletcher sold out his stock of antiques and went back east. There he started a diet cult. His chief tenet was that people don't chew their food fine enough. Bolt it down. Today you'll find even in standard dictionaries the word "to fletcherize," named for him, meaning to masticate what you eat, over and over, not regurgitate, I take it. Strange thing about him. He thought he had solved the problem of digestion through chewing. But the thing, I'm told, that took him off at last was a spell of indigestion. Funny.

Then there was the finding of his Aunt Blanche, a woman who helped bring him up. On the occasion of the University of California charter-day banquet a waiter handed him a note. It was signed "Blanche Eastman." When the poet made his way to her apartment the next day, he was met by a lively, active woman who had kept her beauty through ninety-five years of strenuous life. She called him "Bob" as she had called the little boy she knew nearly seventy years before.

Blanche Eastman, nee Rankin, was the connecting link between Robert Frost and his San Francisco childhood. She alone remained of all those who knew him intimately as a San Francisco boy. She had known Belle Moodie when Robert's mother taught high school in Columbus, Ohio, where she lived with her uncle and her favorite cousin, Jeanie Moodie.

Robert was always sure a cloud must have come over the married life of his father and mother which caused his mother to leave San Francisco when she became pregnant late in 1875 and return to the Frost family in Lawrence early in 1876. One may assume that this visit of Belle Moodie to her husband's parents made her better understand the follies and foibles of her errant husband. William Prescott Frost, Sr., was a dominating tyrant, his wife, Judith Colcord, a termagant. However, despite all this, once there she stayed in the Frost home until the baby came. She gave her the name of Jeanie for a cousin.

There was more to the visit than this. The elder Frosts were none too cordial to their son's wife, blaming her for his irregularities of living, his gambling and drinking. Their attitude sent her back to face whatever had to be faced. She had journeyed to Massachusetts for advice and comfort. She received none of the latter, little of the former. They told her that if she had been a good wife none of the things for which she blamed their impeccable son would have happened. They taunted her with the fact that a fine New England girl had died of a broken heart who would have made him a suitable wife.

It was this eastern trip made by his mother with him along that started off the conversations between Frost and his old nurse.

FROST: I have never understood a certain memory I have. It must have been on our way back to the coast from Ohio, when you came along with us. It is a memory of being dragged out of an upper berth by a leg, and of huddling beside a railroad track in the darkness—pitch darkness. All our luggage was piled about us—a memory of something being badly wrong. Did this, or something like this, happen, or did I just dream it all up?

MRS. EASTMAN: It happened all right. Belle brought you and Jeanie from Lawrence to Columbus, where I lived. She and I were together a great deal, for I had known her before she was married. I kept secretly saying to myself, "I'm going to California—I'm going to California." One day Belle was troubled in her calm way, and said to me, "Blanche, I don't see how I'm ever going to make it back to the coast with these children, all alone without anybody to help me." Then I told her I would be glad to go along and help with the babies. This pleased her very much, and she said if I would she would send to her husband for the money for my ticket and berth. She wrote at once, and I began to make preparations to go along. The money came; we bought the tickets; and then I broke the news to my father. I had been dreading to do it. It was on Thanksgiving day, 1876. The snow lay white on the ground. Belle had taken the children on down to Cincinnati, telling me to follow. So, with my trunk all packed I asked father if he would rope it for me. When I answered his question by telling him I was going to California he was angry and said I shouldn't go. But I was just as firm and said I'd rope it myself, for I was going. Next day I left for Cincinnati. The four of us took the train from there on Saturday morning, December 1, 1876. The memory you have carried all these years was of a thing which happened the first night out. We somehow had got on the wrong train, and in the middle of the night had to change. In our hurry I dragged you out of the upper berth, just as you say you remember. You had already gone to sleep. We were all bundled out into the darkness beside the railroad track, baggage piled all about us, and there we waited for a train to pick us up. You were two years and nine months old—just two years older than Jeanie.

Frost: As I recall Jeanie was crying, I was crying, and we were all cold and uncomfortable and nervous—that is all but my mother. I always remember her as being composed. I haven't too good a recollection of the way she looked then, except her long hair.

Mrs. Eastman: She was always a very calm and quiet woman, but very, very odd. Your memory of her long hair is correct. She wore it in two long braids. The year I lived with your family and took care of you and your sister, Belle and I would go very often to the theater and leave Will as baby-sitter. Being a newspaperman he got tickets to all the plays, just as he got passes on the railroad for you on your summer vacations. She never, to my knowledge, was interested in politics, but she was always interested in the theater. She never, so far as I ever knew, wrote reviews of the plays for the paper, as you say she did. Well, as I was saying, when we would get back from whatever show we had been attending—we went to everything going—late at night we'd find Will sitting in the front room at the table, clippings of all the newspaper exchanges piled all about him, getting ready for the next day's issue. He would be surrounded by empty beer bottles, and his work well done. Belle would start telling him about the play, and would absent-mindedly pull off her hat and coat and pile them right on top of his clippings, so that they would lie in the stale beer spilled on the table. He wouldn't say anything, just lay them aside. I would pick the clothes up and put them carefully away, Belle not even noticing it. She never knew whether her clothes were soiled, or on straight, or not. When she taught in Columbus, I remember her walking down the street, clothes not any too neat, pencil in her hair (done up on top of her head) just as it had been all day. No, she never took care of her clothes. Once she said to me, "Blanche, you know I can't understand how this coat has kept nice so long." I didn't tell her it was because I would pick it up and put it away every time she came home and threw it down just any place, more than likely on the floor.

FROST: My mother must have had a lot to put up with in those days. I have hazy memories of things not altogether right. Maybe all this had its effect on me, I don't know. I couldn't see anything amiss in my father. If he ever had any unprincipled crookedness, it didn't filter down to my knowledge. I was a hero-worshiping son. My grandparents paid us one visit, coming out not too long before my father died. It did them no good, though. They were very anxious to see how we were making out. They wanted to see us children, and of course their own son. They wrote that they were starting west and would be in San Francisco on such and such a day. My father was very angry. He declared he'd not stay to see them. He told my mother he had business over in Sacramento for the paper, and that the business would last till they had gone back east, and for her to let him know when they were actually on the train going east, and then he would come home. They came, visited my mother and us kids, and then went on back home without seeing their own son. They never had another chance on earth to see him alive. He was not what you might call a filial son. As to husband, I have often wondered.

MRS. EASTMAN: Your father was not cruel to Belle, nor could I say he was good to her. As for his showing affection for her, he was too selfish to be affectionate. He certainly was a caution. I can see him now, sitting at the table telling us with a laugh how he used to fool his mother, your grandmother. She wasn't any too easy to get along with. She held a tight rein over her husband and her high-strung son. She insisted on Will being in bed every night by ten o'clock. He would do his lessons, yawn, say good night and go up, presumably to sleep. She would listen. First she heard a shoe drop. Then at just about the proper moment later a second one. She would heave a sigh and go to bed. In a little while, so Will would tell us, he would slip out the window, down a rope ladder, shoes in hand and go out to make a night of it. I would say Will's whole attitude toward life was one of irreverence—irreverence in everything but religion. In that he was indifferent. He was always laughing at people and things, always jesting about everything. He was, of course, head over heels in politics, but he even laughed at that.

FROST: On the matter of my father fooling my grandmother into thinking he was going to bed when he would slip out to make a night of it, he carried the same thing to Harvard. The college authorities caught him running round nights when he got into a very bad scrape, that even his uncle, grandfather's brother, had a terrible time getting him out of. I have never understood why he wasn't expelled. One night he impersonated an officer and tried to shake down the madam of a house of ill-fame, demanding $500 or $1,000 for protection. His scholarship, I suppose, and his uncle's influence, saved him. I have often wondered if perhaps my father's penchant for trying to get rich quick might not have been his downfall in politics. I know it lured him into the game of crooked politics in a city of very crooked, unprincipled politicians, heads I win, tails you lose, sort. I have no proof—only a suspicion—but I have always thought he was a go-between for the politicians and the railroad officials. Maybe that explains all those railroad tickets he used.

MRS. EASTMAN: Yes, he was a problem, Will was. But he did all in his power to make you children happy. There were the summer vacations—Mill Valley, Sausalito, San Jose, Napa, Santa Cruz, Nicasio. You and Jeanie were two summers with me in Napa Valley. I remember well those summers and how you'd ask me to read to you. The reading would bring up all sorts of questions—serious questions for your age—questions about science, history, nature. I'd do the best I could to answer them. You'd look puzzled and say, "Aunt Blanche, wait a minute. Let me get this straight. Say that over slowly for me." And I would repeat. You were always deep in your thinking, but slow to get it.

FROST: I'm still slow.

Thus was painted a backdrop for the stage on which the show might cause the figure of the boy, Robert Frost, to be projected into the man he was to become.

III. POLITICIAN AT ODD SEASONS

ROBERT FROST treasured the memory of the 1884 political campaign in San Francisco as a bright spot of his childhood. He never forgot the wild excitement of the final celebration on Market Street when the tardy returns showed that Blaine had gone down to defeat before Cleveland.

He was not quite ten, but he had had a part in electing a President of the United States. As copy boy in the editorial offices of *The Evening Post,* of which his father had been variously editor, business manager, and political and local editor, he was in the maelstrom of things. The victory, therefore, was his, and his the right to claim spoils. So, he rode on the shoulders of his soul-weary, body-tired father in that parade when unterrified Democrats howled themselves hoarse, walked themselves into exhaustion, and drank themselves into insensibility.

All this did not take place overnight, nor without long preparation and many years' work. Will Frost had scarcely promised to love, honor, and cherish Belle Moodie in Lewistown, when, after the fashion of Frost ancestors before him, he left her at the altar.

The exile's idea was to get as far away from Boston and the strict regimen he had been held to as was humanly possible and still remain on American soil. The city of San Francisco offered new vistas. Its stirring history had begun with the forty-niners, but the city was now vastly changed from the bedraggled hamlet which in 1849 stretched along the bay shore. It had become a fabulous metropolis where anything might happen—usually did.

Financial San Francisco was still fabulous when Will Frost started work on its newspapers in 1873, but by 1881 he saw the boasted stocks worth $200,000,000 dwindle to a paltry $17,000,000. In such a day he began his journalistic career, as cub reporter on *The Bulletin,* and became adept at the use of the current Frisco slang.

Almost synchronous with the arrival of Will Frost was the advent of
Denis Kearney, one of the most picturesque characters of the period.
He was synonymous with sand-lot-ism. The sand-lot meetings held by
Kearney, and covered as one of the earliest assignments for the paper
by Will Frost, had as their object what his battle cry suggested—"Drive
out the chinks."

Early in his career Will Frost came under the influence of Bret Harte
and Mark Twain. Although absent, their ghosts haunted old corners.
A third whose influence was discernible in the New Englander's career
was Henry George, at the moment editing his own journal, *The Evening Post*. Next to Henry George, if not even ahead of him, came Ambrose
Bierce as the great influence in style and disposition.

It is hard to think of the San Francisco of the seventies and eighties
without thinking of Bierce. To seek to give a quantitative analysis of
the influence of Bierce upon Will Frost would be a foolish undertaking.
The two men had nearly everything in common. Both had forsworn
their blood kin; both hated the genealogy that produced them as well
as all members of their immediate family, with one exception—Bierce
had a lingering affection for one brother. Both worshiped the feudalism
of the Old South, wished for the return of status quo ante bellum as
it had obtained in the Old Dominion. Both developed a misanthropic
pessimism that held no good thought for the future of the race.

Will Frost's background was just such as would make him at home
in the rough-and-tumble of San Francisco journalism and politics. All
he ever asked was a fair field and no favors. All he ever got was an
unending series of hard knocks and heartbreaking disappointments.

Not a great while before the ill-starred Tilden-Hayes campaign,
Henry George, gambling in stocks, lost control of his child, *The Post*.
Under the new owners it became a rabid Republican sheet. To such a
newspaper was called as editor Will Frost, a States'-rights Democrat,
unashamed of being dubbed a "Copperhead." Scarcity of money in an
underpaid profession probably caused him to accept every new economic
theory that came along. This doubtless influenced him, as Robert has
said, to take a job on the side, writing for *The State*. While waiting for
his boat to come in, Henry George organized this weekly newspaper

to exploit the single tax. He invited Will Frost to contribute articles. These articles remained unsigned, but in the eleven numbers of the paper from April 5 to June 14, 1879, there were many which were the work of the editor of *The Post*.

Very early a dark shadow fell across the Frost existence.

In the annals of American politics, boss rule of great cities has long been a stench in the nostrils of right-thinking men and women. Will Frost (the authority being no less a person than his illustrious son) was the bond servant of Chris Buckley, the blind Democratic boss of San Francisco.

> I suppose my father was a grafter, boodler. At least he wanted to be whether he ever was able to realize on his desires or not. He associated all the time with crooked politicians. It was taken as a matter of course. In fact, in those days graft was not looked down on. Getting caught was the only crime. However, he never raked in any of the spoils. He had become embittered with life, having been disappointed in everything he tried to accomplish. Such a condition made him an easy mark for a fellow like Buckley. He wanted to be treasurer of San Francisco, county or city —for no other reason I can explain except to have access to the money. How he planned to get any of it I have never figured out.

> All I know is that he soon became the willing slave of the blind boss, rushing to do his every bidding without question. He was always expecting to be named to some important post. The appointment never came. Illness took hold of my father, and that was the end. There were many times when Buckley could have helped him, opened doors. There were many openings filled by mediocre men. But my father stayed out in the cold without reward, a crushed man.

This was the shadow which fell across the Frost threshold. Once in Buckley's power, Will Frost's soul was no longer his own. The clever manipulations of the boss twisted the editor around his little finger, softened the anti-boss policy of *The Post*. "Bosses are bad," an editorial in this newspaper set forth, "but San Francisco, as bosses go, has the best of the lot." This appeared just after Buckley had returned from New York, where his purpose had been division of spoils with the newly elected President of the United States.

It was at the behest of the blind boss that Will Frost entered state politics in 1880. Buckley made it easy for him to become a delegate to both the state and national conventions that year. He had no idea he was being sold down the river.

When a shake-up came in the paper the following year, Will Frost had come of age in journalism. The trustees of *The Post* made him business manager. His salary was increased proportionately. Established as business manager of the paper, Will Frost had time to consider political ambitions. Undoubtedly the boss, after the manner of his kind, held out the hope that he might make the newspaperman county or city treasurer. As late as 1882 the blind boss continued playing with his henchman. He still needed him to represent him at court, and *The Post* was by no means without influence. Later, when the henchman failed to win in his race for congress in the first district, he did not leave *The Post* but was summarily demoted from business manager to "journalist."

It was at this time that Boss Buckley, perhaps as a sop for his pride, called on Will Frost to become city campaign manager for the Democratic party in San Francisco. He threw his whole strength and energy back of the Governor of New York. The job he did in carrying the city for Cleveland showed the force he possessed.

If we grant that surroundings and circumstances and events affect the life and style of the man, we must look to the newspaper offices and free-lunch saloons of Robert Frost's boyhood for whatever contribution they made. One cannot separate the lives of father and son in this period. Although he was under ten, little Bob was the shadow of Will Frost.

During his journalistic career there was one saloon which remained the rendezvous of Will Frost and his friends. It was located on Bush Street, the very center of the newspaper district. His son recalled it in minute detail:

> It was west of Montgomery on Bush, on the left as you went up from the bay. In my memory it all seems marble, glittering with lights, with chandeliers swinging from high ceilings, great mirrors, clinking glasses, lovely pictures. They told me one of the pictures was worth twenty-five thousand dollars. These things are in my memory; of course it was prob-

ably cheap and loud, its pictures bawdy and coarse; but to a nine-year-old boy it was all very grand. There was a long free-lunch counter loaded with the best food anybody ever ate. That was where I had my noonday meal every day, eating mine while my father drank his. I was happy because I didn't have to go to school. I was freed from the drudgery of study and classroom work, and could run my errands in the newspaper office and eat my lunch at the Bush Street saloon. It was all very wonderful for a boy. Whenever I hear people talking about what a horrible place a saloon is, I always call to mind the many happy hours I spent in this one and say: "The saloons *I* knew as a boy in San Francisco were certainly a different sort—rather nice places I should call them. And I ought to know—I grew up in one."

This saloon was run by a fellow named Abe Levy, who, as I remember, had the first Punch and Judy show I ever witnessed. It was the old-fashioned sort with a little stage framed off, the puppets worked from below by the operator's hands. As I recall, it was the kind that came to the west from China with Marco Polo, and not the more classy marionette type of the French, worked from above by wires, or strings. To this day I recall Punch's squeaky voice, how he knocked his wife out, and was himself gobbled up by the devil.

Then, I remember perfectly the war of the kites. The air was filled with them. Just how it all started I never was told, never knew. But everybody had a kite in the air who was anybody. There were American kites and Chinese kites. Probably the Americans stole their ideas from the Chinese, who were always kite fliers. Some put broken glass in the tails of their kites to destroy the enemy's kite. It grew to be almost a craze.

All that year of 1884, with the little boy of nine by his side, the stormy petrel of *The Post* led the Cleveland forces. One of the boy's tasks was to carry campaign cards into saloons and with tack and silver dollar impale them on the ceiling. His father left no trick untried to carry California for Cleveland. In fact, he even engaged in a personal solicitation of votes, trying to persuade the Reverend John Doughty to disregard his lifelong Republicanism and vote for Cleveland.

The day following the election it looked as if all the efforts which cost so much to Will Frost had been in vain. Despite the frenzied exertions of himself and millions of Democrats all over the United States, it appeared that the country had gone for Blaine. With little Robert's hand clutched in his own on the night of November 6, he carried the eight-sheet paper home with him. *The Post* announced that the Democratic leaders had conceded victory to the G.O.P.

Then came the great and heartening reversal. Blaine's majority began to fade, Cleveland's to emerge. When *The Post* came out on November 10 with the headline, "A Glorious Time—San Francisco Democrats celebrate their great Victory—the Streets Alive with Paraders—The Festive Rooster and the Unmelodious Fish-horn—Midnight Scenes," Robert reported proudly to little Jeanie all he had seen and been privy to.

Time, Saturday night at dusk, recounted *The Post*. Democratic hordes rallied. Jovial, jolly, jubilation. The two parties to be congratulated on their actions. All seemed to concede the victory. The parade marched from committee headquarters on Stockton Street, and amid a babel of bands, tin-horns and pans, down Market and Kearney, thence to California by way of Montgomery, back to Market.

Perched on his father's shoulders, Robert was wild with enthusiasm with all the rest. The journalist scarce had strength to receive the congratulations of Boss Buckley for a job well done. This was to be his last public appearance.

It was all very glorious, but something was happening. A long-present enemy had called up re-enforcements. Doctors might advise Will Frost to leave off smoking and drinking, to eat beefsteaks raw, roast beef rawer, to drink cod-liver oil. But there was a shorter way than cod-liver oil and abstemiousness. He would drink fresh blood at the packing-house. So a memory stayed with the poet of going with his father and watching him down glass after glass of the black blood right from the slit throat of cow or steer in the shambles.

Will Frost lingered on all winter following his after-election collapse and well into the spring of 1885. In March he rallied enough to take an interest in the President's inauguration in Washington.

Robert's days of freedom from school were over. Election work finished, he had been hustled back to school on Washington Street. He was far behind his classmates, and, troubled as she was, Belle Moodie helped him nights with his school work. This prepared him for rapid advancement when he entered school in the East the next fall.

In a valiant, though futile and foolish, effort to provide money for his family, Will Frost had played the market and had lost every cent he had. Lying on his bed, the fever-stricken, desperate man thought of the thousand and one things he could do if only he were downtown. The result was that on the fifth day of April, despite the protestations of Belle Moodie, he crawled out of bed and made his way to the cable car. Desperation lent him momentary strength. But that night some men came carrying the delirious man home. He had struggled in vain to recoup his fortunes.

The Reverend John Doughty came to the house to do what he could. Certainly that was little, for the dying man stood on his own, unashamed and unafraid. That he had all his faculties about him is without doubt. He called Robert to him and urged him to make a promise that he would never run around nights.

"He was remembering the trouble he got into," Robert said, "and he wished to save me from it. He held my hand and made me promise. I never broke that promise."

Belle Moodie had prepared herself through her religion for this occasion. She had often talked in her quiet way with the children about the great beyond, and of her spiritual mentor, the great Swedish mystic who had spoken with heavenly beings as men talk face to face with men. Perhaps some of the seed sown in the heart of the small boy, afterwards, looking back to the death of his father, came to fruit in the lines,

> *And a white shimmering concourse rolls*
> *Toward the throne to witness there*
> *The speeding of devoted souls*
> *Which God makes his especial care.*

Surrounded by a few choice friends, Will Frost died that April afternoon. His father was notified. He sent the mony for the three survivors to accompany the body back to Massachusetts. Belle Moodie at once accepted the offer of a home. There were the children, and she was altogether unfitted to carry on in a new country without help.

Had the dead man been consulted, he would have been buried on the slopes of Lone Mountain; Lone Mountain, where only the occasional howl of a wolf or coyote broke the eternal stillness. There were Roman Catholic, Protestant, and Masonic cemeteries there. He had always admired the contour of the peak, and nothing could have pleased him better than to have it stand ward over his grave. But these things were never to be. The New England Frost wanted the Frosts of New England all to lie in death side by side.

So they crossed the bay, the body of the dead man safe in the ferry's hold. Robert gazed back at his beloved city. At Oakland pier there was no time to look back. The long train was waiting under the sheds. One last fleeting glimpse of the silhouetted hills, the rock of Alcatraz, and the snaggle-toothed skyline, then the hustle to catch the train.

The second decade of his life had started.

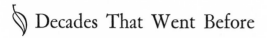

Decades That Went Before

IV. For Mother Eve a Race

Strong, rugged name, Frost.

Just when or from what place it came to England is not clear. It may have been brought over by the Danes under Canute. It may earlier have been a part and parcel of the baggage of Henghist and Horsa, thriving under the Ethel kings, in which case it may originally have been spelled "Forst." It may even have been an emergence after the days of the Conqueror from some older Saxon shade.

Whatever may have been its status in the *Domesday Book,* or beyond, for our present use the first of the line was one Nicholas, or as we occasionally meet it, Nicolaus Frost, an unlettered Devonshire man, who was the first to pull up roots and transplant the stock of the family to the New World.

Apples ripened on trees already gnarled and ancient in Tiverton and the land which lay about when Nicholas Frost grew to manhood in the place of his birth in the early 1600's. When he came to New England, he carried seed in his capacious pockets to sow the gospel of good apples in the uncertain soil of a howling wilderness. Kittery, Eliot, York, and Rye had soil and climate the best for apples. The land thereabout, and even as far as the headwaters of the Sturgeon, was rather on the stony side, reminding one of such soil as the grandson of Nicholas, seven times removed, described:

> *I farm a pasture where the boulders lie*
> *As touching as a basket full of eggs.*

Surely it would not seem far-fetched to send the roots of "The Gold Hesperidee" back to Devon or Dorset, or Cornwall three hundred or more years ago. Matthew Hale himself might have sprung from the first Baron of the Exchequer, and Lord Chief Justice of the King's Bench.

We smile at the spelling and the uncertain flavor of the old record. "Nicholas Frost, Borne Aprille ye 25th, 1585, Tiverton. Nicholas, marride Bertha Cadwalla, Jan'y 1630, ffrom Tavistock, Devon. Bertha Cadwalla Borne ffeb'y ye 14th 1610."

There seems little doubt that shortly after their marriage the new bridegroom decided to leave his bride behind and hurry off to America. Plymouth lies to the southeast of Tiverton, forty miles across the Dartmouth forest—so early do the shadows of "those dark trees" become linked with the poet's life. From Plymouth the restless wayfarer departed, going forth to spy out the land.

Having found it would not be such a bad place to which to bring his new wife, he returned with the good news to Bertha—to meet his new son. He had already made up his mind that as soon as he could dispose of his apple orchard and thatched cottage and gather certain moneys together, he would forsake the old for the new land. However, it was not to be so easy as all that. Being a prolific wife, Bertha shortly made it so that they had to await the services of a midwife, and then for a while after. Thus it was not until well into 1634 that Nicholas and Bertha, with Charles (born July 20, 1631) and John Frost (born August 7, 1633), took passage on the good ship *Wulfrana* and sailed away to their new home.

Little Harbor (later Rye), New Hampshire, missed Maine by half a day's journey. It was here that the *Wulfrana* came to anchor along in June. And here began the history of the Frosts in America, for seven generations fated not to stir more than a day's walk from the place of landing.

If one would see the geographical circumspection of the seven generations in the New World, it is only necessary to take Rye for the center of the half-circle, and Andover, Massachusetts, as its outermost point, thirty-two miles away. This half-circle described, Andover would lie in the periphery. Thus, if we would include Derry, New Hampshire, that point would fall a good four miles inside the periphery, and Eliot, Maine, a good twenty-four.

Perhaps if Bertha Cadwalla had not become pregnant again, Nicholas Frost would have moved from the Rye country sooner. The family remained a whole year at Rye in order that their daughter, Anna, might be born in peaceful surroundings. Her birth is recorded as of 1635.

To complete the picture, we must turn back to the musty records of the contemporary chroniclers. In a deposition taken in 1673 (ten years after the first American Frost passed this life), Phillip Swadden has this to say:

> Thirty-eight or thirty-nine yeares since living then at pischataqua, I do positively know yt Mr. Thomas Wannerton gave to Nicholas Frost a Prcell of Land up in Pischataqua River, now known by the name of Kittery, which pcell of Land was bounded, on the East with a little Cove, Joyneing to the Fort Poynt, on the South West on the River, on the North West Northerly, with a great stumpe called the Mantill-tree stumpe; which is about the middle of the Lane, wch Joynes to ye Land which Major Nicholas Shapleigh now possesseth, & soe runneing into ye woods, as fare backe as the sayd Wannerton's Land went, which Tract of Land Mr. Thomas Wannerton gave to sayd Nicholas Frost to come to bee his neighbor.

Although this well-defined deed to the land never seems to have been successfully contested, it was not sufficient ground for the purposes to which the land seeker would put it. So we find Nicholas Frost purchasing four hundred acres on the north side of Piscataqua, on which he at first built a small log cabin, later enlarging it, using hewn logs, to be a two-story dwelling in 1640. The neighbors, including Alexander Shapleigh and James Treworgie, agreed that there should always be a road out of Nicholas Frost's place to Sturgeon Creek. Still earlier, finding that his neighbor had not sufficient marshland for his cattle, Shapleigh gave Frost five acres additional for grazing purposes.

The family never made this a permanent place of abode, but at least Nicholas impressed himself somewhat upon the town. He was chosen one of the first selectmen, and while serving in the capacity of city father was one of the signers of a petition to the Lord Protector, dated 1657, imploring Cromwell to permit New Hampshire to remain under the government of Massachusetts for moral and religious reasons. That is, he was a signer if you call his manner of affixing his signature signing a petition, for it should be remembered that he could neither read nor write. He signed with a combination of "N" and "F" which passed muster for a signature.

At Eliot, Maine, on the headwaters of Sturgeon Creek, Nicholas lived most of his life, dying there in his bed in 1663. Passing, Nicholas Frost left a will in which his estate was inventoried as "Six hundred forty pounds, fifteen shillings, and seven pence, 1042 acres of land, twenty-seven head of cattle, nineteen hogs, four horses and one negro boy, besides certain personal property."

Nicholas Frost left a son who was foreordained to become a famous character in Colonial days. This was Charles Frost, who married Mary, daughter of Joseph Bolles, of Wells, Maine. She was "Borne in 1646, March 24th." They were married December 27, 1675. He had been commissioned captain July 6, 1668.

Indian fighter was Major Charles—afraid of neither redskins nor witches. He could not have been more than nineteen when the Indians captured his mother and sister, the latter being only fifteen at the time, and made off up the creek with them. Father and son hotly pursued, the son killing a chief and a brave the first day. But by the time they had come up to where the redskins had made camp the next day, all they found was the dead bodies of the two women, which they carried back for burial near the old garrison. Generations later Poet Frost has a word about it.

> I was forever being told what a great ancestry I had come by—Indian fighters, some who had married into shavetail nobility, and such sort—till I found myself in distaste of them. Especially did I learn to harbor a grudge against this Major Charles, because history had recorded that he had a hand in getting the remnants of those Indians who had followed King Philip together on a pretext of a peaceful settlement, and had sold some as slaves, hanging others in Boston. In after years I was to discover that better evidence was produceable showing that he, far from fathering the

scheme, went into it only after he had been deceived over the intent, even then with misgivings. So I have taken him off my black list of relations.

In an important military dispatch dated "Kittorey," February 4, 1694/5, we find Major Frost addressing himself to the lieutenant-governor, one William Stoughton[1] of Massachusetts Bay Colony, urging him to send supplies of food and clothing. We can manage to see why the savages had come to hate and fear him. He had been their inveterate foe for upward of a quarter of a century, and they had taken a vow among themselves not to rest till he had been accounted for. It must be admitted they had long to go without rest for not until the evening of July 4, 1697 was he successfully ambushed and slain. The old chronicle sets it forth in pious phrase: "It hath pleased God to take away Major Frost, the Indens waylaid him last Sabbath day he was cominge whom from metting at night; and killed him and John Heards wife and Denes Downing. It is a Great Loss to the whole Province and espeseley to his famyley."

The third generation of Frosts in America witnessed intermarriage with blue blood—the shavetail nobility mentioned by the poet. The son of Major Charles, the Honorable John Subline Frost, married Mary, sister of Sir William Pepperell, on September 4, 1702, Joseph Hammond, Esq., performing the ceremony. John Subline was born on March 1, 1681/2, and died February 25, 1732/3. He commanded, not without distinction, His Majesty's man-of-war, the *Edward*. Later he became one of the governor's councilors. Wars done, John Subline settled down as a merchant in Newcastle, across the estuary from where his grandfather and his father had landed in the New World. Here were two generations of Frosts not to be forgotten in colonial history.

William Frost (born on Tuesday, August 20, 1705, "at 2 a Clock in ye morning"), the son of the governor's councilor, succeeded to his father's mercantile business in Newcastle. He was distinctly a man of peace, possessing no inclinations toward political power or preferment.

---

[1] Stoughton, who was acting as governor at this time, had his preferment because he was the one judge of the three appointed by Governor Phips for the Salem witch trials (Stoughton, Sewall, and Saltonstall) who prosecuted the trials without shame or regret.

However, he seems to have done his part in raising up a soldier for trying times. It was in this generation that the name Prescott, so intimately connected with our poet, finds its way into the family.

The first William Frost married Elizabeth Prescott—"24th. November, 1750, New Stile." Elizabeth Prescott was born September 15, 1721, and died March 22, 1759, being buried at Newcastle. The soldier referred to above was of this union. He likewise was christened William and was born (as one of the chroniclers has it) at Old Kittery, 1747; or (as another sets it down) November 15, 1754. He became a lieutenant in the Colonial contingent in the war for American freedom, thus giving evidence to the Frost lines, "the land was ours before we were the land's." He served in the notable regiment commanded by Ebenezer Sprouts.

Married to Sarah Holt (so early does the name Holt touch the line!) of Danvers, Massachusetts, December 2, 1777, this William was the first to really leave the family burying grounds of the Frosts in and around Old Kittery. Even so, he traveled no farther than a good horse could pace in a day from the spot on which Nicholas landed more than a century earlier. He was the first Frost of the line in Massachusetts, settling at Andover. Here he spent the better part of his life, raising a son, Samuel Abbott, to manhood. He could not be content, however, to die on "foreign" soil but journeyed back to pass away at York, Maine; which event, according to the chronicler we have elected, occurred September 28, 1836. His wife died September 18, 1841, aged eighty-three years.

It remained for his son, the Samuel Abbott we have mentioned (born July 11, 1795), to hear the call of New Hampshire. While still a young man he packed up his belongings and trekked the thirty-two miles to live in the old neighborhoods. On October 18, 1821, he married Mary Blunt, of Eden, Maine. She outlived him twenty-seven years. The pair had four children, one of whom, in memory of his own grandmother and grandfather, Samuel Abbott insisted on calling William Prescott. This was the grandfather of our poet, and he was born at Kingston, July 11, 1823. Samuel Abbott died at Brentwood, January 11, 1848.

Grown to manhood, the first William Prescott Frost did some backtracking of his own, choosing to return to the terrain his grandfather had selected but making his stand at Lawrence instead of at Andover. He set himself up as a Beau Brummell, taking pride in being known as the dandy of Lawrence. Time settled him down, and a spirit of thrift and innate good sense came to steady his habits. There was another contributing factor to his stabilization. Being married (at Kingston, September 27, 1846) to one of America's earliest feminists of record had something to do with the sobering. For whatever reason, we do know he laid aside his purple and fine linen and became a steady factory foreman.

This woman, nee Judith Colcord, whose influence on Robert was not to be taken lightly, was seven years senior to her husband, having been born in 1816, June 23. It was at Kingston, before their removal to Lawrence, on December 27, 1850, that Judith Colcord gave birth to a son. She named him for his father, William Prescott. He became the father of Robert Frost.

Will Frost by no means had a happy childhood either in the years at Kingston or later at Lawrence. Moving to Lawrence just four years before the Civil War, he spent his entire childhood clouded by the shadows of conflict. In 1857 we find the elder William Prescott Frost an overseer in a print factory. There was little play for the younger Frost. The hard hand of a strong-willed, thwarted man was upon him. There was work to do.

Will Frost was a studious, nervous, weak-lunged child, much given to introspection. How Harvard claimed him; how he went on west to become a newspaperman and a politician; how he was started back to be buried the first one to lie in the family burying-ground at Lawrence —these things we have told. It was to such a scene, into the household of such a grandfather and grandmother, that Belle Moodie and her children were coming.

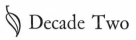 Decade Two

V. EAST-RUNNING BROOK

WHEN ROBERT FROST came to Lawrence to meet his ancestors and take his place among them, he could meet them only in spirit. Although

> *Those stones out under the low-limbed tree*
> *Doubtless bear names that the mosses mar,*

yet in 1885 the name Frost was not among them. The near three hundred years of the family on "our cisatlantic shore" had graves in and around Old Kittery. Will Frost's name was the first to be carved on a stone in Massachusetts, where

> *The living come with grassy tread*
> *To read the gravestones on the hill.*

The repatriate never forgot that April day when the little procession made its slow way out to the hill. There the first clay soil had been turned in the new family plot. The head of the house had his son's gravestone marked "Willie."

The sun broke out suddenly through a rift in the clouds and shone on the tousled head of the little boy. Now all the grief and anguish which travel and excitement had covered for a while came forth in a flood of tears. His mother held one arm about him, one about Jeanie. Then the last requiem was sung, the last silent prayer breathed by Belle Moodie in the faith of her Swedenborgian religion, and the sound of clods falling upon the pine box came dully to his ears. His beloved father was being hidden away forever from his sight:

> *That fallen lance that lies as hurled,*
> *That lies unlifted now, come dew, come rust,*
> *But still lies pointed as it plowed the dust.*

Time did at last heal all the wounds. The nirvana of carefree childhood came to his rescue, and happy days succeeded other happy days. There was a long summer of tramping up and down the Merrimack—an Indian name for the "Place of Islands." He loved the winding stream for its beauty, gliding like a green snake right through the town. He felt a kinship for the silver birches peering over dark banks to catch a glimpse of themselves in the water. Perhaps he swung on the younger, more pliable ones, just as he was to write of them later,

> *When I see birches bend to left and right*
> *Across the lines of straighter darker trees,*
> *I like to think some boy's been swinging them.*

He began to learn his New England at just the season of the year New England should be learned, arriving in Lawrence in time to

> *. . . See the snow all go down hill*
> *In water of a slender April rill*
> *That flashes tail through last year's withered brake*
> *And dead weeds, like a disappearing snake.*

Lawrence was a busy city when Robert Frost came to live at 370 Haverhill with his grandfather. Still famed for its cotton worsteds, it had held its own since it was founded in 1845. The head of the house of Frost, too, had held his own. His steady habits, frugality, and good business sense had kept him regularly employed as foreman of cotton-print factories where others were passed by.

There were many interesting things about the city and its immediate surroundings to attract Robert. One of his favorite resorts was down by the Andover bridge. Wandering to the old stone dam, just where the Merrimack curves about the mills, he would make his way along the old North Canal. He soon learned about the cave under the rock and was seeking the moonshiners' treasure hidden there, as legend had it. He would walk out to the swamp, to the Plains, and to Stevens' Pond. White Pup's bridge was a favorite resort, as well as Bull-dog's Field and Spicket River. Some days he would stroll out to the top of Cemetery Hill, which complacently looked down on the low-lying town. Its three hundred acres of factories (each with uncounted thousands of spools, bobbins, shuttles, and human machines weaving cloth for far-flung markets) made a forest of smokestacks belching flame and soot, poisoning the pure oxygen of the air. Here must have come to his imagination all the horrors of what one inside at work there would have to come to at last. It was a place where

> *The air was full of dust of wool,*
> *A thousand yarns were under pull.*

The young Frost, gazing from his eminence at the sinuous Merrimack winding below, recalled the comforting words of Thoreau concerning the same town and the same river, yes, the very site on which his eye at the moment rested.

"When at length it has escaped from under the last of the factories, it has a level and unmolested passage to the sea, a mere waste of water, as it were, bearing little with it but its fame; its pleasant course revealed by the morning fog which hangs over it, and to the sails of a few vessels which transact the commerce between Haverhill and Newburyport."

It was at this place, at this point that the future poet took account of himself. Discussing it so very long after, he said much:

> When we got back to a place I'd little memory of, scarcely more my mother, for that, we were poorer than we had ever thought we might be when we settled things up out in San Francisco. My father had carried twenty thousand dollars of insurance—life insurance—but in the troublous times the premiums had been neglected, my mother forgetting in her trouble to make the payments. So, there was no insurance to help pay the bills. I don't remember where the money came from to do it—all of it anyway. These matters brought ire out of the older Frosts, who wanted to know why they had not been informed concerning the insurance. They'd have paid it.
>
> You know there's another thing I can't explain. My mother had dear

friends, close friends, back in Ohio who knew her worth as a teacher. They would have found a good place for her in the schools back there, would have given her a home while she was getting over the tragedy. I'll never know. But out of New England my life likely would have gone on in other directions. I'm a fatalist.

We stayed awhile at my grandfather's. But my mother found it too much. Next we went to be with a New Hampshire family headed up by my great-aunt, one Sarah Frost Messer. That was my taste—my first taste—of Amherst village.

When I was eleven,[1] spring of 1886, my mother got a place teaching in a district school in Salem, New Hampshire. The work was trying, the wage small. One good thing was that she had nothing much to keep her from her old natural (and acquired) trait of moving whenever and wherever the urge struck her. So, we moved about from house to house—tenement, farm house, apartment. She was paid nine dollars a week—as money went, not too terrible. The dollar in 1886 was worth about six dollars now (1932), only it was for thirty-six weeks instead of twelve months. Anyway, it sort of kept soul and body together—sort of.

During this period there were jobs young Robert could get helping farmers in planting and harvesting seasons, thus helping his mother.

I think maybe I got as much as a dime an hour—ten hours a day, making a dollar a day—working out. I remember one farmer I worked for whose wife lent me a book (she must have been a Scot, I don't remember —could be) and the book was *Scottish Chiefs*. Good book. I didn't finish it. I knew what the end was going to be.

You know, my mother indoctrinated me in Scottish history and literature. She was a Scotswoman, as you know. She read to me and Jeanie— good poetry—Scott and Burns. She would tell us of her aunt in Scotland who could say most of Scott by heart. I couldn't help but learn something —some little.

But there were things beside reading and listening to tales of the Scottish border as told by my mother who knew 'em all. I began to spread my work-wings. Wanted to do—be able to do—almost everything. Never regretted working with rough men—bad characters. I had my start as you know in California with Balso.

[1] Frost continued to claim 1875 as a birthday until late.

The tyranny of the head of the house of Frost began to be felt by young Frost with the opening of school in September. The old man believed firmly in the Solomonic admonition so often misquoted, more often misapplied. What is more, he was slave to Ben Franklin's "penny saved is tuppence clear; pin a day's a groat a year." Robert and Jeanie were not interested in pennies, pins, and groats. They had come from a land where a penny had no standing; they scarcely knew what a groat was—nor did they care. It galled them, too, that the head of the family insisted on having an account rendered for every nickel expended by anybody connected with the Frost establishment.

Despite his years of laggard truancy, Robert soon caught up with his class. It was perhaps as much his gentleness and the soft look in his grave blue eyes as it was his ability to learn which sent him so far along the curriculum so soon. In the West he had already put on long trousers. All his classmates, even those above him, in Lawrence were still in knee pants upon his arrival. This made him the butt of their sarcasm. But they soon learned he was not to be trifled with. Within three years he had finished with the grammar grades and was ready, in September, 1888, to enter Lawrence High.

During the three years in the lower grades, he came under the influence of the *Franklin Third, Fourth* and *Fifth Readers. Franklin* at the moment was displacing *McGuffey's Readers* generally in New England. Some of the stories and poems in the *Third Reader,* especially, must have been puerile to him. To have to read of little Pearl Honeydew, six years old, listening at the roots of strawberries—"Under the leaves and under the snow/ Waiting to grow"—when he had been reading Shelley, was a blow. However, accounts of frogs and toads, the stretches of the Arabian desert, and the glamour of the frozen North were to become a part of the sum that was to be Robert Frost.

Passing from the *Third* to the *Fourth Reader* bridged quite a gap, as Robert remembered. Here he came upon Turgenev, Stowe, Stoddard, Hawthorne, and Old John Burroughs, whom doubtless he had known already from Belle Moodie. There were poems by Bryant, Cowper, Trowbridge, Longfellow, Emerson, and the rest. But to many he had already been introduced. He never formed the hard and fast habit of finishing a book. He once said to me that he had dipped into, but left unfinished all his life, the *Connecticut Yankee.* Even Mark, he said, couldn't have told why he put all that blood in the final chapters. He had never gone through a book to the last chapter till he was past thirteen. His mother read *Tom Brown* to him, which he would never let her finish because he never wanted to hear any tale to the last page. All his mental processes were doubtless affected by this. He must keep growing.

It is asking too much of human credulity to believe that a precocious youngster who in his teens was reading *Hamlet,* the *Endymion,* and Shelley's poems just for diversion would have been too greatly influenced by his school readers. But reading them as he did was certainly a steppingstone.

When he came to the *Fifth Reader,* which he studied in 1887–88, he had almost attained to his majority in letters. Reading such poems as "The Builders," "Highland Gathering," "The Firmament," "The Bugle Song," and "Under the Greenwood Tree" fixed his attitude.

> I have happy memories of Lawrence. My mother continued to teach at Salem, where we kept on living. I took the commuter's ticket my grandfather got me and rode back and forth from home to school. I had a rebuilt hand-me-down suit made for me out of one of Grandfather's used ones—my grandmother made it over for me, though later, moved by Elihu Colcord, proceeded to get me a new suit out of the store—my very first. And all this while, as I think back over the years, my ambition continued, and I kept plugging away on a path toward carefully written, well-turned poetry.[2]

Sixty years later, Frost went back to his school days at Lawrence in a reminiscent mood concerning the readers he had studied as a boy.

> They were good books, prime. Nothing trivial there. Full of good selections, real literature. No wonder you and I were educated, studying such

[2] In addition to the famous writers appearing in the *Fourth* who likewise appeared in the *Fifth Reader,* were Andersen, Franklin, Kingsley, Irving, Dickens, Ruskin, Aldrich, Goldsmith, Carlyle, Prescott, Addison, Macaulay, Milton, Shakespeare. Frost studied Swinton's geography; Higginson's U.S. history; Metcalfe's *Language and Spelling Book;* as well as music, drawing, and cartography.

as boys. There was "Sennacherib" and "Waterloo" by Byron. Things by Hemans and Tennyson and Whittier and Longfellow. I can still say most of 'em by heart—"Marco Bozzaris" by Halleck, I memorized about this time. "At midnight in his guarded tent . . . ."

I went to New England from the West Coast when I was about eleven, and when I got there I found a new outlook. If we dropped a piece of buttered bread on the floor, butter side down, we were told to pick it up and eat it, since we all had to eat our peck of dirt. It was different in California—I like to think it was, anyway. Winds were blowing, not dust but gold in the Golden State, we were told, and there we ate our peck of gold. I wrote a poem about it—wind always blowing about the town except where seafog laid it down, but I was one of the children told, we all must eat our peck of gold.

The boy Frost had good training in grammar, which stood him as a bulwark a whole lifetime. He studied Patterson his last grammar school year—parsing, analysis, and sentence structure. He might be held up as an example of the worth of these studies. Verbs, adverbs, nouns, and adjectives—just the right word to express the meaning—the finesse of spelling. Grammar it was with laws applied. Later he scolded away at Ripton:

> They don't teach these kids anything constructive at all. We have 'em come here trying to write poetry, unable to spell *anything*. I call their attention to these things. I say, "If you can't spell a word, why don't you learn how?" They look at me open-mouthed, wondering which word they have misspelled. When I point out some word to them, they innocently reply, "But how can we learn which word is misspelled?" "You'll just have to learn." "But how?" They are persistent if nothing else. "Spelling," I tell them, "is something that comes by practice. You must look up words in the dictionary and find out the spelling and meaning at the same time." "But what words shall we look up?" By this time I am getting out of sorts and aggravated and impatient. "Well, begin with *the.* Find out how to spell *the,* and go from there to the others."

September, 1888, when still in his thirteenth year, Robert Frost entered high school. In its day the high-school equipment had been the last word. Then, it was in a constant state of repair. The year Robert finished his course, two classrooms were reconditioned and given new desks and settees. Two others were equipped with water closets.

The four years of his high-school course were happy ones. Robert forgot, in the good times he had at school, the bickerings of the old grandfather at home, the penuriousness displayed when the old miser doled out money. He played on the ball teams, working after classes to get spending money. Most of his spare hours found him curled up somewhere with a book or traipsing through the fields and woods.

Within two years of his arrival at Lawrence, he was regularly and gainfully employed during summer vacation. In 1887 he worked the entire out-of-school period in a shoemaker's shop. He became proficient in the work and could heel and half-sole shoes with the touch of a veteran. But shoemaking was not his line. In future summers there was no end of different jobs and experiences.

The high-school course he found to be a stiff one, with emphasis on the classics. W. C. Bates, who lived at 15 Allison Street, was superintendent of schools.[3] He was a classical scholar and gathered other classical scholars about him. There was no room in the New England schools of that day for short cuts and slipshod education.

Great care went into the choice of collateral reading for the course of study. Latter-day college freshmen would gasp at the required reading a Lawrence high-school student must pursue in the nineties.[4]

It was in high school that Frost had his regard for Longfellow well

[3] During his high school course, Robert Frost had for headmaster Edward R. Goodman, whose salary was $2,500 a year. Goodman taught Latin. Louis H. W. French and Edward S. Riley were the two submasters. Other teachers included Mary A. Newell, Latin and Greek; Katherine O'Keefe, history, rhetoric, and elocution; Emily A. Wetherbee, literature and elocution; Ada A. Lear, classics; Louisa A. Halley, mathematics; Julia A. Underhill, algebra, history, and bookkeeping; and Mary A. Bruce, French and English. Salaries ranged from $700 to $1,200 a year.

[4] The collateral required reading included *Evangeline, Miles Standish, Snow Bound, The Sketch Book, Poems of Freedom, The Autocrat,* "Thanatopsis," "To a Waterfowl," *Ivanhoe, Lay of the Last Minstrel, Enoch Arden, Twice Told Tales,* "Bunker Hill Oration," "Reply to Haines," *The Vision of Sir Launfal,* Grey's "Elegy," *The Princess, Marmion, Lady of the Lake, The Deserted Village, Vicar of Wakefield, Lays of Ancient Rome, As You Like It, Canterbury Tales, Sesame and Lilies, Merchant of Venice, Representative Men,* and Bacon's *Essays.*

established. "He's a pretty good poet, after all," Frost said when he was old. Longfellow's influence had never abated its force upon him. Many a time did he astonish some companion on a long walk by saying a fine line from "Evangeline," or by pointing out some carefully selected, hard and fast rhyme from some other Longfellow verse.

Frost began writing poetry in grammar school. Three times during his high-school course he submitted poems to *The Bulletin,* where they were first published. April, 1890, saw "A Dream of Julius Caesar" in print. It was followed by "Song of the Wave" the next month and by "La Noche Triste" in May, 1891.[5] He relates:

> When I was about twelve I read most of Prescott's *Conquest of Mexico.* Prescott was a relative of the family. My sympathies were with the Indians, maybe still are. I had been grieving about the way Cortez treated Montezuma and his people. I remember it was a windy, dusty March day in Lawrence. My thoughts kept going back to the Indians trying to escape from the Spaniards. Stanzas kept running through my head about the thing, not too good. One of my earliest poems was being born in a wise-sad mood. I called it later, when it was published in the high-school paper, "La Noche Triste." I worked away on it all afternoon and was late for supper at my grandmother's house because of it. This was one of my poems which came out of deep emotion and feeling, being moved by something I had read. I laid this verse aside for four years before I dug it out to be published in 1891. I always have worked that way—from an original mood. One poem I remember writing half of and laying aside for ten years before finishing it. I never tell people which part I wrote first—that's for them to figure out.
>
> My reading has always been erratic in the same way. There was one book I never read in my early days (I never did get round to reading it), but which influenced me. I had heard of *Piers Plowman* all my life but had never read it. I said: "Here is a book about an ordinary individual, so I'm afraid to read it for fear I might write like it." So, a book I never read influenced my writing more than any book I have ever read, or nearly any.

Just when he first encountered that little slip of a girl named Elinor White, who lived at 10 Valley and whose ancestor was Peregrine White,

[5] See Appendix.

44 ·

of Pilgrim fame, nobody could ever quite remember. Her father was Edwin White, a wood turner by trade. On account of Judge Daniel A. White, library donor of Lawrence, the name stood high in all the surrounding community.

Elinor was quick as a flash. She stepped into high school a year later than Robert, caught up with him, and given time would probably have passed him. As it was, her grades tied him for first honors, making it a toss-up who should be valedictorian. The man element won, so it was all settled amicably by Elinor's being chosen to read the essay of valedictory rank, on "Conversation as a Force in Life," while Robert gave the valedictory address with an original declamation on "A Monument to After-thought Unveiled."

Patrons, pupils, and teachers gathered in the old city hall for the graduation exercises that afternoon of July 1, 1892. This structure, erected in 1850, in the words of the Lawrence chronicler, was a "building of bold and impressive outlines, an architectural triumph of its day." Within its walls meetings had been held for forty-two years—religious, civic, educational, cultural, and social. From it departed the men who went away to war in the sixties, and in it, awaiting departure for "the hill," wrapped in the Stars and Stripes, lay Needham, "First blood of the Rebellion."

Towering above the city hall, wings spread as if ready to soar away, was a nine-foot eagle, designed and carved by John M. Smith, one of the town's first selectmen. The commencement speaker saw and remarked about it; here below were little eaglets about to take wing and fly.

As the audience of kinsmen and friends passed into the building, each was handed a printed program containing the class hymn. Robert Frost confessed that he more than once stole a furtive glance at the printed poem. He won high recognition that day. He and Anne Desmond each received the Hood medal of excellence during the whole course of four years. The class hymn, sung by the audience, displayed the by-lines, "Words by Robert L. Frost, Music by Beethoven."

During the golden, more or less idle, years at Lawrence, he had not in vain wandered up and down the banks of the "Place of Island." The hymn had genuine poetry in its lines.

There is a nook among the alders
  Still sleeping in the catbird's "Hush!"
Below, a long stone-bridge is bending
  Above the runnel's silent rush.

A dreamer hither often wanders
  And gathers many a snow-white stone;
He weighs them, poised upon his finger,
  Divining each one's silvery tone.

He drops them! When the stream makes music,
  Fair visions with its vault-voiced swell;
And so, for us, the future rises,
  And thought-stones stir our heart's "Farewell!"

VI. Range Finding

Hanover, New Hampshire, was named after the Electorate of Hanover, through the first George of England. The founders established Dartmouth College there.

Dartmouth was the choice made by the head of the house of Frost in his determination to shape his grandson's life. The failure of his son Will Frost caused him all the more to determine to make something out of the last remaining Frost of the line.

"You will go to Dartmouth," the crusty old grandfather growled, as if an oracle, slightly out of tune, were speaking. "It is a good college, and will prepare you for life as a man of business. You will meet the right kind of boys there, and your training will be suited to the future I have planned for you."

The college at Hanover had had a checkered career. It was founded in 1769, with a charter granted by George III, and was named for its largest donor, the Earl of Dartmouth. When, about 1815, the New Hampshire state legislature decided to pass a law changing the status of the school into a state institution to be called Dartmouth University, the trustees objected. Taking the matter to court and appealing through every appellate division clear to the Supreme Court of the United States,

Chief Justice John Marshall presiding, Daniel Webster representing the trustees, Dartmouth won the decision. This case settled the independence of the small American college.

Hanover in those days lay off the beaten track. The small college on the Connecticut River was rigid in its utter simplicity, almost Colonial in its atmosphere, when Robert L. Frost, carrying his stipend of ten dollars, came into its halls to register the September following his graduation from Lawrence High.

William Prescott Frost, Sr., counted out his money to him and told him he would pay him five dollars a week every week he stayed in college. Robert related the circumstances:

> Since he paid me five dollars a week for my keep, it was only natural, from his viewpoint, that he should desire a return on his investment, usury. He had the New England shrewdness which demanded a dollar back with interest. Now, inasmuch as I got my room for $30.00 a year, meals proportionately reasonable, the five dollars was plenty for ordinary needs. What made it bad was the fact that he insisted on an itemized account for every penny spent, where it went, and what it was for. I rebelled and wanted to tell him to go to hell. But I didn't, I held. It wasn't that I objected to being dependent on him. That sort of thing has never bothered me in the way it has my children, they stew about it. It was just that I hated to keep an account of every little dab I spent.

With this in mind no one can doubt the origin of

> *Never ask of money spent*
> *Where the spender thinks it went.*

In those days Dartmouth had not yet become the college of the outdoors. If custom could be established by the habits of one student, Frost did much to establish it as such. A pioneer, he tramped across the fall hills, down to the old covered bridge spanning the Connecticut. The river flowed peacefully southward through the range of hills, having been "raised in New Hampshire."

Though Robert Frost did it, it certainly was not common to spend time out of doors in his day at Hanover. Winter was a necessary evil.

It sent all indoors to sit about the fire. The students remembered long evenings by a blazing log, which a poet of a previous generation at Dartmouth had made immortal in verse—the widely-known "Hanover Winter Song."

> For the wolf-wind is wailing at the doorways,
> And the snow drifts deep along the road,
> And the ice-gnomes are marching from their Norways,
> And the great white cold walks abroad.

The old traditions here made little impression on Robert. It is true he recalled the funeral of Matthew-Matics, and he never forgot "Wah-Hoo-Wah; Da-di-di-Dartmouth; Wah-Hoo-Wah; Ti-ger-r-r." The cane rush and freshmen beer were in his day only things to be remembered; observance passed in the late eighties, though they were seeking to reinstate the notorious underclassmen fight when he arrived on the campus. The students continued to talk about the Crown Prince and old Eleazar Wheelock's patriotism. The chapel prayers of thanksgiving for "oxygen gas, nitrogen gas, hydrogen gas, and all the other gases," and for the "cerebrum, the cerebellum and the medulla oblongata," good for a laugh in 1892, were to remain the same for generations to come. John Wheelock's turgid illiteracy persisted where the facile culture of others was forgotten; there were "Kib" and "Dan Pratt" and "Lil" and "Bed-bug Alley," for indeed the laureate's cry

> Men of Dartmouth set a watch,
> Lest the old traditions fall

had been faithfully heeded.

While at college Frost lived at Wentworth hall. The names of two men are linked with his—Preston Shirley and Raymond D. Hazen. Once at Wentworth, Frost barricaded himself and a friend, Preston Shirley no doubt, in his quarters because one of them had gotten a box of fruit which they must protect from marauding sophomores. He told how they took turns at slipping out to class and keeping watch for a week over the fruit till it was all eaten.

Then there was the time of which he occasionally spoke in after years with as near a tone of regret as was possible for him, when he helped cut a youthful theolog's hair, leaving a clearly outlined cross made by the bare scalp. The poor student quit Dartmouth between suns. It didn't matter that in later years they were to meet and become friends. The deed had been done which the perpetrator always described as terrible.

In 1915 Frost wrote two letters regarding his Dartmouth days—the first from Littletown, New Hampshire, April 20, the second from Franconia, October 15. They were written to Harold Rugg and give us a picture of a boy full of fun, ready for anything, but one who lived in a world apart. They conveyed his interest in poetry and indicated that the lines later published in "My Butterfly" and "Now Close the Windows" came from that period.

Making choice of the classical course of study, a thing to be expected from the son of a Harvard Phi Beta Kappa, the student soon found it no sinecure. It was a carefully prescribed course much in vogue in the schools of both the Old and the New England of the time. Without taking account, Frost made the plunge into the *Apology* of Plato, into Crito, Livy, and Hebrew history. He took themes in English history; he studied algebra to the theory of equations. He discovered that attendance on morning, forenoon, and afternoon exercises was obligatory. He had to be up and at chapel for prayers at 7:40 A.M. each week day; he must attend public worship every Sunday forenoon and college prayers at 5:30 P.M. These obligations proved onerous to one who had spent his childhood in going to church, and not because it pleased him to go.

Still, all was not work and prayer at Dartmouth. The first week in September with another boy, named Riese, he was chosen monitor for the freshman class, which proved good for his inhibitions. On the night of October 28, being well domiciled, there was a rollicking initiation put on by the Theta Delta Chi, with a banquet at the Wheelock. "R. L. Frost" was one of the initiates.

There were a score of fraternities at Dartmouth; and though his five dollars a week took care of his room and board, banquet tickets and fraternity high jinks do not come without a certain outlay of cash. He was hard-put-to-it to make all ends come together.

Frost was destined to stay but a short time at Hanover—a few months of inconstant study and constant homesickness. The months leading up to December were not wasted ones for the unwilling student. Studying Latin and Greek, he was becoming confirmed in the classics. It was at this period, he once pointed out to me, that something in the *Georgics* of Vergil showed him the way, confirmed him in his poetic purpose. Whatever it was, he saw clearly what poetry meant—not what one thinks, but the way one feels about what one thinks.

Not finding altogether what he was looking for at Hanover, the homesick youth left early in December without taking the term examinations. In fact, no grades were ever recorded for him at Dartmouth, only pencilings on the record, "Left College." "I couldn't make out what the thing I was doing in class and out had to do with what I was after, what I wanted to become."

He must have made more impression on the student body than he ever imagined. A news note in *The Dartmouth* for December 16, 1892, set forth the information that "R. L. Frost has been visiting in Methuen, Mass." This was eased off in the periodical of January 27, 1893, when the reporter stated that "R. L. Frost, '96, is teaching in Massachusetts." The final word was given in *The Dartmouth* for February 24, 1893: "R. L. Frost will not return to college. He is teaching in a grammar school at Methuen, Mass." The curtain had rung down on his career in the college at Hanover.

Called on for an explanation for his leaving Dartmouth, he said he was "roughing it" there and decided he was wasting his time. He felt, he said, that he might as well be at Methuen helping his mother in her school.

He was happy to be back at home for the Christmas holidays, tied to Belle Moodie's apron strings. He saw Elinor White every day, went to one or two parties gotten up by his old high school friends, and spent his afternoons wandering along the banks of his favorite runnel or strolling up and down the Merrimack.

Still he found himself unsettled. There was a livelihood to be thought of, for regardless of poetry, a poet must eat. If he had ever had any delusions of vast wealth coming from the sale of his verse, his first check or two were to disillusion him. The first twenty years of his literary efforts, he said, paid him exactly two hundred dollars.

Frost's pattern of trial-and-error jobs made up a strange hodge podge. He had tried before Dartmouth being bobbin boy, and again night watchman. He took a tramping trip down through the Carolinas, seeking work and finding none. Once when he discussed these various jobs, somebody put in with an irrelevant query about what one thing had most influenced his life.

"When I was a small boy of twelve I worked all summer in a shoe shop, and all that summer I carried little shoe nails in my mouth. I owe everything to the fact that I neither swallowed or inhaled."

With authentic sources at his disposal, Robert Newdick wrote of one of those "jobs." It was the job of light-trimmer in a Lawrence mill. "On dark, cloudy days," said the professor, "his time was taken up completely, but on bright, sunshiny days there was little for him to do. Sometimes he boxed or wrestled with fellow mill-workers in those intervals. Often, however, he went off by himself to read. His favorite reading was his pocket Shakespeare. And as he read he marked the text, as young men will, underlining favorite passages, and making particular record of his judgment as to how this or that speech or passage or line should be read to interpret it aright. This close study of Shakespeare, of course, left its evidence in his early verse, evidence more numerous and significant than his utilization of a phrase out of Macbeth ('Out, out—') as a title of a poem. Frost has said that a young poet must inevitably 'begin with a cloud of all the other poets he ever read.' The reader who knows Shakespeare as intimately as Frost came to know him will encounter not a few wisps of that poet in the 'cloud' of other poets that are to be glimpsed in Frost's early poems."

The history of that pocket text of Shakespeare is interesting. It was misplaced and not found till many years later. When it was finally come upon, the notes were found unnecessary. Shakespeare's word alone was all that was needed. Frost made the discovery that there was only one way each word could be read.

One job came to him during the interval which he especially liked.

He was made editor and gatherer of news for *The Sentinel,* a weekly paper published in Lawrence. He looked on the experience as a step forward in his chosen life work. He was writing, and he had made up his mind to authorship. But here was presented a problem; gathering news meant intruding on other people's lives. Wishing his own privacy respected, he hesitated about invading the privacy of his neighbors.

There was a class of stories he could make use of without outraging his own or anybody else's feelings. This he proceeded to do, as the columns of *The Sentinel* of that period bear witness. Those silhouettes of light and shadow—word pictures of some bird or animal, even of some human, such stories as the one of the eagle shot down from the flagpole by a gun carrier, much to the disgust of the editor; or some glimpse of an individual in the vein of Lafcadio Hearn—almost make one wish he had persevered in that field.

At the time of which we write, Frost was a slight, slim boy, who wished he were more bulky. He told of an incident which happened about that time. He was working with some men, and they decided to find out how much they weighed. While the others were getting on and off the scales, he worked a bit of legerdemain. Unobserved he stooped quickly and picked up some lead pipe which he thrust under his coat to increase his weight.

The college paper in February had announced that Robert Frost would not return to college, that he was teaching in Methuen.

Next to his mother, to whom first honors must always go when we consider Frost's preparation as a teacher, is the Reverend Charles H. Oliphant. It was this Methuenite, "beloved pastor and historian of the town," who gave him his first teaching position. He had left Dartmouth thinking he might be of service to Belle Moodie in helping handle some of the overgrown "toughies." It was necessary for him to come up for examination before Oliphant, and according to Robert he asked but one question.

"How would you go about teaching fractions?"

"I'm so full of algebra," he answered, "I'm afraid I'd have a hard time teaching arithmetic."

"That's a good answer," was his diploma to teach.

"Oliphant had a far greater influence on my life than you might suspect," said Frost later.

The "toughies" he had to teach presented a problem, and always the teacher, who was but little older than they, felt he had solved it poorly, if at all. He tells it.

They were a pretty savage gang Oliphant turned loose on me. As I said, I was a little harsh with them and disciplined them mercilessly, so that I produced a good deal of resistance among them, rebellion like.

I remember one day I started to punish one of them whose back was turned to me. He was known as a rather dangerous character with a strain of Indian in him. Just as I was within reach of him, he turned on me with an open knife in his hand. I was pretty rugged and soon had the knife, which I took to Oliphant with the story. "Do you want me to have this bully sent to a reform school?" he asked me. I didn't want to spoil the boy's whole future, and I said so. Oliphant turned him back to me and I proceeded to deal with him as best I could, but Oliphant kept the knife.

A few weeks after this, the boy's mother (the family lived out in the country from Methuen) invited me out for supper and to stay all night. I suppose she thought I was a good influence on the boy. He could use one. I was about 18 years old, he about 13 or 14. I stayed all night at the farm and was pleased to see that the little ruffian had cooled off enough to treat me civilly. He showed no enmity and didn't draw any knife on me during the visit.

Several years later I met up with Oliphant, who called the incident to my mind and asked if I knew what had become of the boy. I told him I had no knowledge of him, but asked if he had gone on in his life of crime. "No," Oliphant replied, "He became a stable citizen, and is now one of the selectmen of our town."[1]

During the time which elapsed between his taking the job under Oliphant and his going to Harvard, Frost was almost constantly engaged in teaching in private schools with his mother. Belle Moodie was a good teacher. In the nineties there was need for private schools, and she took upon herself the task of providing them. Her schools were

[1] Related by Frost to Carlyle Morgan in 1950.

variously located at 96 Tremont, 316 Essex, corner Jefferson Terrace at Jackson, and in the Collier house on Sumner Street, Lawrence. In them, when he wasn't editing or tramping down south or acting as night watchman, Robert joined his sister Jeanie in giving his mother a hand at teaching.

They were a happy, carefree family of pedagogues. Belle Moodie had charge of the older students; Jeanie taught the youngsters, while in the words of one who studied at Sumner and Jefferson Terrace,[2] "Robert, very handsome with his hair brushed back, causing the hearts of the older girls to flutter, was the most lovable of teachers." He taught Latin primarily.

There was no system. A general feeling of camaraderie pervaded the school morning, noon, and evening. The quarter-hour recess sometimes approximated a full hour when the prankish older boys took advantage of this good fellowship.

This was the sort of school work Robert Frost could always fit into. He did not feel that the teacher's function was to cram a student with so many facts. He stood by the more generally accepted etymology of the word "to educate"—to draw out—and held this to be the prime factor in pedagogy. His idea was the education of the soul and spirit of man, not merely to put something on as a coat, but to absorb it as food.

Yet, authorship, not teaching, was his life, poetry his first love. He had written occasional verse ("My Butterfly," as we have seen, at Dartmouth the fall of 1892 when he was seventeen), but he had not yet published nationally. Later, in one way or another, before he went to Harvard, were to be published "My Butterfly," "Summering," "Twilight," "The Falls," "An Unhistoric Spot," and some now happily lost forever.

His first publication in book form was made solely for the eyes and heart of Elinor White. We know he gave her the only remaining copy of this book after he had modestly destroyed the other of the two printed, and she kept it by her till death. In the fall of 1894, the poet carried the five poems above mentioned to a small job print shop in Lawrence and arranged for the book to be made. The paper was heavy, antique, vellum finished, and the little volume was bound in pebbled leather. It was

[2] Carita Kimball, of Lawrence.

called *Twilight* and was not an altogether uncreditable venture, either in form or content. Its survival at the hands of Elinor Frost is one of the beautiful things in literary history.

Of the poems in *Twilight*, "My Butterfly" was the only one destined to survive, the only one he was willing to stand or fall by. This poem appeared November 8, 1894, in the columns of *The Independent*, a periodical which from 1894 to 1916 was to use many of his poems. It had small circulation, but in those days it was a force in literature. The editor wished to make the young Methuenite his protégé, which nobody ever could do.

When *The Independent* arrived in Lawrence that November afternoon, it found an excited family. Naturally Robert was proud of his first appearance in a national magazine, one which paid real money for contributions. Perhaps it was this first blush of satisfaction which carried him through the years. He continued to include it in all his collections until 1946, when the editors of the Modern Library left it out.

The check for this poem was made out for fifteen dollars. Long after in our home in California he told the story of the poem.

I was over at the Huntington Library the other day, for I had been told that there were some early manuscripts of mine there, bought from the nephew of the woman who was in its later years a ruling spirit in *The Independent*. I didn't remember much about the manuscript of "My Butterfly." It was just a part of a grasshopper's life. When they brought it out of the vault with the others, it all came back to me. I recalled every little detail. The verse had been written on line paper, very cheap. I had at first signed it with my full name—Robert Lee Frost. But already, as I remember, I was turning back from the Lee part of my name. So, as I saw the manuscript, and as I remembered from the past, I had completely obliterated my entire name—inked it out. Then I had signed it with my initials only—R. F. But I had written the street address, 96 Tremont Street, Lawrence, Mass., above the poem. I have wondered how I expected them to get in touch with me without a name. I think, however, they finally persuaded me to sign the three-decker, as that was the way the poem finally appeared—"My Butterfly—an Elegy, by Robert Lee Frost." It was in this way predestined from the original.

That *The Independent*'s editor was captivated by "My Butterfly" is proved by the way it was handled. Placed on the front page, first column left, it occupied the holy of holies, taking three-fourths of a column. Such position, if nothing else, might well have turned the head of young Frost. But he was impervious, even at such an early date, to censure or praise, good fortune or bad.

With the check came a letter of advice and commendation. William Hays Ward, the editor of the magazine, sent with these a copy of Lanier's poems in an edition containing a memorial to the poet written by Ward. He suggested that Frost read the poems and make a study of Lanier— even going so far as to advise him to make the Southerner his model and seek to write in his school. It was natural that Frost should resent the suggestion that a study of Lanier, who wrote with painstaking smoothness, would help to smooth out his irregularity of lines and roughness of meter. All this was fat in the fire to the son of a stubborn "Copperhead" who knew what he knew. "No writer has ever been corrected into importance," he wrote in one of his choice and rare prose prefaces.

The more Robert read Lanier, the less willing he was to consider following his pattern. The editor refused to give up so easily. He wrote to a friend in Lawrence, the Reverend W. A. Wolcott, who came and made friends with the young poet. Mr. Wolcott was a far-seeing, though not an all-seeing critic. He told the budding genius that his verse was good, but that it wasn't poetry. When pressed, he amplified by saying it was more like people talking, carrying on conversation. This, Frost said later, was precisely what he was unconsciously trying to do.

It has already been mentioned that Frost had an early inclination to drop the "Lee" out of his triple-decked name. The metamorphosis from his birthname on through "R. L. Frost," "Robert L. Frost," and finally in 1906 to "Robert Frost," he once outlined for the writer.

Letters kept coming from down south written by people who were interested in Sidney Lanier, as so many Southerners have always been. They must have thought that because I bore the name Robert Lee I had to be in some manner a satellite of Lanier's. I didn't want to be a satellite. I didn't care to be linked up with anybody. It just didn't like the idea, that's all. I don't suppose I ever sat down and reasoned the thing out. You told me that Markham got you to stop to reason about your triple-decked name, advising you to use the shorter, more dignified double-decker, the way he dropped the "Charles" from his own name. Edwin Arlington Robinson managed to survive, you know, with a most awkward name, quite a responsibility. I did it for another reason. I resented being looked on as a Northerner-Southerner, as you might say. I always wanted to stand on my own. Ward, a devotee of Lanier's, looked on "My Butterfly" as being in the Lanier school, which made him partial to it. He kept trying to get me to write under the aegis of the Southern poet. But I was too determined to go my way, stubborn. I wanted to perform, not to conform. (Of course, I'd as soon do neither.) There were things I wanted more than publication. None of my later poems ever pleased Ward as well as my first one. He wanted me to come right down to New York, where he promised to get me a job as reader in a publishing house. There would have been a good salary to it, and I might have given in to his blandishments and the soft words of others. I have always been glad I resisted his appeal and refused to quit Lawrence. My whole life would have been changed, perhaps for the worse. Odd thing about Ward. He was an Amherst man and was for many years a member of the board of trustees. A Congregational preacher, he was a well-known Assyriologist, having published, as I recall, two very scholarly books on archaeology. I often thought of him after I went to Amherst to teach, but he was already dead by then.

Concerning the metamorphosis of Frost's pen name, we can trace it through from the time of his second published poem, "The Birds Do Thus," in *The Independent* for August 20, 1896, which was signed "Robert L. Frost" till the same magazine in 1906 published "Trial by Existence" using only "Robert Frost."[3]

So interested was Ward in his new poet that he wrote a letter to the novelist, Maurice Thompson, seeking to enlist his interest in Frost. An answer came from Crawfordsville, Indiana, commending the poem, but discouraging any poet to continue as a poet if it meant living in poverty.

[3] In the Lawrence High School Bulletin, Frost varied his name and initials. Once it was "F '92," once "R. L. F.," while "La Noche Triste" carried only "'92." Of the hundreds of signed things from Frost to the author, only once (*The Nation*, Feb. 8, 1928) under the poem "Blood" did he sign all three initials—"R. L. F."

All the while, the youthful versifier was innocent of the interest his little poem had aroused concerning his future. Thompson was right. The poem did have "some secret genius between the lines." But he was wrong in wishing to stem the flood of that genius. Frost knew nothing of the fact that a tired man, the famous author of best-selling *Alice of Old Vincennes,* had taken time and trouble to write a very pessimistic letter concerning him, while praising his elegy to the skies, but it would have made no difference if he had known.

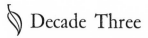 Decade Three

VII. Bond and Free

During the years in high school, the months at Dartmouth, the weeks of desultory ramblings, and on through his teaching with his mother, Robert had kept close to Elinor White. She was then, what she was forever to remain, a genuine helpmeet for him. We have no way of knowing how long it was in his mind to make her his wife. But the final decision was reached in the Ossipee Mountains, above Melvin, New Hampshire, where he had been working on a farm during the summer. The Ossipee interval confirmed him in his love for two things—New Hampshire and Elinor White.

Thus, three days after Christmas in 1895, in the rooms at 316 Essex Street, to which his mother had removed, the young people were married. The bride was the daughter of a Universalist minister and had attended St. Lawrence University. Because of the Swedenborgian faith of Robert's mother, she consented to be married by a minister of the Society of the New Jerusalem. It would seem that this marriage was made in heaven; for through good and evil, wealth and poverty, health and sickness, the two walked hand in hand together for forty-three years.

It was an extremely rainy season in 1896. The Merrimack was at its highest since 1852. The youth, going about the business of living, witnessed much of disaster and ruin as the flood neared its crest. But he had other things than floods to worry about. There were family cares now. As long as the deluge did not disturb his household, he could look on with a characteristic detachment.

Meanwhile, with New England-Scottish economy, Elinor had been added to the teaching staff of the Frost school. Except for the time Robert was teaching at Salem and the two winters Robert and Elinor spent in Cambridge, the whole family lived together from 1895 to 1900. The couple soon had a baby—a son born the first year and named Eliot. The baby was sickly, but the older girl students never minded caring for him.

The restless poet grew still more restless. He had attended Dartmouth to please his grandfather. Now he would go to Harvard to please the memory of his father. Elinor offered no word of protest or complaint when decision was made for him to enter Harvard in the fall of 1897. With a few belongings and his wife and baby, he made his way to the Harvard yard. He continued his classical courses started at Dartmouth, waded through literature, and polished off his Latin.

Frost was to remain a bare two years at Cambridge studying the trivium and quadrivium. He retained pleasant memories of a few professors—Babbitt, later of Trinity College, and Santayana, the successor to William James. Babbitt cut some furrows in his brain, interpreting Greek from the poetic vantage. Santayana, likewise, stirred him up in philosophy, more by process of osmosis than any other way. Once Santayana wrote a letter from Italy, answering one in which I had asked if he remembered having Robert Frost as a student in Harvard. He replied in the negative but expressed pleasure in the knowledge. The "little more" impression was made by George Herbert Palmer, also a philosopher. Frost often spoke of Palmer, who advised him to "bulk up," by which he meant do something big—something epic. But Robert preferred to do what he did at one sitting.

Whatever he may have written at Harvard, he published nothing. The two poems printed in 1897 in *The Independent* were in the hands of the editor before their author was even sure he would go to college. After the printing of "Caesar's Lost Transport Ships" in January and "Warning" the month he entered the university, he was to remain silent for four long years.

Lawrence Thompson has pointed out that Frost went to Harvard mainly to read more widely the classics in the original, a thing he continued to follow to the end of his days. No American poet, Thompson thought, probably ever brought to his work a more thorough knowledge of Greek and Latin writers with as little slavish following of them. My own observation agrees. The first time I met Frost, he had brought along to California with him a copy of Lucretius in the original.

In this same period, Gibson was busy creating "pin-up" girls for the Harvard dormitory walls. George Ade was beginning to write "Fables in Slang." In frivolous moments Harvard students were declaiming "Mighty Casey Had Struck Out!" Weber and Fields were convulsing audiences in New York, and the Floradora Sextette was forgetting to say "when" as they poured into their clothes.

It may have been the birth of his first daughter, Lesley, in 1899, which sent Frost from college back to Lawrence to seek refuge with his mother. Making a living had not been in his thoughts, but now he found he had to face things. He had a wife and two babies. He was a man of twenty-four.

Henry Thoreau and Robert Frost did not grow up in identical surroundings, from identical soils, for nothing. Both went to Harvard, and there both were students of the classics. Frost chose not to be graduated; Thoreau refused to pay five dollars for his diploma, saying it wasn't worth five dollars—or any sum. If Latin turned out a soft spot for the poet, Greek was the same for the philosopher. Both were reincarnate Graeco-Romans who might have written, the earlier, *Walden Pond,* the latter, *North of Boston,* on papyrus a century or two before Christ. Here were two men of today—their day—writing for the many men of tomorrow—any tomorrow.

I am often startled upon coming upon a passage in Thoreau which has in it the soul and genius of Frost. The two men are far more closely related in spirit than is usually granted. I have no slight notion that Frost ever consciously borrowed an idea from the sage of Concord. I only wish to emphasize that both

> *. . . were nursed upon the selfsame hill,*
> *Fed the same flock by fountain shade and rill*

It was inevitable that Frost should hold all his life to Thoreau, just as it was unthinkable that *Walden* should not be a favorite in theme and style all his life long. Had not he himself been a "Self-castaway," a term he applied more than once to Thoreau? There is little doubt in my mind that Thoreau's *Week* left its imprint upon at least two of Frost's better poems. The line in "October"

> *Oh hushed October morning mild,*
> *Thy leaves have ripened to the fall,*

and the lines in "The Cow in Apple Time"

> *She scorns a pasture withering to the root . . .*
> *She bellows on a knoll against the sky.*

These are as near echoes of Thoreau as one might hope to find in a writer who echoes so little.

It was certainly this urge which set him on to the farming adventure— just to show what he could do on his own. Often, both before and after his discussion of the matter in *Books We Like,*[1] he reverted to Thoreau and his Walden Pond experiment in our conversations, just as on rarer occasions he took up the Defoe story of a castaway of another sort— Robinson Crusoe.

It all comes to this: We have ways of knowing that human nature doesn't change much. Maybe it gets worse—maybe not. Only the denouement tells the story, the end. Human intelligence, for all our worship of evolution, stays pretty much the same. We'd be hard put to it to show an intellect in our day the equal of Aristotle's or Immanuel Kant's. These, I take it, appear to be the capstones, at least of their periods, maybe of all time. What has brought about our ability to "do things"? All our adaptability to circumstances? Go back to *Walden* and *Robinson Crusoe*. These experimenters found themselves, when trial came, able to, and *did,* pit themselves naked against an infinitely unfriendly nature, and they provided some part of, no inconsiderable part of, creature comforts sufficient.

I should hate to think we had educated all the animal ability out of ourselves. A little quail skips out of the egg on the run, unfolded by surprise, and never stops. Snakes have to look after themselves from the day they are hatched out, or, in the case of the rattler, after they are born

[1] Subtitled *Sixty-Two Answers* (Boston, 1936).

from their mother. They have no coddling. I have always maintained that we coddle human frailties too much. We encourage the dish to run away with the spoon. Just set a man against the elements. Let him battle. If he's worth his salt he'll make it. If not, it doesn't much matter. He's got to ride like ice on his own melting. He may make a botch of it, but nothing's irredeemable. I often come back to the woman who in the crowd touched the hem of Christ's garment. It was enough.

New Hampshire was calling, and the new experiment of life. The soil had a claim on him. He would use his short-fingered hairy hands to wrest a living from it.

VIII. A Run-Out Mountain Farm

AT THE BEGINNING of the new century Robert Frost had definitely set his mind on being a farmer. During summer vacations he had worked on various "run-out mountain farms" over in New Hampshire. He liked the lay of the land, the rolling hills, the watercourses, the woods, and the little towns. It was as though he had always lived there. A verse written later was to attest his love for the country and its people.

> She's one of the two best states in the Union,
> Vermont's the other.

Those vacation summers confirmed him in his love for these two states and in his love for farming. There was one farm he had seen, worked around, walked across, and learned to love in New Hampshire. He had drunk water from the well in its yard, had nibbled a stray apple "on the bough" in the orchard by the woods. He had looked on that farm as a connoisseur applepicker appraises the fruit he picks, "to touch, cherish in hand, lift down and not let fall." Those of his friends who know the farm, its little rolling hillside, its stone wall (*the* stone wall of all stone walls), its brook and timber, and its saw-tooth skyline well understand why he was determined to hold title to its meager short-thirty acres.

He had tried poetry till Belle Moodie and Elinor White only remained to trust his genius. His mother was never to lose faith in his destiny, but his sister Jeanie, when no one bought his poetry or read it, turned contemptuously from him. His grandfather had evinced his disgust in a number of ways. Why anybody would want to be either a farmer or a poet when there were spools turning in factories was beyond the grasp of the old man. That his grandson should desire to be *both* was almost enough to bring on a stroke.

Determined in his course, Robert laid the whole matter before his grandfather. He would have a farm, live on it, produce his own food with his own labor, and write poetry. After all, the farm he wanted could be bought for a paltry sum, and it would be an easy way to be rid of a nuisance. Up in New Hampshire with his wife and two babies he would have to shift for himself.

The result of the series of conferences on the matter was that Robert and his great-uncle took train for Derry. Arriving at the depot, they walked the two miles out to look on the proposed demesne. The canny old uncle began at once to take inventory of what he saw.

House and barn both needed painting; both needed to be reshingled. Robert could do those chores in between work seasons, thus saving hiring somebody. However, he had his own idea about such things, so for the twelve years he lived on the place he neither painted nor shingled it, and so saved himself the cost as well as the labor. He tells the story:

> The man who lived on the farm had allowed the interest on the mortgage to accumulate, pyramid, until principal and interest became too great a burden for him to lug and make a living too. He had some hay in the mow, and all he asked after my uncle had jewed him down was payment for the hay. He said if we would assume the note on the place (it had snow-balled to the not insignificant sum of $1,700) and give him twenty-five dollars in cash for the hay in the barn, he would make the deed over to us. My uncle saw that the seller had reached the dehydration point and gave in. The poor devil had lived on that farm all those years, and for all his work was getting out with a measly twenty-five dollars. I was moving in, without twenty-five dollars. What I faced, I hadn't the slightest notion. So the deal was closed, the deed signed, the money was paid over, and we went back to Lawrence to get ready to move up to the farm. "I have bought

you a farm, just as you wanted it," my grandfather growled to me. "You've made a failure out of everything else you've tried. Now go up to the farm and die there. That's about all you're fit for anyway."

I suppose my grandfather was right, dead right. I had set up a claim to being a poet, but I was a complete failure—had wasted my life. He was utterly disappointed in me, just as he had been in my father. Perhaps the old curmudgeon was wise and I foolish. Perhaps he knew best. I was very heavy hearted as we packed our scant belongings and made ready to go. The total failure of everything was on my mind, my conscience. I had a wife and children, but there seemed nothing much ahead. It has always seemed strange to me that it was my children (and all of them who lived to man and womanhood except Lesley were born on the farm at Derry) who forced me out into the world and made me try to do something. I was twenty-five when we became farmers. I probably would have gone on writing poetry all my life just for my own amusement and satisfaction, so impossible was it to sell much of the output to the magazines—poetry written with no thought of publication—if it hadn't been for the kids. You see, they got me into debt, and I had to find a way to pay out. I took up teaching again to liquidate, and later, to escape from prosperity and success—financial success—went to England where I published my first book—and here I am.

I think the poet had this in mind when he wrote the preface for the *Bread Loaf Anthology*,[1] where he says; "A writer can live by writing for himself for days and years. Sooner or later he must be read." He continued: "There is nothing so satisfactory in literature as the knockout blow in prizefighting. . . . The scientist has a third proof I have envied for the artist. From the perturbation of a planet in its orbit he predicts exactly where in the sky and at what time of night another planet will be discerned. All telescopes point that way and there the planet is."

Who knows but that he projected himself into the future and discovered himself as a new star in an otherwise dim galaxy. Maybe this sustained him over the barren years.

All this was not without ill effect on William Prescott, Sr. Great bitterness filled his soul—a bitterness he carried to the grave with him a few months later.

[1] *Bread Loaf Anthology* (Middlebury College Press, 1939).

Scarcely had Robert become domiciled in his new farm home till word came that Belle Moodie was not expected to live. Hurrying back to Lawrence, he was there to see her die; and that chill November day, the second day of the month, the procession of hearse, buggies, and carriages wound along toward the home on the hill. They laid her to the south of her husband with the one word "Belle" on the stone. There lay the grandmother, who had died in 1893, Sarah, Willie, and Belle—and the vacant lot at the far end of the geometrically perfect subdivision where they soon were to lay the erratic head of the family. He was to die January 10, 1901.

Derry, Londonderry, East Derry, Derry village, and the depot all taken together barely made one good town when Robert, Elinor, Eliot, and Lesley arrived on the scene in October, 1900. The aggregate population was a scant five thousand people. The Frosts were striking out on their own. Here and there they had gathered up stoves, chairs, tables, and beds. They had loaded these onto a moving van which was to cart them the fifteen miles from Lawrence to the farm.

Winter was already "on the wind" that October. The unprofitable farm, except for the hay in the mow and a few apples on the trees, had been denuded for the year. Spring and seedtime were far in the future.

The unpainted farmhouse stood facing the road from the east, on an eminence overlooking the portion of the country visible through intermittent patches of timber. A birch tree leaned eastward from the lower casement window at the extreme end of the house; and stretching in the same direction, over the hill, was a sturdy, graceful stone wall, destined to have a permanent place in world literature. There in the yard the newcomers looked at the woodbine berries of blue. They saw the dead leaves all huddled and still, while on the upland, a last lone aster lifted its purple blossom. The barn "joined with sheds in a ring-around a dooryard."

None of the poet's unprinted pages of monologue more nearly tell of his life on the farm than his poetry, even though he has recorded that it is hard to "gather biography" from it. In these lines let him describe that moving day when the van came "geeing and hawing" into the drive on the south side of the house and drew up between the porch and the old chain-pump, from which they were to carry water to the house during the next decade. Robert slid the key into the lock, and the squeaking sound it made in turning was full of foreboding. What was in the empty old house? They had the same feeling that late afternoon, which he later expressed in the lines:

> *. . . When we came home*
> *To the dark house after so long an absence,*
> *And the key rattled loudly into place*
> *Seemed to warn someone to be getting out*
> *At one door as we entered at another.*

Soon the moving van was being unloaded, the men piling things here and there wanting to know

> *"Where will I put this walnut bureau, lady?"*

and getting the answer least expected from Elinor, gazing out through the eastern window, her vision skirting the lovely white trunk of the birch tree which faced the sun at morning, as she leaned over the sink to marvel at the weeds made tall by its discharged water;

> *"Put it on top of something that's on top*
> *Of something else," she laughed.*

Still the young wife and mother stood, cape about her shoulders, hat aimlessly held in her hand, seeing the lovely window-tree—slim white birch which other children had ridden down in years that had passed— wall dividing orchard from meadow, spilling into the encroaching woods at the extreme edge of the thirty. The moving men had seldom seen one so detached as this strange woman they had brought from Lawrence. They asked her what she saw through the window, calling her "lady." When she was again "beladied" by a blackened face, and Robert said gently,

> *"What are you seeing out the window, lady?"*

there came a sudden reply, as if all truth were spoken in one swift flight of an arrowed sentence:

What I'll be seeing more of in the years
To come as here I stand and go the round
Of many plates with towels many times . . .

With solicitude the poet queried:

"And yet, you think you like it, dear?"

Then a bang of something heavy upstairs and the tramping of movers shaking the little house on its stone foundation, as if it were none too securely fastened down. There was sadness in her voice as she looked into the coming years, for now the change had come and they were to "give up lighted city streets" they had known "for country darkness."

Husband had gone out for one last look at the place before darkness fell. A new moon tilted through the western woods where lay the road not taken. Elinor called the movers. She would have the stove up before the men left the place, which done, "all turned to with deafening boots and put each other bodily out of the house."

The poem, "In the Home Stretch," illustrated by John Wolcott Adams, was first printed in *The Century* of July, 1916, Frost's first appearance in a magazine in which he had coveted a place. Noted in my copy of the magazine is Frost's opinion of the art: "The place resembles neither the Derry nor the Franconia farm in any least detail."

Life in the Derry household went on after the manner of life in insignificant households everywhere—laughter and tears, birth and death, beginning and end. The very initial season had seen the passing of their first born. Frail Eliot Frost died that summer at the age of four. Now only Lesley, nearly two, remained as winter came on so that the line

I count our strength, two and a child,

becomes very clear.

But others were to take the place of those removed. The year 1902 brought a second man child. He was named Carol, though there was to be little of singing in his life. Tragedy, which had followed so closely after his grandfather, was never to forsake him.

Irma was born in 1903, to be followed in two years by Marjorie—both children of the shadow. In 1907, a girl baby, who received her mother's name with Bettina added, died within twenty-four hours of birth. We would not be far wrong in placing the incident as the genesis of "Home Burial," where the deep, elemental cry

> *Don't, don't, don't, don't!*

echoes an anguish too vast for expression. Truly a man must bury his hopes in a tiny grave before he can write of the ephemeral gold, when

> *. . . Leaf subsides to leaf.*
> *So Eden sank to grief.*
> *So dawn goes down to day.*

How the little family ever lived through those lean years is a mystery. The answer seems to have been chickens. Robert always had pride in his chickens—wanted to propagate a very fine breed, one especially resistant to disease. "About all the money I ever made I made on my chickens," he once said. White Wyandottes predominated, and he had excellent specimens which took prizes at fairs around about New England. It was little wonder that he could write of the winner of the "Blue Ribbon at Amesbury,"

> *Such a fine pullet ought to go*
> *All coiffured to a winter show,*
> *And be exhibited, and win.*
> *The answer is this one has been. . . .*

There is a picture of the late afternoon, toward winter dusk, Lesley wearing her red hood and mittens, leading the toddler Carol by the hand, going out through the snow to the chicken house where the poet-poultry fancier is making his fowl ready for the night. The two children, still hand in hand, jabber to their father and watch the favorite ribbon-bearer, who,

> *Common with the flock again,*
> *Lingers feeding at the trough,*
> *The last to let night drive her off.*

No finer word-etching, autobiographical to the last pinprick, is in the poet's final curtain for the scene:

> *The night is setting in to blow.*
> *It scours the windowpane with snow,*
> *But barely gets from them or her*
> *For comment a complacent chirr.*

With this, shooing Lesley and the toddler out, Robert closes the door, and gathering his son in his arms, leading a small miss in red hood and mittens by the hand, trudges through the drifting snow, up the little hill, past the white birch at the window, around the comforting barn, and into the house.

"What might we be going to have for supper?"

The smell of fresh pork frying on the kitchen stove answers his question. A thoughtful neighbor has come by with a chunk of meat from a day of New England hog-killing just before sundown on the way into Derry village.

Robert and Elinor had turned the corner of destiny. They were farmers now, and one thing they must have taken comfort in, as the culmination of long thinking:

> *The city had withdrawn into itself*
> *And left at last the country to the country.*

There were so many things they didn't know about the soil or about agriculture. There is a story that one day a month after they had acquired a cow, a neighboring farmer asked the new farmer how his cow was doing. He shook his head and replied, "Not so well."

"What time of day do you milk her?" was the next question from the neighbor.

"Whenever we need milk," was Frost's innocent reply.

By no stretch of the imagination could the house where the Frosts lived on the first farm be called attractive. A plain two-story frame structure, without the saving grace even of historical association, it possessed but one angle which might cause a man to glance twice at it. That was across the pump from the corner of the yard. There were two windows on the north, a door and a bay-window on the west with two single windows above. There was a porch whose darkened windows could scarcely be seen on the south and a kitchen window looked out across the farm on the east. To the west lay a few acres of timber—hickory, pine, oak, and birch, with scattered grapevines climbing toward the blue sky. In these woods, west by southwest, lay the road not taken. To the southeast, down a little slope and across a field of rank weeds, lay the brook running west. Pride of possession is seen in the explaining line, concerning another brook and woods to the southeast:

> *And by the brook our woods were there.*

The orchard sprawled away, up grade, down slope, to meet the woods a quarter-mile removed. Baldwins, russets, Ben Davises, Maiden's Blush, and Early Harvest apples grew in abundance.

The minutiae of farm existence must be accepted and fitted into— chickens, a cow, a horse, farming implements, and out-buildings for the animals. For some time they had no dog, which was remedied when a fair mongrel showed up. The horse which came that first year they called "Billy," which was short for Bellerophon. Giving his old plow-horse a name from the classics was Frostian enough. Giving him the name of one who had conquered Pegasus and attempted to ride him to heaven may have been done with a fond hope that Bellerophon might assist in taming the winged horse for him.

And winter and summer, there lay the mountains—not just one mountain, as he has written, but "five ranges one behind the other under the sunset far into Vermont." Hor—it may or may not have been named —intrigued him. It dominated the winter scene. To the poet, that mountain became a symbol of all created things—the epitome of life's hopes and ambitions. It wasn't just one mountain. It was all sorts of mountains. It was real, not fanciful. Not just one mountain, but it helped make a picture. The pasture ran a little way up, then tree trunks; after that tops of trees, everything else hidden by leaves. Only boulders peeked from safe ravines, out through open vistas. I suppose he never climbed it, either from "this side" or from Ladd's. He never went hunting for deer or black bear, but he didn't agree at all with the old man with the oxen who so solemnly declared:

> *"It doesn't seem so much to climb a mountain*
> *You've worked around the foot of all your life."*

Did Frost find the material which went into his verse at his own door? He himself has answered.

> To a large extent the terrain of my poetry is the Derry landscape, the Derry farm. Poems growing out of this, though composite, were built on incidents and are therefore autobiographical. There was something about the experience at Derry which stayed in my mind, and was tapped for poetry in the years that came after. It is all fact—no fancy, but lots of teasing. I never invent for poetic expression. No poet really has to invent, only to record. Some of the poems combine many incidents, many people and places, but all are real. Take the mountain the man "worked around the foot of all his life." That wasn't one, but several mountains. But it was just as real for all its being composite. Those mountains surrounded the Derry farm, and stretched farther than the eye could see.

Strange bundle of contradictions! The same man who wrote, scribbled on the preface to a selection of his poems, that little autobiography is to be found in his writings, except as they came out of the heart and life of one who lived in the country broadly referred to as "North of Boston." The poems themselves, however, are better witnesses to their historiographic character than any afterthought he might have.

IX. PUTTING IN THE SEED

IF THE TERRAIN of Frost's poetry was the Derry landscape, so, also, the weather of New England was embedded in the lines of his poetry. Having spent his early years in the moderate climate of California, the New England weather was something to be adjusted to. In a discussion about Thoreau he had commented

> We coddle human frailties too much. Just set a man against the elements. Let him battle. If he's worth his salt he'll make it.

So on his farm he battled the elements—and his poetry was to prove him "worth his salt."

Have a look at "A Line-storm Song" if you would see a man who has studied his "weather." There you see the flying of tattered line-storm clouds, the roadside flowers too wet for the bee, the silent birds, the rain-fresh goldenrod, and the wheeling east wind; and you share, if you too know your wind and weather, the primordial understanding of the ancient lands "before the age of the fern."

In those Derry days Robert Frost came to know his weather. Turn to what poem you will dealing with concrete things, and his knowledge of weather is to be found. He knew to read its portents with the bridegroom who

> *Came forth into the porch*
> *With, "Let us look at the sky,*
> *And question what of the night to be . . ."*

What profound knowledge there is in the simple line, "out over the crusted snow," or the one which speaks of "the frozen ground-swell." He knew his day—all hours of it—and his night. Witness the phrase in "The Death of the Hired Man,"

> *Part of a moon was falling down the west,*
> *Dragging the whole sky with it to the hills.*

Snow was ever present in the mind of the farmer at Derry. This was unavoidable. It came on early, and it remained late. It filled the woods, obstructed the roads, and banked up the windows. Although his poems were filled with references to snow, it was by no means the only thing he wrote about. The farmers' seasons passed before his eyes, and he set them all down—seedtime and harvest, heat and cold, and summer and winter. It is not strange that *The Old Farmer's Almanac,* published at neighboring Dublin, should use Frost's lines as descriptive of months.

Winter is graphically pictured in "The Runaway," the little Morgan colt, terrified by the strangeness of snow, thundering away in a cloud of dust that will not remain dust long for the snow. It is also caught in another poem in a single line, when he speaks of a time and place

> *Where the sun shines now no warmer than the moon.*

Frost did not forget that the first year of their sojourn at the Derry farm winter had descended upon them with sudden fierceness.

Even in winter, farm work had to be done. Wood was to be cut, corded, and made ready for use at home. The maws of stoves are never filled. He was always

> *Busy outdoors by lantern-light with something*
> *I should have done by daylight, and indeed,*
> *After the ground is frozen, I should have done*
> *Before it froze . . .*

Winter was indoors, too. Poetic thoughts dwelt on Elinor's window flower and the fickle, cruel, neglectful wind which came with icy breath to coquette with the warm blossom and the caged yellow bird singing. The wanton wind gave

> *The sash a shake*
> *As witnessed all within*
> *Who lay that night awake.*

There is a "firelit looking-glass, and a warm stove-window light." But while the flower leaned aside and had nothing to say,

> *Morning found the breeze*
> *A hundred miles away.*

On a mid-December afternoon, the family all safe indoors is listening to the Pan-like voice of the paterfamilias as he reads, Elinor mending before the fire, the children playing on the floor, listening when they choose, just enjoying life, all of them—life that has for boundary the joy which comes from looking out the window at snow on the hillside or the curling smoke from some neighboring chimney. Then a city man pulls into the yard, draws up his team, and just sits there waiting for somebody to come out. The suspense soon sends father and children forth into the cold,

> *A-buttoning coats to ask him who he was.*

He only wanted to buy all the Christmas trees on the place—for three dollars a hundred! Shades of Lucifer and Judas Iscariot! The father refused peremptorily to accept three cents apiece, simply because the trees were

Worth three cents more to give away than sell.

Three cents apiece! When he could look through their limbs cold, cloudless nights and almost touch Orion, Leo, and Canis Major and the Pleiades! Three cents apiece!

But, always there was spring. The poet must

Know that winter death has never tried
The earth but it has failed.

The snow begins to disappear with the longer, warmer-growing days. Soon the white coat has passed from the open fields. Housecleaning, field-furbishing time has come. There is brush to burn, leaves left from autumn to rake, and trees to shear of broken branches where winter's snowy hand has lain too heavy.

Winter's prison has been opened for the farmer—now he will have his oft-repeated wish that the loud southwester may

Turn the poet out of door.

But he can't be too sure. There are still teeth in the old ruin of winter. He may have been talking of himself when he wrote of the fickle April weather, warm at the moment like May,

But if you so much as dare to speak,
A cloud comes over the sunlit arch,
A wind comes off a frozen peak,
And you're two months back in the middle of March.

The dogged farmer—spade, bucket, and rake in hand—goes out to "clear the pasture spring." There stands the dun-colored cow, excited at the sight of the strangely armed biped coming through the patch of withered grass which winter left. The splotched and soiled snow still lies hard under the sheltering oaks along the pasture's southern border.

The orchard is becoming white and pink. The bees are swarming in

· 75

the Baldwin apple tree. There is the nasturtium bed, which is first to spade and get ready for seed.

Yes, spring came on in Derry just as it came on in the England of Chaucer. Each poet experienced his own renascence and set it down for us—the silver peep of the croaker which will not down till winter, birds back for nesting. Winter's spine is broken. How appropriate his lines:

> To think to know the country and not know
> The hillside on the day the sun lets go
> Ten million silver lizards out of snow!

Here of all seasons we have no cause for conjecture about what took place in the fields. The farmer-poet has left his legacy in eternal lines. They all made a little game of it—Robert, Elinor, Lesley, Carol, Irma, and Marjorie. There is the imperishable mezzotint of "The Bonfire." That spring bonfire, with its smells to recur for a lifetime to come, was fun for all the family. But one of those bonfires nearly turned into a catastrophe. In answer to a query, he replied, "Yes, Derry was where I got the scare about a grass fire. I've had a worse one since at Ripton."

So completely was Frost submerged in nature that he more than figuratively passed into the aisles of "those dark trees" and lost himself in an affection which transported him back to the Eocene and Miocene, where it seemed to him the sea returned

> To the ancient lands where it left the shells
> Before the age of the fern.

Spring brought the birds back to Derry. They came winging into his poetry: whippoorwills, blackbirds, sparrows, hawks, thrushes, robins, ovenbirds, swallows, crows, and humming birds. One who could write with such feeling of the meadow left bare after the "cutter had gone over," leaving the open-mouthed fledglings wondering about their mother's deferred return, knew his birds.

The neighbor children have probably passed on the legend about whippoorwills being after little tots who have forgotten to wash their feet. Perhaps the new barefoot Frost children have been warned they'd better wash their feet nights against his coming.

Warm days of spring also found Frost watching the initial appearance of the flowers. More than likely it would be the little rue anemone, beautiful at any season, but coming in March all the lovelier there in its shady place of growth. Or it may have been quite as often the violet which showed under the trees beside the brook. Soon, April dawning, field and forest would be ablaze with pink—the blooming azaleas, with bright red honeysuckles in their copses; the milk-white bloodroot which came up early, wrapped in its sheltering folds, deep in the woods, soon to display a graceful golden center surrounded by red; or the "spring beauty." There was no dearth of color for the flower lover, but one had to wait for the summer ones, or late spring blossoms: the sturdy blue lupines growing beside the wall and the lingering pinkish tinge and light purple of the wild geranium. The white-flowered wood sorrel, too, showed in damp places where the "west-running brook" had influence of wetness.

Perhaps the outstanding event of spring was the thing out of which grew his most quoted poem. He would call to Baptiste, his French-Canadian neighbor, and together they would meet to lay the fallen stones in place, two on a side, just some old game. That wall must be a mecca to ages' end—walling off time from eternity as it were.

Summer brought more flowers to look at, pluck, carry home, and love. In addition to those of spring which he lingered over, he watched for the reappearance of the dull pink petals of the Indian dipper, the sweetbrier rose which ushered in the warm days, growing along slopes of vacant lanes, and alongside woods, the common milkweed with its lavender and pink blossoms, the orange butterfly weed, the damp-loving, sky-blue forget-me-not flaunting its yellow center, the great mullein whose tall blossoms yellowed many an acre of waste and pasture land, the brilliant lobes of the Indian paintbrush, the purple bellflower beside the highway, and the black-eyed Susan and the purple pasture thistle that went along the way with him to Derry village whenever he chanced to pass that road.

Summer at Derry brought the practical side of the impractical man to the fore. He often laughed at a reputation he got among his farm neighbors.

They would see me starting out to work at all hours of the morning—approaching noon, to be more explicit. I always liked to sit up all hours of the night planning some inarticulate crime, going out to work when the spirit moved me, something they shook their heads ominously at, with proper prejudice. They would talk among themselves about my lack of energy. They would all want to be out at work greeting the rising sun in the summer morning, pretty early, that. When they saw me sleeping away the better part of the day—well, it was quite too much for them. They laid it to a lack of energy on my part. I was a failure in their eyes from the start—very start. Certainly I couldn't be a farmer and act like this. Getting into the field at noon! What a farmer! With only one horse between my legs and a cow I kept under cover at milking time.

Most of my earlier poems had to do with country things. So, somebody said my specialty was farm tools, rakes, and hoes and things like that; plows and scythes and axes. But my favorite tool isn't mentioned, not in "The Tuft of Flowers." It does have the hayfork and the scythe. When I was this age I had the fork, and older person the scythe. My idea of poetry is in this poem where it says:

"From sheer morning gladness at the brim."

That's the heart of the whole thing. That's the poem.

A small part of the farm which was set to hay was grazed by cow and horse during off seasons. In the summer were "tall haycocks, lightly piled," a favorite haunt for the poet to "dream upon the opposing lights of the hour." Sometimes the well beside the door would be dry in summer. Surely there would be water in the brook, a giant's stone's throw down the slope, where the woods curtained off the neighbors. Through these woods ran the brook. Armed with pail and can, the two, each laying on other a staying hand, hurry away for water. There, safe within the woods, still doubtful of finding, they listen for the murmur they seek.

Multitudinous tasks there were. Yet, love for the soil, for all these little things, still lured him, ensnared him, and held him in thrall. But he was never so enamored of it that he could not call time out to go to the road for a friendly chat with a passing neighbor (a friend, or perhaps somebody out from the village) who had drawn his horse up by the roadside and beckoned. Frost would stick his hoe into the mellow ground, leaving five feet of handle, leading to the blade end, standing to show him the row he had already finished hoeing. It would have been too bad to work it a second time so soon!

Frost was always living up to his own dictum of "taking what nature is willing to give."

Often he went forth to his unwelcome labors, "scourged as a galley slave," wondering if perhaps the mower had gone who went before him in the morning, saying, "I listened for his whetstone in the breeze." The little children, at play beside the wall, paused to hear his "long scythe whispering to the ground." It was here in this sylvan spot, with yonder

> *A leaping tongue of bloom the scythe had spared*
> *Beside a reedy brook,*

that, on the "height of a naked pasture land," Pan passed by one day to teach him the effect of a new world song. Not for him the old. Not for him a song run long ago into a mold. Pan was with him, listening to

> *The bluejay's screech*
> *And the whimper of hawks beside the sun.*

When Frost first came to the farm, there were many things he didn't understand (as yet), many habits and customs and folkways of the community with which he was unfamiliar. Take "The Code." No hired man in New Hampshire would even take a mild suggestion that a downpour was threatening. He needed no "boss" to tell him about his work or to warn him of weather. He took pride, this mythical hired man, in being a law unto himself. He didn't need to be told to take pains. He *always* took pains with whatever he did. One gets the miniature in lines as hard as steel engraving as the worker, thrusting his pitchfork in the ground, leaves the field for home. And all the hiring farmer had said was something "about taking pains," more to himself than to his men. But he learned something that day in the meadow.

With all his seeming indifference to the far-off harvest, Frost always concerned himself more with reaping than with "putting in the seed."

· 79

His autobiography set forth in his poetry speaks eloquently here. In every spring there is the prophecy of the inevitable autumn. The grasses of April whisper to the southwest wind of the surety of the blustery coming November days.

Autumn, forever sad, is well prefigured in August. Coming up "through the mowing field" where stems, like thatch, lie heavy with dew.

Late summer is berry-picking time. We read the accounts given in these autobiographical lines to his wife on

> *How we used to pick berries: we took one look round*
> *Then sank out of sight like trolls under ground....*

The brief New England summer passes so swiftly, and with it the flowers, for there remains but a single aster flower to be had (October it would seem), and this one for Elinor, never far from his thought. But the aster, while one of the latest to bloom, had as companions the thistles, the goldenrod, and the sturdy vervain.

There are dark days of autumn rain—something he loved. On such occasions the yard was littered with woodbine leaves and winter was "in the wind."

The Frosts loved apples and apple trees. On the Derry farm there were many. With the coming of October work had to be done, back-breaking, arm-aching work. The hectic days had effect even upon the "cow in apple time," inspiring her, having tasted fruit, to scorn the pastures.

It was not the Frost of the earlier winters of the opening century who could create the saw from an old maxim, as he talked to his trees:

> *Good-bye and keep cold,*

advising them in parting to

> *Dread fifty above more than fifty below.*

It took empirical knowledge to arrive at that.

Apple-picking time was a festive season, come autumn and the trees groaning with fruit—some to be sold, some to be stored in barrels down cellar, but all that fell "went surely to the apple-cider heap." The cider mill stood conveniently under a Baldwin tree, and to it went all the spoiled ones, for cider was delicious on a night in autumn.

Yes, the poet had apples in Derry, for all New Hampshire had them.

Thus the cycle of the seasons went on from year to year, Frost learning to drag income from the niggardly soil and poetry out of the land barren of poetry.

X. UNCERTAIN HARVESTS

DURING THE LEAN YEARS at Derry, there were always two harvests, uncertain harvests. Robert Frost could not make up his mind which was the less certain of the two.

Crops were utilized in feeding the growing children, and these were insurable. Then, there was the crop for the children of mankind—soul-stuff—in the form of his poetry. Both were hard to bring to blossom and fruit, and even harder to dispose of when grown.

In 1901, after he had become well established on the farm, he sent forth "The Quest of the Orchis," and it found a place in *The Independent*. It was quite an event on the farm.

We had a family celebration, jubilee. You see, the poet-farmer was still moving forward, remembering the hare and the tortoise. My verse was still printable. It had now been four years between published poems. I was twenty-six, but the eight of my poems in *The Independent* were like rain in summer, rain on growing corn.

There had been days of terrific strain on the farm. You see, I can manage a poem in the singular very well and not feel the strain, not too much. In the midst of my work at the farm I could handle such a task. Sometimes one would grow out of an idea, leaving me relaxed. At other times the idea would produce a second growth, forcing itself as a Siamese twin on its predecessor. That would bring trouble of spirit, and more than likely right in harvest time. I would be in a terrible stew, fever, likely. My legs would ache, my head would ache. Eating was out of the question. Sleep? There wasn't any. I would become grouchy—mean—and bite everybody's head off. The children would have to stay out of reach and sight. Even my wife wouldn't break in on my agony. And that was going too far even for a poet, with or without a publisher. What made it even worse was that I refused to admit I was temperamental on account of my unprincipled crookedness. What did I think I was? After all, what editor would buy even a first poem, much less a second growth, the second growth which brought all the trouble on! As I remember it, "Stopping by Woods on a Snowy Evening" was written in just about that way, after I had been working all night long on "New Hampshire." But I must admit, it was written in a few minutes without any strain.

Critics think I had that sort of all-night struggle before I could write the little poem I'm talking about. They must have heard me say, sometime or other, years back, that I wrote all night, in connection with "Stopping by Woods." But the thing I worked on all night had no struggle in it at all. It's in print, called "New Hampshire." I sat in the same chair and wrote all night. Had a good time writing scatteringly about New Hampshire—how the state has nothing to sell in commercial quantities. Then, having finished "New Hampshire," I went outdoors, got out sideways and didn't disturb anybody in the house, and about nine or ten o'clock went back in and wrote the piece about the snowy evening and the little horse as if I'd had an halucination—little halucination—the one critics write about occasionally. You can't trust these fellows who write what made a poet write what he wrote. We all of us read our pet theories into a poem.

The farm work had to go on, and as I have said the strain was pretty bad—pretty trying. But, what to a poet were stooks of grain from Vermont, across the mountains; or a broken-down fence with a cow bellowing on a knoll against the sky? In such a state I wrote—can't tell how—or even why. The chickens remained unfed, and the rain swept in to spoil the grain.

That which was growing out of all the agony at Derry was his first sheaf (some of his second) of poems, the ones which went into the London-published books. In his words, they all grew out of the Derry soil at a time when he was writing with little hope of publishing. Was there ever, we ask, a poet writing under worse difficulties?

> *Considering the market, there are more*
> *Poems produced than any other thing.*
> *No wonder poets sometimes have to seem*

So much more business-like than business men
Their wares are so much harder to get rid of.

To many of his admirers, his first book of poetry, simple and unassuming as it is, will forever occupy a place by itself, not because it is the first book of a major poet, but because it welled up out of the waters of an unfathomable memory.

The first welling poetry was all so simple—ideas, language, and technique. But don't let it deceive you. It was the simplicity of sophistication, and so original. Frost could learn from Shakespeare, but his tragedies were his own, not Hamlet's, Macbeth's, or Lear's. For comedies, he has Buttons and Falstaffs after the New England pattern. He runs the gamut of created things, from those of the soil to others of the sidereal—from a glance at Canis Major to say,

I looked into the crater of an ant.

It was so utterly simple, and yet so full of bewitching words and manner. There never seemed any reason for the effect on you as you read it. The sorcery it contained was pure Druid. It was elusive as the perfumes of spring woods. Then one day you came upon the treasure hid in a field. It was all hidden in the strange figures, which, because of their naturalness, escape you in all his poetry—some figure, say

Like nothing else by day, like ghosts by night.

Those neighbors of his, along with season and soil, were no small item in the making of his poetry. They are all true New England, all true to New Hampshire life, which goes far to explain their permanence. There were strange families living in those old houses! He knew that his characters were leftovers, "morbid, pursued by phantoms, slowly sinking into insanity." Amy Lowell's summing up is worth remembering:

" 'Home Burial,' " she wrote, "gives the morbidness of death in those remote places; a woman unable to take up her life again when her only child has died. The charming idyll, 'After Apple-picking' is dusted over with something uncanny, and then 'The Fear' is a horrible revelation of those undercurrents which go on as much in the country as in the city, and with remorse eating away whatever satisfaction the following of desire may have brought. There is also the theme of 'The Housekeeper,' while 'Generations of Men' shows that foolish pride in a useless race which is so strange a characteristic of these people. It is all here—the book is the epitome of decaying New England."

Frost knew all this, but he inserted the sly, restrained, chuckling sense of humor for which he became famous. Stirred up by a woman poet who had given up her home in Dublin, he asks what ails New Hampshire.

> *She said she couldn't stand the people in it,*
> *The little men (it's Massachusetts speaking).*
> *And when I asked to know what ailed the people,*
> *She said, "Go read your own books and find out."*

Frost had a feeling of pity and compassion for these thought-inbreeding people and regretted their dwindling population. Of a deserted house in a desert of swamps, where no one "could tell the time of year when every tree that could have dropped a leaf was down itself," he had to declare it filled him with melancholy that the census taker had

> *To count souls*
> *Where they grow fewer and fewer every year.*

Then there was the gum gatherer who was neighbor to him, whose stuff was "golden brown" at picking, "but comes to pink between the teeth." The poet saw something in that sort of life to admire. All the work one had to do was

> *To loose the resin and take it down*
> *And bring it to market when you please.*

And there was, to take another at random, Meserve—he of "the wretched little Racker Sect." New Hampshire always had its quota of men looking to get up a miracle—daring the Almighty in a blizzard.

There was also the neighbors left over with houses full of bric-a-brac, claimed naturally as a *Mayflower* cargo. On the walls, as in "The Black Cottage," were atrocious enlargements of stern forebears.

> *A buttoned hair-cloth lounge spread scrolling arms*
> *Under a crayon portrait on the wall,*
> *Done sadly from an old daguerreotype.*

Neighbors, too, like the ones who went afield for blueberries—whoever's berries they found first. Of this fellow Loren, head of the blueberry-picking family, the poet could say,

> *He seems to be thrifty; and hasn't he need*
> *With the mouths of all those young Lorens to feed?*

From these neighbors Frost knew what blood-inbreeding and thought-inbreeding (thought incest) had accomplished in New England since the Puritan days. The story of all the intermarrying and the re-intermarrying that had been going on, one of his characters in "Generations of Men" tells with a laugh. When his cousin pulled his passport and said, "I'm a Stark," she tossed her head, having already declared that she herself bore the name, with,

> *I only mean my mother was a Stark*
> *Several times over, and by marrying father*
> *No more than brought us back into the name.*

Another neighbor who was good for a laugh was the old woman in "The Housekeeper," who had grown so big sitting in the house she was sure they could never get her out through the door, for she said,

> *I've been built in here like a big church organ.*
> *We've been here fifteen years.*

It was a time of great production—but the harvest was indeed small. During the twenty years which ended with his leaving Derry, he received pay for a meager thirteen poems.

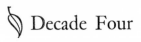# Decade Four

XI. A Dole of Bread

One cannot know Frost without an acquaintance with Derry village. This hamlet, as distinguished from Derry Depot, was the home of the true Derryites, descendants of the old inhabitants of Londonderry, including the Pinkertons and the Chases. Its people were ultra-conservative, to put it mildly.

Derry village, where Pinkerton Academy was located, had refused the railroad permission to profane their sacred precincts. Not to be defeated, the railway officials changed their right-of-way and built the depot a mile to the west of the academy. The new village, given proper impetus by the coming of the "iron horse," started to grow. Industry came in—not that Derry village had no such, for the Chase family made their wealth out of manufacturing tags with little wires attached to fasten to new fruit trees for identification. Londonderry, the oldest settlement, was a separate entity. The three, Londonderry on the north, the Village (East Derry on the maps) at the east, and the depot on the west, formed a proper triangle.

The people of Derry village maintained an academy to which they sent their children and grandchildren—and a good academy it was, with Christian influence. They supported their churches and owned the final word in religion.

It was President Eliot of Harvard who dubbed Major John and Elder James Pinkerton "Old-time merchants of Londonderry." The phrase was placed on the bronze memorial tablet on the façade of the Pinkerton main building in 1906. The Pinkerton brothers, who in 1815 gave sufficient endowment to carry on the work of the academy and John M., son of Elder James Pinkerton, who at his death in 1881 left a second large bequest, were all men of foresight.

The academy began work shortly after its incorporation in 1814. It was founded for the purpose of "promoting piety and virtue, and the education of youth in science, language and the liberal arts." At the turn of the century, patriarchal George Bingham, academy principal, taught Latin and carried out the finest traditions of the school. To old-timers bent on tradition, the chief end of man, next to worshiping deity, was to work hard at getting an education. Latin and Greek—the classics in general—and logic and philosophy were of the first importance.

Pinkerton campus was always a beautiful spot. The old brick building with its great open windows was inviting enough, but the pine trees and town made the picture complete. In the early days of the century, the graduating class each spring planted a tree with due solemnity. A row of elms graced the south side, and there stood two delightful blue spruces. At the southern entrance, toward which the whole campus sloped gently, stood two stately cottonwoods.

Socialized medicine was unheard of in New Hampshire in the early days of the 1900's. When sickness came to the home it was every family for itself. There were two results: the doctor either gouged his patients and collected fees from the willing and able, or he took produce for his services from the moneyless.

At the Frost homestead, chickens were about the only things that naturally took the place of money—chickens and eggs. Just as chickens fed the growing family and gave them what clothes they had, so chickens paid the doctor for his incessant calls.

Those doctor bills! All of them might have been sick at the same time, but nature refused to co-operate, and their spells of sickness came tandem fashion. Old Dobbin drew the village doctor down the two miles of turnpike so often the old horse learned to pull into the driveway every time he reached the Frost house. How Frost remembered it in after years!

It was quite a day when it came to me what I had to do to keep life in the body and bones of my family—doctor bills, clothes, food required for growing kids—these things demanded money. My income had stayed about the same, no change. We had plenty to eat, for we raised a great deal on the farm and had poultry; but we were not getting any farther ahead.

When my grandfather's estate was wound up I got a little driblet of money now and then. I would go to the bank at Derry, an institution to then unknown to me. To tell the truth, until I got that first installment of the inheritance in the form of a check, I had never done business with a bank in my life. It was an entirely new experience. The banker very pompously said to me when I presented my check, "How will you have your hard-earned money?" meaning of course, would I have it in cash or leave it on deposit. There wasn't enough to deposit as I was always behind with everything before I got it. I remember I signed my name Robert Frost. The banker looked at the signature and said, "Since it doesn't cost you anything, we would like your full name." It hurt my feelings. You told me once that you saw my name signed to a legal document with the full name—Robert Lee Frost—and that the Lee was written much smaller. It was not done on purpose, or even consciously. The Lee had already become atrophied through disuse.

There are other memories of our home life at this time. I was beginning to train Lesley in the art of poetry-writing. I was very careful what I taught her, and for all the years before we went to England I was keeping a little notebook in which I wrote things she must learn. She never became a poet, something I should have foreseen. She was not the sort, and you can't teach a child poetry-writing, or a bird to sing. The verb has no imperative. She lived in the world. It remained for Marjorie and Carol, the first two to leave the world, to write the poetry of the family, though as I recall, every one of the kids took a hand at writing verse first and last.

Well, in the summer of 1905, one day I drove Old Billy down to Derry depot with two of the kids with me, to get some meat for supper, we had to eat. The butcher came sneering out, knowing very well what I was after, and remembering my account-payable. He eyed the horse up and down, asking if anybody had a lien on him. That determined me as to what I should, or rather *must* do. It was my first clash with realism.

There I was with four children and a wife to feed and clothe and doctor —something I was not knowing rascal enough to put across well, at all. I was thirty years old and as great a failure as anybody ever was at the turn of life. Up to that day I had sold exactly five poems. I had written many others which had been laid away to jell. There I was like the old woman who lived in a shoe—I had so many children—and poems—I didn't know what to do. As a financial wizard I could have learned a lot from that fellow Lawson who was writing about his *Frenzied Finance* at the time. My finances were frenzied enough, though I furnished the frenzy through lack of them. It took all night for me to bring myself to do what I had to do. I had driven home from the village without meat that afternoon—but with my determination set, though my mind was not yet reconciled, even though made up. I had not had time to think it all through. I was an unsocial being afraid of another man's shadow. Many a time I have stood in the middle room at the Derry farmhouse looking out the window across the porch to where some man would be standing in the yard by the pump, one who had come to buy chickens or a calf; biting my lips till they bled before I could force myself out the door to talk business with him, chicken and egg business. Yes, I was unsocial.

Times had been unusually bad, and we were getting deeper and deeper in debt—with all those infernal doctor bills. I knew I must supplement my farm income from some additional work. The children were coming along, and we needed more and more money for them. So, as I lay thinking, awake in bed that night, I became reconciled to my fate. I decided to do what I hated to do—and what I didn't want to do, what I had never liked to do—go back to the drudgery of teaching. I had not made a bad job of it. I let my wife sleep, while I tossed, and didn't bother her with the problem all night. I lay awake till morning, my heart thumping, dreading to have to go and see somebody about a job. But finally I screwed up my courage to a point where I was willing to make a try at it, one try.

Next morning, with rather red eyes, when I brought up the subject to my wife, I convinced her that I was right, and she urged me to carry it out. So I went down to Lawrence, where I knew there would be those who would remember my work as a teacher. I ran into a man on the street almost immediately, who knew of my work. He remembered my poems in *The Independent.* So it was that my poetry made a breach for me, as it continued to do all my life. If I couldn't sell poetry, at least it was forever my opening wedge. This man listened to my suggestion that I must have a teaching job. He asked me why I didn't try to get into the faculty of the academy at Derry—Pinkerton. He asked me if I knew the principal or any of the teachers. Of course I had to say no, for I had scarcely so much as even heard of the school.

There I had lived within two miles of the academy for five years and hadn't made the acquaintance of anybody connected with it, which would be hard to explain when I got back and asked them for a job, I told him. But he had a friend, the Reverend Charles Merriam, an able preacher, who was a member of the board; so he told me he would write this friend all about me, introduce me. He advised me to wait a week or two, then go into the village and talk with the preacher. I went on back to Derry and followed his advice. In a reasonable time I went into the village and called on Merriam. I went ahead telling my story, and he sat there looking straight through me, as much as to say, "Why haven't you done anything in your life? Why are you here like this?" And he was right, three strikes. A man at thirty should have done one little constructive thing, made some sort of success out of something. I had never succeeded at any job I tackled —that is as the world looks on success.

But Merriam was kind. He said there was going to be an annual meeting of the school board at his church, the Congregational church at the village, and that all the trustees and their wives would be there. He said I should write a poem and get up and read it before the diners. That would introduce me to the trustees. The meeting was a thing they always made quite an event of, and it would, he assured me, make a good opening for me. When I got to thinking of having to get up and read a poem before all those strangers, my heart failed me. I told him that wouldn't do. I never could get up and read my poem. Very well, he said, then I should write one and he would read it. After that we would talk with Bingham, the principal.

I went home, and instead of writing a poem for the occasion (a thing I was never guilty of in all my life, except an occasional doggerel in fun), I dug up one that was finished off pretty well. It was "The Tuft of Flowers," one I always considered one of my best. I took it to the meeting with me and sat there on needles and pins while Merriam read it. It would have been a great deal better for me to read it, for I had to listen while he did a bad job of it. But it made a hit, and again my poetry saved me. Sort of modern magic, you see. Not black, or white. Just modern.

Most interesting, this meeting at Derry's Congregational meeting house that night in 1905. Here was a writer, unknown, unrecognized, unpublished, his poem being bungled and fumbled by a kindly, well-intentioned man; and a crowd of diners, some of them bored, others

plainly impressed. Of the latter was Chase, who became a lifelong sup-
porter, and Principal Bingham. Thus did "The Tuft of Flowers" do its
work. Frost goes on:

Coming up to the board, the members turned the matter of hiring me
over to Bingham, a long-whiskered, white-headed—could as truthfully
say long-headed, white-whiskered—New Hampshire educator of the old
school. Good man. He had plenty of New England shrewdness, as I was
to learn. I plainly was no match in wits for him. For you see I was a babe
in the woods. There we had lived in the farmhouse all those years, and
only twice during all the time had we been away from home later than
eight o'clock at night. I couldn't meet him on his own grounds, as the
sequel showed. However, in the years to come, during our association together, I learned to like and respect him. He grew on me.

The day I went to call on him he beckoned me in from the hall and
said, "Well, I understand you only want to teach part of the time." I agreed.
"How would an hour a day suit you?" I nodded. My timidity closed my
mouth against speech. "Let me see. That would figure one fifth of a teaching load. How would $1,000 or $1,200 suit as base pay?" I choked at the
figure, thinking I would get that much for my work and grunted agreement. He put that down and added a phrase that sealed my doom. "One
fifth a teaching load, base pay $1,000 a year. That will be about $200 a
year for your work. How is that?" I could only do what I had done at
every turn of his monologue. I accepted my fate. But my doctor bills
amounted to more than that every year!

It was in this manner that I became a teacher in historic Pinkerton
Academy. Every day I trudged to school, rain, shine or snow, exposed myself, almost caught pneumonia, for which I was paid $200. Naturally at
the end of a twelfth-month I had come out the little end of the horn.

Next summer, that was 1906, I said to Preacher Merriam, with whom
I had formed a close friendship and who really wanted to help me all he
could, that I wasn't being treated right. "Here," I said to him, "I am teaching about as much as any regular faculty member, and I've only gotten this
pitiful sum. I must have more money." He saw the light—at least a glim-
mer—and next season I was paid $350. By 1907 I was really getting up
in the world for they had raised me to $1,200, and later, when Bingham
resigned, they offered me the principalship at $3,000 a year and a house
to live in—a good house. But I got scared, so I said to the trustees, "You

folks don't want me to be principal. Think how it would look for the head of this famous old school to have his name printed in the catalog, to go out everywhere, with no degree showing after it. Just let me continue teaching as I have been, and you get another principal." You see, I wanted to work for awhile yet, as legally the farm was not mine till I had lived ten years on it, and I couldn't afford to make the Pinkerton people mad, just yet, anyway. I had to be soft spoken. They took my advice and called another man as principal.

Robert Frost was remembering his Horace. He would not become involved. If Pinkerton was his Macaenas, and accepting its patronage meant a surrender of a noble freedom, he would say, "Farewell to fortune and welcome adversity."

Frost's first mark of genius as a teacher is to be looked for in his ability to inspire students to learn and do. The experience of John Bartlett, so long editor of *Editor and Journalist,* who was at Pinkerton from 1907 to 1910, is perhaps typical. That Frost affected his whole life is not to say too much. Of Bartlett the teacher speaks in his longest poem, "New Hampshire," concerning friends:

> *I'd sure had no such friends in Massachusetts*
> *As Hall of Wyndham, Gay of Atkinson,*
> *Bartlett of Raymond (now of Colorado),*
> *Harris of Derry, and Lynch of Bethlehem.*

When things got difficult at Pinkerton, it was always Bartlett who went to bat for him. That friendship came about because of the perfect understanding which naturally sprang up between them. A slight composition had been handed in by a new boy, and on the ball field the teacher had taken time to tell him he had done a fine piece of work, that he had the stuff in him. John Bartlett never forgot. Here was a teacher who understood and appreciated, a teacher who played with the boys— coat off, shirt sleeves rolled up—on the diamond, swatted and caught balls, attended their games with rival teams and rooted, and wrote songs for their victories.

Bartlett became ring leader of the gang which tagged Frost around the countryside at Derry. There were long walks across the hills, through the woods, and along the streams.

Frost discovered athletics long before athletics discovered him. Often he has talked of the beauty of athletic sports in our presence, to us. The nearest thing to the arts is the gymnasium, the ball field, and the track. The Greeks knew this. Their Olympic games expressed beauty to them the same way that architecture and sculpture did. Fifty years after Derry, he had come to be recognized for what he was—an old Greek out of Homer. In 1956, *Sports Illustrated* proved such recognition by inviting him to become a "visiting columnist" to represent them at an All Star baseball game. They dubbed him "America's leading living poet." The result was one of Frost's few but inimitable ventures into prose, with subdued sallies of humor, just as Frostian as "The Witch of Coös."

The girls at Pinkerton remembered him too. There was Christine Feinaner, later married to Augustus Buttman. She never forgot his unorthodox methods of teaching. Walking up and down in the room talking all the while, writing in an exceedingly fine hand his choice of poems on the board for the pupils to copy, Frost rarely asked a question which he himself could answer. This led to no end of investigation, talk, and curiosity to go forward.

On the first day after he began teaching in the academy, his pupils turned in their written work in English composition. He gathered them all up, and holding them aloft asked if anybody wanted theirs back after he had read them. After a little hesitation on their part, there was a chorus of "no, no." "Very well, then," he said as he dropped the whole batch in the wastebasket, "here goes. I don't intend to become a reader perfunctory of perfunctory writing."

We may learn somewhat of those mysterious methods of pedagogy engaged in by Frost at Pinkerton by looking into the notebooks of one of the students of his day and his classes. It would not be hard to re-create the classroom of the teacher by judicious use of the imagination. He would probably read a chapter from *A Connecticut Yankee*—crouched and slouched in his chair, tie off, shirt unfastened at the top, unruly hair, his paradoxical voice—soft, gentle, but firm, high pitched—rambling along, putting more humor into Mark Twain than Mark ever dreamed could be found there. The class would be in convulsions of laughter. Then he would lay the book down and start talking.

He runs the gamut from "The Cuckoo Song" to the twentieth century. He talks about names and shows how beautiful names help make beautiful poetry, prose as well. Then he is off on the choice of words—something at which even Housman was never more adept. The springboard is Cowley's poem, "The Swallow." He has quoted the opening lines. Then he pauses.

"Foolish prater *what dost thou?"*

"Cowley might have called the twittering swallow a silly twitterer, or a silly or idle talker, or an endless chatterer. But he has a fine choice of nouns and adjectives in mind. He may have discarded a dozen or fifteen of each before he arrived at that which satisfied his taste—foolish *prater*. They are clever words—especially the noun. It grows on you as any well-selected adjective, adverb, or noun will. But the greatest beauty of this poem is its central part. It is a little extravagant, but, let that pass. At least we have here a fresh observation. Strange that an experience so common has not elsewhere been written about—it has not been, at least to my knowledge."

Dialect comes in for discussion—dialect into which he seldom lapsed —unless the homely philosophy of his New Hampshire and Vermont characters might be called "thought dialect."

On the day of which we are thinking, in the itinerant classroom of the farmer-poet-teacher, perhaps he was adverting to his own life "without a name" as he chalked Scott's poem "Lucy Ashton's Song" on the board.

"Sound, sound the clarion, fill the fife,
To all the sensual world proclaim:
One crowded hour of glorious life
Is worth an age without a name."

During the term the choice made by Frost for writing on the blackboard included Keats's "Nightingale," Emerson's "Brahma," Barnes's *"Mater Dolorosa,"* Tennyson's "Lotus Eaters," Christina Rossetti's "Wind," Brown's "My Garden," and Kipling's "There Never was a King Like Solomon."

Glancing through *The Critic,* Pinkerton's student publication, one cannot but wonder which poems published there were inspired by Frost, what unfathered ones might be his own. John Bartlett is authority that the teacher-critic did write some of the unsigned ones, in addition to those published over his signature. Shakespeare was the god of Pinkerton, and *The Critic* shows that not only was he taken seriously, but that blood and tears were shed in bringing out his plays. It is safe to wager that the itinerant teacher had nothing to do with their production—not because he did not like Shakespeare, but because he believed in modern plays for modern players. He encouraged the dramatic classes to produce some of the moderns, including Shaw, Barrie, and Yeats. He made fun and pleasure out of the matter of producing these plays, taking it out of the tedium of classroom drudgery. When he was met on the street by someone in authority and was told he might use the communion service of the church for props in the scene showing Circe's palace in Milton's *Comus,* he had received real recognition.

Then there were the coaching days at Derry—coaching in debating and oratory. One never knew how much tongue-in-cheek went into R. F.'s description of his work in these fields. He made odd claims more than once.

It wasn't too hard to win debates—take all the prizes at oratory. I had a good plan worked out—fool proof. Maybe I was fooling.

You see, I got my men picked right off who were to win the debates. I started 'em off by saying they'd best give up claiming any original, brilliant thoughts. There was always Daniel Webster to quote. So, I'd tell 'em when they had a good idea to ascribe it to Webster, which would win the judges. Not all of 'em to Webster—to somebody just as noted. That'd fool the judges. It worked. We won.

But my way of handling the oratory contest was even a greater success. Some donor put up the dough for the prizes. I picked the ten competitors and asked each to write an oration. The first drafts were pretty bad, and I made a suggestion or so and asked 'em to rewrite and hand in. This went on and on till I had changes enough to have an entirely new oration for each boy. Then they memorized 'em, orated 'em to the judge (me) and the judge (I) picked the winner. I was congratulated by the man who gave the prize for the five orations I had wormed out of the ten youngsters. I hadn't read about Ellis and the Olympics for nothing. I got to be quite Elean—good idea.

During all the dreary months of teaching there were remarkably few days marked by the appearance of a poem in some magazine. "The Trial by Existence" occupied nearly a whole page in *The Independent* on October 11, 1906. It was the first poem he ever published which brought him a letter from some unknown reader—in itself a thrill. *The New England Magazine* presented "A Line-storm Song" in October, 1907. Another year passed before *The Independent* again opened its columns to print "Across the Atlantic," March 26, 1908—his thirty-fourth birthday. It was judiciously dropped by him from all his lists of poems chosen for inclusion in collections. On my copy of the magazine containing this poem, he has written the confession, "Negligible accident."

In the May, 1909, number of *The New England Magazine* appeared the poem "Into Mine Own"—the title changed in his books to read "Into My Own." This poem had been in process for a long time, a log of youthful adventure into the wide, new world. The same month, *The Youth's Companion* published "The Flower Boat" with a picture on the editorial page. The ending line of this carried further the theme of "Into Mine Own," for it spoke of his wish to "seek the Happy Isles together." After this—silence for three barren years!

Things had not gone smoothly. The long trip into town, in the days when two miles were more than a Sabbath Day's journey, had been trying to the teacher. The New England winter had taken its toll of suffering added to hard work. At last he rented a house in Derry village, a couple of blocks from the academy, southward down the hill. It was a delightful old white frame building, two stories in height, with evergreens and elms bordering the lawn. The Russell family shared the house. A common sight for passers-by that school year was Frost on the porch or under the yard trees, seated in a Morris chair, a writing board in front of him.

"I can see him now, and feel all the old affection for him which I felt in those days. His stubborn hair in the wind, his serious face, set off by a quizzical smile which occasionally lighted up, sitting there on the porch in the sun. Frost's poetry to many people has been hard to understand. I found it difficult at first. Aside from the subject matter with its constant reference to farm work, fields, and woods, the style made it even more difficult. But I early discovered that one way to master and overcome it was to read the poems aloud for a few times. Of a sudden they would become clear as day."

This was the memory of an old neighbor who lived across the street and who saw him every day in school and at home.

The house in town never took the place in the affection of Robert and Elinor Frost which the farmhouse occupied for them to the end. Long after, Elinor confided to a scion of the Pinkerton house that no other place had ever seemed home to her—that she loved the Derry farmhouse above all others. There her husband found himself, there their children were born—there two of them died. It was the memory of the farm and of the woods and brook, which long after, when his life companion had died, brought the poet back to wander alone through the fields.

Often during the Pinkerton days he took walks afield with the village men. If Sylvia Clark's memory is a good one, it was on such a trip to the woods northwest of Derry village that Robert strayed to a "sequestered spot" in company with Edward Pettee. There they came upon a bed of orchises, out of which probably came "Rose Pogonias."

She also tells of a time when the poet-teacher, walking back to the farm, would pause at the Clark house and be fed by her mother. This he vigorously denied, warning us not to believe all they said around Derry.

> I was never in the Clark house to eat but one time, just once. They invited two other men teachers and myself to dinner. We ate, never said a word, listening only to the incessant talk of the women, of which they monopolized the whole. They showed us the bric-a-brac (the hickory-dickory clock up which the mouse ran) supposed to have come over in the *Mayflower* or to have been owned by some Clark ancestor who was a famous Indian fighter or something, I don't know. I recall one time when Sylvia Clark's sister drove me home to the farm in a buggy, for lunch, for

my lunch. We went into the house, and there on the table was a single wooden dish, such as grocers sell cottage cheese in. It contained one lone pickle. It looked as if that was to be my lunch. I saw that her eye was taking in the whole situation. She looked very queerly at the pickle. We always had plenty to eat, such as it was—not much variety but of what we had there was never a real lack. Maybe she connected my general sourness with that pickle. Could be.

Frost was the object of much jealousy during his days at Pinkerton. He had no settled classroom—taught where he was placed by the exigencies of the moment. He was an interloper, in other words. He was younger than most of the other teachers, did not abide by the rules, came and went as he pleased, did not attend chapel, and was conspicuous by his absence from church. In short, he lived his own life.

Compulsion was the power which moved the wheels at Pinkerton. There were hours set for study; there was a requirement of attendance upon "divine service"; playing cards were strictly forbidden. For a boy to escort a member of the "opposite sex" was unheard of. All students had to be in their rooms at seven o'clock every night except Friday. One might as well be in jail, was Frost's summing up of the matter.

There never seems to have been any criticism of his nonattendance at church. The undeniable goodness of the man seems to have disarmed completely whatever critic might have excoriated him for this matter of default in things spiritual. He always took for granted that such attendance was purely personal. To Frost, religion was not a matter of some creed "made to order," but a vast, elemental possession of the human soul.

On this whole matter of professional jealousy and the problems which came out of it, the bard appears to have claims for rebuttal.

When Sylvia Clark says it was my sensitiveness which called up in my mind the existence of a jealousy that was nonexistent, she is far from hitting the nail on the head. Ask Bartlett. For, it was not only the faculty that was jealous, it was the farmers about Derry as well. I remember what happened when I was being talked of as the successor to Bingham as principal. I knew what was good for me—that it would never do for me to accept the post—even aside from what success as an educator would do for my poetry. Those farm neighbors of ours would have said, "He's only a hen-man, and now they have made him principal of an academy. What is education coming to!" No, it would not have worked. Resentment in the faculty—jealousy and suspicion among the farmers. When Sylvia Clark so glibly denies the existence of jealousy at Pinkerton, she is just closing her memory to things which happened time and time again. There was plenty of it—and bitter jealousy, too, among the teachers. They weren't careful to conceal it, either. But I got my revenge on one of them. Vengeance was mine.

You see, I'm like an Indian. I never forget a wrong. I may forget a right, but not a wrong. Now I seldom stoop to do a downright mean thing, though occasionally I have been guilty. Being insulted is the one thing I can't stand. Once when I was teaching at Derry, four of us went to the city to attend a conference of teachers. I was sitting in the hotel lobby talking philosophy with several other men. One of my fellow teachers at Pinkerton who had been in the English department until I started to teach, but who had been switched to the history department, came up to where we were, insult plain on his face, and not helping his face any.

"You didn't stay at Harvard long enough to get a football ticket, did you, Frost?" I didn't answer him, but right there I determined to lay for him. I knew my time for revenge would come sooner or later.

Some time later Bingham resigned, and they were looking around for a man to take his place after I had refused to accept it. Chase, the ramrod of the trustees, the real life of the school, called me in and said they were considering this history teacher for the principalship. He asked me what I thought about it. I hesitated and countered with a good solid question that carried a dart loaded with poison. "Do you think" I asked, "that he is a man of sufficient calibre?" I used that word calibre because I knew it would stir Chase up. "Sufficient calibre."

"Then you don't think he is a big enough man?" he asked. "Now, I didn't say that," I came back. "I was only asking if you thought him a man of sufficient calibre." But I saw that doubt had been planted in his mind, so that I wasn't at all surprised later on when they didn't elect him to the job. That finished his career. He went to another school and later on came back to Pinkerton in a subordinate position. I won't be insulted without striking back.

Ernest Silver, a Pinkerton graduate of 1894, succeeded Bingham as principal. I got on well with Silver, for he understood what I was trying to do. By this time, though, my plans were understood more generally, and my methods were not so strange. Silver, however, only stayed at Derry a little while before he got a call to head up the State Normal at Plymouth, New Hampshire, and put at me to go along and teach psychology. Now I really didn't know much psychology, except maybe by osmosis from James and Santayana in Harvard. But I told him I would go, under one condition and one only: That I should stay just one year—no more. You see I had lived my necessary ten years on the farm, which now legally was mine to do with as I pleased, plow or sell. I hadn't sold it yet, though it was on the market. He consented to the one year tenure, probably thinking if he didn't like my psychology he would have an ace in the hole to get rid of me painlessly, and if he did he could easily talk me into staying on. But in 1912, when I left Plymouth to go to England, keeping my end of the bargain to the letter, I made an enemy of him. In 1938 I spoke at Plymouth at his invitation. He introduced me with flowery words. When I got up to speak I turned to him and said, "Come on now, Silver. 'Fess up. After I had taught a year for you in this school back in 1911–12, weren't you getting just a bit uneasy having me on the faculty?" He squirmed in his seat and turned red.

XII. To Seek the Happy Isles

THE MONTHS FROST SPENT at Plymouth teaching psychology were by no means wasted, not that he read much psychology. He was busy reading modern plays, some of them aloud to his family and friends. One of the friends who heard him read was Sidney Cox, a fellow Plymouth citizen and professor. Speaking of that experience, Cox later said that his bias toward at least two modern plays, *Arms and the Man,* by Shaw, and *Playboy of the Western World,* by Synge, had been fixed by hearing the reading. He averred that he knew of no one who could do the Irish better.

This same Sidney Cox has left us a full-length portrait[1] of the wise-cracking poet whom he met in 1911 at the normal. At first he thought Frost uncouth, but he changed his mind as he knew him better. He says: "We were at a dance, and he wore an unpressed suit and a gray, soft-

[1] Sidney Cox, *Robert Frost: Original Ordinary Man* (Henry Holt & Co., 1929).

collared shirt, and he sat with crossed knees and poked fun. After that when he and I had long talks together, and I felt the world growing larger and stranger and more challenging in his company, I still detected in his speech and in his attitude an absence of conformity. There was something earthy and imperfectly tamed about him."

Here we see him, listen to him, feel his presence in this remarkable etching made by his fellow at Plymouth: "Lax but strong and muscular figure—blunt—but, sensitive and interpretive,—hairy-backed fingers—massive oval head—serious and passionate soul and changeful face—tender, unsubdued blue eyes, with deep recesses and wide brows—broad, slightly impudent nose—thick, sensuous, often mocking, oftener questioning lips—touseled brown and gray hair, deliberately rumpled—his come-one-come-all chin saved from being forbidding by the quizzical cock of head and eye, now and then. His voice a marvelous medium when he is going well. Elfin, ribald, gargoylesque, serene, sinister, utterly convinced, altogether skeptical, tender like firm fingers pressing soil around a delicate plant, and full of emotion and hilarity. A fringe of little vibrations around it that have suggestions of mystery and power like the vibrations of a great dynamo. The undisputed organ of an uncowed human being."

Once when Frost was teacher at the Normal, Cox noted, he received a letter from an anxious mother, desiring to know if her son were doing the required reading for entrance into the school of technology. His answer was a line out of Pan: "I don't know, but if he isn't he'd better be."

We are forever indebted to Cox for reporting Frost's definition of God—just such a definition as would be expected from him. "God," so his friend quotes him, "is that which a man is sure cares, and will save him, no matter how many times or how completely he has failed." Once he made a scale of existence in the following curve: "Religion, goodness, beauty, property, crime." Religion at the top, but all three merging into and decomposing one another.

This was the man who followed Ernest Silver to Plymouth to teach psychology. How graphically he tells of the end of the tenure:

> After we had stayed our year at Plymouth, ending in June, 1912, my mind was made up. I would stop teaching. It was not for me. Why keep

on working when you get nowhere for the effort? Why have only your labor for your pains? I said to my wife, "It'll never do to go on like this. I'll just turn into a machine, and what will happen to my poetry? We must get away somewhere, anywhere—only away." I wanted to be as far away from the nosey relatives down Lawrence way as I could get, clear off. For by this time word had percolated down there that I was becoming a man of respectability, quite a change, perhaps I might even one day head up a big institution of learning. Had they not already offered me a principalship—even though I had foolishly declined it? The people who had been giving me work had an interest in me, my welfare. They were good people who honestly were trying to save me from myself. I had no choice but to run away somewhere and hide.

Now we were ready to sell the farm and had a buyer for it. I have always looked on the sale of the Derry farm as my greatest financial achievement. You see my grandfather originally paid $1,700 for it, not counting the war tax for hay in the mow of $25. Well, I didn't take my uncle's advice and repaint the house, nor did I reshingle any of the roofs, so I saved these expenditures. In fact, I never spent a red cent on upkeep all the years I was there—taxes only excepted, and nothing can beat the tax collector. I left things exactly as I found them, not any worse, not any better. The roof never leaked, though I can't explain why, and the house managed to stand up all those years without a new coat of paint. I made a living—not a big one, or even a good one—but it was enough to keep body and soul together for ten years, paying our thirty dollars more or less every year for taxes. Thus, even counting the money for the hay, I expended in the ten years some $300 and not another cent, no more. That brought the entire cost of the buying the place and keeping it going for ten years, up to an even $2,000. I sold it for $1,900, so that we had our living for ten years at a total cost of $100—not counting what work I did, which wasn't much to count, not much.

Now we were set on going. Where to go? That was it. It finally simmered down to a choice between British Columbia and the British Isles. John Bartlett was in Vancouver. There was nobody in all England known to us.

"We'll toss for it," I said, when decision had not been arrived at. We tossed and England won—or lost, lost I guess. You see, in those days crossing the Atlantic was a rather simple matter if you were willing to travel third class. Passage was only $50 for grownups, and nothing for children accompanied by their parents, and we were going along. Moreover, the food cost nothing, and we had a place to sleep.

So, England it was. Great excitement! The children (thirteen, ten, nine, and seven years old), dominated by Lesley, eagerly planned the ocean voyage and the things they would take in when they had arrived in the old country. The voyage was to be all pleasure. There would be London, and the Cathedral towns, and Stratford, the home of Shakespeare.

This excitement never quite reached the heart of Robert. It was not till his little family were all safe on board ship that he breathed freely. He was an urchin playing truant from the schoolhouse—a boy running away from some slight at home—fearful every minute that a hand might reach out from the darkness and a strong arm whisk him back to servitude. But once at sea he took on new life. The ship they sailed in was a "little boat" of the Allen line, Boston to Glasgow. He was to see his mother's country first, after that the homeland of the Frosts. There were so few passengers aboard that the captain was irritable, Frost has recorded.

Glasgow finished, they took train to London. When he landed in the world's metropolis that autumn day of 1912, he had no desire to meet literary men. He was no literary or social climber. In the United States he had met few men of letters. Why start now?

The first few days in London, not knowing my way around, and being in the biggest city of the world, a stranger in a very strange land, it was by the merest turn of the wheel that I ran into an ex-bobby who gave me some good advice, and was fated to give me more of the same kind of good advice later on. He had quit the London police force to devote himself, as he said, "to literachoor." At the moment his literary endeavors consisted in "corresponding" for the Tay Pay O'Connor *Weekly*. It was his job to write a weekly column, after the British manner, on some place or another near London, where people could go on picnics and sight-seeing trips, London people. It was a sort of one man travel bureau in a periodical that was rather widely circulated. He was a friendly, obliging fellow, as Britishers are apt to be, on rare occasions, good sort. I told him that we were hiding from ourselves, or from something else not the law, and that we didn't care to stay on in London, not long. I asked where we could find a place near enough to the city, and yet quite out in the country, where living was cheap and all that.

The bobby never hesitated a second. "You want to go down into Buckinghamshire—'Bucks' we calls it—being a 'ome county," he told me. "Beaconsfield's the place for you—the very place. Quiet, cheap livin', just as you requested, and the grave of William Penn, the noted British Quaker who founded Pennsylvania and Philadelphia, right hard by, no more than two mile walk it is from the town's center any time."

Though I've always had a weakness for epitaphs out of the ordinary, noted men's graves were never a point of pilgrimage for me. But the sound of Beaconsfield and Bucks as a 'ome county, fresh air, rich grazing lands, the Chiltern hills, and withal reasonable cost for food and lodging, these things decided me. We found Beaconsfield on the Great Western railway, a matter of twenty-one miles out from London—fare four and sixpence, I recall.

Thus we came to Beaconsfield. And though we were in Gilbert Chesterton's own town, almost his near neighbor, in his big house all windows, nearly all, I am not sure I even knew it till we had moved away. I don't know that I ever saw him, big as he was. We stayed there a year, but eggs and butter and meat and rent and bread were all about the same price we would pay for them in America, so the Londoner's boast of cheap living was not forthcoming in Beaconsfield. We did have a pretty good year of it and saw the sights thereabout, among them the seat of the Earl of Beaconsfield. This was also the burying place of Edmund Burke.

Aside from his one great triumph, the months at Beaconsfield were silent ones, punctuated only by everyday happenings. There is one pleasing incident surviving from the period. It was the poet's birthday, and the children wanted to remember the day with something for their father. They had no money with which to buy a present, so each youngster wrote him a poem. The Beaconsfield poems were all warm, cheery, and welcome. The children were doing something for father, even though it may have savored of carrying poems to Stratford or something. Nothing in Lamb's life is more poignantly, sweetly sad than this picture.

Beaconsfield now has an additional fame. According to his own word, it was here that he wrote "more than a few poems." Some of these were to be kept and later included in *Mountain Interval,* some even being saved for use in *New Hampshire*. It was here, likewise, that he made the selection of poems which were to go into his first book. He had carried these verses overseas with him.

He related it all in his own inimitable autobiographical conversation, in my own front room, on a tiny footstool, so that he looked almost like a great contented frog ready to jump. It was in such fashion in his Beaconsfield cottage that he seated himself in front of his little fire and mulled over his few poems. Especially on this occasion in my home did he discuss some changes which had made such vast improvement in his already spell-enchanted lines. It may have been because the changes were so marked in two of my favorites that they came in for special attention. We saw by comparison how the author lifted "My November Guest" from its magazine form in *Forum* for November, 1912, to the finished product in *A Boy's Will* and how the same thing was repeated for the poem "Into My Own," which appeared first in *New England Magazine* for May, 1909, with "Mine" for "My."

There is skill in the improvements effected in some of these lines. Even Frost could never explain the processes which brought about the transformation. "She loved both bare and withered tree" in the first poem, becomes the smooth, satisfying, "She loves the bare, the withered tree." The line, "The fallen, bird-forsaken trees" he changed into "The desolate, deserted trees." Turning to the poem, "Into My Own," we are amazed to see such slight change accomplish such improved artistry. The touch of the master turns the line "Or highway where the slow wheels pour the sand" into "Or highway where the slow wheel pours the sand," while the line "I should not be deterred" is transformed into "I should not be withheld."

He told us how he made some of these alterations that night in his Beaconsfield cottage and how he wrote the marginal notes which accompanied the poems in the first book and continued in its succeeding editions until the appearance of *Collected Poems* when they were omitted.

In addition to some baker's dozen poems published in magazines, I took to England with me a sheaf of others which had not made the market. These I had continued to keep by me, now and then burning one that hadn't jelled, or had soured, usually writing another in its place. When a poem hangs fire I customarily burn it, though I leave it to cure if it will. I try to keep to my standards. The little pile of lyrics which went into my first book had stayed all the time around thirty, what with burning one and writing another. When I went to England I not only carried these but all that went into my second book as well, and more than half of my third. But my nonsuccess with the editors had kept the idea of a book out of my head. They about had me bluffed. I had not yet accomplished what I had set out so boldly to do when I left Harvard and went to Derry.

During the years on the farm I had given all the good magazines a chance at my work. The office readers were dead set against me. One will never know just what good poetry the damn fool manuscript readers keep from ever being printed. There was an old bitch on the *Atlantic* staff who kept my verse out of the magazine for ten years. Once I sat by her at a dinner given by the Poetry Society of America. She confessed that she had read poetry sent to the *Atlantic* for years. My books were already famous when she told me this. I didn't tell her she had done her best to keep me down. I didn't think it worth the effort.

I sent the manuscripts of some of the best poems which were later included in *North of Boston* to the *Atlantic* my first year in England. They were returned with the comment that they seemed a bit too vigorous for *Atlantic* readers.[2] I had my revenge.

One night that first winter in Beaconsfield I was sitting in front of the fire, on the floor, my little sheaf of poems spread out around me, reading them through. "Storm Fear" was the youngest of the lot, the last finished before publication. As I sat there I even made some marginal notes, setting forth what each poem stood for. It seemed to me, though, that there was too personal a note in them—too much of Robert Frost in these marginal identifications. Timidity caused me to shrink back from this, false modesty. They represented a curve from the days I taught with my mother at Methuen, on through the Derry farm days and the Pinkerton interlude,

---

[2] Ellery Sedgwick, *Atlantic* editor during these years of rejection, once wrote me in defense of the attitude of the magazine that it was the *Atlantic* which in an article by Garnett first voiced a "comprehensive and understanding praise" of Frost's poetry. However he added that of his "professed *theories* of poetry I had and have my doubts. I hold *North of Boston* brightest and best of the sons of his morning. Concerning Job, I prefer the original." Since the Garnett article came out in 1915, this did not in any wise explain the rejection of the submitted verse the ten years preceding.

to the time we left for England. That curve represented my flight away
from and back to people, just as my second book was to be the curve of
my forgiving people for being people. So, I rewrote the marginal notes,
taking the capital "I" out, and stressing the third person, transferring
them thus over to an imaginary individual. You can never tell which person I am writing under. "I" sometimes means "he," while "he," as in
this case, means "I." We'll leave "we" out of the consideration. It was
surprising what turned up out of the heap that night. I found many tending
toward the unity of one meaning.

"I think I shall run up to London tomorrow and find a publisher," I
said jokingly to my wife. Her instant encouragement confirmed me in my
bold adventure. We discussed the title which I had long intended should
be from Longfellow's poem about a boy's will, and a boy's thoughts being
long, long thoughts.[3] So, *A Boy's Will* was agreed on as the name of my
book. I was up bright and early next morning waiting for the London
Express on the Great Western. I went at once to look up my friend, the
Weekly correspondent, to explain what I had in mind. Big event.

When I told him I had come up to London to get myself a publisher for
my book of poems, he laughed uproariously, for he looked on the whole
thing as fantastic. A stranger from a faraway land, coming to a country
of great poets, and hoping to find a publisher for his unknown wares! The
idea *was* fantastic. Nobody knew it better than I. But I was obstinate. When
I asked for suggestions as to what publisher to call on, he mentioned three
or four of the larger houses, which I knew to be out of the question. So
I said, "No, I want to see somebody less pretentious." Then he mentioned
a firm that would publish if the author paid for it. I shook my head and
answered, "No, for that would stamp me at once, just as Badger in Boston
would do." He thought awhile and said, "David Nutt might take it on.
He's a small publisher, but he's 'ad some good poets—'Enley amongst
'em." I had always liked Henley, so the thought appealed to me.

I went to the office of David Nutt, 17 Grape Street, New Oxford. I
didn't find any David Nutt. Instead I found myself talking to a woman,
a Frenchwoman, too, of the most erratic, erotic, exotic type imaginable.
It appeared that her husband, who had founded the company, had died,
and she, for business purposes, had become "Mr." David Nutt. She was

[3] That he had long toyed with the idea of a boy's will from the Longfellow
philosophy is shown by a poem Frost published in the Pinkerton *Critic* of March,
1907. He called it "The Later Minstrel."

the widow (still in weeds) of David Nutt, the man who had published Henley. I must admit she eyed me suspiciously when I mentioned that I wanted a book of poetry published; she had a right to. And she was form-idably enough dressed in her black outfit to have scared most anybody, almost scared me. No market for poetry! Nobody would buy it! Nobody would read it, even if they bought it! After all, the day of poetry was past, and all that. Then, having as she thought disarmed me, she said she might, she just barely *might,* publish it if I would pay part of the costs. I told her emphatically no. I would never do it. So, I started to gather up my manuscript, which till then she had scarcely even glanced at, very firmly telling her I had never stooped to paying to have my poems published, and I would never do it.

Seeing I was firm she softened a bit and told me to leave the manuscript and let her have a look at the poems. "If they're good I'll take a chance," she said, adding, "but you'll change your mind and help bear expenses." Again I said no I wouldn't, and after receiving her assurance that she would make her decision soon and notify me down at Beaconsfield, I took the train back home, very doubtful of the outcome, very doubtful. But, you see, I was used to disappointment, having had only four or five editors to send me checks over a period of a score of years of trying to sell. Mrs. Nutt kept her word with me. She dropped me a line asking me to come in and sign a royalty contract. I went up to London in a day or so and looked over the contract. Since it was a straight royalty agreement calling for me to have twelve percent, I signed and left the matter in her hand. There were just thirty-two poems in the collection.

This precious tome, so sought after by collectors, came off the press of Spottiswoode and Company, Ltd., early in 1913. They printed a lim-ited number of sets. The Leighton Straker Bookbinding Company, Ltd., prepared a few copies of the book for its final form—bound in brown pebbled cloth, sheets octavo, five by seven and a half inches. Mrs. Nutt was feeling out her public. She was risking as little as pos-sible. If these went, she'd have more bound. The author has described his reactions.

> I take it I have seldom been prouder of anything. You see, I had turned the trick, done it. I had found myself a publisher. It was not that I had any reason to expect the book to have a warm reception. Who can judge the

public? And here was a public that had been surfeited with poets since Chaucer's day. But I had a book. My little poems were printed, and I hadn't put up anything to have it done. I had proved what I had contended with my grandfather, that I was a poet, and a poet who some day would be read. Here was my first little proof, or part proof. As I remember, it sold for a shilling six, and was one of the Series of Modern Poets. That ought to hold my critics back in Derry, Plymouth, and Lawrence. I was one of the Modern Poets—it said so in plain English and good, clear type. What was more, it had been exactly twenty years since I had set my limit of twenty years with my grandfather. Maybe a divinity was shaping my rough-hewn ends, maybe. Like most books of publishers undertaking unknown poets, this was limited to a small edition, and sold, I am told, five hundred copies at once, the other five hundred coming straggling along for many years, five hundred or fewer. And because of this it has since brought ridiculous prices at auctions where multi-millionaires send their agents to pick up rare things. But nevertheless, its later prices have caused me to exult a bit.

A Boy's Will actually was an instant success. But I must give the credit to those deserving it. It was all due to the fine reviews it had. You see, I had picked up a few friends among the reviewers, and these, out of the kindness of their hearts, and seeing me sort of like a lost puppy straying far from friends and relations, felt sorry for me and praised the book above its due. I can say this, but I wouldn't like anybody else to agree with me. Perhaps Edward Thomas should head the list. At the time he wrote reviews for a string of papers and for a few magazines. He was able to do a writer a great deal of good in this way. Then I had met Wilfrid Gibson, and through him, later on, Lascelles Abercrombie. These added their voices in praise, and gave their pens in my cause. The combined efforts of these new friends sent my little book on its way, and found new friends for it and for me. A few were not so kind in their reviews, though honest; I recall one in the London *Bookman* who said that *A Boy's Will* suggested young work. That was right. I wrote it when I was young.

He was Frost. He stood in no need of epistles of commendation to the literary lions of London, nor did he require letters of commendation from them, though he welcomed their friendly reviews. His circle of friends widened as each new friend presented him to another. There was his meeting with F. S. Flint, and through him with Ezra Pound,

two men as removed from himself as fate could possibly contrive. Pound
had not yet forsworn his native land, nor had he become quite the cantankerous egotist he was later to grow into. Fascism was far afuture. In
Frost, however different the two men were, at the moment he found a
kindred spirit. How they met, Americans in exile, Frost tells:

> During one stay in London we took rooms by a pure accident over the
> Bookshop run by Harold Monro, at 35 Devonshire Street, Theobald Road.
> Maybe fate directed me to the place, seeing the original Frosts came from
> Devon. Monro gathered the known as well as the unknown to his place, and
> through his conniving many struggling poets became known.
>
> Admission to the meetings was had by ticket found in his magazine,
> *Poetry and Drama*. I was there at the first meeting, when a crowd gathered
> on a certain fateful night, and sat uncomfortably on the stairs. There was
> a thin-faced fellow there who could tell nationality by shoes. Not much of
> a feat to pick out a pair of American shoes in a crowd of English ones. He
> was rather friendly, and introduced himself as F. S. Flint. He was one of
> the Imagist group. The result of our little talk was to turn out to have
> significance, though I was not to learn of it for some time. He asked me
> if I knew my fellow-American, also then in London, Ezra Pound. I asked
> who Ezra Pound was. He very seriously advised me never to let Pound
> know I had asked such a question. He informed me that Pound was an
> American poet from Idaho, who had come to London from Philadelphia.
> He said he was a voice in poetry to be reckoned with. I dismissed the matter
> from my mind as being of small importance, until a few days later a post-
> card came to me from Pound saying he would be glad to have me drop
> in at his place sometime. The address, 10 Church Street, Kensington W.
> London, and the names were all printed in red ink. I took my time and
> didn't show up for several weeks. He wasn't very friendly at first, but he
> warmed up as we talked. I told him I had a book coming out by Nutts,
> and that I understood the proof sheets were ready for me to go over.
> Nothing would do but we must go right over for them—not a far journey,
> as I remember, to Nutts on Grape Street. When we got back to his lodgings
> he sat right down and read the poems twice through, completely ignoring
> my presence, making a few notes as he read. Then he remembered me,
> and said he had some work to do, gave me back my proof sheets after
> scribbling a few more notes, and showed me the door. I thought his
> manner rather brusque; but when long after I read his review in the May

number of *Poetry: A Magazine of Verse,* Harriet Monroe's magazine, I forgave him. Meanwhile he had proceeded to pass temporarily out of my life till my book came out, though he did me the good turn of sending my poem, "The Code" to Harriet, who gave it a place in the periodical for the following February.

Harold Monro was doing a good turn to poets and poetry. It was a time when new forms of verse were developing, and to find a group of men gathering to discuss art in a serious manner was refreshing, agree or not. It was just like Alfred Noyes to sneer at the gatherings and say that young poets from the country came to Monro's with long hair and flowing neckties to pose and read their verses, and thus give the man on the street a contempt for all poetry. Somebody wrote that I had come from the country, but that I did not have long hair or wear a flowing necktie.

It is with unusual pleasure that one turns to Harriet Monroe's magazine in the copy Frost mentions to find Pound, in the first notice the poet had in an American publication, informing his prospective audience that:

> There is another personality in the realm of verse, another American found, as usual, on this side of the water, by an English publisher long known as a lover of good letters. David Nutt published at his own expense *A Boy's Will* by Robert Frost, the latter having been long scorned by the "great American editors." It is the old story.

> Mr. Frost's book is a little raw, and has in it a number of infelicities; underneath them it has the tang of the New Hampshire woods, and it has just this utter sincerity.

The review went on to praise some of the lines and expressions, such as

The whimper of hawks beside the sun.

I have no doubt that when it first came to his attention Frost appreciated it. But in future years, in the light of Pound's fascism, he wrote in my copy of *Poetry* containing this review: "Ezra did this sort of thing badly. Poor old Ezra, as he seems now in 1944." Opposite Pound's statement of manufactured information that "his grandfather and uncle disinherited him of a comfortable fortune and left him in poverty because he was a useless poet instead of a money-getter," the subject scribbled, "Not true."

It is very easy to underestimate the effect of this visit the American paid to Monro's salon—an influence that continued with him throughout the coming years. Unknown in his native land, of a sudden, in a far country, a country of long established traditions, he found himself meeting with powerful names in literature. Not, of course, Kipling, or Barrie, or Shaw, or Housman, or even Noyes, but a coterie of intellectuals, good writers, and influential critics. His impressions of the men in contemporary literary London are not unimportant parentheses:

> I liked Walter de la Mare very much. I mean first as a poet, second as a man. You can like a man as a poet and hate him as a man, I take it. You can be indifferent to him as a poet and like him as a man. But I found Walter de la Mare a fine fellow, one who never felt called on to buy a high hat. His poetry was worth reading, still is. But I must say that William Butler Yeats was the world's first egotist. I have never met his equal at it. Nor have I, on the other hand, ever known a conversationalist to match him, except George William Russell.

> As to Housman, he is not I think the first of the English poets of our time—though good. Certainly I should place him far ahead of Masefield who writes poetry with a meat ax, cleaver. I don't doubt that Housman wrote poetry under great stress, as he suggests in the preface to *Last Poems.* When he wrote his first book he stopped writing and maintained silence for thirty years. No word in all that time, in all that generation, came out of Cambridge. There he was, a classicist and a good one, a fine Latin scholar, and he didn't want to talk about his book. He snubbed all who came to talk to him about it. Then it was announced that the silence of the ages was about to be broken after thirty years. With everybody else I said, "Now we're going to have something really good. We will listen to something very much worth listening to." But when *Last Poems* belatedly followed *A Shropshire Lad,* instead of being any different, the poems were merely others just like the first. Some of them even sounded as if they had been left out of the first collection for lack of space, turned up out of the heap to be used in the second. I shouldn't probably say all this, but it seems true to me.

We reverted in conversation to Yeats and his egotism. I wanted to know, in the light of his statement that Yeats was the world's first egotist, if it could be he was as great a one as George Sylvester Viereck. He laughed sardonically and grunted:

"You're asking the impossible, even for Yeats. Nobody could be that bad."

When I pointed out that Viereck had written many beautiful poems, and quoted in support lines from "Nightfall," "Finale," and "The Ballad of King David," he exploded. Viereck was one of his sore spots.

"That pride of his in tracing his kinship as a cousin to the Kaiser, taking joy in being a whoreson, sticks out all over in all he writes and says. It's too much for me. And this thing of sodomy and perversion in poetry doesn't strike me right. It is all an unnecessary cess pool."

Accident had once more cast adventure in the path of the wanderer. He had enlisted a jousting champion of the first order in grouchy, conceited, egocentric, erotic, cultured, psychotic Ezra Pound, who talked to him about a very rich woman from Boston whom he had taken under his wing to convert to the tradition of free verse. Her name was Amy Lowell, he said. "It all began just like that," Frost told me. There were luncheons and parties to which his mentor dragged him—necessitating frequent trips on the Great Western up to London. There were evenings at Hulme's, something to be sought after. Here was Frost thoroughly enjoying himself with social events, mixing up with his fellows, having a good time with Pound and Flint and Abercrombie and Gibson and de la Mare. He had opportunity to meet some truly big lions in literature, so many in fact that his head might well have been turned. But the "bridge pier in the middle of the river" was impervious to drouth, flood, freshet, cloud burst, or tornado. Did he have a look into Adelphi Square with Barrie and Shaw calling to one another across the spaces in between?

Though he may not have met them in person, he saw their handiwork —even the triple bill which included *Overruled,* a Shavian sex-morality play; *The Widow of Wasdale Heath,* by Pinero; and the irresistable, irrepressible *Rosalind*—the latter being Barrie's. Since his Punch-and-Judy days in San Francisco, Frost had held a sneaking love for the theater. He had put on modern plays at Pinkerton. He made a point of seeing the best ones in London.

It was in February, 1913, that Frost met the man who was to become his closest friend of a lifetime. At the home of Dorothy and Vivian Locke Ellis he came face to face with Edward Thomas. A year later, in London, E. T. held teas at St. George's Rest, in St. Martin's Lane—"through a little side door to the right, up two flights of brass-lined stairs, through a door with 'Smoking' on it, to the chess room, where he presided over another gathering at tea." Here Frost, Rupert Brooke, de la Mare, John Freeman, and Arthur Ransome were among the guests.

During those months in London and Beaconsfield, Frost did not completely sever the cords which bound him to his friends back in America. He probably felt the need of being anchored to something or to somebody. His correspondence was slight—but it was always that—just an occasional letter to an occasional friend and intimate. One of these was Sidney Cox. In December of his first winter we find him writing from "Bunghole," Beaconsfield, Buckinghamshire, England, to his old Plymouth interval colleague. His letters were so scarce we might almost think he had forsworn his native land. It is little wonder that later on he was so completely unaware of what was going on in New York City.

With all his meeting famous Englishmen things didn't move any too smoothly at the publishers. That is, not financially. He wasn't getting his per cent of the "swag."

Mrs. Nutt was a funny individual. From the start we didn't hit it off together. In fact, in all my dealings with men and women I have never dealt with a person so hard to get on with. Very peculiar woman. *A Boy's Will,* so far as I was able to judge, sold quite readily. So much so that she asked me not long after publishing it if I didn't have enough poems for another book. I grinned and told her I had enough for several, by assortment. She shook her head and said we'd cross one bridge at a time. That if I had enough poems for a second book, to get them in shape, and bring them in. If not, to write enough and she'd bring out another collection. My contract with her called for my next four books following the first. The reviews had made a success of it with comparatively small sale. England is so compact one can become famous over there by selling a few hundred copies of a work. I took my time in getting out *North of Boston,* delivering it to her in February, 1914. Nothing random in it. It was the gathering in of a larger design. When she had read it she told me it was better than the first. I agreed. In the collection were poems I had been working on for ten years. There was "The Code," which Pound had sent to *Poetry* (the printing of which pleased Harriet's vanity after the fact), and which was printed without too much time to spare before it came out in the book. I was satisfied with the contents—and I've never been called on to change my mind.

But, so far, I had never received as much as a shilling, much less a pound, from royalties on the sale of my first book, and here she was getting out a second. I knew there were sales. So many people talking about it. They couldn't all borrow. Somebody had to own one. You can see what that leads to. I kept at her to give me a reckoning on my twelve percent. I was getting hard up. My money was going pretty fast, never was much. If it kept up I'd have to turn out a Tom Tom the Piper's Son or starve. We were far from any sort of a base of supplies. But whenever I would bring up the subject of money she would flare up with, "Just like you dollar-grabbing Americans—always talking about money." It did no good to point out that I hadn't been much of a dollar grabber, that she hadn't held a dollar within grabbing reach, not even a tuppence. Later, when *North of Boston* came out, it went tumbling after *A Boy's Will.* I had nothing out of her on royalties from either one.

In this state of financial embarrassment and fiscal insolvency, the poet had to scratch his head. He had met Wilfred Gibson and with that charm of his which drew and bound men to him had made a friend of the noted poet-critic. At once the North Country dreamer began to besiege him to pick up his family and household goods, however few the latter, and move down into Gloucestershire where he knew the very place for them. It was a little farm he could till for food, located near Leadington. It had a very romantic name, that farm—Little Iddens. It was a parcel of ground with a pretty little yellow, timbered cottage, to the north of Dymock. Lascelles Abercrombie had gone down three or four years before, and Gibson had followed. When the three got together it would be a great company.

For what had they come to England but to seek the happy isles together? When the Frost money ran lower and lower and it seemed imperative for them to do something to supplement their diminishing income, Robert turned to the only thing he knew besides teaching—tilling the unwilling soil. With a prescience known only to poets, lured by the siren voice of his friend, he turned to the beautiful flowery West Midlands and sought shelter in a dwelling whose rooms were so tiny that the housewife had to set all the furniture out in the yard to sweep the floors. This cottage and its location are best described by one who was familiar with it at the time, John W. Haines, Gloucester solicitor and littérateur. I leave his words below as he wrote them to me in letters, before I saw it for myself:

> Little Iddens was a small brick and half timber cottage situated on a byroad leading from Dymock, Gloucestershire, to Ledbury in Herefordshire, and some distance back from it. It was quite small with a garden in front and a small orchard alongside of it. In all I should think not more than half an acre. He did not cultivate the place except that he looked after the orcharding and spent much of his time in it. It was there in a chair that he read to me many of his poems.
>
> Since then the cottage has been made very attractive, painted white, and it is now (1949) a good deal more than a farm labourer's cottage which it originally was. It was there that he lived when he and Edward Thomas had their early meetings and the latter took rooms in a farm (Brook's Farm) near by.[4] Lascelles Abercrombie, the poet, lived at The Gallows (Callows) Ryton a couple of miles away in a magnificent double cottage thatched almost to the ground, and they constantly met.

North of Boston (three shillings six) was to be much talked about and written about that summer, copies of the green buckram volume printed at Ballentyne, Hanson and Company, Edinburgh, for David Nutt coming down into the country. All three of his new-found friends wrote reviews of it—and good reviews. Perhaps Frost was as proud of it as he had been of his first book. The author held happy memories of that summer.

When we decided at Beaconsfield to go further down into the country

---

[4] In a later communication Haines corrected this. "Yes, you are right about Brook Farm which I mixed up strangely with the farm at which Thomas stayed near Robert Frost. This is really called Chandler's farm."

it was with a dual purpose (always aside from my country inclinations), perhaps with a number of purposes. There were the friends we had made; there was the urge to be with those who spoke our language and understood our thoughts; then there was the money—the root of most of our evils. We had never lived among poets before, working poets. In fact I had known very few poets in America and had met comparatively few since coming to England [*sic*]. It was a new experience for us in every way. Maybe it stirred me up, roused me. There were the country folks among whom we were to live. In Beaconsfield we had seen few such. In our new location we had them on all sides. They were the curds and whey population of England—the remnants of the old Saxons, like the mountain whites of our American south, living with prejudices that were the accumulation of the years.

And while you are talking about poverty in America, or poverty most anywhere on the planet, don't forget: Those English in the hamlets and open county, the genuinely submerged classes, can give you some pointers on destitution, depression, and dejection that are age-lasting. They are used to living on black bread and rancid cheese, mitey cheese. Now and then we would run into one of them in the fields poaching for a hare. We would see the gamekeeper following after, waiting for a chance to nab the poacher and hustle him off to prison. We found that like as not the gamekeeper had his eye on us, squinting out from under his cap. One had to show a birth certificate to prove he wasn't a poacher and avoid arrest; and because one didn't have on knee breeches and a red coat they suspected the worst. Those poor devils in the country go around with snares to catch rabbits just to get one little taste of meat for their families to take away the infernal smell of rancid cheese or worse out of their nostrils. The authorities were forever invoking the laws of William Rufus and the New Forest—laws that made it safer, as Emerson says, to kill a man than to kill a hare. At first this knowledge came to me as a shock. But it turned later into a spirit of railery when, during the days of prohibition in the United States, I would listen to a Britisher razzing us about our liquor laws, and sneeringly ask about prohibition, as Chesterton did, "When does it start?" I would remember their prohibiting those half-starved devils from having a bite of meat, and would get a glimpse in my memory of a furtive figure slinking through the narrow lanes and hedge-rows, with a fat, sleek, well-kept gamekeeper following to entrap him. So I always sneered back that they weren't any better with their own game laws that were just as bad as our liquor laws—maybe worse.

But, considering everything we made shift, got on. We liked the common people among whom our lot was cast; though, not only could we never succeed in getting acquainted with them, not really, but they never came to know us at all, or understand us. Full of native prejudice they thought there must be something wrong or we wouldn't be there. When they found out that if I had any religion, which I didn't much, I would be a nonconformist, their worst suspicions were confirmed. They thought that everybody in the United States who was anybody was a member of the American branch of the Church of England. Why, in the early days of the war they got to spreading stories about me, saying I was a German spy, at least sympathizer. This was as it happened. They told that I would go down cellar, and shut myself up to sing German songs. They had no knowledge that "God Save the King" had for tune an old German drinking song. The provincials would talk all around about me. They watched every move I made, day and night. They even got the constabulary down to investigate me. I was to them always an utter stranger.

This was the sort of people Thomas Hardy knew, and lived among, and wrote his novels about. Their lives were eked out miserably, held as they were in caste subjection so that few could rise above it.

These were the modern counterparts of Langland's *Piers Plowman* people, for he lived among these same rolling hills, the Malverns. Seeing the cowmen with their two-tined forks, dressed in filthy short-coat (too small to button on them), leggins, with a helmet-hat on their heads, and thin, scraggly hair blowing in the wind, cleaning out the cowstalls or pitching manure into the corner of the cowlot, almost brought me to read Langland. But I didn't yield. There must always be something left undone. *Piers Plowman* is mine. In the fields, where I sometimes wandered, it was a joy to see the farmers and farm laborers making hay on a pleasant summer afternoon. It was interesting to remember that this very field had been plowed and harrowed and harvested since the Neolithic man whose tools of stone are still come upon, thrown up by the plow. Celts, Romans, Saxons, Normans, English, each in turn had farmed it, and still the crops came to harvest, and men lived by the fruit of their toil —lived after a fashion. Perhaps the most precious quality of the life here was its continuity. When we were there in 1914, times were still medieval, even if not Neolithic. Between our going away in 1915 and our return in

1928, the small farmers who had been renters bought the land from the lords and things happened. Temporary prosperity had risen out of the ground. What these farmers did with their new toy is quite another story. Anyway, they did more with it than their "betters" had ever done—put it to more uses.

In those days we found, still sticking like burrs, the old regard on the part of the common people toward these "betters." We came upon the use of the word "obedience," used for "obeisance," which was new to us. The older women, meeting a superior, would bend the knee and made a low bow. They called this (by an understandable evolution) their "obedience." For people who like that sort of attitude on the part of the submerged, I take it, it was a very pretty performance.

They are right who say we were happy there. It was a lovely land, and we had gotten together with poet friends—English men who were no more a part of the countryside than ourselves—men as little understood by their neighbors as ourselves. With these friends there went on endless talk on high themes, and as we strolled singly, in pairs, or in groups about the hills and valleys to the far Cotswolds and beyond, looking for flowers—botanizing they called it—vasculum in hand, our bonds of friendship tightened. One remembers incidents like the walk with Edward Thomas on a hot afternoon in summer, after a thunder shower, and the Bath apples, pretty as New Hampshire, under the trees where the wind had felled them. And though we never made much out of farming (gardening in a small way) in that country of strange agriculture to us, farming so different from what we had known in New Hampshire, we yet managed somehow to muddle through, our money all the time experiencing the law of diminishing returns—only it didn't return. It all came out right in the end, though, and we chalked it up to experience—something which, first and last, no matter where we lived, we had plenty of.

I must admit that the country, though lovely, never impelled me to poetry. Or if it might have on few and far-between occasions (as at Ryton when we moved there) the unmistakable voice was that of the New England. It was not of England, or of the West Midlands, or of Gloucestershire that the voice spoke to me. I always drew for my poetry, wherever I might find myself, or what might put something into my head, on the experiences of my past, long ago, out of that and out of Derry.

Yes, we were happy there, but they are wrong who say we went to England with a desire to have a book published in the country of a great literary tradition. I may have said something like that once in a teasing way; but I was always anxious to have my book published in my own country, for it was American to the core and didn't belong to England, much less to London. I always had to laugh when the provincially-minded English thought I was writing about some place north of the English Boston in my second book.

I couldn't find it in my heart to be such an ingrate as to fail to give the English and Scotch due credit for giving me my start there—though it was only a matter of happen so—fate you might say. I am under obligation to them—to some certain of them at least—for life. But to show that there is no rule, it ends there.

There was something very homey about the little triangle of towns where Frost lived among his new friends. Looking for the first time across the brown hills, the American saw orchards in riot of bloom—apple, cherry, peach, pear, and plum. Stretched out were the valleys of the Why and the Lugg. For itself, Leadington was a black and white town. Here once builded John Abel, "King's Carpenter," as he labored and wrought over and through all the surrounding shires. Here, on the tiny Little Iddens farm, with its shining apple-trees in full blossom, later in fruit, under which he often sat with his friends and carried on talk on "high themes," Robert came to learn tillage again, making use of the lessons he had so well learned and mastered in the old New England to wrest a living from the soil of the new Old one.

Probably he never knew it, unless by chance Gibson or Abercrombie or Thomas or Brooke dropped a hint, but nearby, two or three miles distant at Ledbury in Herefordshire, John Masefield was born. He had little good to say of the craftsmanship of Masefield, though it was with a more delicate implement than a meat ax which Frost accused him of employing for a pen, that the laureate wrote of this same land in the finest lyric poetry in the language.

> It's a warm wind, the west wind, full of birds' cries;
> I never hear the west wind, but tears are in my eyes.
> For it comes from the westlands, the old brown hills,
> And April's in the west wind and daffodils.

Nor was it likely that he knew that "Hope End" where Elizabeth Barrett spent an unhappy young womanhood was quite near at hand. He never bothered with such inconsequentials.

Again and again he looked on the lovely sights, heard the same unforgettable sounds described by Stanley Baldwin in the days of his pre-enoblement, when, politically and otherwise, he was rooted here in this same soil: "The tinkle of the hammer on the anvil in a country smithy, the corn crake on a dewy morning, the sound of the scythe against the whetstone, and the sight of the plough team coming over the brow of the hill, the sight that has been seen in England since England was a land. . . . The one eternal sight of England. The wild anemones in the woods in April, the last load at night of hay being drawn down a lane as the twilight comes on, when you can scarcely distinguish the figures of the horses as they take it home to the farm, and above all, the most subtle, most penetrating, most moving, the smell of woodsmoke that our ancestors, tens of thousands of years ago, must have caught on the air when they were coming home with the results of the day's forage, when they were still nomads, and when they were still roaming the forests and plains of Europe."

These were the influences surrounding the American poet come back to the land of his forefathers—a history that went back to the beginnings of modern life. And all over the lands bordering the Welsh marches, wherever he went, the golden daffodils carpeted the countryside with a fairer covering than Henry and Francis knew of the Field of the Cloth of Gold.

XIII. A Relation of Elected Friends

When, somehow, as if a future wind had blown before its time and acquainted him with the fate that was to be his when the "dust whom England bore, shaped, made aware," was to mix with another dust in "some corner of a foreign land," Rupert Brooke penned "The Soldier," may we not believe he had reference to the quintet of poets of which he was a transient member?

I cannot but think that when he wrote of "this heart, all evil shed away," which

> *Gives somewhere back the thoughts by England given;*
> *Her sights and sounds; dreams happy as her day;*
> *And laughter learnt of friends; and gentleness,*
> *In hearts at peace, under an English heaven,*

there passed through his mind those soft summer days when the poets wandered the valleys and hills together or talked all night in the Old Nailshop at the Greenway.

At the first of the season, the little group was made up of three families—the Gibsons, the Abercrombies, and the Frosts. Both Gibson and Abercrombie had a teasing sense of humor. They delighted in chafing Robert about American mores. Nor were they always gentle in the chafing. The camaraderie existing among them could not be better proved than by their willingness to poke fun at one another. Frost had the better of the game before summer was over, in an incident presaging another great adventure in his life. He always snickered in relating it.

Abercrombie and Gibson both had American readers, and both got "fan mail" from America. Nothing pleased them better than to get a bit of poorly written correspondence from some illiterate American, asking foolish questions in execrable grammar. This they invariably tucked away in their pockets and brought along to plague me with.

"Such spelling," they would say, "such diction. Don't you have any schools in the United States? What an illiterate nation you must be. No wonder you ran away from the States to come to a civilized land." And so they would go.

But one day, after *North of Boston* had a chance to reach America and be read, along in midsummer I had a letter from the States about my book, which I stuck in my pocket to use when the time came. It came from a town named Stowe in Vermont and was written on crested stationery, with the legend "Four Winds Farm" engraved in the corner. The penmanship was beautiful, the letter a perfect gem of good writing, well worded, carefully phrased, and what was more, it showed insight and discrimination, revealing a power of judicious criticism on the part of the writer. Signed to it was the name Holt.

The letter went on to say (it was written by a woman) that the writer and her mother had experienced a great deal of pleasure in reading my book. It said that her mother knew the people I had written of, but that though she did not know them in the way her mother did, she yet appreciated the pictures almost as though she did. The letter was unimpeachable in every way. I knew I was going to have fun with my friends. "I'll fix those two," I said to my wife.

Next time we met I drew my letter out of my pocket and said, "Of course I'm not responsible for the literacy or learning of the sort of people who read your poetry in the States; but here is a sample of the kind who read mine. Just take a look and judge for yourself between the quality of my readers and your own." That put a stop to it. They never again twitted me about American illiteracy.

Frost's letter from an American reader was indicative of what literary people in the United States were thinking of his poetry. The poems in his second book were making a significant impression on those who really counted for something where a writer was concerned. Sarah Cleghorn tells of Dorothy Canfield Fisher reading the poems of *North of Boston* to her on a summer evening in 1914. "Mending Wall" was the first, and then came one after another of the truly important poems in that astonishing collection, so that this newcomer to his poetry felt an enforced intensity rising around her.

Critics often compare Frost with Wordsworth. Both, they say, were close to the soil, Frost delineating the New as Wordsworth did the Old Englanders. Both had a passionate love for nature, with a gentleness that considered all created things. But there stands another likeness between these two noted English-writing poets not often mentioned. This likeness lies in the similarity between the Lake Poets, with the laureate as the center, and the Triangle Poets, gathered, as Haines has so well put it, in the Gloucestershire towns, with Gibson in the Old Nailshop at The Greenway; Frost at Little Iddens, adjoining Leadington, two miles removed; and Abercrombie in a thatched cottage, the Callows—the Gallows he preferred to call it, and so it came to be—two miles farther away at Ryton's edge; "so that the three lived, as it were, within a triangle, with Dymock in the middle."

· 123

Edward Thomas later on came to join the group with his son, Merfyn. Helen, with whom, through the intercession of the American, he had become reconciled, came still later with the little daughters, Bonwell and Myfanwy. She writes of the late weeks of the summer, calling her husband David and her son Philip:

> Then war came. David and Philip had cycled into Gloucestershire, staying with friends on the way, taking a week or more to reach the little village beyond Ledbury where some Americans David had lately met were staying, and where later the two girls and myself came to join them. . . . We did not then realize all that brooded over our lives. We spent those happy weeks in the open air, in the evenings sitting with our friends and talking—talking of people and life and poetry, for our friend was a poet, and between him and David a most wonderful friendship grew up. He believed in David and loved him, understanding, as no other man had understood, his strange complex temperament. The influence of this man on David was profound, and to it alone of outside influences is to be attributed that final and fullest expression of himself which David now found in writing poetry. There began during that holiday a kind of spiritual and intellectual fulfilment which was to culminate two years later in his death. In that short time, most of it spent in the army, David was to pour out in poetry all the splendid experience of sadness and beauty; and in his poems is expressed forever the tender loveliness of the English country. . . . Our friends sailed back to America taking Philip with them for a year. . . .[1]

Rupert Brooke returned to his native land by way of America in June. He paused to be feted by Harriet Monroe and a group of her poets in Chicago. Reaching Liverpool, he hurried on down to visit his former associates in *New Numbers,* which with Abercrombie, Gibson, and John Drinkwater he had founded the previous year. This magazine was devoted to the poetry of its four founders. Only three numbers were issued from the press before it was discontinued.

The Thomases moved into a farmhouse with the family of a small farmer adjoining Little Iddens. The friendship between Robert and Edward had become well established even before the Georgians gathered in the West Midlands. It was but natural that they be much together.

[1] *World Without End* (Harper & Brothers, 1931).

The two have separately memorialized their walks afield, Frost in his "Iris by Night,"[2] Thomas in "The Sun Used to Shine." Those long walks together, with talks about the war, brought them to the gate of one or the other to linger till darkness overtook them and the same stars shone on them that shone on "soldiers in the East."

Padraic Colum has written of the influence which he felt was exerted on the American by the group of Georgians. It was not that the form of his poetry was altered or that the subject matter was changed; both were already well established before he went to England. It was a more subtle influence, one that came from seeing a crowd of brilliant young men feeling that they were accomplishing something worthwhile, writing as they saw fit rather than devoting themselves to business.

Of this group Colum writes that he "saw them as a real society—quarreling went on among them, to be sure, but they formed a society, a kind of brotherhood." Hulme is not often mentioned with the others, though he had his place among them. Frost was often in his London house.

Whether it was when the quintet gathered in the "cozy cream-washed living-room" of the Old Nailshop, at the Gallows beneath the Ryton firs, or in the apple orchard bordering Little Iddens which looked up on May Hill, it was always, as Gibson has written, Robert Frost who,

> Kept on and on and on
> In his slow New England fashion for our delight,
> Holding us with shrewd turns and racy quips
> And the rare twinkle of his grave blue eyes. . . .[3]

In this connection one might profitably dwell on certain marginalia of the poet. "The Golden Room" was printed in the *Atlantic* for February, 1926. On one of my copies of the poem, R. F. has written: "I owe Wilfrid Gibson much kindness for so much kindness, don't I?"

On the manuscript of "The Golden Room," which I have, beneath Gibson's signature R. F. has written, "We must admit this was terribly nice of Wilfrid. He and I were neighbors away down in the country

[2] See Louis Mertins, *Intervals of Robert Frost* (University of California Press, 1947), 26.
[3] *Ibid.*

in 1913–14. I wonder how you found this copy of his poem all done out in his own hand."[4]

What sort of men were these with whom the American poet consorted? One would appreciate a picture of such a gathering—a subject worthy of Rembrandt's brush. There sits modest, rugged, determined Abercrombie, the real leader of the Georgian movement in poetry. Slouched forward, thus accentuating his stoop of shoulder, with his high forehead and unshorn hair (not a little of the Sandburg in him, especially the Neanderthal-Heidelburg Sandburg), he wears a slouch tie and old-fashioned, thin-rimmed gold spectacles, held by broad, flat ears. Across the table, slightly turned aside, sits Rupert Brooke. There is something suggestive of Frost about him. His lips are thinner than the American's, the hair more wavy, perhaps less unruly in other ways. Always conscious of himself, he has the same indifference to what some might call the niceties in all but art so apparent in Frost. Both are shy as birds, both weather beaten—one by the suns of the South Seas, the other by the elements of Gloucestershire. Thomas, delicate, airy, almost feminine, sits worshiping his new-found friend. The smoke of conflict still hovers as a wraith about his devoted head. Gibson, lover of a practical joke, is the poseur of the quintet. He sits in the picture but is somehow apart from it. His declining ears seem discouraged and beaten down. Here is a dreamer with an undertone of scheming, one who looks right through things—and people. There is one paramount thought in his busy brain. "What are they thinking of me?" Hovering over all, in his role of Arcadian jester, his hairy, stubby hands expressive of his thought even as they lie motionless on his knees, or while his fingers toy with a paper, Robert Frost dominated the group.

Those halcyon days were not to last forever. Man was bent on war—the pastime of kings—and Rupert Brooke had a rendezvous with fate somewhere beside the isles of the Aegean, where, "in a place forever England" he was destined to consecrate a soil eternally, buried by torchlight on the top of the stony mountains of Skyros, in an olive dell, his grave covered with slabs of white marble which lay about in profusion.

[4] *Ibid.*

For himself, Edward Thomas was, after long consideration, to go away "to meet the shell's embrace of fire" at Vimy Ridge.

When in August of that summer hell burst forth along a line which extended from London to the Levant, Thomas felt his first impulse to become a soldier. But he waited. Brooke went to join up in Piccadilly. Soon Gibson went away from the Old Nailshop, leaving the Golden Room behind but carrying imperishable memories. Abercrombie sought solace "in a bleak northern town beneath glowering smoke."

Robert Frost never doubted, then or later, the place Edward Thomas was to occupy in English letters. He never quite forgave the others for a half-concealed "group snobbery" which, without word or deed, denied E. T. a place among them. Frost was sure of the place to be occupied by his friend's work and resented this. Many times he was to say that Thomas was to write better than any of them for the too little time left him to write.

During that July they were all together, *The Bookman* published Gibson's review of *North of Boston*. The reviewer showed rare insight into the worth of his American companion, not the least proof being his choice of a title—"Simplicity and Sophistication." "Mr. Frost," he wrote, "has turned the living speech of men and women into poetry. To the unsophisticated reader it may seem an unsophisticated production . . . of a naïve and ingenuous mind. . . . Mr. Frost's poems are American, and they are his own."

One can scarcely believe, without some reservation, R. F.'s statement, "Nope, I never saw it before," written on my copy of *The Bookman*. Yet, he actually may have neglected to see a review in so prominent a magazine, written by a famous critic friend. Abercrombie also wrote a review of the book in which he said that "most of Mr. Frost's subjects are in some way connected with farming, the few that touch anything urban have the atmosphere of country towns—nothing in the book, at any rate, suggests in the least a nation of dwellers in vast, roaring, hurly-burly cities."

In Gloucestershire, Robert Frost came up against something he had scarcely met in New England, despite the fact that his ancestors in the New World had lived up to his description of a grindstone. This was the absolute historical continuity of life. England in the West Midlands of 1914 was well-nigh unchanged and unchanging, as he himself forever remained; he was yet untouched by the land and the people. His writings offer scarcely a suggestion of his sojourn among the apple blossoms. Many have thought that "The Sound of the Trees" may have been written about his days at Abercrombie's cottage. This is stated categorically by Haines. The fact that it was printed in *Poetry and Drama* in December, 1914, is good argument against it.[5]

Occasionally through the years I sought to gather a bit of biographical or critical data from the poet. Concerning the foregoing, I once asked him obliquely if the poems printed in *Poetry and Drama* in December of his stay in the West Midlands ("The Sound of the Trees," "The Cow in Apple Time," "Putting in the Seed," and "The Smile") were products of the Ryton sojourn. He merely scribbled a Delphian answer on my copy of the magazine, "You ask if any of these are English in spirit. That would not be for me but for someone else to say."

I have stated that there was scarcely a suggestion of Gloucestershire in any of his poems; yet, on the page of *The Virginia Quarterly Review* containing "Iris by Night," Frost has written, "Once with E. T." Inasmuch as he was never with Thomas, except in England, it stands to reason this is an exception. No part of the poem is traceable for its English origin except where he speaks of the two "groping down a Malvern side."

Further, there seems no question but that he was writing of the borrowed cottage owned by Lascelles Abercrombie when he penned the lines in "The Thatch" with the unforgettable picture of the night walk, when "the world was a black, invisible field." That, of course, suggests

[5] "A word about the trees. Written at Dymock for Lascelles Abercrombie, but *not* in connection with the *Ryton Firs* of L. A.'s poem. These were on a hill some way beyond the Gallows and cut down earlier. R. F. told me so, adding that at the back of his mind were a group of trees near his old home in America— I assumed New England. John W. Haines." (From a letter.) When the trees were destroyed, Haines wrote to E. T. about it, getting the reply: "I don't think I shall regret the trees cut down till after it's all over, if I regret anything then."

it, while the birds nesting in it, flushed out of winter hermitage to shiver in the rain all night by

Trusting feathers and inward fire,
Till daylight made it safe for a flyer

completes the picture, clinching the truth.

Still, the best evidence of the Ryton origin (The poem was first printed in *West-Running Brook*.) is to be found in the lines:

They tell me the cottage where we dwelt,
Its wind-torn thatch goes now unmended;
Its life of hundreds of years has ended
By letting the rain I knew outdoors
In on to the upper chamber floors.

During the early summer, another visitor came to the Triangle to become a part of the company of poets, though himself not a poet. This was John W. Haines, whom we have mentioned. Those who love Frost's poetry owe a great debt to this remarkable Gloucester solicitor. Except for Gibson's "The Golden Room" and a few verses by Edward Thomas, Haines, alone of his intimates in England at the time, has left pictures of what went on among them. Following a breakdown in health in 1949 and a resulting blindness which continued to the end, Haines wrote me many letters of his memories of the summer and fall of 1914. As he admits, "It is true that only Gibson and I can recall much of the Dymock Triangle." Then he launches out upon a fine description, which shall be given with only a catalytic paragraph here and there:

I had known Abercrombie for a good many years when he was at Ryton, and indeed he had lived with us for a month or more whilst his wife was having an operation in Gloucester. On one occasion when I had walked over to see Lascelles, I found him away and The Gallows loaned to Wilfrid W. Gibson, the north country poet, who welcomed us and we became intimate with him, and his wife, also, when they went on to the Old Nailshop, at the Greenway, in Dymock, two miles from Ryton. One day Gibson told me of Robert Frost coming to live at Little Iddens at his suggestion, and asked me to call on him. I walked there from Dymock station one day carrying my big vasculum as a keen field botanist, and when I got near my destination I called a man I met in the road where Mr. Robert Frost lived and he replied, "I am Robert Frost."

He seemed to know of me and invited me in and we had a splendid time in the cottage and orchard talking all the time and after serving me some tea (all the family were there) walked back with me to the station. The botanical tie was a lucky accident since we had a common ground at once in the quest of wild plants of which he was very knowledgeable. This was in early spring 1914, and we later had many walks and talks together and found many flowers together on May Hill and around it—the one considerable hill in the neighborhood, 1,000 feet or so. We talked of poetry, his own and that of others, and he wanted me to wait till *North of Boston* came out and not judge him on *A Boy's Will* alone. These meetings were fairly frequent till some weeks after war broke out, after which I was for a time too tied to Gloucester, and not renewed (though I think he came over to us) until he went to The Gallows in the autumn. Lascelles lent it to R. F. and his family, and R. F. resided there till he left England for the U.S.A. in March [*sic*] 1915. At The Gallows there was a large garden, but no other land.

The people around Little Iddens were chiefly busy farmers and farm labourers. There were few educated people in a cultural sense and there was not a great deal of fraternization, but this he did not much miss as the Gibsons and Abercrombies were close by, and they had friends stopping with them, such as the poets W. H. Davies, John Drinkwater and Rupert Brooke. The Frost children spent most of their time in education. They were educated entirely at home and did not go to school. I think this question of the education of the younger three children worried Elinor a good deal and was one of the reasons behind her wish to return to the U.S.A. The children no doubt played with the Thomas children and with Abercrombie's though these last were tiny. I know Thomas used to read them his then unpublished stories in "Four-and-Twenty Blackbirds."

Haines had a memory of a portable typewriter in the house at Little Iddens, "for," he says, "I saw it, and it was small and semi-circular." However, he said he had no knowledge of the user, whether Frost or one of the children. Robert once told me that in his early days he always typed his poems out before sending them to editors, a habit he gave up in later years. Even his letters were seldom written in any form except longhand. Concerning the typewriter, the Frost children and the Thomas youngsters worked on some little books, Lesley doing the typing, with E. T. looking on and having fun watching. These books, or magazines, were bound in green paper backs. There were poems by R. F., which were signed mysteriously "Anonymous," and two of E. T.'s things, "Nettles" and "The Combe," in a later issue. There were drawings by "The Staff." Mrs. Frost preserved these early attempts at literature for many years.

Always a talker as well as walker, Robert Frost could never resist the lure of conversation. Haines again:

> There was hardly any subject he did not talk upon. Philosophy and psychology (his brands of course); and New England, particularly the old farming country interests, and the mountains and inhabitants, especially the farmers. He was full of anecdotes, many set out in his own poems. He talked a great deal about his own poetry, especially his technical theory of the "spoken word," and read many incomplete ones to us. He talked too of some American poets, Whitman, Lanier, and E. Arlington Robinson, and of the Imagists poets he knew in London, Flint, Aldington, Tancred, Hulme, Pound; though I fancy he did not greatly admire their work then. He also talked of the American critics and of the Georgian English poets, Brooke, Drinkwater, Abercrombie, Gibson and the rest, especially of Abercrombie whose work he liked best, though he was critical of its technique in the psychic drama. The wild flowers of our different countries were constant topics, notably the orchids he had found in New England. I spent a week end with R. F. at The Gallows, with Edward Thomas, and had long walks and talks with them. He was of course very full of Edward then and later of his work and personality. This was in latish autumn 1914, and after the period at Little Iddens when these two had their famous talks. We talked late and R. F. quizzed me in lively fashion over G. B. Shaw and also the Irish political question. It was largely fun but I had to call on E. T. for support of the English point of view, and got it.
>
> R. F., as he told me once, came to England to get his poems published where "The Golden Treasury" had been,[6] and I think what he chiefly got from England was just self-confidence. You see, Abercrombie and Gibson

---

[6] Frost denied this to me. Elinor may have said it, or at least expressed a wish "to live under thatch."

were well-known critics as well as poets. Garnett was the most influential critic in England and not a personal friend as the others were. I do not think that R. F. was influenced in any way by the writings of the English Imagists or the Georgians.

Robert Frost in 1914 was a very fine looking man indeed. He was of medium height but had a splendid physique and especially broad-shouldered. His eyes were an attractive shade of jade blue, and extremely penetrating, and he looked what he had been—an athlete. He often talked about his games of American Rugger (football) at the university and we compared it with our much milder Rugger in England at which I played a good deal. In disposition he was happy and cheerful. He talked much and well but liked occasional long silences and specially late at night enjoyed giving slow, long soliloquies on psychological and philosophical subjects. He enjoyed staying up late and hated early rising. His hair was fair and there was much of it and he usually liked to keep it rumpled.

His sense of humor pervaded all his talk and he could be sarcastic if he wanted to, though usually his humor was kindly and he had a great sense of fun.

There was little running around for the Frosts. Money was too scarce. Haines declared that "whilst at Little Iddens the family kept pretty close to it for it was an out of the way spot. They did," he goes on, "run up to Gloucester now and again to see the (Norman Perpendicular) Cathedral and other sights." On one occasion the family splurged. The famous fair at Gloucester drew them. At Haines chronicles it:

> Once the whole family came over for a day to visit the Barton Fair at the end of September, and Elinor and the children had tea with us at St. Helens and Robert too, I think. Tea was not a meal they were used to at our early hour and they were a bit puzzled over its being celebrated as a somewhat heavy meal.

Haines's fine picture of the family is too excellent to mar by paraphrasing.

> We found Elinor and the children quite charming and very easy to get on with. They were most interested in everything we told them. Lesley at 15 was nearly grown up and well educated and very handsome. I fancy she read a great deal. The youngest girl (Marjorie) was very quiet and shy.

Irma and Carol were most delightful children, very talkative and lively. Irma looked fragile but was lively enough and was the one who asked the most questions about everything. She was the most American of the four, I thought, but Carol might have been an English boy except for his ability to "jerk" stones across the little River Leadon, at which he licked me hollow, as at least one of the girls; and R. F. himself was prodigious at it. Robert stayed with us more than once and Lesley came with him on one occasion. We then lived in a very small house, St. Helen's Hollow road, Huccelcote.

I did not find the family at all given to sickness. Robert was not too well just before they left England and Elinor was a good deal worried. I think they all thought we took the war too philosophically and were not bloodthirsty enough.

What Haines says somewhere of how the poet used to sit in a chair in the orchard at Little Iddens, where he frequently read his poems to visitors, is worth remembering. The poem "Putting in the Seed," he says, was used by Frost as an example of his technique. "I had a newspaper," Haines continues, "on which he scribbled symbols indicating how it should be read."

Again Haines tells of receiving a letter from Frost dated March 2, 1923, enclosing a poem which was then entitled "Nature's First Green," sent from Ann Arbor. This poem was the beginnings of "Nothing Gold Can Stay." Haines chronicles: " 'Swinging Birches' he often read to us in 1914 and my wife and I have often thought that when published it was a great deal shortened."

Whenever I chance upon some description of the "botanizing" proclivities of Robert Frost, as for example, in the typically English article by Haines,[7] telling how he and the poet wandered all over the Gloucestershire hills, hunting ferns "by match-light under the steep bank of the Leadon," walking "in the Leadon Valley by Ketford Mill," through Dymock, Newent, Ryton, Clifford Mesne, and Oxenhall and Bayford Bridge, a series of recurrent memories crowd the mind. One ceases to wonder that Wilfrid Gibson should have referred to Haines as a repository of Frost incidents.

[7] *Gloucester Journal,* February 2, 1935.

One recalls a day at Laguna Beach, California, with hours of talks-walking together, when Frost took boyish delight in tossing stones at objects near and distant with almost unerring marksmanship, his lax body giving itself to each heave, recoiling with the grace of a striking serpent.

Memories recur of walking in and around Monrovia, Palm Springs, and Redlands with touches of desert flowers and trees, where he would compare the old world flora with the new, and of long walks across the Vermont hills at Bread Loaf and Ripton, where conversation ranged from gossip over current idols to flowers, birds, and trees.

Thus one understands what the Englishman meant when he related how Frost would compare the British and the New England flowers, and be thrilled when now and again they coincided. On one of those Vermont walks I, who loving flowers had never become a true botanist, plucked a dainty blossom from his August pasture land, unfenced save for the mountains on the one hand and the woods and turbulent river on the other, and casually asked what it might be. "This flower," R. F. replied, "was named for your college. It is a Jewel flower."

I have looked in vain through the issues of Harold Monro's *Poetry and Drama* printed during Frost's sojourn in England for any editorial mention of the newly discovered poet. But of his verse there is a proper representation.

In December, 1913, Monro used two of the best poems Frost ever produced, "A Hundred Collars" and "The Fear." In the same issue, Robert Bridges, just crowned with the laurel wreath, is publishing "Fly-catchers," his first poem since he accepted the laureate tun of wine and other honorarium from the king. Walter de la Mare makes offer of "The Enchanted Hill"; Rupert Brooke, "The Funeral of Youth." Monro modestly includes himself last of all with "Children of Love."

To Edward Thomas we must always turn in discussing the genuine friendships of Robert Frost. Here was the man who most influenced the American, granting that he *was* influenced. It was of Thomas that he thought in the closing days before he turned from England back to the States. Through the years Frost's mind often went back to dwell upon the sweet, sad memories he held of his friend. He seldom mentioned Rupert Brooke, who was at most only a visitor for a few days at the Triangle before he gave up England for immortality. Thomas was exceedingly close. There was always a gentle note in his voice when he spoke of E. T. "He was my greatest friend since boyhood," he has said. In my copy of *Yale Review* for April 1920, where the now-famous poem "To E. T." appears, Frost has written, "The second stanza comes back oftenest."

Frost said that he wrote the poem "The Road Not Taken" for his friend and sent it to him in France, getting the reply, "What are you trying to do with me?"

While discussing what Haines had written of Thomas, R. F. and I read together what the same man had set down concerning May Hill and Leadington, where the Englishman said: "Perhaps Robert Frost thinks sometimes of the night we hunted ferns together by matchlight."

"Haines is a romanticist," R. F. ventured. "He writes not wisely but too well."

Then, thinking better of it, he went on: "Sure I remember all the walks he writes about, the flowers, the trees, the valley stretching out from May Hill. The flowers he mentions so unlike our new world blossoms—the Little Tresses, the Little Teazel, and the others. Though not strictly of our group, Haines was a good walking companion, and we had good times together." Then getting back to Thomas. "He did much for me, and I can never repay his memory. When I first met E. T. he was living quite alone, his wife and son living apart from him. I didn't like it. Mrs. Thomas wrote it all up in her book which made quite a roar in this country. The two were exact opposites. She was the vigorous type, always effusive about everything. Reading her book it is easy to see who was being chased by whom. Edward was quiet and modest and undemonstrative; but like still waters there was nothing shallow about him. She nearly ran him distracted taking on over him all the time. A poor reward for modesty. Whenever he got an order for a piece she would just go on and on, and he, being a neurotic, couldn't abide it. I set about trying to reconcile them, and finally got them back together.

Thomas and I had become so inseparable that we came to be looked on as some sort of literary Siamese twins in a literary sense, with a spiritual bond holding us together. When I first met him he was writing reviews for a string of newspapers with a few magazines like *The Bookman*. He didn't have as many as he once had, but enough so that he could write up a book and do the author a great deal of good. Perhaps he had a dozen at the time. He was a sort of amateur naturalist. I wanted him to try his effect in verse. Before I started him to writing poetry he turned out page after page of drab nature description. It went sour on him. Once in so often men of other cliques would say to me, "Why did you start Thomas off writing poetry? God knows his prose was bad enough?"

Frost in 1925 wrote a letter to H. R. Brennan concerning this friendship. "Edward Thomas," the letter stated, "had about lost patience with the minor poetry it was his business to review. He was suffering from a life of subordination to his inferiors. Right at that moment he was writing as good poetry as anybody alive, but in prose form where it did not declare itself and gain him recognition. I referred him to paragraphs in his book, *The Pursuit of Spring* and told him to write it in verse form in exactly the same cadence. That's all there was to it. His poetry declared itself in verse form, and in the year before he died he took his place where he belonged among the English poets."

I had the manuscript of Frederick Niven's "In Memoriam," an ode to the memory of Edward Thomas, an item which I valued highly. I had also Niven's *A Lover of the Land* inscribed and sent to me from far-away British Columbia; having an extra, unsigned copy of the book containing the poem Niven had given me in manuscript, I thought Frost might prize it. When I mentioned it he merely said:

> I don't think I'd care to own it. I'm as much concerned as possible in forgetting all about it. There is a war raging in England now over which started writing my kind of verse—Frost or Thomas. The books show, of course, which of us it entitled to priority, as mine came out long before his. But it must be admitted some of his *do* sound like some of mine, only he had plenty that didn't sound like mine at all, quite his own. He used to read me one and say, "That's just like Frost." But it wasn't, either

in look, tone, or manner. One of my worst enemies in England recently wrote that since the books showed mine to have come out first, it was undoubtedly a case of dual style, simultaneous style—though he never explained what that might be.

The English interval was drawing to a close as the year 1915 approached. The urge had become strong for America. There was nothing tangible, it would seem, to lure them back, but the American scene was calling. With every fiber and cord of his being, Frost loved his native land. As much as anything else his English sojourn had given him contact with the Georgian movement in poetry. England had recognized him when America almost completely ignored him.

> Our money was about all gone as winter waned. We had been living in a cottage borrowed from Abercrombie. We were getting in a financial strain, worried. At last I went to London for a final showdown with Mrs. Nutt. I again approached her on the thing I had urged on her the year before. "Why don't you get in touch with a good publisher in New York to bring out my books over across?" I asked her. "You would be just that much ahead, for you would have a part of all the profits over there, sharing on all that were sold." It did no good. She only flared up again and called me a money grubber, and forbade me to deal directly with any American house. When I asked her when she would pay me my 12 per cent royalty, overdue, she nearly exploded. "You're going to be sorry one of these days when I pick up and go back to the States," I told her. "You'll lose a good author." But it never bothered her any so far as I could see. She was hard as nails.

The poet's words to his publisher were more promise than threat. Already the family was counting its pence and shillings to find funds sufficient for the voyage over. With a friend he had kept in touch with in New Hampshire looking out for him, a farm had been located at Franconia. They booked passage on the SS *St. Paul,* and on February 13, 1915, they sailed from Liverpool to New York, navy convoyed. Submarines lurked menacingly everywhere. Six persons had been in the party going over; seven were returning. Helen Thomas had asked them to bring Merfyn along, to leave in the care of an English friend, Russell

Scott, at Alstead, near Keene, New Hampshire. It was planned for the boy to take lessons at the forge, to get away from the easy and sheltered life he had known at home. There had been some talk of Edward Thomas coming along to farm in New Hampshire. At first he was so inclined, but he gave it over. The war was on his conscience.

 Decade Five

XIV. By the Highway Home

CORNELIUS WEYGANDT tells us only a part-truth when he says that it was only after Frost's "transplantation to England that he attained masterful ease in his speech and his own augustness of tone." We must not forget that the one book which after decades still is the essence of Robert Frost, the one work which stands above his other collections, is *North of Boston;* and this book was written wholly at Derry and Plymouth before the runaway booked passage in 1912.

Perhaps Wilfrid Gibson, who was qualified better than most to evaluate for us what the Dymock Interval had done for his friend, should be heard in this connection. In a letter he said: "I doubt if Frost's visit to England had any influence on the essential quality of his work; but I do think it helped to give him reassurance as a writer. One of the proudest moments of my life was when I heard him declare to a Philadelphia audience that I was the first person who had given him any encouragement to write poetry! I suspect this was a friendly exaggeration; but I have little doubt that the sympathetic appreciation of such men as Lascelles Abercrombie and Thomas did much to stimulate his self-confidence."

When his ship docked in New York and Robert Frost, Elinor, Carol, Lesley, Irma, and Marjorie, accompanied by young Thomas, landed in the United States, to all intents and purposes it was the same country. But actually it was a new and strange and different country. Different that is, insofar as Frost and his relation to it were concerned.

· 139

By now the children were getting to be good-sized youngsters. Lesley was sixteen, Carol thirteen, Irma twelve, and Marjorie ten. The eldest was approaching college age. Regardless of their continuous movings about, the Frost children, like their father, would learn, even if Robert had to teach them—a thing he did well.

Robert was turning forty. No hope was in his heart for the homecoming. He was completely disillusioned by his English sojourn. His poetry, though published and read and made over, did not provide food for his family.

A certain poem, "Lodged," together with the marginalia he has scribbled on my copy of *The New Republic* for February 6, 1924, shows his disappointment. Reading the short six lines telling how the rain and wind conspired to destroy the garden bed, till

> *... the flowers actually knelt,*
> *And lay lodged—though not dead,*

one feels for the flowers, and one feels, too, for the poet who has added:

> *I know how the flowers felt.*

The returning wanderer was in the depth. Later he was to write over against this verse: "Interesting to know I felt this way as early as thirty years ago when this was written," which authenticated the date of the poem as being the year he returned to America.

On landing, he faced the immigration agents regarding Merfyn Thomas. It didn't seem to matter that young Thomas had a letter from Lloyd George certifying him as what he represented himself. They forced him to spend a horribly upsetting night at Ellis Island. Frost continues the story:

> After getting Ellis Island off our minds, I found my shore legs, bought tickets for the whole party up into New Hampshire—where we planned to visit an Irish friend of ours till we investigated a farm I had wind of near Franconia—and when I counted up my cash in hand it had dwindled to a mere four bits. But that fifty cents was destined to buy me more satisfaction than any other half-dollar I had ever broke to spend.
>
> After I had safely deposited the family and our rather bedraggled guest

on board the train, I went out to stroll round a bit, to see what an American city looked like after the English ones. Passing a newsstand, I saw a new magazine—new and unheard of to me. It was called *The New Republic,* and it looked good to me from the cover. I remember a phrase on the outside. The war had been going on for six months, and of course was in everybody's mind. The phrase quoted a lead article in the magazine and said: "The United States may have been the indirect cause of the present European war." I resented that. I even recall the feeling of resentment which came over me. I had long been fed up with British arrogance abroad. To meet such a statement on my return home was too much, last straw. But I bought the magazine, climbed leisurely back onto the train, and found my seat in the coach. Soon we started moving, and I settled back to read.

I must admit I enjoyed the magazine. It was well written, not too highbrow. But it turned out to mean more to me than just another magazine —for when I came to the book section, right there before my eyes was a review that actually shook me out of my seat. It was of my second book, *North of Boston,* and was written by somebody who ought to have known poetry when she read it—Amy Lowell. When I devoured that, proudly displaying it to my wife and having her enjoy it with me, I said Amy might smoke all the big black cigars she was a mind to, or more. Ezra Pound had not biased me any in her favor, but now I forgot all that. Though I must confirm the not too infrequently expressed opinion I have held of her that by and large she was an evil influence in poetry. Yet when nine million dollars speak you have to listen. Amy came to tell of how I assured her that when I saw her review it seemed to me that America was holding out friendly hands to welcome me. Perhaps I did, I don't remember.

I can still recall the pleasure I got out of her clear understanding of what I was up to. I was even willing to have her gloss over the fact that no publisher in America had been willing to chance my work, saying that it was an accident that I was published in England and no reflection on the perspicacity of American editors. That was far from the truth, but I let it pass. What she had observed that pleased me especially was that I had caught a fleeting epoch and stamped it into print, of a people purely American. That was what I had unconsciously tried to do.

I was delighted to see that the fine old firm of Henry Holt and Company of New York was my American publisher. I suppose no wandering poet ever came home to a happier welcome. This friendly review was a balm from Gilead to deferred hopes. I had gone to England unknown. I had found there a publisher who believed in my wares—though not enough to pay for them in pound sterling. I had come home to America to find that a publisher here was already printing me, and I was more sure now of a proper financial recognition. Perhaps I could even get an advance on royalties, which would be a new thing for me.

As we rode onward toward New Hampshire, my mind went back to that letter I had received from "Four Winds Farm," signed by the woman named Holt. I at once suspected there must have been some connection between the two incidents—her letter and the owl of the Holt colophon. It was to be some time before I was able to confirm this.

I was all excited about running back to New York to get acquainted with my publishers. I was proud, you see, for an American publisher was what I wanted. I never fancied exoticism either in poetry or publication.

When I did get back to the big city I found the Holts fine people to deal with. I had lunch with Holt, and we talked over my future. I told him frankly all about Mrs. Nutt's actions, and he declared I was absolved from every legal and ethical responsibility because of her breach of contract in not paying me any of the royalties agreed on. Moreover, he said the David Nutt Company was now in bankruptcy, and if I but said the word he'd take over my publication rights and get an associate publisher in England to handle the trade there. That was what we did without further ado. The London firm he got was Longmans.

Then he told me the history of my book in America. It would seem that I had stirred up Mrs. Nutt by urging her to get a New York publisher to co-operate with her, for she was willing to talk business when the chance came.

The actual way it all happened was related to me by Alfred Harcourt. He was Holt's first reader at that time, long before he broke away and founded his own company. He never got on well with Mrs. Holt, who was much younger than her husband. One day, he said, she came breezing in with a book she had been reading with her mother. It was published in London, but the author evidently was an American, so she told him. She thought the firm should bring out the American edition. The book was *North of Boston*. She related how she had written the author, then residing in England, telling him she and her mother had like the poetry and that her mother, especially, knew the sort of characters up in New Hampshire, which he described so well. That was the letter from "Four Winds Farm."

Harcourt was an independent fellow; the minute her back was turned he took the book she had left and dropped it into the wastebasket.

Well, Alfred said the obnoxious *North of Boston* lay in its bed of discarded paper and books in that basket for some little time. But curiosity got the better of him, and he fished it out and read it straight through. By now he had forgotten that Mrs. Holt had anything to do with the recommending of it for publication, and inasmuch as he had brought it out of the basket, he looked on himself as the discoverer. He took it right in and O.K.'d it for the Holt list. That was back in 1914. Holts wrote to David Nutt and Company and bought 150 unbound sheets. These they bound in cloth and tipped in their own title page to replace that of the original publisher. This explains why all those books first sold in America of *North of Boston* have never been first American editions. Only those published in 1915 with a Holt imprint are that. If the people who figure out numbers of copies of books printed and sold know what they are talking about with reference to *North of Boston,* I can't help but wonder what became of the 550 copies of the first London 1,000 still unaccounted for.

From that day on Holt has been my publisher. Aside from stray little things which didn't actually count, I have only stepped aside once, which was done with their disapproval—that was when Knopf printed *A Lone Striker.*

I became very friendly with Harcourt, and whenever I was down in New York we would always go out for lunch together. As his friendship for me waxed warm, Mrs. Holt's waned and became chillier and chillier. She and I didn't have any break but just grew farther and farther apart. Then Harcourt drew out of the firm and started his own concern. He wanted me to go with him, and I was really inclined to do it. But I thought the thing through and because I knew that one day I would want all my poems together in one volume, which would make complications if I divided publishers, I refrained. Sandburg and others left Holt with Harcourt, but I have never been sorry I stayed with them.

Amy Lowell was not the only critic who recognized Frost upon his return to America. In April, the Chicago *Evening Post* permitted the man who was to remain the poet's greatest champion on this side the Atlantic to clarion *North of Boston.* That voice was never silenced.

Louis Untermeyer was mindful of Robert Frost long before that April in 1915 when he printed his first review. As far back as 1913 he

had come upon the name in *Poetry and Drama,* signed to two poems—
"The Fear" and "A Hundred Collars." He could not reconcile, he has
said, such verses with an English author. Later he was again to see the
name associated with groups of Georgians headed by Abercrombie,
which mystified him all the more.

Nor was Frost without awareness of his future champion during his
years of expatriation. "I have known you long before you knew me,"
he said to the critic when they met for the first time. That was after
Untermeyer had reviewed *North of Boston* for *The Post.* Lascelles Abercrombie living "under a certain thatch roof in Ryton, Dymock, Gloucestershire" had often spoken of L. U. to him in the days of his sojourn
in the West Midlands. Untermeyer summed up Frost with rare discrimination when he spoke of him in his prepublication days as "not
beaten but resigned to obscurity."

Thus we find the poet and critic opening one of the most notable
friendships in the history of letters. I recall something R. F. said to me
about that friendship which once came near the breaking point over
Virginia Moore. "We had been so close," he said, recalling how he attended the funeral of Louis's suicided son, "that I would have had to go
to his hanging." For his part, he realized that Untermeyer carried a
useful torch for him, so he tolerated many things. This devotion was
clearly not altogether an unselfish one, perhaps no less so on the critic's
part. Poetry made strange bedfellows.

Once or twice it was my good fortune to be with them together so
that I was able quietly to make appraisal of the two unlike men. There
they were, poet and critic—the poet on one occasion listening to the
honeyed words of the critic as he told what somebody the day before
had said of some of the later verse, ear-marked for *A Witness Tree.*
Critic and poet; Jew and gentile; urbanite and ruralist; shallow and
deep; eclectic and original; flighty and steadfast; vacillating and un-
bending; cackler and chuckler—in all things these men were truly each
the antithesis of the other.

Yet, if Louis Untermeyer ever really loved anybody, selfishly or un-
selfishly, he loved Frost. No matter what rival momentarily appeared
on the literary horizon, he never relinquished the torch he carried for

his friend. On Frost's part, certainly, the relationship was not completely altruistic, even beyond the bearing of torches. Finding Louis willing to work, eager to please his friend, in New York, at Bread Loaf, elsewhere, he called on him time out of number for various services. Little tasks of drudgery which needed to be done were shunned by the poet and left for the critic to perform. "When they wanted to turn the poetry department at Bread Loaf over to me," Frost told me as we discussed Untermeyer, "making me the final judge of verse written in the summer school of English, I consented with the understanding that I should get Louis to help me. He agreed, and now he reads all the poems through. When he finds one that is not too terrible he passes it on to me. I like to work this way by proxy."

The volume of correspondence between Frost and Untermeyer demonstrates the depth of their friendship. To have received two hundred letters from a non-letter writer is certainly a man-sized achievement. Robert even grew to despise the sound of the postman's whistle, he hated so to get letters, some of which had to be answered.

Untermeyer mentions a letter received by him the first year of their friendship, revealing the Pan-like humor which pervaded Frost's thinking. A great many poets were seeking the Chautauqua audiences in those days, getting out florid prospectuses of their work, quoting what people had said of them, setting forth what they could do in the entertainment field and how well they could do it. Frost prepared one in a facetious manner for himself—not printed, of course, but written in his broad hand—and sent it to Untermeyer. "Immersing myself in White Wyandottes," he sets forth as his principal bid to fame. Such a letter, in such a spirit, multiplied by two hundred, speaks more loudly than multiplied words.

About the time Robert Frost gained his first recognition in America, another poet, six years his senior, flashed across the literary sky. This was Edgar Lee Masters, the New Englander's absolute opposite in character, training, and art. Many years later I talked with Frost about the work of his quondam rival, as compared with his own. I related my conversations with Masters as we sat in Chicago, and of Masters' hatred for his law partner, Darrow, of whom he once said bitterly to me: "Darrow wouldn't steal the pennies from the eyes of his dead mother, nor rob his old blind grandfather of his porridge, or dig into his brother's grave to steal the brass off his coffin, but any other crime in the catalogue he would be guilty of," so bitter did he feel toward his former associate in law. Frost took the thread:

> Masters could never understand the great fuss being raised over me about the same time people were talking about his *Spoon River Anthology*. In his eyes I was a simple, wornout farmer, a dumb old fellow who wrote verses of the quieter sort. As to my being a genuine poet, he never credited me with that at all. It may be, as you say, that some of his poems are pretty good stuff. But to me they are just so-so. What you said awhile ago about my poetry being like well water, which you meant, and I took, as a compliment, would be taken up by Masters who would say it was well put. My verse to him is like water, as compared with the strong drink he distils—I should say the stagnant stuff he spigots out by the gallon.

What a change came into the fortunes of Masters and Frost as age came on. Frost had starved in lean years but came at last into certain affluence. Masters had his good things early in life, and so came to eat the bread of suffering, dying in want.

Frost *would* have another farm. He had more than a passing knowledge of the acres he had heard were for sale up around Franconia. He had worked in the community as a boy in summer fields and knew both the people and the land.

Franconia is on the Boston and Maine Railway. It is just such a community as one would expect Frost to seek out. Lafayette Mountain, the highest peak in New Hampshire, shoulders out the sky more than a mile above sea level. Garnet Mountain lies near at hand. The farm Frost had chosen for his own was almost in sight of the Great Stone Face on Profile Mountain. A few miles away flowed the unruffled Connecticut.

A European Continental,[1] who knew his America, has set down concerning this new venture: "He bought a farm at Franconia in one of those fertile 'intervals' that the rivers have made among the mountain chains of New England and there he buried his fame."

[1] Albert Feuillerat, *Revue des deux mondes,* September 1, 1923.

Robert Frost, 1960

Jim Sloan

At the Organization of the California Writers' Guild, 1932. *Seated:* Louis Dodge, novelist, Robert Frost, and Louis Mertins. *Standing:* President Remsen Bird, Occidental College, and Lee Shippey, columnist.

Robert Frost, recently returned from England and wearing an English suit, with a friend.

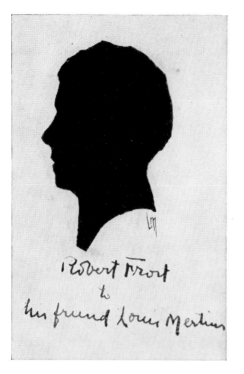

Silhouette of Robert Frost as a young man.

Silhouette of Robert Frost in later life.

A caricature of Robert Frost shown in *Punch*.

Punch, London

The Old Nailshop, Greenway, Dymock, where Wilfred Gibson lived
in England as a neighbor to Robert Frost.

Rev. J. E. Gethyn-Jones

Farmhouse in which the Frost family lived in Derry, New Hampshire.

Little Iddens, Leadington, Dymock, where Robert Frost
lived in England.

Rev. J. E. Gethyn-Jones

This farm very nearly met Frost's requirements. He loved to spend time there, often taking advantage of such rustication to catch up with his belated correspondence. September 11, 1935, he wrote me an eight-page letter from Franconia—the longest I ever had from him. There was something about the surrounding mountains, the rolling hills, and the boulder-filled pastures that he loved.

The house on this place was quite like the house on the Derry farm, only smaller. Standing on a sloping hillside, it was no more than one story and an attic. It was a shingle-roofed, frame structure with two chimneys. To it the Frost family found their way shortly after their return from England.

Money was now more plentiful in the household, but the farmer in Frost sent him back again farming, and all the children worked in the fields. It was at Franconia that Lesley became the "foreman." She was a good one. In fact Robert called her a veritable Simon Legree. The parents would see the four children working away in a distant field, really getting things accomplished. What they didn't know then, but were later to learn from the younger children, was that the oldest of the flock had appointed herself overseer and that she had not read *Uncle Tom* for nothing. When they didn't move fast enough, Robert said, she'd knock them "galley west."

His first summer at Franconia sent a man Frost's way—Professor Morris P. Tilley. The professor had been in the habit of spending his vacations from work in the University of Michigan in the White Mountains, and he found it easy that summer to be a daily companion to Frost, seated nightly, as Sidney Cox recalled, under the soft glow of the round-wicked lamp.

That same season Cornelius Weygandt went up to Franconia with a carload of children and adults. He has left for us a happy picture of the visit: the friendliness of Robert Frost, the Frost children playing with the visiting youngsters—"knockout and catch and moving up." There is a warmth about this picture which is illuminating. The Frosts had come upon good friends who spoke their language in England. Now they were glad to welcome the same sort of friends in their own homeland. The Dymock Interval had taught the poet that the having of friends who understood his speech, and whose speech he understood in return, was a very necessary thing. Already *North of Boston* had made him almost a legendary figure, and more and more Franconia was to become a "must" for literary people. Because of his innate friendliness and good manners, they were all well received and hospitably entertained. If among them were climbers, Frost knew how to handle them, too.

As he felt the need of friends, he felt also the need of enemies. If the latter were not in evidence, he fancied them. This trait was a thing he never managed to overcome.

Fall came and the children entered school at Franconia, Lesley in Franconia high, the others in the grades. Lesley stepped into the junior class. Her father's work as tutor during the English visit had been well done. He had made a classicist of her—as he himself had been, as his father before him had been.

A new book was in the offing. The poet, spurred on by his publishers, who were anxious to make hay while the literary sun shone, had started the arrangement of the poems new and old that were to go into it. At long last he had sold three poems to the *Atlantic Monthly* which were published in the August number. The year was most fruitful in reviews of *North of Boston*. Not until 1936 was any year to exceed it in regard to reviews of his books. Every month magazines found their way up to the Franconia farmhouse with articles about him. Sylvester Baxter had a word in the April *American Review of Reviews;* William Aspenwall Bradley came out in *The Bookman,* the same month; William Stanley Braithwaite puffed him in *The Boston Transcript;* Zoe Akins placed him well with the shadow of Parnassus in Reedy's *Mirror;* Jessie B. Rittenhouse did her stint in the New York *Times;* O. W. Firkins, in *The Nation;* R. M. Alden, in *The Dial;* and even in faraway Los Angeles, Eunice Tietjens wrote of him in *The Graphic.* But for Bostonian, as well as for other reasons, that which pleased him most was the appearance in the August *Atlantic* of an article, called "A New American Poet," by Edward Garnett. It was refreshing for him to find a famous English critic, unknown to him, who caught so well his spirit. Garnett quoted Goethe to effect: "What do we want with so much reflection? A lively feeling of situations and an aptitude to describe them makes a poet." Frost rebelled against pigeonholing. When cornered, he would ask to be called a synecdochist, as he was always taking the whole for a part or a part for the whole.

When the September issue of *Harper's* came out, the dean of American Letters, William Dean Howells, had risen to prophesy from the Delphian *Editor's Easy Chair*. He wrote:

> Prophecy is not our job, or not our present job, but we have a fancy that when it comes to our next book of shredded prose it will not be so eagerly welcomed as some next book by Mr. Robert Frost. . . . Mr. Frost's volumes, *A Boy's Will* and *North of Boston,* have already made their public on both sides of the Atlantic, and they merit the favor they have won. . . . When we say that Mr. Frost's book is unaffectedly expressive of New England life, we do not mean that it is unconsciously expressive; we do not much believe in unconscious art, and we rather think that his fine intelligence tingles with a sense of that life and beautifully knows what it is at in dealing with it.

In my copy of the magazine Frost has written: "I never read this."

One day that first Mountain Interval year, a letter came from Bryn Mawr inviting the author to come and stay on the campus for two weeks and speak to the students. Being one of his first experiences in being "loaned out," Frost always remembered the circumstances to a detail. When he arrived on the scene he found that a Bryn Mawr student named Kathleen (she was afterward to become Mrs. Theodore Morrison) had stirred up the other girls to raising money to procure the "fee" they must pay. He loved to talk with young people, and he went away charmed with his sojourn among the girls at the college.

This was the beginning of a friendship that was to mean much to him in the years to come. Pan was laughing behind a clump of trees. Perhaps he even persuaded his colleague, Eros, to come to his aid. At any rate, the name Kathleen Morrison comes to have a real meaning for us; the initials K. M. take on true importance.

In that good year 1915, Tufts College invited him to read the Phi Beta Kappa poem there. With money coming in from royalties, life was somewhat easier. The farm was more successful than either the Derry farm or the Little Iddens venture had been. A speaking engagement now and then was for the moment looked on as a blessing—unmixed. *North of Boston* had sold twenty thousand copies with five printings.

Thus passed the first year at Franconia. Through the winter he had not forgotten that the Phi Beta Kappa poem must be read by him at Harvard in the summer. Well chosen indeed for the occasion was "The Axe-Helve," read in June of 1916. It was not printed until September, 1917, in the *Atlantic*. This would seem to be Frost's first attempt at any sort of dialect. Not having seen the poem before she published her *Tendencies*, Amy Lowell could not have known of its existence. "Mr. Frost," she said, "does not deal with the changed population, with the Canadians and the Finns who are taking up the deserted farms." Such a far-flung statement was dangerous. "The Axe-Helve" was the French-Canadian dialect of a near neighbor.

It was the summer of 1916 that James Chapin came to the farm to discuss illustrating *North of Boston* for a special edition. Frost was of the opinion that poetry was better without attempt at graphic interpretation, but he went into the matter with Chapin, and the thing eventuated in the illustrated book.

With their early protégé rising to international fame, *The Independent,* in its issue of May 22, 1916, reprinted "My Butterfly" from the November 8, 1894, issue. Its long-time editor—more than any other person entitled to fame as the discoverer of Robert Frost—William Hayes Ward, had severed his connection with the magazine the year *A Boy's Will* was published. It was no small satisfaction that came to the octogenerian in his Maine home to know of the success which followed his protégé. He did not live to see the publication of *Mountain Interval,* dying August 29, 1916.

Frost's third book, his first to be published originally in America, came out in November of his second year at home. In *Mountain Interval* many verses saw print for the first time, though nearly half had previously appeared in magazines in 1914, 1915, and 1916. *Poetry and Drama* had used four in December, 1914—"The Sound of the Trees," "The Cow in Apple Time," "Putting in the Seed," and "The Smile." *Yale Review,*

McClure's, and *Century* each printed one in 1916. *The Independent* had given space to his poem, "The Telephone," on October 9, just a month before the publication of the new book. "Snow" found a place in *Poetry* the month the book was out. On my copy of the magazine containing this poem, he has chuckled in writing: "This was when Harriet had forgiven me for her mistake in not having discovered me herself." *The Craftsman,* one of the best edited, most artistic periodicals of the day, printed "The Vanishing Red" in July, 1916. On my copy of the magazine Frost has written something of rare critical import. "The place," he says, "was Acton, Mass., a hundred or more years ago. This was not intended for any kind of verse. It wanted to scan but I wouldn't let it."

Mountain Interval was destined to become one of the rarest of Robert Frost's volumes. It frequently reached the high prices attained by *North of Boston.* When it showed up at the farm, dressed in its modest coat of blue cloth, looking very much like its American predecessors, the poet was almost as proud of it as he had been of his first book in London. It contained some of his loveliest lyrics. It failed, however, to stir up the excitement of his second book.

In the dearth of good notices, that of Harriet Monroe, in *Poetry* for January, 1917, stands out as more deserving than Frost would ever admit. Unquestionably the thing that troubled him was the company in which Harriet Monroe had placed him; for she had reviewed *Mountain Interval,* by Frost, and *The Great Valley,* by Masters, in one article. She did, however, show great discernment of character, summing up the two poets—Frost, who wrote meagerly—Masters dashing off lines whole-sale; each depicting life as he best knew it: the one in the niggardly New England soil, the other in the fertile, prolific Middle West.

The biographer reads with no little interest the dedication of *Mountain Interval*—the history of the Frost farm places. "To you who least need reminding," could mean but one person—that one to whom he faithfully dedicated nearly all of the books of poetry he published during her lifetime. He continues, "that before this interval of the South Branch under the black mountain, there was another interval, the Upper at Plymouth, where we walked in spring beyond the covered bridge; but that the first interval of all was the old farm, our brook interval, so called by the man we had it from in sale."

After another summer on the Franconia farm, Lesley was ready for college. Her choice was Wellesley, but she was not to be too happy there. Our entry into the first World War had something to do with it, but by no means was that the most important contributing cause of her dissatisfaction. Robert detailed the events:

I taught Lesley to read Latin in the days of our visit to England, when I took great pains and much time. I taught her to read well and rapidly, but her translations all had a bit of slang of her own contriving, and I could easily recognize them anywhere. She had a teacher at Wellesley with whom she didn't get on well. I suppose Lesley was a bit too independent for her. The teacher accused her of copying another girl's paper in the Latin class because the two papers were alike.

Lesley came home and told me the whole story. So, I went to Boston to investigate. When I saw the paper in controversy I knew very well which one had written it, which had been guilty of copying. It was full of Lesley's own style of slang. Well, I called in the dean and the teacher and demanded to know of the teacher whether she has accused the other girl at the same time she accused my daughter. She said that had nothing to do with it. I insisted that it had everything to do with it, for I knew that at some time or other Lesley had crossed her and made her mad. The teacher calmed down in a minute or so and said she had intended to question the other girl. "Well," I said to her, "six weeks or more have passed and you haven't spoken to her yet. So, Lesley must go into another class, or go back with me." The dean was horribly shocked and said that could never be allowed, as it would be against all the rules of the college. "Well, then, she goes back home with me today," I answered. When I returned home I went alone, as they had broken all the rules and put Lesley into another class.

But Lesley's greatest unhappiness, perhaps, in any event her reason for leaving Wellesley for Barnard the next fall, was because she felt herself a prisoner at Wellesley. Being like me, she didn't want to be penned in, and they wouldn't permit the students to read the daily papers. Knowing the world was at war, she was anxious to get the low-down and be out in the midst of the melee of things, and not remain shut up in a cell, cut off from all knowledge of what was taking place. So, the next year we packed her off to another school, at the same time sending Irma to Wellesley preparatory school.

One sees the irate father, his daughter falsely accused, rushing off in a boiling state to have it out with the accusing teacher. Insult brought out a streak of meanness in him of which none suspected him capable. He became inexorable in his hatred. No Indian was ever more implacable. Ask a few who still live, who, because of dereliction on their part, have felt the sting of his poisoned arrows—the hammerblows of his right arm—the thud of his mailed fist. Point is given by such a picture to Frost's own statement: "One should have all kinds of feelings, for he lives in all kinds of a world."

There were pleasant as well as unpleasant happenings in those days. A group of artists and authors had founded an unusual magazine called *The Seven Arts*. Motivated by high purposes, this periodical sought to allow poets and playwrights and essayists to express themselves as they would on its pages. Frost was made one of the arbiters of the literary tendencies by being placed on its board. Of course, insofar as his duties called for any exertion, services rendered were few. His influence, however, was far from insignificant. He printed excellent work in the magazine, to mention only two items—"A Way Out" and "The Bonfire."

Pleasant things out of the past called, too. Plymouth Normal had him back. Weygandt tells us that he was present at Plymouth in 1916 "on a wild day of wind and rain" and saw with what pride his old school welcomed back as poet him they had known as teacher five years before.

Recognition of a higher degree came also. Perhaps William Dean Howells did more than review his books. As the recognized leader of the American Academy, Howells' voice carried weight. In 1916 Frost was elected to membership in the National Institute.

With all his moving about, his interest in things American grew and expanded so that before he was aware, Robert had found England slipping out of thought. Edward Thomas was not so forgotten. Even after the latter had signed up in 1917 the two exchanged letters. Thomas wrote some rather extensive correspondence during his last days, enclosing poems on which he had been working right up to the end of his life. Some of these Frost sent on to Harriet Monroe for use in *Poetry*.

Thomas had finished his collection of *Poems* and sent it to the publisher before he went to France early in 1917. He never got to read the proof sheets. This book, signed "Edward Estaway," was dedicated to Robert Frost. It was published by Selwyn and Blount, London. When he donned uniform and left for the front, Thomas carried two books with him: a pocket Shakespeare and a copy of Frost's *Mountain Interval*. On Easter Sunday he was regulating the fire of the 244th Siege Battery from an advance post. In the very moment when victory was theirs, he was killed by a direct hit from a shell, though his body was left unmarred.

Long after, grief still in his heart, Frost was to publish the poem in memory of his best friend in lines that speak of affection and sorrow.

> *You went to meet the shell's embrace of fire*
> *On Vimy Ridge . . .*

XV. Unless a College

AMHERST COLLEGE, since its founding in 1821, had gone on its way, a small-town school, in a measure church-related to the Congregationalists. In 1912 a new force came, stirring up even the ghost of shy Emily Dickinson. A man of vision and outlook became president of the school.

Alexander Meiklejohn was a recognized philosopher. His ambition was to transform Amherst into the outstanding small college, or at least into one of the few such, in the union. He had high ideals of scholarship. He wanted to make each department a force in American education. To do this, he had to man each department with the best scholars available.

Thus it was that he began to "steal" good professors from the faculties of other colleges and universities. The very first year of his tenure he set about building a staff of teachers that has often been referred to as one of the strongest of any college in the history of small colleges. The school, from the start of his meteoric career, grew in scholarship, gained in standing.

Meiklejohn believed that the teacher was everything in education. To build a great faculty meant building a great school after the Mark Hopkins formula. He wished to bring outstanding men together whether they were to teach or merely to give atmosphere to campus and classroom.

To use a pertinent example, he wished to recognize poetry. Who was the most talked-of poet in the country? At the moment, thanks to *North of Boston,* this happened to be Robert Frost.

Meiklejohn was attracted to Frost when he saw him in action on the Amherst campus in 1916. Stark Young had engineered the first visit, which was a tremendous success. Frost read his poetry to a small group that gathered in the Christian Association room. This, as later on Whicher pointed out with great nostalgia, was the forerunner of many such events. When he finished his visit he went back to Franconia. That was spring. When, that summer, overtures came, he immediately accepted them. He was made professor and at once removed his family to Amherst.

It was not without mental reservations that he took on the onerous duties of professor of English. He remembered the days of slavery at Derry, continued at Plymouth. For a long time, now, he had been free from the serfdom of classwork. But Meiklejohn assured him such slavery was not to be imposed at Amherst; and an admission is due the college administration that during all his years there, barring certain teaching which he did at the start, the promise was faithfully, though occasionally grudgingly, kept.

No one single person associated with Frost is more fitted to recount the tale of the Amherst years than Meiklejohn:

> When we were building our faculty at Amherst from 1912 on, I made up my mind that teachers were more important than research doctors of philosophy. The large proportion of the new faculty members I chose were ordinary Masters of Arts, some bachelors, some like Frost with no college degree at all. Stark Young, who was really responsible for Frost's coming to us, talked it all over with me. We decided that here was a man who

was doing something about literature. He was not merely a fellow who could use a scalpel on a work of literature, tear it apart, show how it was put together. He had the positive approach. He could and did produce it from his own mind. He was a coming man, though neither Stark Young nor myself realized how far he was coming before he stopped. He was pretty hard up when he came to us. Of course he was getting money from royalties on *North of Boston,* but he was educating his children, who came and went, and he was always short of money. Lesley was about the only one of them I learned to know well.

He stirred up considerable jealousy in the Amherst years. He was full of the war spirit, and felt that the rest of us were not. He worked well with Stark Young in the English department. They were as different as two men could well be. Frost was always interested in the athletic games, and would attend. Young never went, but when they had a rally the athletes would ask him to come and give them a "pep talk." He would quote the Greek authors in the original to them at such rallies. Young was a fine student of the classics, which he knew by heart. Frost was pure American. He grew out of the soil of New England, regardless of having been born in California. He never quoted Greek. He never quoted anything. He simply said what was in his heart. It was all his own. He was out of the earth. Young was the greater teacher. But he was the sophisticate. They complemented and supplemented one another perfectly.

When R. F. came to us at Amherst in 1916, right at the start he laid down certain laws for his classes in literature. In his first talk to his English class he said there would be writing and studying literature. "But," he said, "I want it understood right now that we don't intend to do anything with any piece of literature that the writer of it didn't intend to have done."

After he had been with us for some time Frost came to my office one morning and said he had a complaint to make to me. I asked him to state his complaint. "Well, Meiklejohn," he said, "it's that you've robbed the boys of their right to rebel. You're always just a bit too far to the left— just a bit farther than they. Thus they are thwarted. They want to rebel and can't. Of course you don't intend to do it, but you're the cause of their frustration. They never can quite catch up with you."

We talked all morning. Then we went to lunch together. Then I took him home to dinner with me, and after dinner we talked till midnight. We didn't get it all settled, but the experience was a warm one.

I've never understood Robert's stand on politics and economics. He always seemed to be a confirmed rightist, but one wonders. About 1946 I went to Dartmouth to lecture. I was in the Hanover Inn having lunch with a professor. We got up and started out and there sat Robert. He got to his feet, we greeted one another, and I started out. He followed me. He seemed embarrassed, finding it hard to say what he wanted to get off his chest. Finally he blurted out: "Alec, I've been thinking a lot about my actions when we used to be together at Amherst. I've decided there are two sorts of people, the stupid and the crazy, and I've come to a conclusion and want you to know my conclusion. In my attitude toward you in the past I was of the stupid. Now I want you to know I'm on the other side."

He was so honest, so sincere, that by the time he had got it out tears were running down my cheeks. It took a vast amount of sublimation for him to bring himself to tell me that. It showed the greatness of the man to do it.

I found out one thing about Robert. When he made up his mind he didn't want to do something, then you might just as well make up *your* mind he wouldn't do it.

When he had been with us a year or two the question came up about buying him a home. I suggested a house in Amherst near the college. He vetoed this. He didn't want a house right in town, but one at the edge, close enough to walk in to the college and the post office and the library, but far enough for him to have the feel of being in the country. I remember well how we climbed into my buggy and drove all around the countryside one afternoon accomplishing nothing but have a good talk. We never seemed to find just the thing to suit him, so nothing came of it. He finally bought a home on Sunset, but that was long after my day. He didn't live in it very long, for he soon passed on to Harvard.

Wise old Amherst! Astute Alexander Meiklejohn! The latter, for all his Scottish traits, was perhaps unaware of the truly wise thing he had done. It is likely that the English alone actually plumbed the depth of the matter, and they, through their provincialism, thought this isolated case a thing of general practice in America. We find the editor voicing such an idea in the introduction to *Selected Poems,* by Frost, published in London in 1932, where he states:

"America, which does so many things better than we do, has dealt wisely with Frost. American universities think that a poet may be worth hearing on poetry, and Robert Frost holds a chair of poetry at one of the most individual of colleges. Really his job is that of resident poet. What is required of him is not a minimum of set lectures, but that he should be on the spot when the farmer's season permits. . . . The best teachers . . . have accomplished their influence by being extant and accessible. Amherst is lucky in its professor of poetry, for no one is more unmistakably a man of genius in his conversation, which is thinking aloud, informed with shrewdness, honesty and imagination."

Withdrawing itself on a little knoll, which nine steps were required to surmount, the house in which the Frosts lived at Amherst was the handsomest of any they so far had called home. There was a garret, and below this two full stories. The house was commodious enough for all family needs. A mammoth tree stood directly in front of the steps, and vines covered the little porch. The familiar New England shutters were on all windows. A homelike atmosphere pervaded. This, like the other Amherst houses in which he lived (it was purchased not long before he left Amherst, first), was quite removed from whatever commotion a small college town might suffer. At the Sunset house David Grayson was a near neighbor.

Trained in scholarly traditions, the Amherst faculty understood and respected Frost's desire for privacy. They left him to his own devices. They admired, as the students adored him. Some jealousy existed among the professors who had to buckle down to work while the poet-in-residence failed to live up to his title. They were envious of his life of leisure, but they knew such a life was productive of genuine literature; and they gave few, if any, evidences of such envy. His standing with the faculty is revealed by the evidence they gave in conferring on him his first honorary degree in 1917. At that time they made him a Master of Arts.

The granting of this degree did not come without knowledge of his having done at least one scholastic thing extremely well. In the spring of 1917 he was commandeered to carry on for Professor George Churchill, a noted Shakespearean scholar and an international authority on the sources of *Richard III*. Churchill's subsequent career in politics ended tragically. Frost taught in this course *Hamlet* and the rest. There were doubts on the part of such as thought Shakespeare should be taught in the light of seventeenth century research—dates, figures, and facts—not as a living, breathing thing. The pinch hitter shocked some who came to visit the class "over at College Hall," to find the boys acting one-hour cuttings of the drama. (The cuttings were by the students.) At least one Amherstian was not slow to observe the movement of straws. "For us the breezes were blowing," he said. Frost was still the teacher original.

Librarian Greene, of the Jones Library, always enjoyed a homey anecdote of Frost's early Amherst days. R. F. had a boon companion, a real-estate man who had as much New England flavor about him as the poet. One day Frost's friend asked his wife how she would like a little buggy ride. She demurred saying she was not dressed for it. "Nobody'll see us," he said. "Come on." They rode around for an hour, and pulling up at a house he said, "Suppose we go in here and have dinner with these folks." She was shocked at the thought, but he insisted. She told him she wasn't dressed, and anyway they couldn't just barge in on a household like that and stay for dinner. But he was firm, saying it would be all right. It *was* all right, too. The house was Frost's, and the poet had invited them to dinner.

From 1916 on, for at least four years, Robert knew peace. In those years he was associated with Everett Glass in advanced composition. This, however, was largely a front. He was professor-at-large, the world his field, humanity his subject. With a perennial flair for the legitimate drama, he conceived a one-act play, which was completed and finally published in *Seven Arts,* February, 1917. It lay for two years untouched before "The Maskers," college players, decided to try a hand at producing it. February 24, 1919, it was given at the Academy of Music in Northampton, across the river. The author was codirector with Mrs. R. G. Gettell, and though it went no further, it was cordially received at its Northampton appearance. In his dedication of the printed play in book form, Frost gave credit to the Amherst junior who took the leading role of Asa, in the words:

To
Roland A. Wood
Who created the part of Asie
"The Maskers" of the college put on the play.

"A Way Out" was a fine psychological study, written as cleverly as any one of his poems. Ten years after it was produced at Northampton, it was published in book form by the Harbor Press.

The year 1919 is further memorable because at this time Frost bought a farm near South Shaftsbury, Vermont—a place in after years to be the setting for tragedy. New Hampshire had been his first love. Now Vermont beckoned. Unless his memory failed him, he found it as hard to take root among the Vermonters as it earlier had been to ingratiate himself with his neighbors in New Hampshire.

"The people of Vermont never mention New Hampshire. When they have to talk about me and where I'm from they say: 'He's from off somewhere.' "

Laughingly Frost recounts an incident which happened at a meeting of Vermont poets somewhere around 1919, after he bought the property at South Shaftsbury.

> There I was, a farm owner, and tax payer, in Vermont. They had gathered together their versifiers, bad and indifferent, who proceeded to read their effusions to one another; and they introduced as many nobodies as man ever saw assembled under one roof. At last the old fellow in charge looked over his glasses and said, "It has been brought to my attention that there is a fellow named Frost here today who writes verse." And that was all the introduction or recognition this fellow named Frost had from them.

Vermont poets may have seen him only as "a fellow named Frost who writes verse," but over the state, taking it by and large, it was quite different—especially in scholastic and critical circles. At Middlebury, Vermont, where long an institution of the higher learning had existed, some kindred spirits hit on the idea of a summer school of English and writing to be conducted at nearby Bread Loaf. Frost was inveigled into becoming a co-founder and teacher.

The Bread Loaf School of English got under way in 1920. In the prose preface to *Bread Loaf Anthology* he wrote: "You who are as concerned as I over the future of Bread Loaf will agree with me that once in so often it is to be redefined if it is to be kept from degenerating into a mere summer resort for routine education in English, or worse still for the encouragement of a vain ambition in literature. We go there, not for correction or improvement. No writer has ever been corrected into importance."

Harriet Monroe that summer conceived the idea of celebrating the tenth anniversary of *Poetry: A Magazine of Verse.* She wished to publish the works of noted poets still living, making the restriction that the poem must be one written before the author was twenty-three. Frost, among other contributors, was asked, and submitted "Flower Boat," which had been published in *Youth's Companion* May 20, 1909. It was printed in the anniversary number in August, 1920.

Regardless of the auspicious beginnings, things were not to go on placidly at Amherst. They began to cloud up quite early—not for the poet, except insofar as he was a Meiklejohn product, but for the administration. Two factions naturally arose—pre-Meiklejohn, and pro-Meiklejohn. Things were beginning to get warm as 1920 arrived. Frost was destined to make a radical change in this year.

President Burton, in the University of Michigan, felt there should be a greater recognition of the creative arts by leading state universities. He therefore invited Frost to come to Ann Arbor as poet-in-residence. He would have no duties to perform but would merely hold himself in readiness, accessible on the campus. Perhaps the fear that things were going to explode at Amherst helped him to a decision. He accepted the proposition and removed to Michigan. Burton fully kept his word. Frost was given his own time with no clock to punch. He was allowed to work or loaf as he wished. He slept all he wanted to, stayed up all hours of the night, got up when he pleased, and lived just the sort of life he always favored.

Being geographically removed from his children did not keep him from carrying their burdens. "The trouble with kinfolks is," he once said, "they are always calling you on the telephone, collect."

Lesley, so far, had not found herself. She changed with the phases of the moon, a thing that always troubled her father. His months at Ann Arbor were occupied in thinking something out for her. In the end he hit on the idea that she should be a bookseller. She loved books and was a good salesman. But he had to learn more about it. He fastened himself upon two young women who ran a bookstore in Detroit, going over nearly every day to talk with them about the book business, pumping them dry on the commercial end while they pumped him dry on the artistic.

"It took us no little time to find out what his 'racket' was," one of the girls admitted. "But when, one day, he said he believed his eldest daughter would be a good bookseller, the truth was out. After that we freely told him all we knew about the book business, which wasn't too much. And this he passed on to Lesley."

Lesley, forever a plunger, accepted her father's advice and went into the business headlong. She was not content to do it the orthodox way. She hit onto the plan of selling by book caravan, hauling the merchandise from town to town in a truck. This didn't last long. Soon she located in one place with a central store, which became a feeder for smaller stores in other towns, till at last she had a whole string of bookstores. In time she drew Marjorie into the business. Her father had a word about it:

> Lesley is a born fighter. She is always in a scrap with somebody or other. She is not happy unless she is waging a campaign. She carries works of art in her stores, especially fine prints. This now and then opens an opportunity for a fight on her part. She had one very fine picture in her store awhile ago, which she seems to have priced too low. A man came along and said he'd take the picture, but didn't make any down payment to bind the bargain. After he had gone she discovered her mistake, and marked the price up. Then he came for his picture and she wouldn't let him have it at the original price marked. She pointed out to him that he hadn't paid anything, and so the bargain had never been sealed. He took it to court to force delivery. She told the whole thing to the judge, who, nevertheless, ruled against her. She appealed the case, and the higher court held that she was right. No money payment, no bargain sealed, and she was in no wise obliged to deliver.

President Burton might promise all the freedom on earth, but there turned out to be something to reckon with at Ann Arbor which neither president nor poet foresaw.

Frost was a famous man. Lionizing became an epidemic.

There were social functions, pink teas, a thousand demands upon his time. Before he was aware of it he had become involved in the social whirl. Ordinarily he could not have put up with this sort of thing. Just why he felt differently about it at Ann Arbor he could never explain. Perhaps the reason was that he had good listeners. Always a good talker, he always had an audience. Moreover, the students, bent on hearing him talk, tagged after him all the time. Said he:

> I always remember an incident at Ann Arbor. There wasn't any literary magazine in the university, which I thought was a shame. Of course literary magazines in college or out are the hardest things to make pay. Sex and mystery and crime and western stuff have easy sledding. We learned that when we tried to make a go of *Seven Arts*. Weeds grow without trouble. Flowers take a lot of water and digging.

> Well, there was a Japanese girl at Ann Arbor, named, if I remember right, Yupiasiwa. She came to me one day with the sad story that there was no medium through which good literary writing could be published. She said nobody was interested in a literary magazine. She had picked up the information that somebody would come along and start one, it would run awhile and then be given up. The ones who were managing it wouldn't put any money into it, and they couldn't get anybody else to put in any. She was all excited about getting one going.

> I told her there was an old German who ran a bookstore in town. He might be interested. At least it would pay to go and see him. She did, he got interested and the result was that he put his money into a losing game and started a literary magazine. A Japanese girl getting a German bookseller to put money into a literary magazine in an American college!

There was publication, too. Joseph Anthony, of *Harpers,* came after something from him. He had published "The Runaway" in *The Amherst Monthly* in 1918 and nothing else until 1920. In July, Anthony put "Fragmentary Blue," "Place for a Third," "Good-bye and Keep Cold," and "For Once, Then, Something" into the magazine. He emphasized the two years of utter voicelessness with a note.

"After being almost unheard for two years Robert Frost is speaking again in the old strain that will be unmistakable to readers of his *North of Boston*. But Mr. Frost has not really been silent during this period. He has been producing more work of the type that has made him regarded on both sides of the Atlantic as one of the authentic voices. In the group of new poems which he here presents the broad range of his work is represented. As Mr. Frost himself put it, 'big bear, little bear and middle-sized bear.' "

On my copy of *Harpers,* containing these poems and the note, Frost has inserted: "Sounds like a revival."

In December appeared another group in *Harpers*—a most distinguished group including "Fire and Ice," "Wild Grapes," "The Valley's Singing Day," and "The Need of Being Versed in Country Things." "Joseph Anthony came after these and gave me a new send-off with the magazine public," Frost wrote on my copy. In fact, 1920 saw the magazines publishing no fewer than ten poems—*Yale Review* using "To E. T." in the spring number and *The London Mercury,* "A Favour" in December.

Great surprise was expressed at the end of the first year at Ann Arbor when Burton announced that Frost was returning for another term. The surprise was as great that he accepted as that the invitation had been given. He explained carefully that he felt his work had not been finished. He had ideas for the coming year, including the gathering in of voluntary students who wanted to write, who were willing to take the course without credit. He said he had plans for bringing outstanding poets to the campus and listed Edna Millay, Sara Teasdale, E. A. Robinson, Witter Bynner, and others.

Michigan followed the lead of Amherst in making the poet an honorary Master of Arts at the end of his first year. That same season saw him elected to membership in the International P.E.N. club and receiving the doubtful honor of being chosen poet laureate of the Vermont League of Women's clubs. He was further recognized when the "The Witch of Coös" received the Levinson Prize. At commencement time he spoke to the graduating class of the State University of Vermont and received his first doctor's degree, an L.H.D.

After two years at the University of Michigan, his two great friends at the helm at Amherst, President Olds and Dwight Morrow, put at him to come back home. He would not consent until one thing was clear; he would teach only when he had something to teach. When this very satisfactory arrangement had been agreed on by candidate and college, the prodigal returned in 1922.

Frost never used the term "South Shaftsbury Interval," though he well might have done so. Dorothy Canfield Fisher was a near neighbor of his here; Carol had married a neighborhood girl and was living the year round on the farm. The old house on the place was constructed of great square blocks of stone and known through the decades as the Peleg Cole house. Built of native stone, "just as it was flaked off under the quarryman's hammer," by the father-in-law of Peleg Cole in the eighties of the eighteenth century, it was tenanted intermittently. When Frost had heard that the house could be bought and it was hinted that it had a ghost, he didn't hesitate a moment. In addition to the fine view and the old house, there was a substantial barn surrounded by an apple orchard. The cider mill went with the place.

Dorothy Canfield Fisher, very happy over the situation, probably thought that everybody in the community looked on it in the way she did. She writes:[1] "Everybody up and down our valley is silently and intensely proud of the fact that Robert Frost has chosen a home among us." The whole story is told in the words "silently proud." She continues: "To us the house looks not at all grim and sombre, but homelike and strong and cheerful and protecting when we look up at it as we climb the Peleg Cole hill, with its old lilac and syringa bushes, and the lily-of-the-valley bed, earlier to bloom than in any of our gardens, because of the sun's warmth reflected from the grey stone walls against which it is planted. As we pass we crane our necks about, with the humane country interest in other people's lives (called meddling curiosity by city folks), and comment to each other on the things we see, important in the round of the seasons; as, 'They've got their new corn planted already,' or, 'My, how far Lillian's sweet peas are up!' or with the deep approval

[1] *Bookman*, December, 1926, p. 403.

Vermonters feel for provident winter preparations, 'Oh, just look at all that nice wood that Carol has split and stacked!' "

For his part, Frost admired the Fisher home just as they admired his. A great bond of friendship grew up between the poet and the novelist. A quarter-century after, Dorothy said to us with a tone of pride: "Robert and I are the only members of committees down in New York City these days who have rural delivery addresses. We fly down to New York on business, but we can't fly back fast enough. Years ago, when Robert was our permanent neighbor here in the Battenkill valley, one day he walked with me across the Fisher forest. 'You know, Dorothy,' he said, 'you've done the right thing. Every person should learn to love trees before he's thirty, so he'll have friends when he's sixty.' Then he added, 'I talk and write about trees, you *do* something about them.' "

What Dorothy and John Fisher had done about trees was to set out tiny sprouts no taller than a span—hundreds and hundreds of them—on the barren hills of the Canfield patrimony. The forest for years was the butt of neighborly jokes because the weeds were higher than the trees, but the sprouts grew into woods that were "lovely, dark and deep," with underfoot a carpet of moss that silenced all footsteps.

For a long time Frost had been planning a fourth book. He wanted it to be different, not only from his other books, but from *any* other book of poetry. At Franconia, at Amherst, at Ann Arbor, at South Shaftsbury, wherever he found himself, always he had the idea of a book which he had determined to christen *New Hampshire*.

Such a title was well chosen, for Frost wrote much poetry both in and about New Hampshire. "You won't believe she said it, but she said it," might well have been the text for this unusual book. It all had to be built around New Hampshire, "one of the two best states in the Union—Vermont's the other." Since he was to dedicate the book to Michigan, he must have intended to hint that Michigan was third in line.

Probably in no other one of his books did Frost have so much fun with himself as in *New Hampshire*. What chuckles he must have indulged in over the footnotes. One must own a first edition to have a look at this fun. If they served any purpose, these footnotes, it was only as a commentary on the magnum opus he designed the title poem to be.

Frost's account of the preparation of this manuscript is a genuine segment of out literary heritage.

> I used to carefully type my manuscripts when I was having hard sledding getting rid of them to the editors. But when the time arrived that it was a question would I please give them a poem for their pages, I just wrote them out in longhand and sent them in, letting it go at that. When I had just about brought *New Hampshire* to a place I was willing to leave it— as willing as I ever am to leave a book—and was ready to collect it in order, I did what I always did, thinking nothing of it. I went out and bought a fifteen-cent composition book and wrote it out. I have always been more comfortable writing on line paper from the time when I first wrote "My Butterfly" for publication. This composition book was a cheap affair, having a red cover, bright red. My whole thought was to write it up as soon as possible and get it off my hands, done with it. So I just scribbled the poems in the notebook and sent it down to the publishers. They hurt my feelings by writing a news story about my manuscript. They have it all bound up now and put away to show, exhibit "A." Later on they sent me several blank books of the finest paper, done up in lovely bindings, saying I used such horrible paper they wanted to see me with a good stock for once.

Holts got Lankes to do the woodcuts, and typical Lankes landscapes, "like nothing else by day," resulted.

The illustrations for *New Hampshire* and others of Lankes's caused a sort of misunderstanding to grow up between poet and artist, with neighbor Dorothy piping up from the sidelines and being piped up about from the ring. Lankes tells how he had been sketching over in eastern Ohio when he was approached by Lincoln MacVeagh, in charge of the new book, who asked him if he would like to "do" *New Hampshire*. Never having been in New Hampshire and having some sketches of eastern Ohio already finished, he accepted the assignment, and more than one Ohio landscape resulted in the book. It may be of some interest that the famous grindstone and tree which appeared as tailpiece to *New Hampshire* and was made into a bookplate for Frost was made from a tree and grindstone in the elder Lankes's orchard. The artist has affirmed this under his own hand in my copy of *The Month at Goodspeed's*.

Since Lankes has busied himself on occasion with the Frost legend, illustrating books and articles about the poet, his story of his early meeting with the man he was to collaborate with has been passed on by Goodspeed's:

Robert Frost lived in this house [the Peleg Cole house] when I sketched it in 1923 or 1924 [really 1924]. I was very ambitious when it was cut. I wanted the house to look like the home of a poet, which in itself was a big order. I also wanted to suggest the flavor of his poetry. Dorothy Canfield Fisher used this woodcut to illustrate an article in *Bookman* about this house. She complained that my job did not do the house justice, for to her it looked sunny and gay, whereas I had it otherwise—"grim, sombre." It is a house of tragedy.

Shortly after Robert Frost bought The Gulley, near South Shaftsbury, I came up to spend some six or eight weeks on the place while it was in process of renovation. On the first walk around the farm we passed through this gate [referring to his picture "Calf Pasture Gate"] Frost remarking that the enclosure was called "the calf pasture." The gate is the kind intended to be weighted with a rock as a counterbalance and it looked to me for all the world like a calf bawling for his (her) ma.

On my first visit to the Peleg Cole place I was met at the South Shaftsbury station by Frost and his son, with a buggy. The seat was the typically narrow seat which justified young men holding their girls from falling off. A real necessity as all old girls know. The son drove. I was bidden to sit beside him. Well, that left no room for Frost. So he sat on the quarter-inch-wide edge of the "box" in the rear while the horse slowly jogged up the hill. The road was later made into a highway to Montreal. . . . Well, we reached the house at 6 P.M. Had supper (dinner elsewhere) and talk started. Little by little the members of the family disappeared until finally only F. and I remained. "Now we can talk," he said, drawing his chair closer and adjusting the kerosene lamp. I had been up the night before in New York talking to an old art school companion until two and had as usual waked up early. Finally I had to "call" it and staggered off to bed as the birds commenced to carol. A few hours later I was wakened by a churn, so got up and prowled around the farm. It was drizzling but I made the sketches from which these cuts were made. F. was on the lawn when I returned to the house, I planned to take the noon train. Talk started again. Presently the noon train whistled down at the station. So talk went on unremittingly until 1 A.M. Again I had to cry, "Hold, enough!" I've always needed more than two hours sleep a night.

It would appear that the mild feud which grew up between writer and illustrator caused the latter to have a little fun at the expense of the former, as in the case where, because he had heard Frost make some derogatory remark about sheep, he put some in his upper pasture. "His neighbor in the Gulley," the artist added, "raised sheep. The shepherd is my invention."

Lankes knew and remembered the pasture he pictured all right. On my copy of *The Bookman* containing Dorothy Canfield Fisher's article on Frost, he has written under his woodcut, "When I saw this pasture ten years later I couldn't recognize it for the trees." Continuing his account of his relations with Frost, Lankes says:

> I complained to Frost one day about the unfairness of the system that permitted a poet to write his poems untrammeled by the decorations or pictures to go into his book. It should be the other way round, I insisted. Let the poet write around the pictures and see how he likes it. After a good deal of insistence for the galley proofs of *West-Running Brook* and getting nowhere, I concluded Frost was handing out rope to see how well I could hang myself. It amused me to read a review in which the critic referred to the success the artist had in capturing the spirit of the Sycamore tree. I didn't see the poems till they were on the market.

Frost's comeback to Lankes's argument referred to what the artist had said about his quarrel with Mrs. Fisher concerning the picture of "the Peleg Cole house" used in *The Bookman,* the matter of the churn, and the conversation was:

> I don't know what to say to the twist he gives this. Does he mean the flavor of my poetry is essentially grim and somber—tragic? . . . There has never been a churn in any of my farmhouses. Much of this is pure literary extravagance. Some people have been kinder about my conversations. . . . This [referring to what Lankes says about illustrating *West-Running Brook*] gives a false impression, probably unintentional. I have always done what I could to keep my books from being illustrated. I only let the artist into them with the express understanding that he wasn't to

try to repeat the poems with pictures. The stipulation with James Chapin was that he should decorate *North of Boston,* not illustrate it. He didn't keep to the agreement as closely as Lankes did.

In 1944, on my copy of Goodspeed's catalog containing the conversation about Robert Frost, the poet has written: "Lankes was one of my greatest friends."

New Hampshire, bound in green and gold, made its appearance in October, 1923.

 Decade Six

XVI. As Pedagogue to Pedagogue

It was a happy event, that beginning of the sixth decade on the cabalistic five in 1925 with a gathering at the Hotel Brevoort in New York City to celebrate the fiftieth anniversary of the birthday of Robert Frost.

Four friends joined in sending out the "Invitation for a Birthday Dinner to Robert Frost." These four were Amy Lowell, Frederic Melcher, Louis Untermeyer, and Irita Van Doren. The invitation read: "A few friends of Robert Frost are planning a dinner in his honor on March twenty-sixth. The occasion—his fiftieth birthday—seems to them an appropriate one on which to express a little of the admiration and affection they have long felt for him."

That night of March 26 saw a gay crowd seated at table. Carl Van Doren was toastmaster. Pan sat grinning slyly. He had something up his sleeve.

Dorothy Canfield Fisher revealed sidelights of her fellow Vermonter which astonished no one—they seemed so like him—but brought peals of laughter.

"And when I came upon this distinguished poet playing a love game of tennis, toeing it with the agility of a cat, I was not surprised to find he was playing in his stocking feet."

We see him that night through Elizabeth Sergeant's eyes. ". . . he wore at first this marble Dantesque mask, colored really like Carrara marble, with mauve and golden shadow, and shining with a clear Renaissance beauty of the Christian sort. . . . Yet it took only a featherweight of affection to make tenderness flicker like flame over the still features, and shape itself in facial line."

Of the crowd itself, Mark Van Doren said: "The guests included, in addition to many persons who could not have been considered literary at all, representatives of every conceivable fashion in criticism."

Pan played the role of sphinx that night. He knew what he knew. When time came for him, it was announced that he would read a new one-act play he had just finished in New England dialect. A ripple of excitement followed, heightened when the author's interpretation of that dialect turned out to be Irish. This play was his now famous "The Cow's in the Corn"—one of the shortest of short shorts. The *Dearborn Independent* was to publish it June 18, two years later, with a full-page drawing to illustrate it.

Frost never did a more artistic piece than this, nor was a play ever read better than he read it that night for his friends. James and Hilda Wells printed it with a foreword by Frost in 1929. "This," he sets forth, "my sole contribution to the Celtic Drama (no one so unromantic as not to have made at least one) illustrates the latter day tendency of all drama to become smaller and smaller to be acted in smaller and smaller theatres to smaller and smaller audiences."

As the decade came on and the year 1925 dawned, Frost found he was still a pedagogue. He had not broken with the cap and gown. He was again seeking the halls of the University of Michigan. This time his title was to be "fellow in letters."

Word reached him at Ann Arbor that Carol and Lillian had a son. In the old "Peleg Cole house," into which the couple had moved when the elder Frosts bought the white house in the Gulley, the cry of a new-born babe had been heard. Robert may have appeared indifferent to the call of posterity, as he had to the call of ancestry. But it was not indifference when, looking back to Nicholas Frost and forward to Frosts yet to come, he wrote

> *It is turning three hundred years*
> *On our cisatlantic shore*
> *For family after family name.*
> *We'll make it three hundred more . . .*

The first William Prescott Frost had been named in memory of a maternal grandmother, Elizabeth Prescott, and her husband the first William Frost. The second was the poet's father. Now Carol and Lillian went back to it and named their son William Prescott, III. In all the long years ahead, following sorrow, tragedy, and disaster—dogged by the three fates—the rugged grandfather was to stand by him, look after him, and hold in him all hopes for future Frosts.

Was it the call of lineage, or the pull of New England which drew him from Ann Arbor the second time. Apparently the high plans and purposes held by Burton for his fellow-in-letters were coming to naught. So, when his second tenure ended in the spring of 1926, and after he had been duly "doctored" by Bowdoin, we find him accepting an ephemeral post at Wesleyan on the George Slocum Bennett Foundation. We also find him, just as he secretly wished all along, again connected with Amherst, in a connection that was to round out a full decade.

President Olds was still at the helm when, at the close of his term at Michigan, Frost returned to Amherst to teach on the John Woodruff Simpson Foundation, in which capacity he was to be heard in classes in English, Greek, and philosophy. "During those years," he said, "I was a sort of poetic radiator." While resident professor, he gave a course in ideals, out of which grew the evening discussions that came to mean so much to the college. Always he seemed more interested in the ordinary student than in the ones who planned writing careers. Now and again he would find a boy who was a dead ringer for literary success. He would then reverse his interest.

There is a story of the Amherst days when Frost was good for ten straight hours of talk. Stacy May took the Frosts by his home for a little chat which went on until supper. Pressure was brought, and he consented to stay for supper on promise of going right after, because he had an engagement at the house of a former pupil. Supper over, the talk still ran high, and the diners retired to the sitting room. Ten o'clock came, and Mrs. Frost warned him. He drew his watch partly out of his pocket and furtively glanced at it, saying, "It's only about eight o'clock." Finally at midnight they left the house. When they got to the former pupil's home they found a very angry host, whose guests, invited to meet Robert, were all gone.

Next morning, Frost met May in the hall. He said he was sorry it happened that way, but it was all on account of his watch. "I was given a very fine watch costing about a hundred dollars. It was out of order and had to be taken back to the jewelers. So I bought an Ingersoll. It keeps good time, but I'm sort of ashamed of it. When I look at the time I never pull it out very far, and always shove it right back. So, last night I mistook what time it was."

There were a few Amherst students such as Charlie Foster, who elected to attend Amherst just because Frost was on the campus. Foster had been a Frost idol-worshiper from his adolescent days. A great and life-lasting friendship grew up between the two. He was close to his idol during the days of the feud that went on later between President King on the one hand and Robert Frost and nearly everybody else on the other.

Foster, who in 1938 was to become the first to hold the Elinor White Frost Fellowship at Bread Loaf, has given us a picture of the all night talks—one, two, three, four o'clock, sometimes till dawn—with Frost, George Whicher, and a selected band of boys listening as the poet rambled on and on. Seminars were something else. There the poet-teacher wanted the boys to ask and answer questions. Often there would be teachers in the room, much to Frost's chagrin. Finally he told the teachers they'd have to stay away. Once the place was cleared of professors he felt more at ease and was able to precipitate a free-for-all with the students.

Another student who sat under Frost at Amherst was W. G. Rogers, who was to climb to the top as critic for the Associated Press. The teaching of this man was unlike the teaching done by any other professor, Rogers declared, and had for him "made all the difference."

Olds was succeeded as president by Arthur Stanley Pease, a genuine scholar, later to become professor of Latin in Harvard. He was president of Amherst from 1927 to 1932. The inauguration of Pease occasioned the production of a favorite poem, "One Step Backward Taken." "So many of my poems have Amherst memories," R. F. said. "This one remembers the time of the big flood when I set out to see Mr. Pease inaugurated here and didn't get here."

Under both Olds and Pease the poet had made his position in the college clear. It was under the man who succeeded Pease in 1932 that he fretted. Never were two men of more different outlooks and dispositions than Robert Frost and Stanley King. Eight years the junior of his poet-in-residence, the president in few things saw eye to eye with his "fellow-worker." King was a representative of big business. Trained as a lawyer and man of affairs, he had been general manager of the International Shoe Company before assuming the presidency of the college. The biggest business Frost had ever handled was a one-horse, one-cow farm in New Hampshire.

All in all Frost was happy and content at Amherst until the coming of the businessman for president. Then he found himself stirred up most of the time.

When *West-Running Brook* appeared in 1928, garbed like *New Hampshire* in green and gold, it was dedicated to E. M. F. as its predecessors had been. From the chorus of silence greeting its coming out, one would be led to believe that the author was passing into eclipse. Louis Untermeyer wrote of it in *The Saturday Review,* Percy Hutchinson in the *New York Times Book Review,* and Franklin E. Pierce in *Yale Review.* Other notices were few and far between. Those who did write were mainly concerned over the fact that he had surrendered the monologue manner of *North of Boston* and had affected the lyric. They failed to consider that his first writing was purely lyric and that he was only returning to his first love. However, the praise, what there was of it, was not stinted. Here were lyrics of the highest quality. A book of verse containing "Once by the Pacific," "Tree at My Window," and "A Winter Eden" needed no apology.

A most unaccountable hiatus is to be looked for in the period beginning in 1929 and ending January 1, 1934. Not one magazine carried his poetry during that period. Laziness may have overwhelmed him. Or he may have been in a huff with the editors. This hiatus followed the appearance of *West-Running Brook.* Could the editors have become discouraged over this latter-book?

Just what tempted our poet to revisit England in 1928? John Haines has asserted that the trip was undertaken in part to fulfill a promise he had made to revisit his old friends of 1914. Four years after that trip, he showed disappointment over it. Things were not what he had looked for. Nearly all his old cronies were gone—the Old Nailshop, the farmhouse of Little Iddens, and the Gallows were all emptied of their lively inhabitants. Scattered was the group of famous Georgians. Abercrombie was teaching, Gibson writing poetry elsewhere, and Thomas and Brooke dead on the fields of war, their graves, even if known, unvisited. Only Haines was there to greet him.

This good friend was of the opinion that the visit was made partly on behalf of Marjorie, whose health was bad. At least the trip to France, which was finished first and consumed six weeks of their time, was undoubtedly made for Marjorie's sake. When Frost got to England along in August, he was very critical of France and the French. He had not been happy or comfortable there at all. On the other hand, he was amazed at conditions in England, finding them so much better than his memory recorded of what they were before the war.

In late August he went down into the West Midlands where he stayed with the Haines family at Midhurst Huccelcote, Gloucestershire. Once again he looked with sweet-sad memories over the "rich pastoral country of slow streams, and marl and low broken hills . . . pierced by one small river, the Leadon, a tributary of the Severn." Haines wrote to me of the visit:

> We drove R. F. and Elinor over to the Dymock country and took him to Little Iddens where the folk living there showed him round and were very nice to him. We took him also to the outside of The Gallows, but he did not go in, and the place was then getting dilapidated. The Gallows in recent years deteriorated and much of the place was more or less fallen down and was so when I took R. F. to see it in 1928. Once again we walked the Cotswolds together, and later sat on Churchdown Hill, whilst he expounded the inner origins of his poetical themes, and once again we climbed May Hill and gazed round that astonishing ring of country from the Brecon Beacons to Shropshire, and from the northernmost Cotswolds to the Channel's rim . . . but the wraith of that dead friend was ever before us, "and a tender grace of a day that is dead" could never come back to us.

Then there was the trip to Ireland, which proved a very satisfying one. He always liked the Irish, never objected to having people say he looked Irish. He had a fine Irish brogue when he wanted to assume it. But it was nothing of this sort that attracted him to make the trip to Eire. Haines says it was a desire to see Æ (George William Russell) and Yeats that took him across the stormy channel.

"During his short visit to Ireland (I think he stayed about a fortnight) he met Yeats and Æ and went there for that purpose. I was not present at Frost's meeting with Yeats and Æ. I afterward gathered from what he said that he was charmed by Æ and he showed me a picture in blue tints Æ had painted and given him."

Whenever Frost in after years had occasion to refer to that visit to Eire, it was not of the Irish landscape, or of Irish farming, or of the Irish peasantry, or of the Sinn Feiners, or of the Eire Republic, or of de Valera that he talked. These things scarcely formed a backdrop. It was always of the other-worldly conversation he held with the two Irish mystics—men of the older Ireland—such talk, he said, "as nowhere else on earth have I ever heard the like of. These men took ordinary conversation and lifted it into the realm of pure literature."

In Dublin, likewise, he met Padraic Colum, Irish-American poet. Colum has one incident to relate, which he has given his word to, concerning this visit—an incident which pictures a carefree Frost full of fun and ready for a frolic.

I was showing the American some of the sights. We drove into a courtyard and Robert wanted to know where we were. "Dublin Castle," I told him. "What does one do in Dublin Castle?" "If one is an American one goes into the office and asks for his genealogy and coat of arms." A twinkling gleam was in his devil-may-care eye. "I'll do it." So, in we went and when he gave his name the genealogical expert asked, "Lincolnshire or Somersetshire Frosts?" He didn't know. He was asked what names were common in the family and gave his own—certainly not common in the family. "Lincolnshire Frosts. There are tombstones with the name in various places." "What arms do I get with the Lincolnshire Frosts?" "A gray squirrel and a pine tree." "Nothing better."

On his way back to London from Ireland, Frost, traveling alone, stopped for a few days with Haines. They made arrangements to meet again for a farewell visit in London late in September before the Americans sailed for home.

After all the running round in France and Ireland and the revisiting of old scenes in the West Midlands—all night talks with the only accessible remaining link that bound him to his old cronies of distant days—there were invitations to be considered in London. Harold Monro and the Bookshop people wanted to give a dinner for him so that he might again see Flint and others and meet some more whom he had never seen.

He made his way rather wearily to the metropolis, went the rounds with Monro, met new people, and renewed old friendships. The verve was gone. It was not that he was averse to seeing his old and meeting new friends. It was only that he was "a little weary of all the inconsequentialities of literary matters."

In September, Haines ran down to London twice by prearrangement. On the first visit Frost was registered at the New Imperial Hotel in Russell Square, London's west end. Haines describes the hotel "as I remember very hot and stuffy for an Englishman." In 1949 he wrote:

"It may interest you that I have just found a letter from Robert received September 23, 1928 from the Imperial hotel, Russell square, where I stayed with him, concerning 'The Night Light,' put into his head by a talk we had. I do not know anything about the origin of the poem. It bore the postmark London, Sep. 21, 1928, and was sent off no doubt a day or two after my stay with him, except that we must have been talking about night lights, as there was precious little we didn't talk about. The letter ran:

" 'Dear Jack: This is a small one put into my head by our talk about the night light.' Then follows the manuscript of the poem he had written with his initials."

The second visit was to a flat in Jeremy Square which the Frosts had taken, and it occurred just before the three sailed for home. Haines was disconsolate at the parting, and he says, "We talked all the time and I don't think went any place."

Thus Frost satisfied himself with the futility of it all, gained a greater distaste for the English which grew almost into an obsession, increased his regard for America as a thoroughly satisfying place, and so returned to Amherst perfectly content to roam abroad no more. The pedagogue had a new message for pedagogues after all.

XVII. I'VE BEEN LONG AWAY

FEW PRODIGALS, however long absent from their childhood haunts, come back more completely established as world characters than Robert Frost on his return to California after nearly one-half century of expatriation.

Unheralded, one day he dropped into the state of his birth. Almost until he was ready to pack up for his return to America, his presence, except to a few, was unknown or unnoted. Naturally, this was his choice. For those Californians, mostly from "off someplace," the surprise was that the poet of New England was a native son of the Golden State. Born in California, in a great city, he had lived most of his life as a rural New Englander. The double paradox, for the few who even bothered about it, was startling.

The New Deal decade was to see Frost a victim of recurrent sorrow. One after another the blows fell, transforming him from a joking, mocking Californian visitor into a confirmed New Englander, whose conversations, however spiced, turned invariably toward the seamy side. For the first time, it would seem, his poetry and his outward attitude coincide. One after another he saw his loved ones buried under earth or behind walls. In any case it was tragedy to which, while knowing sorrow, he had been half a stranger.

The thirties opened auspiciously. The year 1930 had seen the publication of the Random House volume of his Pulitzer Prize-winning *Collected Poems*. Of this he was understandably proud. Moreover, he had three other books, current but comparatively minor, selling in the shops—*Selected Poems, West-Running Brook,* and *A Way Out*. These he looked on with little more than a "sidelong glance."

Another milestone was passed in 1930 with his election to membership in the American Academy. While he might scoff at the "empty honor," all the same he was pleased to see his name in the *World Almanac*

among the variable Brahman Immortals, in the same column with Elihu
Root, Henry Van Dyke, Owen Wister, Charles Dana Gibson, Edith
Wharton, and William Lyon Phelps. His friends took his railing at the
Academy with a grain of salt.

Marjorie had been helped in health by the trip overseas, but at South
Shaftsbury, the Old Peleg Cole house echoed distress and anxiety. Lillian, plagued with the scourge of tuberculosis (which she brought into
a family already burdened with it), was gradually growing worse. The
rigorous Vermont climate, however native she may have been to it,
proved too severe for her.

After a family council which went into all the *if*'s and *and*'s Frost
advised Southern California, though without any personal knowledge
since he had never been south of San Jose. Lillian had been slowly
fading, and in the summer of 1932 it was thought she had little chance,
so Carol and seven-year-old Prescott came out west with her, landing
in San Bernardino, sixty miles east of Los Angeles. Robert tells the story.

My wife and I, uneasy about matters in Carol's family, came on out
west in mid-summer. We landed in San Bernardino on what I remember
as the hottest day I ever lived through. We took a room in an air-con-
ditioned hotel, which we afterward regretted. When we got out in the heat
again it seemed four times hotter.

Lillian was pretty sick, bad shape, and we really never expected her to
pull through. My son had a Model A Ford, and he and I got into it, took
Prescott along, and drove around trying to find a more suitable place in
which to locate them.

I had heard that the foothills around Arcadia and Monrovia had a good
climate for pulmonary patients. We drove down. I pointed out to Carol
that Monrovia, right on the slope of the mountains, was near enough to
Los Angeles for all purposes, and that the Community Players were at
nearby Pasadena. Even in New England we had heard of the work done
by this group. We became their regular fans. In Vermont we mostly had
to run clear to New York to see a play. Our Broadway was within ten
miles of our home in California.

The upshot was that we rented the house at 261 North Canyon and
moved down from San Bernardino. All five of us stayed together at this
house for several weeks. But I have always held that a single roof that

sheds water for one will leak on two families. My wife and I looked round and rented a house on Greystone. We moved about the first of September but continued to take our meals at Carol's, having a community kitchen.

My son was greatly upset over his wife. I tried to get him to look for a place in the country, some sort of farm. We drove round quite a lot, short distances. But more and more I became convinced that California farming wasn't in our line, too involved. During the summer we took in the Olympics, which kept our thoughts away from trouble—kept Carol from worrying about his wife and about finding something he could do for a livelihood.

His first visit to his native state since he left it in the spring of 1885, thus turned out to be a harassed one. If other than worry and illness had drawn him he would have had only pleasant remembrances. Lillian was always a favorite with him. She called him father with great show of affection. Moreover, she was the mother of his only hope for cognominal immortality.

"In spite of my early criminal training in San Francisco," he growled, when the native son first met the migrant Californian, "I *would* have to write you an answer and give away my presence in the Southland. A really good crook worth his salt, would have sent the answer back to New England to be forwarded to you. *I* had to wire straight."

The letter mentioned had been forwarded from Amherst to Frost in Monrovia and answered by him from there. This revealed that the poet was only thirty miles away. An immediate reply invited him to be guest at a meeting of the Beloved Vagabonds in Long Beach. The occasion was a writers' night, and inviting him a perfectly natural procedure.

Came answer by return telegraph:

> Just found your letter on returning from desert where interested in claim. Appreciate friendliness, but absolutely not available for anything social out here till after September 15th. Too deep in family affairs. Extorted doctor's permission to rest. Hiding out in Seabury case. Name Sherwood. For the present, 261 N. Canyon, Monrovia.

The month was August. "I always remember when I first met you," he said many years later. "The Olympic games were being held in Los Angeles, and Jimmie Walker was being held—in hot water."

It will be recalled by those who boast good public-scandal memories, that considerable buzzing was going the rounds over Gotham's mayor, and one Sherwood, who was alleged to have absconded with the only key to a certain safety deposit box containing allegedly incriminating documents. Thus, the first word from Frost was a mischievous one.

It was intended to respect his desire to be left alone until September 15, but certain events gave excuse to be admitted a fortnight before the proscription was removed. Then came days of getting acquainted. He was hiding for sure, but he had no key to any safety deposit box.

On this matter of Frost's "hiding" from something, one can't help thinking that he used his various rural retreats ("I have as many addresses as a gangster has aliases!") much as the "Drumlin Woodchuck" used his farm.

For some time prior to Frost's first visit to the West, a few Southern California writers had been planning to organize a writers' guild. It seemed propitious to call an organization meeting at one of the colleges and have Robert Frost as the *pièce de résistance*.

Occidental College, near Los Angeles, was chosen. Taking matters in hand, on the way to Monrovia, the self-appointed delegate stopped at the campus to see Professor Benjamin Stelter, head of the Department of English, to tell him of the plans and to suggest that Occidental had been elected capital. Robert Frost would be guest of honor. The college was offered at once. Thus was made sure a place of meeting. But as yet there was no promise that the promised guest of honor (not yet consulted, or even seen) would be amenable to vicarious promises.

The car stopped at the house on North Canyon Drive. The delegate took in the roses in the dooryard, the stately deodar and oaks, the ubiquitous pepper trees, and the lone maple.

A Ford car, Model A, stood under the shade of the yard trees. A little boy was playing about. An English-appearing young man, whose speech was as British as his looks, watered the lawn.

"Does Mr. Frost live here?"

"Robert Frost?" the young man countered, questioning, revealing. When the answer was yes he shook his head.

"He doesn't live here any more."

"He wired us to Long Beach that he was hiding out on the Seabury case."

A smile very nearly broke out on his face, but he checked it and went on:

"Yes, he told me about the wire. He will be glad to see you. Go down Greystone, the street above, and you'll find him at 219. He's at home this afternoon—alone. I'm his son, Carol."

Thus the child of tragedy entered the picture. Something in his fine face suggested portraits of the poet come upon occasionally and indistinctly remembered. Without reasoning, the visitor felt depressed. Trouble flashed across the mind. As these thoughts crowded, eyes sought out the little boy nearby.

"Prescott, my son," was all Carol said.

On Greystone the car drew up to a rambling, southward-facing house on a sloping hillside, surrounded by trees growing out from between the toes of the mountain. A bushy-headed, unkempt man opened the door a crack's breadth, one wisp of graying hair fanned in the wind.

"Well," he said with unmistakable rising inflection.

"I'm the fellow who wrote you from Long Beach—to whom you sent the Seabury wire."

"Come round to the other door," he greeted in a changed voice.

Thus simply began a friendship which was to last till curtain fall without intervening shadow. Conversation started that afternoon which, with necessary intermissions, went on till his death; each talk, regardless of time between, appeared to take up where it had been left off. In those California weeks not only did the listener get acquainted with Frost, but with all the Starks and Lorens and Asies that filled his lines of incomparable verse.

There sat the poet calling for appraisal. Chunkily built, active as a tiger, his expressive hands were never used to gesture any meaning which words might of themselves convey. His eyes twinkled, his raspy voice sparkled and sprawled. Alternately it was sandbag and saber thrust. He poked fun at THE SOUTHLAND, as the *Times* called Southern California. He razzed Hollywood in adjectives not found in home magazines.

The suppliant tried to rescue the literati from the visitor's sarcasm in time to get round to inviting him to sit down with the diners at Occidental. The whole plan almost turned out a debacle.

To begin with, there was Hamlin Garland, whose pride in being referred to as "The Dean of American Letters," was inordinate, and whose jealousy of any rival boundless. Later on, it was he who did all he could to wreck plans for the organization meeting. Yet it developed that it was the agitation of the "rebel of the nineties," rather than anybody's urging, which stirred up Frost to aid in the venture. At that first meeting, when he learned he was to be invited as guest at Occidental, he accepted at once. (Later on he wavered and nearly backed out.)

He was told he might be called on to say a poem or so, and it was suggested that inasmuch as he and Garland were the only members of the American Academy on the coast, except Stewart Edward White at Burlingame, it might be arranged for him to sit by the rebel. His waggishness came out.

"What about your sitting with me—I'm two-sided?"

Having obtained the use of a college on promise of a poet, then the poet on the assurance of a place of meeting, it remained to bring together other poets, with novelists and nonfiction writers, to greet the former at the latter.

When, on the meeting day, September 27, 1932, the car went to pick up the noted visitor, he was found all slicked out with tie and coat! But to keep the record straight, his clothes were as unpressed as they had been in the old Plymouth days when Sidney Cox so graphically described the way he dressed for a dance.

He hadn't ridden a block before he blurted out, "Garland won't be *there*." "Why?" he was asked.

> Well, the other day I went over to see Ham, to have lunch with him. I thought it only right that I should. He started right in on me not to have anything to do with "that thing"—that is just what he called this meeting—"that thing." "I wouldn't go to that thing," he said, "if I were you. There aren't three respectable persons connected with it. They are just trying to use you. You must be careful what kind of a crowd you get in with out here or they'll ruin you. Now I know what ones to associate

with. There's Rupert Hughes and Irvin Cobb, and others, I am proud to call my friends. They have a group in Hollywood called The Authors. That crowd would do you some good."

Old Ham had already been out to the University of Southern California where I am to speak next week, stirring up his namesake, Garland Greever. He got me nervous talking about it. If I hadn't been worried about my children and their health, I wouldn't have paid any attention to him. But he just kept on raving at such a rate he made my head ache. My wife tried to get me settled, straightened out. She says that Ham is just jealous because I am to be guest of honor, rather than himself. Maybe he is jealous. It's just like him. She said that was all that was ailing him—envy and jealousy. But, he said he wasn't coming, wouldn't be there. I tried to kid him, but you know he hasn't the slightest sense of humor. I said to him, "Now, Garland, you and I are the only members of the American Academy out here, and you ought to stand by a fellow Academician." But he never saw any joke in what I said. It was just wasted breath on my part. So, I took the trouble to go out to the University of Southern California and talk to Greever. Then the two of us went to Occidental and talked to President Bird. I hadn't been with them two minutes till I realized that everything was all right and that Ham was just imagining things. Now, suppose we forget all about Garland and talk about something interesting.

Though he seemed to try to keep the irascible Ham out of his thought, he would always come back to him:

You folks out here have got Garland all wrong. He's just an old snob, vain and egotistical. I know one thing, and I have it on good authority: he kept me from being elected to membership in the American Academy for years. I had belonged to the National Institute for a long while, and that without paying any dues. I actually thought I had been dropped for nonpayment. When I was elected to the Academy, the first thing they did was give me a prize of a thousand dollars. I paid up my dues, and when I sent them I said if they wanted me to pay again they'd have to award me another cash prize. Dues are only nominal, really, trivial, wouldn't break me. They are so heavily endowed they don't need the money. They have a fine building erected out of the Huntington millions. Dues, thus, in the light of endowment and other things, are a mere item.

Getting back to Garland, which we said we wouldn't do; he was talking about the sales of his books the other day, and I let him go on braggin' and strutting and preening himself. Then I came out and punctured his balloon. "Just how much of a sale, if it's a fair question," I said to him, "did your best book have?" "What would you call my best book," he countered. "Oh, *Son of the Middle Border,* say." "I wouldn't call that my best book," he sulked. I thought I wasn't going to get an answer, but he finally grudged, "The greatest sale I ever had was on that book, and it sold 40,000 copies." Now I'd not call that too much for a novel. *North of Boston* I think reached that figure, or went a little above it, quite a little. I only tell you this to show how naïve Old Ham is. He wrote me that whenever he went East he always wrote to all the universities and colleges en route that he was coming, and suggested they have him deliver a lecture. "I always clean up a good percentage of lecture dates in this way," he told me, adding, "I always feel I am doing them a favor."

That afternoon I came to understand Frost's fear at Ann Arbor. "Hero worship scares me," he said. "Whenever you talk about me I always keep my fingers crossed. What I want is a friend who will stand by me through thick and thin. I don't want friends who when things are going well and everybody full of praise will join in the chorus, but who, when things flop, are on the other side. I don't want any of this 'I told you so,' after the fact."

Pan was indeed with us at Occidental. To carry out the figure, we heard the shrill notes of his syrinx and caught the merry peal of his laughter as fellow travelers were panic-stricken by his antics. (At least we heard a New England watered-down peal.)

Olympos came against his word just as the diners sat down. Even then the furry-eared made Zeus look more pretentious than divine. We were to learn Frost's method of allowing a god of pomposity to swell up to the bursting point, when, in a flash, he thrust in a thorn and only a limp toad remained.

Louis Dodge, the novelist, and Ralph Waldo Trine, of *In Tune* notoriety, spoke preceding Frost's reading. President Bird sat by Trine. Frost whispered, "You know Trine's a billionaire, or something. Look at Bird coddling up to him, trying to coax a couple of millions out of him for the college."

"No, he's trying to get him to put up your salary as poet-in-residence."
His voice echoed the rasping of file on saw.

"He's what?"

"Bird said he had somebody in mind to give him the money to pay
your salary, I wondered why he insisted on inviting Trine. Now I see
through it. He's getting the money lined up and you lined up with the
giver. Simple."

"It can't all be settled as easy as that. We'll have to wait for Amherst.
They are my Simon Legree—owning me body and soul."

Garland sat through the whole evening (up to his premature departure) glowering more darkly moment by moment as he listened
while Frost read two of his best-known, best-loved poems—"Mending
Wall" and the one he referred to as the short poem with the long name,
"Stopping by Woods on a Snowy Evening."

After guild officers had been named, including Frost as honorary
president, Garland was asked to say a word. It was planned that he
should do honor to his fellow. Instead he slowly rose to his feet and
gave birth to a single sentence.

"As this meeting has been called to honor Robert Frost, I will only
say I am glad to be here." And down he sat. Before the evening was
finished he stood up lugubriously, said he was getting to be an old man,
begged leave to go home, and stalked out with Greever, who had brought
him over.

Elinor Frost's prediction had turned out correct.

We who for the first time were allowed to be close to America's number-one poet were to be forgiven our efforts to reclaim the renegade son
of California. We were likewise to be forgiven for wondering why, as
little by little the knowledge leaked out that he was in our part of the
world, people should remain so unimpressed. Did he not by birth and
early childhood belong to California? What right had New England
to him, even though the blood of Colonial America flowed in his veins!
At that, only half his blood was American. His mother contributed a
strain of Moodie Scottish. So we reasoned, and so reasoning some of us
laid aside ordinary, everyday affairs and devoted ourselves exclusively

to listening as he talked. If, as he said, he had his first experience in listening to genuine conversation when he heard Æ and Yeats talk together in Ireland, it must be admitted he learned late but well.

During those days and nights before the poet returned to face Stanley King in October 1932, he laid bare so very, very much of his early life. Being in California, his mind seemed to turn more to his early childhood than to any later period of his life. Those hours of conversation (largely one-sided) resulted in a clear picture of his early San Francisco days being revealed and recorded. Fifteen years later, when he was again in his native state and in the city of his birth looking over old scenes and boyhood haunts, and as earlier, only then, did his conversation begin and end in California.

But, this is a tale already told. . . .

Humor was always a staple literature of the poet's idle hours. Many times his talk turned on it.

I've always liked Mark Twain. When I taught at Pinkerton I was in the habit of reading him to my classes, "The Jumping Frog." Some of Mark is as funny as anything ever written—especially I have in mind the first half of the *Connecticut Yankee*. That's the sort of fun-making that makes you fall out of your chair and roll on the floor. Just what he meant, though, by putting all that blood and gore in the last part of the book is a mystery. It isn't funny, and I don't think he himself had it analysed. Maybe he just wanted to get the book done and so killed 'em all off that way.

I used to enjoy Josiah Allen's wife when I was younger. A bit localized in time and geography, but, in broken doses, good. Not all of her, of course; but I've enjoyed her homely philosophy—so purely American. Pretty dead now.

Then, there's Artemus Ward. You know how he went over to England and lectured in Aeolian Hall.[1] The audience, which didn't know what to expect, sat very silent when he came onto the stage. He quietly stepped to the front and stood there with hands folded on his vest, not saying a word. The house was like a tomb for silence. Then after he had waited a long time he lifted his hands and said, "Now that the applause has died down I will begin my lecture!" That won their hearts.

I'm not much on pilgrimages just to see the house where somebody was

[1] We suggested that it was Egyptian Hall.

born or where a man lived and died. But once I was riding with a fellow in Maine, who pointed out the house where Artemus grew up on the old Browne homestead. Even though a pilgrimage meant nothing to me, I must admit when I saw the old house and gazed on it in passing (for I wouldn't let him stop), and remembered the sad life of this true humorist, a tear came into my eye. I recalled how when he was sick over in England, far from home, about ready to give up the struggle and die, that a friend brought his medicine and begged him to take it, and he refused. "Take this medicine just for me, won't you, Browne?" the friend pleaded. "You know I'd do anything on earth for you." Ward's face brightened. "Would you, really?—would you do anything on earth for me?" "You know I would." "Then," Ward said dryly, "you take it."

Interested in everything that is life he turned the talk to the Sacco-Vanzetti case. At the time (1932) it was much in the news. He had opinions.

I have no sympathy with them. They may not have been guilty of the specific crime with which they were charged; but it was just as well. They intended to commit some similar crime, carrying firearms to do it. They claimed to be Tolstoyan nonresidents. But that subterfuge was thin stuff— didn't go well with their gun-totin'. They said they carried hundreds of dollars with them all the time and had to go armed for self-protection. The judge who tried them was a hard-boiled conservative, and the Massa-chusetts laws are such that any appeal for retrial must come up before the judge in whose court it was tried first. This judge always denied the appeal. When it came to the governor, who was a businessman, and had no un-derstanding of the men at all, he shifted the responsibility, passed the buck, and put Lowell of Harvard and two others to try it for him. They denied it. Edna Millay, and others of the parlor-pink variety of bolsheviks kept picketing the governor's mansion and the state house, telling the governor to be honest for once. But it did no good. The lawyer who pleaded their case overstepped the bounds of propriety and tried it out of court in the public prints, cheap way. No lawyer has a right to do that. It made against him in the end, helped lose.

After the passage of years one remembers conversations and poems later to be made public property. Though he remained anticommunist in print and daily talk, he was never rabid. Once, the night following his eightieth birthday (new style) in his Brewster Street house in Cambridge, he had a word. A senator, at the time much in the public eye for his committee on subversion in government, irked him. Somebody asked him what he thought of the man. "Do we *have* to bring him into this conversation?" he half snarled.

I've been close to a few friends who flirted harmlessly with the Russian brand. Louis Untermeyer, Joe Blumenthal, both went through a phase of left-wingism. These people who make a career of anticommunism are bad as, or worse than, the commies themselves. I admired the communists in the Medina trial. They stood up and fought back in court. They may have been wrong, but they didn't take their medicine lying down. I don't know. Maybe in Russia, even, they are doing some good, maybe.

You can never accuse me of being a pro-red. There are my books, my poems. Over the years they have stood against the Kremlin. Just read "Build Soil" and you'll see. Awhile ago I won a bet made in Florida. I bet a friend that Beria would be the next Soviet top brass to be liquidated. When the loser sent me the swag from Florida he asked how I knew. I just used my head.

Some of us had been trying to ferret out a few Frost books in Los Angeles shops without much success. We found only one reasonably cheap first—at ten dollars. None of his current books were available. When the news was passed he was stirred up.

This is neither right nor fair. They should keep my books in stock at all times so that people who want them may have a chance to buy. I'm going to wire Holts that in a city of a million and a half people no book of mine is to be had in the stores. For you, you needn't worry about a book. But just keep on asking and maybe they'll stock up on 'em. When I get back home I'll send you a *Collected Poems* and write a poem on the fly for you. Here's a first edition that'll keep you till then. It's a selection I made for the Augustan Series of Modern Poets, published in London by Benns.

A plain, square, spindle-legged parlor table with books of travel, borrowed at the Monrovia library, lying on it; a few chairs, one or two pictures and a calendar on the wall—these things made up the appointments of the room. Frost was finishing his supper. From the bedroom came the sound of a woman coughing. It was Lillian.

When he had finished eating, Frost came into the room. He wore the same old rumpled coat and unpressed white trousers, or rather cotton pants. We went to the car to drive over to the Greystone house for our talk. During the evening, word was dropped that he had been beaten out of a doctor's degree at Occidental. Stelter suggested they might confer one but was told he already had honorary degrees from Amherst, Wesleyan, Vermont, Michigan, Yale, Middlebury, Bowdoin, Columbia, and Williams.

"You shouldn't have done that," he scolded. I never refuse degrees of honor from any reputable school, however big or little. I have them from small colleges and great universities. I hope you didn't offend them at Occidental."

Memories like patches of snow or of sunlight recur. . . .

Once he brought out Gorham B. Munson's *Robert Frost: A Study in Sensibility*. This was the first attempt made on a biography. Neither he nor his wife ever showed enthusiasm for it.

> It isn't that we object to it, only that we would have preferred a more sympathetic book. It seems inadequate. Munson came up to the farm one night, and we talked practically till morning, which gave him the information about my life. Then he consulted some books on genealogy, read some reviews and wrote the book.

Once he asked if he might be dropped by the market to do some shopping. He had made quite a list and it was observed he had signed it "Frost, 261 North Canyon." When he had left the store, the avid collector asked the market man to keep the bill to be picked up later. He looked his surprise. How was he to know it was a valuable document— a grocery list in the hand of America's first poet, signed. Robert Frost was not even a personality to him, just a customer. As a footnote it might be interesting that the family stocked up on calories and starches that day. The list called for white potatoes, grape juice, cream of wheat, wheat bread, *fresh* eggs (he was still a farmer in taste, which explained the underscoring of fresh), celery, rice, soda crackers, nabiscos, 4 lb.

peas, 5 grapefruit, 1 lb. best prunes, 100 percent wheat, (crossed out), few apples . . .

When we got back to the Greystone house, he mixed a pleasant concoction of grape juice and ginger ale, and with cakes to munch we sat gossiping from one to five-fifteen. He told of a Western Union messenger in a small town who stopped him on the street one day and asked him to write a poem to be used as an epitaph on his wife's gravestone. "Once only kings could demand such a thing," he laughed. "Today the ordinary citizen in our democracy can make a demand, and if he doesn't like the efforts can turn them down with a wave of the hand."

. . . So the memories of golden days continue to recur.

XVIII. THE MUSE TAKES CARE

NIGHT WAS COMING ON. In the gloaming, Frost began to tell, in that slow, easy, unforgettable manner that was his, of some semihumorous verse he was working on. There was one where he talks with a man about the evening star, being assured by this "literate farmer" that it was not a star but only a light Edison had hung up in the sky and that it was taken in early every night.

"I have that thing here some place," he said, fumbling in the mass of papers about his Morris chair.

At last he found it and in the half-light managed to read it out. There were the rememberable lines,

> *In short, you think that star a patent medicine,*
> *Put up to cure the world by Mr. Edison.*

The manuscript was so changed and interlined and blotted out, it was hard to decipher. And there was failure to bring out the meaning by the intonation of his voice, which may have come through his fear of being elocutionary—something he criticized Markham so severely for being. However, this manner of reading his verse changed with the years, for in the end he gave it emphasis and strength rarely equaled.

This poem, later to find a place in *A Witness Tree,* he had projected just six years before he read it to me. The note, published with it, said, "A dated Popular Science Medley on a Mysterious Light recently Discovered in the Western Sky at Evening," and one line of the poem gave its date

Marvelous world in nineteen-twenty-six.

In 1945 he wrote on the page containing it in *Atlantic,* "Just to think of it. I had read this to Louis Mertins ten years before I sent it to be printed." Thus it is clear it was in process from 1926 to 1941.

After he had finished with the electric-light fantasy he shambled to his feet with:

"I'm going to get these poems I've been at this summer out here and read some of them to you—a thing I seldom do, but you've been so damned nice to me. So, I'll just shut this door to keep anybody from hearing me."

Coming back he carried a notebook in which he had written poems for the volume he said was to come out in a year or two. This manuscript-book was written in one of the blank books made up of very fine paper, furnished by Holts. He explained:

"I want to call it *Talks-Walking*—but then I'm always playing with titles of which nothing ever comes. I feel that Holts owe me another book—one in addition to and apart from my *Collected Poems,* to stand along with them. When Knopfs planned to bring out a long poem of mine, 'A Lone Striker,' in the Borzoi Chap Book series, Holts heard of it and wrote my wife they were very put out, for they said if I had any more to be published they should get them. So, I am getting a book ready for them now—working on it here in California. This is it."

He had wanted to call the volume *Talks-Walking*. Instead, when Holts published some of these poems (others were held over for a succeeding book) in 1936 (the Book of the Month selection—and Pulitzer Prize-winning book), it was given another name—*A Further Range*.

However, the poet was not yet through with his pet title. In the Contributor's Column of the *Atlantic* for March, 1941, we read an editorial note. "In his rooms on Boston's Beacon Hill, and on his perambulations at Bread Loaf Mountain, and along the Esplanade, Robert Frost has been gathering the poems for his new book, *Talks-Walking,* which is to appear this autumn." But fate decreed otherwise. In 1942 "Talks-Walking" became *A Witness Tree.* It contained most of the poems he had read to the visitor that night in Monrovia which had been left out of *A Further Range.*

"These poems are not all new ones," he explained. "In fact, some of them go back as far as thirty years to my farming days at Derry. But they are a bit funnier than poems of a poet of my advertised standing should be."

Then he laughed wryly and started reading the poems that went into one of the noblest books in literature. Some of these poems were humorous, with that sly fun-making that is Frost, some infinitely sad, some of characterization, some of incident; but others were of scenes, snow and mountains, and moon and stars.

"Now which of these do you like best?"

When told that the choice was the one that dealt with the two old shoes in a closet, one wet with the waters of the Atlantic, and the other with the waters of the Pacific, he replied:

"I'll see that you get the manuscript."

He kept that promise to keep—unkept. A notation he made on a copy of *The Atlantic* for May, 1936, containing it in its first printed form, makes one doubt it was completed in 1932. He has written, "Read and partly written at the dinner for T. S. Eliot at St. Belophe [*sic*] club."

Frost often said that his autobiographical poems as a rule were composite. He has given an enlightening marginalia to the line "In a Vermont bedroom closet," by adding "South Shaftsbury." Opposite the line "At the Cliff House," after underlining "Cliff House," he has written "Long Beach, rather." This suggests that the California sojourn, even his visit with us in Long Beach, had its effect on the poem.

Another poem of composite origin grew out of this visit. On a copy of *Yale Review,* spring 1934, beside the poem "Neither Out Far Nor in Deep" Frost has written, "This is one of my few Californian poems. But it is made up of mixed memories. Take good care of the MS. of it I gave you, Louis." Where the poem appears in its first anthology,

Contemporary American Men Poets, the author on our copy has written "To Louis Mertins to remind him of the day we rode down the coast together."

In this connection there is the bibliographical evidence of the California origin of another poem Frost wrote that Olympic year. In *Yale Review* for autumn 1934 appeared "Moon Compasses," "A Missive Missile" and "After-flakes." On our copy he has written, "L. M. I believe I wrote the third of these in California when we were round together. R. F."

But there were other than California subjects dealt with that Monrovia night. There were things both in verse and talk about old kings who punished the bearers of evil tidings.

"The old kings used to have a fine way of treating such," Robert laughed. "The general would send a runner on ahead with the bad news of retreat or defeat; and when the message was delivered the messenger would be taken out and killed. I like that, original. Some teachers, one of them one of my best friends, but a fellow who is obsessed with the mistaken idea he must always come to my rescue and run to me with all sorts of bad news, was telling me how a college boy in one of his classes had said of me that I wasn't for America. 'Frost,' this student said, 'laughs too much. America takes her poetry seriously.' Now of course he completely missed the point. You know I don't laugh at all, except slyly—mostly at myself."

I recall how greatly exercised Frost was over the fact that the encyclopedias were trying to take the honor of the first heavier-than-air flight away from the Wright brothers.

"Why," he sputtered, "when all this thing is written, that about Lindbergh and all, there will still remain only the Wright boys, the Columbuses of the air. Orville is eating his heart out over in Dayton because of what's being done and what is not being done. Shabby treatment."

Asked if he thought Orville would be willing to bring his plane back from Europe to the Smithsonian Institution if Congress would give him the credit for making the first flight, he continued:

"Of course he would. Why, they have a little insignificant contraption in the institute marked as the one which made the first flight, when all it was ever able to do was nose up and take a dive into the bay, and that without a pilot. I wanted to do all I could to help establish them in their rights. So I wrote a poem about our long having wheelwrights, wainwrights, and now we've got wingwrights. I want to print it and do what I can to help."

It was this poem, greatly changed, published in *A Further Range,* which he called "The Wrights' Biplane," having the stinger at the end concerning the invention and perfection of flying:

> . . . *Time cannot get that wrong,*
> *For it was writ in heaven doubly Wright.*

He lived to see the plane brought back, and a long while after.

It was but natural that his children should enter the discussion.

"Lesley, of course, wrote poetry off and on, but her interest has not been that form of writing. She takes to prose. Last year she wrote a florid detective tale, full of literary value, but not quite the thing, too something. She hasn't found herself yet. None of the rest have ever done much writing. They have all scribbled, though, at odd seasons. Marjorie, the youngest, is engaged to a man working with Earl Morris in ethnological research down in the Southwest. She writes poetry furtively."

The time passed unnoticed. Suddenly he exclaimed:

"My, my, how the hours have gone. I want to drive Carol over to Pasadena to see the Community players tonight, so we'll have to move fast. That is one thing I always try to take in wherever I am—good plays. I have always loved the stage. Nothing I have ever done anywhere has given me more satisfaction than that I got from directing the plays at Pinkerton."

As we started to go he called:

"Look at the moon. Isn't it lovely?"

When the departing guest was almost a block away, he came hurrying after, calling, "Come back Monday at one-thirty. We'll talk all afternoon."

Without our asking a question Frost talked of his poetry, outlining those things we wished to know.

Perhaps when that preacher friend of Ward's looked me up shortly after my first poem appeared in *The Independent* and talked with me about it, something providential was happening to me. I'm sure the old gentleman didn't have the slightest idea he was having any effect on a very stubborn youngster who thought he knew what he knew. But something he said actually changed the whole course of my writing. It all became purposeful.

One day as we talked he said to me that when he read my poems it was just like hearing me talk. I didn't know until then what it was I was after. When he said that to me it all became clear. I was after poetry that talked. If my poems were talking poems—if to read one of them you heard a voice—that would be to my liking! So, I went to the great poets, from Chaucer and Shakespeare to Coleridge and Wordsworth. And looked for this very thing in their lines. I will admit, when I have been quoted on the matter I have been made to speak rather mistily. But one thing must always be kept in mind: Whenever I write a line it is because that line has already spoken clearly by a voice within my mind, audible voice.

There has been a great hue and cry raised over what I have had to say regarding voice posturing, or as I have sometimes called it, the sound of sense. When I first began to write poetry—before the illumination of what possibilities there are in the sound of sense came to me—I was writing largely, though not exclusively, after the pattern of the past. For every poet begins that way—following some pattern, or group of patterns. It is only when he has outgrown the pattern and sees clearly for himself his own way that he has really started to become. You may go back to all those early poems of mine in *A Boy's Will,* and some that are left out of it. You will find me there using the traditional cliches. Even "Into My Own" has an "as't were." In "Stars" there is a line "O'er the tumultuous snow"; while in my very first poem, "My Butterfly," I was even guilty of "theeing" and "thouing," a crime I have not committed since. For sentiment, perhaps, I have left all of these as first printed, though I have made one change, it will be observed, even in "My Butterfly" as it appears in *The Collected Poems,* transforming " 'wildered" into "bewildered." The young poet is prone to echo all the pleasing sounds he has heard in his scattered reading. He is apt to look on the musical value of the lines, the metrical perfection, as all that matters. He has not listened for the voice within his mind, speaking the lines and giving them the value of sound.

There is another angle to this. It is suggested by a proneness to the unique. It is the value of current words in writing poetry. It has been a long time since I consciously fell into any of the clichés so common in verse. It has been a long time since I used any word not common in everyday speech. For example, I would never think of using the word "casement" for window in general. Whenever I have used that word, which I have occasionally, it was because I was writing about *that* kind of a window—never for window as such. In this, perhaps, I have unconsciously tried to do just what Chaucer did when the language was young and untried and virile. I have sought only those words I had met up with as a boy in New Hampshire, working on farms during the summer vacations. I listened to the men with whom I worked, and found that I could make out their conversation as they talked together out of ear-shot, even when I had not plainly heard the words they spoke. When I started to carry their conversation over into poetry, I could hear their voices, and the sound posture differentiated between one and the other. It was the sense of sound I have been talking about. In some sort of way like this I have been able to write poetry, where characters talk, and, though not without infinite pains, to make it plain to the reader which character is saying the lines, without having to place his name before it, as is done in the drama.

Because I have been, what some might call, careless about the so-called proper beat and rhythm of my lines, there have been those who think I write free verse. Now, I am not dead set against *vers libre;* but you know there is no idea you cannot express beautifully and satisfactorily in the iambic pentameter. Much of my verse is written in this form—blank, unrimed verse. I have always maintained that it takes form to properly perform, and free verse has no form, and so its performance is meager. These fellows, old Carl and the rest, think they are being free, but they aren't. The greatest freedom poetry can attain is having form, a frame, to work in. Free verse is batting a ball into space and wondering why it doesn't return to the batter. Poetry written in form is like batting a ball against the side of a wall and feeling it return to the bat. A picture frame with its four simple lines is necessary to the showing of a picture. Try it and see. The frame thus becomes a part, even, of the picture. Old Carl tries hard to write without form, but he has a form without knowing it. When he repeats himself, as he sometimes does, he is following a certain form, a slight form.

But with all of this as I look over my later things, these I have been boring you with, and others you have escaped, I wonder if I have really grown up. The things I wrote on the farm twenty-five years ago are about like the things I write today. I suppose one should not write poetry after fifty.

Often since the days of our early conversations on poetry, we have recalled in this connection the words of Lord Dunsany delivered before the London Poetry Club in 1912, where the dramatist-poet summed up his ideas of what poetry is made of.

"No man in his lifetime indeed can understand it, and I do not think that any poet would claim to or would pretend to know more than any other man; but then at moments unknown, always unexpected, there comes that clear voice into his mind, and with a feeling surely of ignorance and of awe, he finds himself speaking of cities he has known and byways he has trod in lands where the desert has long since covered all, coming back to its own, where the historian can only guess and the traveler durst not go. He speaks of things that were before cities began, and of gods that walked with him in the prime of the stars. The voice passes (like the wind in the Gospel of John) and he is only a man again, with a man's humiliations."

Frost was shortly returning to Amherst to take up his burden, and he was scheduled to lecture a few times on his journey eastward. He gave a history of his histrionics.

I try to patch out my income by giving ten lectures a year. I have always kept my price reasonably low—two hundred dollars a lecture. I have never deviated. It has been that or nothing. I have demanded my pound of flesh, unless there were reasons why I should not charge, when I gave my services gratis. I have never cut price. I am willing to lecture when I can do it without being troubled about it. But I hate to lecture and won't do it when I can get out of it. Once a senior at Dartmouth wrote me that they wanted me to lecture, and told me they would meet my expenses. I misunderstood what he was trying to say, as I was to discover later on.

He really intended to tell me they were willing to meet my terms and pay my fee, whatever my fee was. Not knowing this, I wrote back that about all the pleasure I ever got out of lecturing was carrying away my two hundred dollars after the performance, so I could never bring myself to talk just for the fun of talking. I never heard from him again. I suppose I made him an enemy.

A great many poets are putting on dog, giving themselves airs, getting up-stage all out of proportion. They have very high opinions of themselves. I have never taken myself very seriously, have always managed to laugh occasionally.

Old Ham likes lecturing. It gives him a feeling of propping up. He can wear his Mark Twain hair to fine advantage. Some of these fellows do such things simply because they have had hard beginnings and need this to make them forget. Ham had a hard life in Dakota—lived meanly. So we must forgive him for trying to live above mean memories. If lecturing helps, then let him lecture. What Ham forgets in feeling sorry for himself is that his hard life on the frontier was worth all it cost. America was expanding in the greatest of all centuries, and he was a part of the expansion. Such a thing can never happen in this world again. On Venus, or Mars— who knows. Not here.

Markham does it for the sake of money to live on. He isn't like Ham who worships money as money, rich men because they have money and power. Old Ham frankly says he's all for big business and millionaires who use their money for the good of their fellow-beings—whatever he means by that. Quite a change from the Hamlin Garland who barnstormed for the Populist cause in Kansas during the nineties—the rebel seems to have rebelled against rebellion. He's like the D. A. R.

One thing we can say good for Masters—he's never done much lecturing as compared with some. I suppose his legal training and experience have combined against it, or when money was plentiful he didn't care to lecture. Some people like it, every man to his taste, every man for his reason, yes and no. I'm one of the "no" kind; I suppose as much as anything else because I have to get screwed up to lecture and then get unscrewed after it's over. I actually go through agony getting ready. It's hard for me. If I could lecture the way I talk and let the slips fall where they will, I suppose I wouldn't mind. To me lecturing is writing with the words spoken, and writing takes lots out of me. That, I take it, is about the whole matter.

After all, the muse takes care!

One night at the California Institute of Technology, when many had come to hear Frost say his poems, Robert A. Millikan, finding no seat, sat down on the floor in front of the visiting poet. Looking into the round smiling face of Millikan, Frost bantered:

"Dr. Millikan, this is as it should be: Science sitting at the feet of poetry."

XIX. The Gift of Idle Hours

At Laguna Beach we came upon a place where the arm of the sea cut into the land—a cove where the water was so green, and the sky so blue, and the winds so soft, and the air so sweet that Pan was carried away.

> Sea waves are green and wet,
> But up from where they die,
> Rise others vaster yet,
> And these are brown and dry.

There he stood, the wind blowing his unruly hair, his devil-may-care jaw set, his eyes taking note of all that lay along the horizon. It was then that one understood why he knew nature so intimately. There was no wave, no identation, no strange rock, sand bar, fossil remains, no unusual shell that he did not see and investigate. The "petrified" fish which protruded from the soft stone face of the cliff; the hard, granite-like surface of the green-brown, wave-beset crags; the various formations interlined with slate and sandstone—all intrigued and interested him. The changes in the sea's coloring, the low-lying fogs, the wind that left its mark upon the distant surface of the waters—nothing escaped him.

We had come to visit certain also of our poets and artists at the Laguna Beach colony. When we reached the house of Frank Cuprien, we found him "hard at work," as he expressed it, digging a cesspool and preparing to reline it with brick. Frost was greatly interested in the roots from yard trees which had filled the pool almost to capacity, squirming like so many writhing serpents out of the broken wall and twisting about inside the cavity, leaving all dry within, with no trace of odor.

Inside Cuprien's studio the painter began to exhibit his work, from the lovely seascapes which he held at five thousand dollars each, to the tiny ones, just as lovely but less costly. When he saw Frost admiring one about fourteen by twenty inches, of moonlight on the surface of waters, the artist said

"That would look pretty back at Amherst, wouldn't it?"

"Sure," said Frost.

"Then, it is yours."

"You mustn't do that," Frost scolded.

But Cuprien said he would frame it and ship it back to him. Later Frost took us to task for what he suspected.

"You shouldn't have asked him to give me a picture. I was only kidding when I said he might give me one."

To Cuprien's gift Robert offered a buffer, saying he would send him a book when he got back to Amherst. In 1941 at Bread Loaf Frost remembered:

"That artist down at Laguna Beach, the one with the picture, 'The Bait House,' never did send the painting to me."

We never learned whether Frost had sent the book.

After a visit to see Steve Chalmers, national secretary of the Robert Louis Stevenson Society, who owned much Stevensoniana, the Tahiti flute among them, we were on our way. "A season-ending wind there blew," and Frost was chill. He was afraid he might catch cold—a thing he couldn't have happen because he had to lecture two or three times on the way back East. We turned back to Cuprien's place. The artist was a big, bulky man, whose overcoat would have been ample for one's cold friend. But Frank had fled, and we hurried on to Steve's. He let us have his overcoat, small enough, and thin and darned, but in a measure warm. On our way to Long Beach Frost chose to wrap himself in silence, nursing his throat, a little cross about the fear of taking cold before his tour East.

The warm glow of a cozy house greeted us. A most appetizing meal was ready, and as the dinner progressed the visitor became more and more genial. After a third helping of the sirloin we went to sit before the fire. Starting in at the beginning he talked out, smoking a single cigarette—the only one the writer was ever to see him indulge in. Elinor was the smoker of the two.

There was a word about his farms.

> I have a young poet living on one, nobody you would know. He's from Detroit. Ford, Model T. He has written a few poems which show promise, has published a thin volume of verse. His folks wanted him to be something worthwhile, but he cut loose from them (which probably gave us a common bond of understanding) and decided to be a tramp poet, tramp part's easy. He borrowed a few hundred dollars from me to buy a farm with. It was an acre. It had a house on it, but it was rather shabby and open. So he got some lumber here and there and patched it and built a lean-to. He had met a girl who wrote for the newspapers, and as the depression had come, they thought it a good idea to get married and pool their troubles. Two can starve as cheaply as one. His house, at best, was comfortless and cold, and was really no fit place to spend a winter in. So, I said for them to move over to our house during the cold weather. They took me up and live there now.

Frost usually was drawn to the underdog, especially one who so nearly followed in his own footsteps. Yet, he could say, as he did say, that writers are encouraging only so long as the one needing it is down and out. The minute he is on the way up, a likely rival with the editors, the writer is the first to give such an aspirant a swift kick. Perhaps he exaggerated. Not that he was himself free from it. He was jealous of rivals too. But a rival who was discriminated against enlisted him as champion—just as he became Dreiser's champion when the author of *Sister Carrie* was being kicked and cuffed about by the Anthony Comstocks. He has doggereled about it—dogs threatening to bite senatorial toga-togs.

It has been rumored that a barefoot burglar had been active in and around Monrovia, and Frost turned to telling us about him.

"You know they got to thinking that maybe I was the barefoot pad. I go prowling round nights, and somebody started a rumor that I was the miscreant. It was so in England in the early days of the war when they called me a German spy. Up at Monrovia the other day I was down at the market and they got to talking behind my back, and one fellow said, 'There—that's the guy—there.'"

The very next day the police captured a "barefoot burglar" in Long Beach. He was not an amateur, but a real burglar—no poet at all.

On the way that night to Monrovia he asked concerning two young fellows who recently had interviewed him. He said laughingly that they had asked, very soberly, what in his opinion America stood for, what it was.

> I answered, also very soberly, "Certain great names—Jefferson, Emerson, Lincoln, Wilson—just something to give continuity." "What about the present?" one of them asked. "What name would you suggest?" "Well," I said, "why not say Robert Frost?" They very seriously wrote it down. You know it's terribly dangerous to answer nonhumorous people humorously. They never quite get you, quite understand what you're driving at. A newspaper interview is a most unsatisfactory medium of making one's thought known. The interviewer puts more of himself into it than of the person interviewed. "Mark Twain and the Interviewer is a story that has a lot of advice in it. I've felt just like doing that myself many times. The interviewer seldom gets your statements right. When he does, he puts in only half of what he has on hand, and a half statement is a deadly thing.

He went on to advise, just as he had probably advised often before, and many times thereafter, many new friends and old. He had himself felt the security of a college back of him. In years to come his championship of "certain also of our (younger) poets," accomplished wonders. Especially one recalls Edward Weismiller and Peter Viereck. There were others, too. He went all out for young Viereck, regardless of the way he had felt toward his father always. Peter's proximity to Amherst was probably something in his favor. Being lazier even than R. F. the Californian never followed the matter up to its conclusion. At any rate his advice was good. But it must be said that no real poet, certainly not Robert Frost, was ever "coddled" into success by any help given as subsidy by any college. However, literature will never know the debt it

THE GIFT OF IDLE HOURS

owes to those colleges which took Robert Frost and gave him a hand when he needed it so badly.

You ought to get a college back of you, just as I got Amherst and Michigan. Of course there are two angles to the thing, as I find it. First, in your case, you might persuade some college that you wrote good poetry, quite unrecognized it is true, but good nonetheless. This might not be easy to put over, but it's worth trying. Colleges are pretty set. Good salesmanship on the part of an old Chautauqua campaigner might turn it. Secondly, you might try approaching them from the angle of a young poet with promise, one who only needed encouragement and bread and butter and leisure to write. I wasn't so well known when Amherst took me on—though *North of Boston* was going pretty strong. They have always felt that, because of taking me, I was their investment in the art of the nation. Last year I recommended a woman poet to a college on these terms and they took her on. I'm willing to do something, if I can, for you.

Here's what I want you to do. Go over your poetry and pick out that which has no echo of any other poet, every poem you are sure is entirely original. There is that poem "Cornstalk Fiddle and Shoestring Bow" which I told you might suggest Steve Benet's "Georgia Fiddler" but which you tell me was printed long before Benet's. But that's the thing you've got to watch like a hawk, similarity. Get all these together and send them on to me at Amherst.

When we arrived at the Greystone house, I suggested to Robert that I had not during all our days together had a chance to meet his wife Elinor. He hurried into the house but came back with the information she was already abed and asleep. In this manner it came about that only dimly, as through a half-open door, was ever her presence manifest. But she was so intertwined in Robert's life that one felt her visible, living presence, just as if she had been in every conversation carried on.

Now and then during our talks, from the distance would come the sound of her voice reasoning with Prescott when we were at the Greystone house, or sometimes at the North Canyon. Occasionally we heard her talking with one whose identity it was not mine to know, or inquire about, as the two of us sat together. A quiet, shy, modulated voice, never insistent, always in command of itself. Nobody hurried through what he was doing because of it.

Again it would drift in from the yard, from under the trees, lifted a little now to be heard over the winds sighing through the evergreens clustered about the roots of the mountains. But even then it still remained only a voice. It never obtruded—scarcely insinuated. Thought went on and speech, as if the poet knew that all was well. If she spoke, he knew she was there. If she maintained silence, still all was well. Thus they progressed understandingly for their forty years together. Might it not have been Frost's theory of the voice within the mind which spoke his unwritten lines to him in Daimonic cadence, a voice over which he had no control, in some manner connected with this Voice?

Surrounded during those passing days by the Voice, the visitor yet was never to see the one whose medium it was. When he saw Robert again, the poet walked alone.

Came our farewell.

"I have had a good time of it, I want you to know," he said.

"I won't tell you what it has meant to me," the other responded. "If there is at any time something I can do for you after you get back to Amherst, call on me."

He studied a moment before replying.

"Well, there is something you can do for me. You know a little bit of Carol's background, of his unsocial nature. His wife's physical condition seems beyond cure. Prescott is often sick. For himself Carol is always aloof from everybody. He is trying hard to dig into something out here. Your friendship, if you could only get him to accept it, would mean much. I wish you would come up now and then and get him to make friends with you. Don't try to have him meet other folks. Just pass the time of day with him. Nothing you could do would be better than this."

We shook hands, almost in covenant.

And Carol?

In a week or so we drove up to see him, to find how he was getting on. Somehow he was frozen up. Hardness was in his face, terror stared out from his sad, burdened eyes.

"There is nothing you can do—anybody can do."

Again, within a week or so we sought to help him. It was of no use. He had drawn back into his social armorplate and had shut the door between us. He had taken a path, as we were later to be told by his father, from which he never deviated till the day of tragedy.

XX. A BRIDGE PIER IN THE MIDDLE OF THE RIVER

DURING SUCCEEDING MONTHS all we of California had of our native son in exile was the name "Robert Frost" as honorary president on the stationery of the California Writers' Guild. But one thing was a solace: This was one of the few organizations he admitted membership in.

When the second annual meeting of the guild was held at Occidental College, Frost in his capacity as honorary president sent greetings to the group, one of the first of his characteristic slaps at the sudden trend in national affairs.

> Bennington, Vt. Oct. 3, 1933
>
> Please disregard any cheap three cent letter you may or may not have received from me in my capacity as prose jester, and take it from this serious telegram in rhyme and meter how much strengthened I feel in my claim to being a Californian by this invitation. I greet you tonight in absentia. Be of loud cheers. Let us, as authors, refuse to be held accountable for anything that may happen in politics. Literature never undertook to give a country prosperity. The extent of its obligation is to insure a few people against being made fools of by either riches or poverty. It is no wrangler in an emergency. Its influence is over the years, like the Constitution, which will keep America American after other countries have all broken down and run together from mutual imitation.
>
> ROBERT FROST

It would appear that for the moment poet had turned prophet. It was not to be long before writers were to be paid by the government and set to work on projects of authorship. He never became reconciled to these things, looking on them as shrewd bribes for political support.

That famous American who was the inventor of these schemes (just coming into an era to be named for him in history) in true Roosevelt fashion also sent greetings to the guild. In the coming years F.D.R. and the New Deal were to provide many hours of conversation for R. F.

and many lines of his most provocative poetry, in which he almost himself became a "wrangler in an emergency." As a States' Rights Democrat, his soul was burdened by the centralization of power in Washington and all the alphabetical agencies which sprang up almost overnight.

How he must have been torn in his mind at this time between his allegiance to a capitalistic tycoon at Amherst and a wider allegiance to a socialistic politician in Washington! Some of the finest lines in one of the noblest books of poetry in the language (the book he had read portions of to us in manuscript the previous year) were hammered out at white heat during this battle of allegiances.

When Robert and Elinor quitted California on October 7, 1932, and returned to Amherst to face the unknown, we had been left with a partial promise we would see them back in California one day. It was because of such assurance that a few of us entered with zest into an attempt to get him a place in one of the colleges. At the time, we had no more than a hint of conditions at Amherst. His anxiety, as was to come out long after, was because of the new president, Stanley King, and what would be a poet's place in the new set-up. His forebodings were to be realized with compound interest.

Later we were to learn that any inclination Frost might have had toward us arose from the uncertainty following the coming of King. During all the time that followed, both Frost and Remsen Bird, president of Occidental, kept us in utter ignorance of the nearness to success that had followed our efforts. A letter from Frost revealed this.

In this letter, he wrote Bird that he was in bed with a temperature when he telegraphed. He had to get up and about and have a talk with King before writing the promised letter. He said he wanted to go out to California and that King, who planned a trip west that winter also, wanted him to go. But Frost was uneasy because of his lagging strength and suggested that in addition to consulting King, he had to take his own health into account. He declared there were limits to his energy. "An expedition to Texas has just taught me that I am not up to one unbroken series of events, entertaining and being entertained." But, being diplomatic, he expressed assurance such was not in Bird's mind.

"You intend to distribute me humanely over some weeks, devote me largely to the undergraduates and protect me from too much hospitality," he wrote. Then he called for particulars. How many colleges involved? Would he like the January, February, and March weather in California? Or some other months. "I have the happiest memories of my day with you on the campus." he concluded.

We heard again from Frost in 1934. His letter clarified many things and let us know what he had been up to, what sorrows he had borne.

DEAR MERTINS:

I wish we might see each other for a talk. But look where I am this time for some one's health. We have had a great sadness since I saw you last. My daughter, Marjorie, who wrote good poetry, but sad, died tragically at the birth of her first child last spring. That was in Billings, Montana. We were there a long time with her at the end. It seems my wife would never be the same again. The daughter-in-law who lay sick at Monrovia for two years has completely recovered. Carol is back on his New England farm with her. There was always a chance while they were in California that Carol would find a foothold as a farmer in California, and by settling there make a Californian of me again. But farming is so different in California from what he grew up to in New Hampshire and Vermont that he never seemed to know how to go about it. Some of you friends out there ought to have connived a little at our getting a start on the coast. I don't altogether give up the idea yet. Don't take it as a promise that commits me in the least, but you might see me out there at your big table in November, though this is a trifle early for my plans, (very, very vague as yet). I should like to see you more than a little. And I should like to see Garver[1] and Shippey and Garland. I can get cross with Garland about small things. (He's been saying in a recent book that he found me impractical as he expected to find me. Dad blame it, he'll spoil me for getting a job with the CWA if he doesn't look out.) But he's a fine old timer, and I'm getting old myself.

I wish I had—I wish you'd send me your daughter's whole name so I could send her a selection I have just made from my five books to amuse myself and anyone else who may wonder what my self-preferences are. Her having espoused my cause at U.C.L.A. must not go unrewarded.

[1] Frost refers here to Garland Greever.

I enjoyed your Longfellowan sonnets about Chaucer and about your old teacher. The gentleness of your nature comes out in them. We must swap a poem now and then. Here's one of mine called "Two Tramps in Mudtime," and I consider it to be against having hobbies. I don't know what you consider it to be.

Ever yours,
ROBERT FROST

KEY WEST, FLORIDA, December 26, 1934

When we read "Two Tramps in Mud Time," the similarity between its first line and the first line of Lanier's "Trees and the Master" struck us. We remembered how careful he was in the beginning to avoid writing in the Lanier school. He probably had no memory of the Lanier poem, but, notwithstanding, there was great similarity.

South Shaftsbury had become the center of the Frosts again, with Carol, Lillian, and Prescott tilling the Vermont acres atop Peleg Cole's hill. Robert and Elinor lived summers in the house in the Gulley. Lillian was better—though not as Frost had written, "completely recovered." Carol's growing restlessness kept her unsettled. For a time he seemed to be improving amid the old scenes he knew, but with his sister's death, and later on his mother's he reacted unfavorably.

At the request of President Sproul, of the University of California, we wrote Frost in January of 1935 to see if he would come out to deliver the Charter Day address at the University, the honorarium to be five hundred dollars, expenses cared for. A reply came by wire:

Key West, Fla. Jan. 30, 1935

Money, friendship, and honor, but I can't yield to the temptation this spring. All tied up engagements at Amherst, Yale, etc. etc. Thank President Sproul from my heart.

ROBERT FROST.

Letters followed but all our sophomorics failed to move him. He wrote:

DEAR MERTINS:

Is the idea to rush me off my feet out of New England, back into my native state?

Sometimes publishers try to rush me off my feet into their enthusiasm for their latest, greatest book in the history of literature. Ask them how deep in the silt of ages I am planted. I am a bridge pier in the middle of the river.

You were in too much of a hurry to see me again. An amiable fault. I most of all should be able to excuse you for it.

But if you will quiet down and listen for a moment without answering you will hear that what I am saying is: You would have been more sure to see more of me as a visitor out there if you or somebody had been able to locate my son out there on some kind of ranch. I said that partly from the fun of it to tease you. I had been pretty well satisfied myself there were no ranches in the SOUTHLAND within our means, and no kind of farming within our education and experience.

You chose to infer that I was hunting a job for myself in some one or all the colleges in California. Goodness, my child, I am not in need of a job. Haven't I told you all that Amherst college does to bind me to her in lifelong gratitude? I am a full professor at Amherst with no obligations or duties, but to stay in residence three months a year, deliver a lecture, or perhaps two a year, and go on having a book of verse every few years.

What I might thank you and the Californians for (you put it in my head) is an invitation to spend a week at a few of your colleges next winter at five hundred dollars a week. I would give one public lecture, go to two or three classes, and conduct two round tables of the chosen. Let's not look beyond next winter. I can see several kinds of advantages in the arrangement like that if you care to work it up. I shall have to be getting out of the cold again, they tell me; and it had better be in my native state than down here among the FERAL Floridites. No reflection on Florida is intended. I merely mean California has a claim on me, and I have a leaning of the sentiments toward my native state. And please don't put yourself or anybody else about too much for me. You may see me out there uninvited and for nothing anyway.

I am sending the book to Mrs. Virginia de Vries.

Ever yours
ROBERT FROST

KEY WEST, FLORIDA
February 12, 1935

When a letter was written apologizing for enthusiasm, he made reply:

DEAR MERTINS:

Don't bow your head in shame before me, but in my affairs try not to be so headlong. Nothing is important at our age, you know. Why try to get the fussy details right when everything is coming right in a lump so soon. Let me not scare you. I am not fey. I merely mean that in fifty years from now we'll be about at the end of our old age pensions. The oldest person I could find in the Key West graveyard yesterday (Sunday) was a veteran of the War of 1812 who died in Key West at 108 years. But many have lived to be older than that. His inscription wound up "A good citizen for 65 years." He must have been a bad citizen for 43 years then. That's what undermined him and shortened his life.

I hope your daughter got the book.

Ever yours,
ROBERT FROST

KEY WEST, FLORIDA
March 3, 1935

There can be little doubt that he was writing the poem in *A Witness Tree* called "The Lesson for Today" when he scribbled the above letter. The lines are echoes of it.

> *It sent me to the graves the other day . . .*
> *But I was only there to read the stones.*

Faithful to his suggestion that we swap a poem occasionally, one still in progress was forwarded to him. With his reply there came one of his, later to be published in the group "Ten Mills" in *Poetry,* where it was titled "Untried," then in *A Further Range,* and called "Waspish." In the original manuscript it was "Name Unnamed."

DEAR MERTINS:

Your poems r'c'd and contents noted with pleasure and interest. Poem also noted with the same. Interest at the old rates. That's especially good about the pop and yellow bantam. In reply would enclose one called Name Unnamed.

Now about these engagements. I wish you would lay off the colleges out there. By insensible degrees I am already in so deep with colleges back here that it looks as if my year, my winter, was wholly accounted for. I have practically agreed to go to Wesleyan, Texas, Iowa, Yale, and Miami.

That's for the group thing I told you about, and with the scattered one night things is too much as it is for my health. Oh and I forgot my series at the New School of Social Research[2] in New York and opening the new literature house at the City College of New York. And you may have forgotten Amherst but I haven't. You don't want to kill me. And you don't want to make a plague and pest to the whole Pacific Coast by insisting on me to excess. You can have my friendship without getting me engagements. Always bear that in mind. I want less rather than more engagements. I have difficulty in persuading the agents of that fact. Get lectures for Hamlin. He asks for them and he likes people to ask for them for him. My best information is that his condescension toward his rivals though kindly seems rather to hurt than help them. But never mind. Be magnanimous. Put your time in for him. I seem more than provided for. Let's think of these things no more. You will suspect me of high hatting you if you force me to keep on about my prosperity. Mind you it has been you forcing. And I could tell you of an affluence that doesn't matter to me either way anyway. My ambition lies far other where than in lecturing. You are forbidden to be anything but bucolic with me henceforth. I don't want to hear about lectures or literary societies any more. Keep pegging away at information about Californian farming and perhaps sooner or later you will hit on something that will fetch me out there to buy land. Be good now if you don't want to offend me.

Ever yours,
ROBERT FROST

FRANCONIA, NEW HAMPSHIRE
September 10, 1935

Persistency went on. The next letter had a tone of finality.

DEAR MERTINS:

Don't worry about losing my friendship. You can't lose it. But I wish you would understand how you make me look with your everlasting insistence on their having me out there to visit their colleges. Learn to let them seek us, my boy. I have never asked a chance to lecture in my life

---

[2] Frost's new venture was the New School of Social Research. Harry Hansen has reminisced about how Alvin Johnson used to place Frost in a circle of students and give him free rein to do as he would. It wasn't long, he says, before the room was surcharged with a spirit—a feeling of common understanding superinduced by the elemental and profound wisdom of the teacher.

and I doubt if anyone but you has asked a chance for me. You forgot that you lay us both open to the charge of politics. Another thing to consider: My friend and fellow Academician[3] does more to keep me away with one well-planted word than you can do to bring me by all the words in the language.

Let us forget these things. You will see me out there sooner or later. Lectures do not determine my movements.

Best wishes. Stay happy.

Faithfully yours,
ROBERT FROST

AMHERST, MASS.
October 16, 1935

The poet did not write again until a letter came from the Lone Star State, prompted by an Associated Press story about our collection at William Jewell College.

DEAR MERTINS:

The first time you ever had anything to do with me I was hiding—from subpoena, wasn't it? Now I'm hiding again, but from never mind what. I don't myself know. Other poets of my standing hide their meaning. I don't hide my meaning, so I have to hide my head. It may be a vestigial psychological necessity to hide something. See my poem on the subject in my very earliest book. I'm hiding this time at 947 West Agarita Avenue, San Antonio in the vast state of Texas.

Will you give me your President's full name at William Jewell college? I shall be glad to speak for you there.

This climate is nothing to make California jealous. Southern Texas, Florida and California are all a trifle citrous with jealousy of each other I'm told. Well, they're so much in. Just as I am not seeing people, so also I am not writing letters. This isn't a letter. You'll have to bear with me.

Ever yours,
ROBERT FROST

January 19, 1937

Nothing came of the attempt to bring him to the coast, except the letters he wrote, revealing his heart, portraying his character. These were worth all the effort they cost.

[3] Hamlin Garland.

In all this correspondence one is conscious of an undertone of tension. What was going on at Amherst? He certainly was doing his best to fit into Stanley King's plans. But these plans were so at variance with anything for which he had a taste that such collaboration would seem a spiritual impossibility. The president failed to realize the independence that was R. F. An example: Only once during King's tenure was Frost known to attend a meeting of the faculty family dinner in the old barn where the Faculty Club met. It happened this way.

President King's ambition was to make of the administration and teachers one big, happy family, as he had made his staff at the International Shoe Factory. He had on this faculty some of the original teaching staff of the pro-Meiklejohn days. Then there were a few which he had been responsible for. Thus, with a good faculty at hand he wanted to go further by having every person connected with Amherst know every other person. To do this he effected frequent get-togethers.

Once a month he assembled the faculty at their clubhouse for dinner. But the poet-in-residence never came! This irked the President.

One evening two fellow faculty members were dutifully driving over for the monthly dinner, when they came upon Frost and asked him if he didn't want a lift. He climbed in and one of his confreres asked how he was feeling. They got the grudging and unwilling reply:

"I'm not feeling like any sort of a man tonight. This afternoon King called me on the phone and as we talked along on a number of things he suddenly said to me out of a clear sky, 'Well, Mr. Frost, I'll see you at the faculty dinner tonight, won't I?' 'That's fine,' he said, and hung up the receiver. So, I had to come against my will, just because I wasn't man enough to stand up for my rights and say I had no intention of being there."

The efficiency expert in Stanley King would have liked to set the poet doing manual tasks. "He looked on me as a sort of fifth wheel, ornamental, but having no use," Frost grumbled in reminiscence.

From the days of Meiklejohn until 1932, Frost had been found doing more or less regular class work. Eventually this had turned into seminars of the elect. He would meet with groups of boys, or with individual students, interested in writing, on the campus or in his home.

If Frost was a fifth wheel to King, he was an outsider to the other staff members. It was hard for them to accept him as a teacher on an equal footing. He was so different, his status so unlike theirs. This difference was in more than tasks performed. It may be illustrated by looking at two poets, friends, often seen together on the Amherst campus—Robert Frost and David Morton. Morton taught regular classes, but as a poet he stood high. He took his meed of toil along with the regular teachers. Physically a wide difference existed between the two. Morton was a giant of a fellow, towering over his friend. To the students, seeing them thus together, the two professors lived on completely different and separated planes.

R. F. was always a much sought after guest for dinner parties, where talk was the thing. His encyclopedic knowledge of world affairs and his utter uncompromising opposition to that which he knew to be inevitable made him tremendously popular in any conversation. When a student mentioned "social thinking," he exploded. "Social thinking! Huh! What does he mean by social thinking? Does he mean we've got to sit with our arms around one another's neck and think?"

From 1926 to 1936, the poet was a recurrent lecturer at Wesleyan University, Middletown, Connecticut. It really began in 1924, when he received a doctor of letters there.

His work at Wesleyan was quite different from his tasks at Amherst. The plan was for him to come onto the campus once in every college generation, so that theoretically every student might have a chance to become infected. When he first came to Wesleyan as visitor in 1926, he was the guest of the Wilbert Snows.

At the time of this first visit, he was greatly troubled about his sister Jeanie. She had a checkered career. A born Bohemian, she had gone down to New York City to become an artist's model. When she became too old for this, Robert was seeking to care for her in the best possible way. It was just three years later that she died in the state mental hospital and was buried out on the hill at Lawrence.

When, on this 1926 visit, the time came to catch the train it developed that the host's car wouldn't start. There were Robert and Elinor five miles out from Middletown with no way to get to the depot. The fear of missing a train had stayed with Robert all his life, and he grew very excited. They had been poor so long that calling a taxi never occurred to them, so Mrs. Snow persuaded a student at the college to come for them.

In another of these periodic visits, Frost found himself strapped for cash. He didn't make the discovery until he was ready to leave, so he borrowed twenty-five dollars from Mrs. Snow, promising to send it back the minute he got home. Mrs. Snow allowed him sufficient time to get the money to her—she needed it for buying groceries—and then wrote him a letter calling his attention to it. Immediately he called on the phone. "Do I owe you twenty-five dollars?" he demanded. When she explained, he was crestfallen and apologetic and sent the money at once.

Snow's third book of verse, *Down East,* came out in 1932. He sent Frost a copy, which brought a letter of warm appreciation which Snow passed along. (Postmarked Amherst, Mass., May 18, 1833). His preference for lyrics and sonnets as opposed to poems "against anything or anybody" was clearly indicated.

In the Snows' delightful old Colonial house north of Middletown, Frost became a frequent guest. There were friendly arguments, though warm, between poet and poet, first over New Deal, later over Fair Deal politics. Frost did not share Snow's high opinion of F.D.R. as a messiah any more than he shared his friend's enthusiasm over Truman as a "miracle man." "What we need is a new deck, not a new deal," Frost told his friend.

It was in this same old house that the Snows lived when the Wesleyan professor entered practical politics, landing briefly in the governor's chair. When he first ran for office as lieutenant-governor in 1944, Frost wrote a letter to the "Secretary for the Snow for Lieutenant-Governor Club of Wesleyan," inclosing a five-dollar contribution for his campaign fund and indicating his willingness to give a thousand dollars if he were running for president of the United States. Snow, he commented, had nothing to hide about himself in the campaign—other than that he was a poet.

A celebration held at Wesleyan in 1936 was designed to mark the end of a decade of Frost at that campus. An unusual exhibit collected from several private collections was held in the Olin Memorial library.

The exhibit was soon dismantled and its treasures returned to their owners; but Lawrance Thompson and other Wesleyan professors preserved the composite knowledge thus made possible in a book published that year.[4] Nothing printed about Frost up to that time more clearly demonstrated the deep regard and affection he commanded in people. He always sought to deny that people loved him for himself. Once he made a categorical statement that none of his children loved him—were only proud of what he had accomplished. He would never admit that people more than admired him.

In this Wesleyan book, the picture Larry Thompson paints of the tragic fire which destroyed East Hall and Professor Snow's room in which he housed his Frost treasures—how "the sight of charred book pages with inscriptions, and books with water-stained covers, will recall the tragic morning . . . when he groped, heart-broken, among the ruins of that room to recover what was left of his precious library"—is a proof of genuine affection.

One item exhibited in the Wesleyan display was a holograph of "Nothing Gold Can Stay," written in a copy of the first edition of *Mountain Interval.* To show the power possessed by Frost in perfecting his lines, we place this first, or early, draft of the poem alongside the final form as it appears in all published versions—just as it was placed in the Wesleyan volume.

Nature's first green is gold,	*Nature's first green is gold,*
Her hardest hue to hold.	*Her hardest hue to hold.*
Her early leaves are flowers;	*Her early leaf's a flower;*
But only so for hours.	*But only so an hour.*
Then leaves subside to leaves.	*Then leaf subsides to leaf.*
In autumn she achieves	*So Eden sank to grief,*
A still more golden blaze.	*So dawn goes down to day.*
But nothing golden stays.	*Nothing gold can stay.*

[4] *Robert Frost: A Chronological Survey* (Middletown, University Library, Connecticut, 1936).

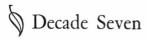 Decade Seven

XXI. Some Shares in Harvard College

IT WAS AT THE BEGINNING of the seventh decade, late in 1935, that Harvard beckoned for Frost to give a series of lectures under the Charles Eliot Norton Foundation.

Frost has confessed that he had long held a hope that one day he might go to Harvard. It was to him a matter of pride. Yale had recognized him by making him associate fellow in Pierson College in 1933, which was continued over the years. Harvard was his real intellectual alma mater. Going to Cambridge was another vindication.

When on March 4, 1936, Frost opened his series of talks on poetry at Harvard, a most complimentary audience greeted him. John Holmes has written of it in a warm, sympathetic manner, describing the audience as "not only friendly, but warm with anticipation and understanding, and with love for a great, kindly, simple figure of a man." "There can have been," Holmes adds, "very few occasions in the history of such public events in Greater Boston in our times when there was so much friendliness concentrated under one roof and directed at one man."

Regardless of what president and visiting lecturer came to think of one another in later years of association, James Bryant Conant, accompanied by his wife, was present the first night of the series.

The topics discussed by Frost in this series were selected with thoughtful care. Those who knew his poetry knew his genius for selecting titles, "The Old Way to the New" opened the series, to be followed in the coming weeks by "Vocal Imagination, the Merger of Form and Content," "Before the Beginning of a Poem," and "After the End of a Poem."

The Charles Eliot Norton Fellowship could not remain the possession of any one lecturer. Harvard was not without funds—having more than could well be spent—but strings were attached to each bequest so that the overseers (Frost was to serve as an overseer himself in 1938–39, and in this way could understand) might not always do what their own personal inclinations moved toward.

After two more years at Amherst, the poet returned to Harvard in 1939–41 as the Ralph Waldo Emerson Fellow. The tenure of these fellowships was less than tenuous. Could it have been that in Harvard the poet was homesick for the halls of Amherst? A pensive note came into his voice once when he talked about the change. How, after all the years, could he fail to miss Amherst? But in the next breath he would tell how well Cambridge treated him.

> As each new president came and went at Amherst some would know what to do with me, some not, most not. At last it came to a place where the presidents were stymied about what to do with me—what I was there for. Harvard invited me in 1938, and I came. I only lecture eight or ten times a year at as many colleges or houses. There is the Eliot House where I have talked. It was not named for T. S., though he has been there and is their god. While an undergraduate at Harvard he studied under Babbitt. His old teacher was very proud of him and of his part in making him what he turned out to be. As for Eliot, he always referred to Babbitt in his letters to him as "My Master," though in private he spoke slightingly of him. I didn't suppose the Eliot House would care to hear me under the circumstances, but they seemed to accept me graciously, different as I must have appeared. One can't forget the years, they're there. One can't take a home, or a companion, or a college out of his heart without leaving a great void, great empty place.

Indeed he could not forget the years when he busied himself on the teacher's platform "steering his classes toward the reading of Emerson by asking them to define an idealist." Frost has said that he wanted to stay on at Harvard, that he was ready to make the break at Amherst. These things had to right themselves.

In his Harvard lectures Robert Frost quoted from two unpublished books—both of which were to win Pulitzer Prizes. He admonished his listeners that he was just talking sense. For those who know the first of the two volumes well, talking sense by merely quoting its lines is inevitable. The two books were *A Further Range* and *A Witness Tree*.

In 1936 we received from the author a copy of the limited edition of *A Further Range*. On the fly he wrote:

> To Louis Mertins, this my secretly published
> (as distinguished from privately printed) book about
> California among other places.
>
> > From his friend,
> > ROBERT FROST

No book from his pen up to that time had created more widespread interest. There was a chorus of praise—largely indiscriminate. The critics puffed it because it was the thing to do. It deserved the praise given it, though a more careful analysis of its better points would have given more standing to the criticisms. Some of the poet's finest work was collated in it, some of his most truly great lines to be looked for here.

Not all agreed that Frost had again struck thirteen, though rare indeed those criticisms like that of Irvin Haas in *A Book-Collector's Journal* for July, 1936. Frost wasn't very happy over this review and refused to initial it for us, something quite unusual for him, though not unique. Haas wrote:

> Reading the reviews of this book in the large journals I found the perfect example of damming [*sic*] a writer with faint praise and I am sorry to say I can't blame the reviewers. They faced the prospect of reviewing a book inferior to any that Frost has written, and they preferred to write an essay on Robert Frost and his past work. This work proved my contention that Frost is not a sustained poet. E. A. Robinson, for example, was ever the great creator to his last volume, and in it we found new meaning and new beauties in spite of a long life in writing. He did not perish of creative exhaustion. Frost, on the other hand, who is so often coupled with Robinson, shows in this book that he is staggering.

Could it be the critic failed to read "Build Soil" in this volume—or was that the snag on which the ship sank?

Writing a more friendly review in an editorial in the Long Beach *Sun* at the time, his California friend set down:

"In *A Further Range* one finds Frost leaving the quiet valleys and apple-orchards of New England, and looking in thought beyond the White Mountains to the Green, and beyond them to the Rockies and the Sierras, and finally to the further range of the Andes and Himalayas ...

"That curve which runs from the first to the last book is unmistakable. While the first dealt with things, those that followed had to do with persons, personalities and incident. The last he placed on the higher plane of abstract thought, as expressed in the dedication to his wife, 'and even to the realm of government and religion ...' "

In this book the poet has relieved himself of a number of ironies, especially against the New Deal. He found much to laugh about in the Roosevelt regime, and never stopped. There was, likewise, much to laugh about in religion. He could understand how the Europeans might make sport of the foolish little (and big) sects rampant in the Land of the Free, though certainly he wanted to do the ribbing, denying that luxury to all outsiders, especially to the English.

Yes, Pan laughed when he wrote,

> *Let me be the one*
> *To do what is done,*

for that was the way he liked to work.

There are chuckles throughout "Build Soil" for one who can see that the author is poking fun at more people than the Stalinists, though he never leaves them out. There are more than chuckles—there is wisdom, older than Vergil, older than Olympos, old indeed as Arcadia, in the reasoning which Meliboeus, the potato man, imparts to Tityrus, the bucolic poet:

> *I'm done forever with potato crops*
> *At thirty cents a bushel. Give me sheep.*
> *I'll dress up in sheep's clothing and eat sheep.*
> *The Muse takes care of you. You live by writing*
> *Your poems on a farm and call that farming.*

Then he speaks of the Russians who are not content to keep their communism in Russia.

> *Friends crowd around me with their five year plans*
> *That Soviet Russia has made fashionable.*

Then he turns to socialism, contrasting it, perhaps, with communism. Meliboeus asks,

> *Is socialism needed, do you think?*

getting the reply from the poet,

> *We have it now. For socialism is*
> *An element in any government.*

Now he talks in his sunlit study, on the eve of Pearl Harbor, sitting in his chair, poems piled on the floor all around him, as he says:

Now with all this talk about Russia [1941] and taking on over making allies with them and of them, and sending Harry Hopkins over there to have his picture taken with Joe Stalin—I never objected to Russia and the Comintern so long as they kept it safe in Russia, sterilized in Moscow. That was their affair. But when they tried to carry on their Third Internationale in other countries—especially in ours—it became an entirely different matter. Naziism started out as a protest against Communism. It may be bad, but to me it isn't as bad as the latter. England is always trying to get somebody to fight her wars for her. I have no specific distaste for the British Empire; but when they own the world and say, "What's the use of fighting? We own it all anyway"—they hated us after the first world war and said we did little to win it. I've always said I wished we could have another world war and let us stay out and let England see how quickly she would win it by herself. Maybe I'll get my wish, I keep at it. Only I don't suppose we'll stay out—not with Harry Hopkins and F.D.R. running the ring around a rosy.

Sure, I know we're funny. Nobody better. Nobody has a smaller opinion of Congress than I—that is, Congress as Congress. We've had our flings with Presidents. We've even had Cal—a good Vermonter, stingy in more ways than vocabulary, too. Just how he ever got to be vice-president, thus placing him in line to lead the nation, is beyond comprehension, mine anyway. Certainly he had none of the requirements. It's exactly as you say, no use trying to figure out what Cal was thinking about when he sat and looked dumb. He just wasn't thinking. He had turned off the process.

I was sitting in the living room of Dwight Morrow's house one morning about two o'clock, in front of the fireplace. We had been talking on all night. In the midst of our talk the phone rang far off someplace, and Morrow went to answer it. He was one of the most absent-minded men I ever knew. One of the family jokes about his lack of memory had to do with being on the train and losing his ticket. The conductor helped him look for it, but couldn't find it. Recognizing who he was the trainman said, "That's all right, Mr. Morrow, you can just give it to me when you find it." "But," Dwight replied, "if I haven't a ticket how'll I know where to get off the train?"

Well, that morning Morrow went to the phone. He came back and stood in the doorway, a faraway look in his backward-gazing eyes. In a moment he came softly back to the fireplace and leaned over the mantle-piece to announce, "Calvin Coolidge is President of the United States." Which was his way of announcing the mysterious death of President Harding.

Morrow liked Coolidge. He told me once that when they were all in college at Amherst together, he himself got every vote but one in an election to determine the opinion of the student body as to which Amherstian had the best chance to attain success in life. "Of course," he chuckled, "I couldn't vote for myself, so I voted for Cal Coolidge." I wanted to say to him, "Yes, you wanted to wish one thing off on the college." They still tell at Amherst the single joke perpetrated by Coolidge. The first morning he was there they had sausage for breakfast. So, right off when the future statesman saw the sausage on the table he demanded to see the dog, nor would he let up until they brought in the dog for inspection, for he said he wouldn't eat till he saw the dog. When he got a good look, and found the animal was still alive, he said "Now it's all right, I'll eat the sausage." Which was the beginning and the end of his college humor.

Morrow wanted to get Cal to do something nice for me while he was in the White House. He told me the story, and so I had it straight. He was down in Washington and approached the President. "Why don't you invite Robert Frost to the White House? Incidentally it would be a fine thing for poetry, and for literature in general for a president to recognize the leading poet of the nation. It would be doubly nice in the case of Frost.

You are both Amherst men—you an alumnus, he a professor, and you'd be doing a good turn for the college." "Well, Cal got an absent look in his eye. He seemed completely immersed in study for a whole minute. Then he came out with this astonishing reply, which was no reply in any wise: "When I was governor of Massachusetts there was a fellow named Dennis McCarthy who hung around the State House, who wrote poetry." And that was all the President of the United States had to say about doing something for American letters.

Coolidge said he had read ten books in his lifetime, just for the sake of reading. It is amazing to look the list over. All but two of the ten are purely Vermont. There are two by Thompson, one being *Green Mountain Boys,* absolutely local and New England. He said he had read Cicero's *Orations,* which I have always doubted. His reading that of all things, when we take into account the limited reading he otherwise boasted of, just doesn't make sense. He barely got admitted to Amherst as a freshman, being turned down on this first application, and only making it after another year of preparatory study at an academy.

During the early years of the seventh decade things were very pleasant at Harvard. Frost liked his work and enjoyed his home at 35 Brewster. True, he had more than one spell of ill health and found it necessary to get out of the winter cold. As usual it was Florida. There he at last bought himself a house out in the country.

By this time he was seized with the idea of having much real estate. There was the house at Amherst, bought on the very eve of his leaving that school; there was the farm at South Shaftsbury; there were other places that he owned or held title to, which first and last Carol also laid claim to; and finally there was the Ripton farm, where he spent his summers while playing at teaching at the Bread Loaf school.

Surely we may discover a specific reason back of all this farm buying. It cannot have been merely because he wanted more room in which to expand; perhaps he grew tired of one place and wanted the feel of a new one. This may approximate the truth, for when was ever poet or peasant, prince or pauper, more restless than Robert Frost? He did not require more room, for surely even the Arcadian could disport himself on fewer acres.

Improvidence? That must have been the trouble. He never needed but one farm at a time. He managed always to get along with one suit of clothes (two at the most), "Sufficient unto each existence is the farm thereof." Improvidence moved him. He would gather a few thousand dollars together. Heigh-ho, he must have another farm. Then another. Still another. He little dreamed that the time might come when he would have need for all the money he was tying up in real estate, prodigally squandering on land.

His farms and his children. To these permanent investments went his easy money. He could never say no when one of his children asked for cash. There were janglings and bickerings, but he always yielded. They came first, however he may have begrudged it.

His fame, meanwhile, knew no stock-market fluctuations. It rose steadily. Gone were the preterit rivals, rivals who had never troubled him greatly. Little by little he had distanced them in the race. First he was a major poet, with others ranked above him. Then the critics deigned to place him on a level with the others. Finally, especially after Robinson's death, he held his unassailed position at the head of living poets, with many a critic placing him at the head of his generation, and no few who gave him first rank in American poetry since the beginning of our letters. It was not uncommon for him to be referred to while William Butler Yeats was living as the unquestioned English-writing poet after the Irishman. Yeat's death left his place unchallenged.

The old Cambridge school had found its poet and was proud. The poet had a few shares in Harvard College and was satisfied.

XXII. Now Close the Windows

Death and tragedy became the alembic of change for Robert. It was after the hard hand of sorrow had been laid upon his head that we talked about the geometric plot of earth "out on the hill" at Lawrence where the five Frost dead lay—old William Prescott and his wife, Willie, Belle, and Jeanie—the gravestones so primly set in a row.

But when age came on to bring the ordeals and tragedies of life, to show the realities of existence—and of the ceasing of it—somehow he softened. A new note came into his voice when he spoke of death and burial. Graves took on a new meaning for him. All the laughter was gone from his voice when he spoke.

"Time brings about a different attitude toward these matters. I feel far from the way I once felt about them. I have only two out of five children left. We must set out stones and then go away to forget."

As we have already set down, Marjorie died in the spring of 1934 at Billings, Montana.

Elinor never got over the death of her daughter. She grieved and mourned like Rachel of old, and there came a hurrying hither and thither, now as much for Elinor's as for Robert's sake—Texas, Florida, Colorado, and Utah. A cloud had settled upon the one who so long and so faithfully had stood by Robert's side.

Thus it came about that down in Gainesville, Florida, Robert closed the eyes of Elinor Frost and turned his face again toward Amherst, carrying the simple urn that contained her ashes home for the last long sleep.

He told me, long after, how the family lived together-apart in Gainesville. They occupied two houses close together, so the whole tribe was united and close to one another. Robert and Elinor had the upstairs of a house shared by Lesley and her flock downstairs. Carol, Lillian, and Prescott and Marjorie's daughter, Robin, lived in another more commodious house close by. Robert had an attack of the "flu" and was cared for by Elinor. Then, like a thunder bolt, on March 20, 1938, she was struck with a heart attack and died suddenly without any warning. The printed announcement mailed in the handwriting of one of the family came to me from Gainesville, Florida. The funeral services were to be held at Amherst, so long identified with the Frost family. Far away from New England he was turning back again, as a little boy he had done fifty years before to bring the body of his father for a peaceful sleep after the long day was over.

> *Then I arose and silently wandered home,*
> *And I for one*
> *Said that the fall might come and whirl of leaves,*
> *For summer was done.*

The ceremonies in the Memorial Chapel at Amherst, April 22, 1938, were simple but full of dignity. Those who knew Frost best looked on his white head, bowed with grief, the tangles of his hair unruly as ever, and knew what was behind that tearless sorrow. They knew how much Elinor White had meant to him for forty years and could not but wonder how he would manage as he walked the future alone.

Elinor had loved the farm at Derry above all the other places where they had made their home. Here her children were born—here two had been buried. It was one spot in a kaleidoscopic existence which, despite all transfer of deeds, remained their property in spirit.

The place had passed through many ownerships during the quarter-century the Frosts had been wandering over the world. The present owner was a widow, who with her husband had farmed the land till his death. Now she lived alone. One day a stranger knocked on her front door and modestly suggested that he once had owned the farm.

"I lived here as a young man," he said to her by way of explaining his presence. "I wonder if you would mind if I went out and looked around."

She gave consent and watched him as he walked away, lingering eastward past the wall, through the orchard, back southward, till she lost him as he entered the woods.

The thoughts which crowded the mind of that returning tenant-owner must remain forever sealed. When the woman lost sight of Robert Frost as he passed into the woods "beside the brook"—the woods that Elinor had loved—she little suspected his mission. He carried with him, hidden under his coat, the container holding Elinor's ashes. Once out of sight of prying eyes, hidden by the trees, he strewed those ashes beside the brook and left her in a spot she loved almost beyond all others. Then he turned back to the living. He had fulfilled her wish.

Maybe the poet cried out, there in the woods where once they had been so happy,

> *"Look me in the stars*
> *And tell me truly, men of earth,*
> *If all the soul-and-body scars*
> *Were not too much to pay for birth."*

After Elinor died, Robert seemed unable to talk of her for a long time. The grief was so poignant. But in due course when we came together for long talks-walking he turned naturally to the memory of the only love he had known.

> She was my greatest critic. I suppose an imperfect line, or flash of beauty spoiled, hurt her worse, both physically and spiritually, than I ever knew. This was the only goad I needed—her opinion. You see, when you've gone through high school in love with some one, when you marry her and face the future with her, and put yourself through agonies to write that which you think—which you hope—will meet up with her approval, and then she goes away, and you've not got her to sympathize with you, to advise with you—it's just about the end of the row. It was with me. How could I ever dedicate one of my books to anybody else? She always showed her mind and heart the perfect judge of art. What was left me after all those years—years at Derry, at "Little Iddens," out there in California, at the Gulley, South Shaftsbury, anywhere? Just one thing—to write poetry as she would have it—poetry she thought was not only *my* best, but *the* best. But I knew that life must go on living. You can't give up—you can't quit. But in those days and weeks it seemed I was on the verge. The outcome of it all was right, though, and things shaped up—with help.

It was a long speech, and it sufficed. Now it could be understood what the poet might have meant when he wrote those haunting lines in that very early poem about the search for the purple-fringed.

One cannot but wonder how much Elinor's death had to do with the chain of circumstances leading, two years later, to the tragic death of the one next to go.

During the years I had personal knowledge of that shaping tragedy. At the start, in 1932 in California, I watched it when it appeared a cloud no bigger than a man's hand. Had I not, in my little way, tried to circumvent its action?

The newspapers were kind in the case of Carol's death, just as they had been in the case of Louis Untermeyer's son's suicide, committed at Yale. I had seen in neither case a line concerning either. But on our way to Ripton, people kept hinting that something was mysterious about his death, conjecturing suicide. Arriving at Ripton, we stopped by the meeting house in the village, services on. A man came out of the church building, and we asked him where the poet might be found. He advised us to inquire at the big house on the north side of the road, west of the meeting house. A young woman stood in the doorway. When we told her we were looking for Robert Frost she said,

"I am Carol's wife. I noticed your California license."

She pointed out Prescott standing in the yard and told us he would be ready for high school at Bennington in September.

"He wants to be a mechanic," she told us, "and is preparing to enter M.I.T. You know Carol killed himself last fall. Father is all broken up. I thought you ought to know about it before seeing him. It might be easier for you to talk to him."

Seated in his study at the cabin that afternoon, R. F. told the strange sad story.

I suppose you know about Carol. You knew him in California. I remember how hard you tried to get next to him, to help him. Nobody could. He was one of the most unsocial of beings. He just wouldn't make friends, just wouldn't talk, couldn't talk. He would close right up the minute somebody started to make themselves friendly, or started leading into a conversation. No matter where he lived he never got acquainted with any of the neighbors. They usually started in trying to be neighborly, but he would rebuff all their kindly advances.

I went along for years thinking nothing about it, or noticing that his actions were more than a freakish turn of disposition. But things Lillian told me afterward made me see it all clearly, made me remember other little things which escaped note at the time. He was always suspicious. I recall that once I asked him if he knew his next-door neighbors. He told me he didn't. "Haven't they ever called on you?" I asked. "Yes, but I knew when they did what they were after." "What was that?" "Why, they called on us so we would call on them and they could have a chance to snub us." Now of course nothing like that had ever happened to him. Nobody had ever tried to snub them that I ever heard anything about. Nobody.

Once when he was a youngster he and I were walking down the road together. I would wave my hand at every passer-by. The first time I did it he spoke right up. "Do you know him?" I told him no. "Then aren't you afraid he'll think you're trying to get on the good side of him by speaking to him when you don't know him?" Well, maybe I was trying to get on the good side of him. No harm in that. Not a bad idea.

So, when the tragedy came, I talked with Lillian, and she told me the whole story. She had improved in health, as I wrote you at one time, but later took a bad turn, so the doctor gave her up and said she couldn't live. They really thought she was dying. It was this that made Carol take his own life. Cared for by his mother, just as I had been cared for by mine, and like myself married to a woman he leaned on and depended on, the thought of facing a big, unfriendly world alone overwhelmed him. It was too much. You see, Carol was a perfect example of a man unfitted to battle the world. Knowing only farming, he came to a time when farming was the hardest of all work to make a go of. It was too big a problem to face.

It all showed up in his inability to push himself. He had no knack for asking for a job, or for any sort of favor. Out in California all he did was garden a little. He took to writing poetry for want of something better to do. He always felt irked when forced to be dependent on me. With a sick wife, no income, no job, he developed a greater inferiority complex than ever.

You see, he started out as a perfectionist. He had a slight case of tuberculosis when a boy, and the doctor said he could avoid going to a sanitarium if he would carefully follow a certain formula, stiff one. He started in with the routine and got the habit of trying to be perfect in whatever he did. The result was a perfectionist complex. He was never satisfied with anything that wasn't perfect—and he could never be quite sure whether it was or wasn't perfect. He never overcame this. Anything imperfect was a trouble to him.

I recall a case which clearly reveals a certain attitude or state of mind in which he was most of the time. In New England we share line fences. Carol on one occasion told me that he had kept his share of the fence religiously but that his neighbor wouldn't do anything for his share, so that the stock got more and more breachy. I asked him why he didn't go ahead and mend the part of the fence neglected by the neighbor. He was all nervous even at the suggestion. Too bad he didn't have a French-Canadian neighbor to help mend wall, and have a good time doing it.

Dorothy Canfield told me a member of her family drove by the Peleg Cole house the afternoon before the suicide. Lillian was in the hospital not expected to live, and this neighbor drove by and stopped to pass the time of day. He said Carol talked queerly, in an incoherent manner, muddled, though at the time he attributed it to worry over his wife. He asked my son what method he used in cultivating apples, just to get his mind off his anxiety. He asked if he cultivated around the trees or mulched. Carol shook his head and replied, "My life is so mixed up I don't know which I do."

A thought flashed across the mind as Robert talked, a thought born of a memory of his own poem germane to the subject. Is there something the dead are keeping back? Something even the living refrained from telling while alive, leaving it to go unsaid to the grave with them? Who knows but that through the bare rooms of the stone house on top of Peleg Cole hill, a white blanket of cold snow spreading across the Green mountains, wandering like another set of bones out of "The Witch of Coös," a restless spirit goes forever searching for hidden wires that might reveal secrets (secrets now unutterable and eternal) whispered in the bedchamber!

XXIII. Time Out

AFTER THE DEATH OF ELINOR, Robert's ailments which he had pooh-poohed took a turn for the worse. The doctors hustled him off to the hospital. When the Associated Press looked him up for a statement, he grinned from his pillow, "Just say I'm in the hospital for a legal operation."

There came out of this experience something the world of letters should be grateful for. All that he wrote and published after this date, according to his own statement, he owed to a turn of events which dated back to Bryn Mawr shortly after his return from England in 1915.

Already we have mentioned an undergraduate in Bryn Mawr who got her fellow students to save their pennies in order to bring Frost to the campus. This girl became the lifelong friend of the poet.

Grown to be a woman, she had married Ted Morrison, of Harvard's freshman English department.

The inscription on our Clymer and Green *Bibliography* tells that Robert Frost and Kathleen Morrison jointly presented the owner with the book—"it was her copy." Printed on the dedicatory page of *A Witness Tree* we find

To K. M.
For Her Part In It.

He has affirmed briefly, but with great feeling:

> I owe everything in the world to her. She found me in the gutter, hopeless, sick, run down. She bundled me up and carted me to her home and cared for me like a child, sick child. Without her I would today be in my grave. If I have done anything since I came out of the hospital, it is all due to her.

In 1942 he wrote us from Coconut Grove, Florida:

> I am in Florida for a week or more, but the best place to address any further suggestions you may have to make would be 35 Brewster st., Cambridge, Massachusetts, where I wish you could see how comfortably I have been provided for by the friendship of the lady who either writes my letters or forces me to write them myself. . . .

All his life long there went on this unceasing battle between dependence and independence. "I was forever tied to somebody's apron string," he put it. First it was his mother. Then it was Elinor to whom he transferred allegiance and a sense of complete dependence.

After he had recovered through K. M.'s nursing, her kindliness continued. The Morrisons spent their summer at the Frost farm near Bread Loaf (in New England fashion called the Homer Noble farm for a former owner), occupying the large house and leaving the small logcabin for Frost. He prepared his own breakfast at the cabin, though he ate dinner (the noon meal) with the family.

Pan as a little boy gazed away on Tamalpais and Lone Mountain, trampled up and down the Merrimack; boy grown up, he roamed the Derry woods seeking hidden dales of orchises, hunted ferns by matchlight on the Malvern Hills, hurled stones at nothing on the sands at Laguna Beach.

From the Frost cabin at Ripton, which "just divides the desert from the sown," the government land stretches away to the Green Mountains, haze-hidden humps in the distance. Yonder is Bread Loaf, joined on the horizon by peak companions, standing in a semicircle northwest to southeast. Everywhere is the hardhack—steeple bush, Robert called it, as his readers know—and jewel flowers—while on all sides the tall mullein stands sentinel, with the stubby lavendar blossoms of the thistle serving infantry in an undeclared war. Cawing crows, a half-dozen in concert, their shiny backs glinting off the sun, sweep gracefully toward the trees in the pasture.

As we attain the commanding position of the heights, we turn and look back toward the southwest. The village lies hidden among the trees, only betrayed by ascending columns of smoke from many chimneys. We trace the tumbling stream by the dark foliage of its forest. To the southeast lies the summer camp at Bread Loaf.

In the immediate foreground stands Frost's cabin, built of smooth pine logs, with shingle roof and cobblestone chimney. Defined by its border of natural trees—flanked by a stone wall, thrown carelessly together to serve no purpose other than to get the stones off the field—the cabin fits its locale as naturally as a bird's nest does a clump of bush. About the stone wall, gargantuan ferns toss under the sighing trees. Over all the tranquil scene August hovers, but the native knows only too well that "autumn, yes winter, is on the wind." The Baltimore oriole dodging in and out is aware of this, too. The "fragmentary blue" of the indigo bunting striking against the gray background speaks of summer passing with the flowers.

To the left, toward the eastern slopes of the mountains, lies the fenced pasture, where sleek, mild-eyed cows are kept within bound. We can trace a disused road, for the untrodden years have not brought back the full growth to the beaten wagon tracks. Lined with goldenrod, the old road can almost be traced by the yellow blossoms. The culvert is tumbled in, a snare for the wary cows who shun it as a plague.

Down the slope, ten rods from the cabin, stands the rambling, low-roofed farmhouse. Here the Morrisons live in summer, caring for the creature needs of the farm owner. Across the eroded, weed-choked right-of-way is the garden, where beans, potatoes, peas, and corn grow with abandoned luxuriance in the short Green Mountain summer. A single wire strung to alternate steel and wooden posts surrounds the whole. The deceptive wire, R. F. informed us, is there to keep the Green Mountain deer from destroying the vegetables. The secret lies in the black, oblong box at the northwest corner post, to each end of which the wire is attached. When the deer comes smelling the wire to see if all is safe, a galvanic explosion strikes like an atom bomb, and he finds himself with business in the next county.

When we drew into the yard of the old farmhouse in the middle of the forenoon, Mrs. Morrison informed us that Robert was not yet about. While we waited, she went to tell him we were there. Soon he came, walking with an unwonted display of enthusiasm and warmness, greeting us like long-lost relatives, or better.

In the littered sunlit room of his cabin, facing downhill toward the farmhouse, the trees forming a frame for the picture, we started the talk that went on without interruption. Across the arms of his Morris chair, tied with a cord, was the cardboard rest on which he had done many a literary stint. His picture in one of the old *Independents,* taken a little while after his return from England, shows him seated in just such a chair, with just such a cardboard shelf for writing. Yes, there was talk that wanted talking.

New book coming out. I thought perhaps when I had *A Further Range* to stand alongside the *Collected* that it would be the last. But, no, here I am with another. Some of the poems are old ones. One of them at least forty years old. Certainly that one poem has had plenty of time to cure. I shall be glad for another book to stand beside the Halcyon House *Collected,* which as you know contains *A Further Range* in addition to the earlier books. Maybe someday there'll be another *Collected* to contain this newest one. And where it stops, nobody knows. You'll find a great many poems you've met up with before in this. Some I read to you nine years ago—some you have probably come across in magazines. For, now and then I manage to get myself screwed up to send some out.

As I have told you before, my children have all first and last tried their hand at writing—some with, most without, much success. Lesley was writing florid detective-mystery stories when I met you first, you may remember. The editors were interested in them, but she and I talked it over and decided she'd better wait to go on her own. We now know it was a mistake. She should have gone ahead. Lesley's full of energy, but she wastes it on nonessentials—bad marriages and divorces. But she goes right along thinking up something new.

She has a project now which is quite an innovation. She reasons that a lot of people, women especially, would like to go on with their education, not to get a degree or to amass grades, but just to learn. She plans to start a school in Washington, D.C., charge a stiff matriculation fee, get a good faculty to attract them. It has a good chance I think. Maybe she could educate some of our lawmakers—which I suppose is asking too much—much too much.

Conversation was interrupted by the dinner bell, so we trudged down the path to the farmhouse, talking all the way on interesting and entirely unrelated trivia.

In addition to the Morrisons there was a stranger at the board. She was the artist painting the poet's picture. As we recall, she was a refugee from the Nazis. The first fruits of the garden were on the table, the corn being a bit crowded into season. ("I have to have my sugar corn," he put in.)

Robert kept strangely quiet at the dinner table, the Morrison children occupying most of the attention. We stooped to a pun by saying that it was told that Vermont had frost every month in the year except August, "Which," we added, "we suppose is why Robert comes up in August, just to help the climate keep it unanimous." He growled that he had been called everything but *Jack* Frost.

Dinner over, we went out past the car, on our way to the garden. We furtively took the camera from the back seat.

"Not here, not here," he objected. "I can't let you take my picture here with all these people looking on."

"Maybe we just wanted to take the garden," we answered.

"Yes, with me in it. You embarrass me."

Leaving the family and the artist behind, we made our way across the rise northeast of the cabin, which, he told us was government land.

Gillie, the black Border Collie followed upon the low command of his master.

We talked our way slowly up the rutted roadway, overgrown with weeds (the desert, at least, if not "the woods come back to the mowing field"), until we reached an eminence overlooking the distant mountains—Bread Loaf and the other peaks. The path was indifferent, though once, long ago, white settlers had probably made a road where the Indian trail had been and over it had hauled their hay to mow. Now the boulders and small undergrowth made it difficult to follow with comfort. A few flowers were peeking through the wild grass, Robert walking carefully not to crush them. When we had come to a secluded spot where he felt himself free from prying eyes, his master called Gillie to him and patted his head as we took a snapshot. The dog, he informed us, was given the name Gillie, which is a Scottish word for servant, especially a huntsman's attendant, sentimentally.

On our way back from our desert walk he told us about the portrait painter. She worked, he said, in water color.

"I'm sorry, but I'll have to steal some time away from you two, this sitting has already taken a lot more time than she told me it would at the start. They always edge up on you that way. They always swear it will be done on such and such a day, but they never say what week, or month, or year, and it is never done at the time we understood it would be. You two go on now and come back at five. Come right on up to the house, and that'll give me a good excuse to get rid of her. Sitting for a portrait is a horrible nuisance. She'll be showing up any minute now. I'll go in and try to make up my mind to stand her."

At that moment she came round the corner, past the clump of trees. We never knew whether she heard him or not. We went away for a ride around Bread Loaf, leaving artist and subject to battle it out. When we got back she was still painting. He called out to us:

"Lesley's down at the house with Kay Morrison. Go send her up to me. She's got something to talk about that she says won't wait. I've arranged for you to stay at a house down in the village and get your meals there. We'll all go to Bread Loaf for the lecture right after supper. You always look after me in California. I should look after you in New England."

At the supper table we found a teacher in the Bread Loaf school made the subject of conversation among the students, who seemed talking for our benefit. This teacher was an English woman who didn't think much of Frost's poetry. She said he was not of this period. One student said she dismissed him with scant words, devoting her time to certain of the younger faddists.

After supper we drove to the Little Theater where the announced "lecture" turned out in good old New England fashion to be a concert. Louis Untermeyer was there with his new wife. Harriet Eells, mezzo-soprano, the evening's artist, had driven up with them. She sang acceptably, with the finesse of a fine Jewish artist. In her group of songs was one Frost lyric—"The Pasture," music by Naginski. Robert had applauded everything till she came to this. He had displayed enthusiasm and showed that he appreciated the well-rendered program. He sat like a statue when she finished "The Pasture." We thought the silence was because of a fear that he might be looked on as applauding his own poetry, but as we walked out to the car to return to the cabin, he volunteered that his stuff didn't go well with music, just as it didn't lend itself to illustrating.

I have always thought that Homer went about in his blindness saying his poetry, rather than singing it. You see, to say it is natural, for human speech tones are so much more beautiful than any singing can ever be. Singing came in with the shamans and witch doctors, who chanted or sang their abracadabra. Homer was more artistic. He said his poems and made known the story that Tall Troy was down, and why.

When we reached the cabin he began on us right off. He was unmincing in his words.

Now, I'm going to scold you children. You've been poking round in my past, digging up things at Lawrence and Derry, and I don't like it. It's alright for you to look up things out there in California. I don't mind that. But when you come back here where I am living and start nosing about in the years that are over—well, I don't at all like it. I'm sort of like an ostrich, head hider. What's faraway and out of sight doesn't trouble me. When it's near is different.

I went through all this with Newdick. I suppose I killed him. You see, he was going everywhere, always carrying a big brief case packed and jammed with notes about me—notes gathered here, there and every place. He had amassed no end of stuff—and it *was* stuff, nothing else much. There must have been over a million words of it. Much of it was made up of newspaper interviews, and a newspaper story makes the worst sort of biographical material. Reporters rarely get a thing down right, and if by chance they get it down right, and write it into the story right, the editor, who always knows so much more about anything on earth than the man who writes the story, changes it to some inane thing, giving a wrong sense to what you are supposed to have said. A man's biography made up out of one's repeated speeches, or interviews, would be a horrifying mess.

Yes, I suppose I killed Newdick. I remember speaking at Ohio State, at Columbus, and riding on the train with him. I scolded him for digging up my past, as I have you two. I told him I wouldn't stand for it, and he'd have to stop it. It broke his heart and he died.

Of course I didn't exactly kill him. He died during an appendectomy, but I didn't help him any. He died very young. Now his wife is sitting on his manuscript. Holts wanted to buy it from her, but she demanded an outrageous price for it. She wants somebody to collaborate and finish the book, giving her husband due credit—giving her due cash.

All through the evening Frost kept looking about searching for something. At last he explained.

"I've been trying to find something to give you—some manuscript I've finished with—but I can't seem to lay my hands on anything. I'll wait till I sign these things you're going to leave here with me. Then I'll get you the *Bibliography* and *Recognition,* and when I get back to Cambridge I'll gather up all the Christmas cards I haven't sent you, and mail the whole batch with some scraps of manuscripts."

Then holding up the first American edition of *A Boy's Will* we had brought along for him to sign, he said, "Are you sure you want me to keep this to sign and fill out the dates of poems?"

Assuring him we would be glad to gamble all or nothing, he laid it down and went on:

"I'll not forget. I'll find the dates I have set down somewhere and write them in for you."

The fact that all these things came safe and sound to us—though minus the promised dates and not without a long wait—showed he had remembered.

The evening had been chilly, for all its being August. He had wrapped himself in a blanket and so had sat under the lamplight, which fell in eerie softness over his rumpled white hair. When time came to go we said to him:

"Seeing you has been to us the shadow of a great rock in a weary land." Quickly he spoke up, "Don't say that. You'll make me cry."

Upon our return to California we immediately wrote a long letter to Untermeyer suggesting that the Derry farm be made a shrine for Robert Frost. He answered briefly, succinctly, but without equivocation. He did not approve of the scheme. It was not practical. The poet was still living. His shrine was in his books. He (Untermeyer) did not have the time for such—and asking for money would be undignified and embarrassing.

XXIV. The Great White Cold Walks Abroad

As EARLY AS 1941 things were becoming unpleasant for him in Harvard. He told us at Bread Loaf that he was already in a strait betwixt two. He wanted to stay on, but he didn't want to stay unless President Conant was 100 per cent for him. The percentages were much lower than that.

His long tenure at Amherst (however often broken for brief intervals at other schools) had given him a feeling of continuous security. All other things being equal, he would have preferred to stay on at Harvard as long as he lived, as he told us in so many words. A master of oblique statement, Frost at times could speak out and call a spade by its real name.

Everything was fine for a long while at Harvard. At first, so the poet said, he got on well with Conant. Then he took up the tale:

He even came to hear my early talks. But oil and water have a way of separating. Quit stirring, and there you are.

He was proud of being called Dr. James Bryant Conant, twenty-third president of Harvard College. To begin with, what place has a scientist as the head of a university? A scientist sees only science, his own. A researchist thinks all that matters is found in the precipitation at the bottom of a test tube. I told Conant once that it was mighty little he knew about humanities, or about poetry, or even about philosophy—with his nose stuck in a test tube. That's the trouble with scientists. They compute everything in milligrams on their tiny scales. They discount and discredit everything not reducible to an algebraic equation. But I've managed to slip in a little word of rebuttal in my books now and then, and don't you forget it, ever.

I remember one night at a party. Conant had been laying it on pretty thick, even for Conant. "The trouble with the nonscientific mind," he said, looking slyly at me, "is its inability to be practical. On the other hand, the scientist is a practical thinker." "Hold on, Conant," I put in, for I knew what he was driving at, slapping me over somebody else's shoulder. "Hold on. Don't tell me a poet is impractical or I'll get up and go home."

With all his science—research at Harvard, University of Chicago, Cal. Tech.—with all his learning, which nobody begrudges or denies him, Conant was always a very "proper" individual, a Puritan and a prude if not a prig. He tried to regulate the lives of all his faculty—a task even a New Deal bureaucrat would have found strenuous. He tried to interfere with their mores. I have always felt that we should allow to every man his own manners. For myself I won't be shoved around. What's more to the point, I refuse to be directed by any outside force. My propulsion has got to come from inside myself. I'm a gyroscope, not a string top.

There was Bernard DeVoto, a very original thinker, teacher, and writer, but rough in his speech, unpolished in his manners. Not at all proper the way Conant measured propriety. Conant was hot on his trail to be well rid of him, I suppose because he considered him a boor. He wasn't being advanced as rapidly as some, so DeVoto went to the president about it, to ask concerning his Harvard future. He told him he had a chance to go to *The Saturday Review of Literature*. Conant was sarcastic. "If you really *have* such a chance," he said, "I'd advise you to take it." DeVoto left Harvard very bitter in spirit, almost at once, and went to *SRL*. He was already on the "Editor's Easy Chair" at *Harper's Magazine*.

DeVoto always has to have some girl on the string, tagging her around. His wife always laughed it off and talked about it, for it really never was anything out of the way—just silly. Now I could never do that sort of thing that way. I would be more dangerous than that.

I don't know how things are going to turn out for me at Harvard. I can stand just so much. Conant could find ways and means of keeping me there very easily. They've got plenty of money available. I'd like to stay on. I'm comfortable there, and reasonably happy. Only time will tell.

The book he told us about on which he was working in 1941, came out in the spring of 1942. His 1941 Christmas card with the poem "I Could Give All to Time" had a picture of a tree by J. J. Lankes. Frost wrote on our copy the legend, "A Witness Tree"—the foretaste of the 1942 volume of that title. This became another Pulitzer Prize book.

In this, his seventh book, Frost went back over time and selected poems which had been curing and uncuring for forty years or more. There was "The Quest of the Purple-Fringed" which grew out of the Lawrence Interval, published first in *The Independent* for June 27, 1901, as "The Quest of the Orchis."[1] This poem was one of the finest examples of good editing Frost ever did.

The introductory poem, "Beech," sets us at rest concerning something critics long have been troubled over. The question is asked, "Was the poet circumscribed, or was he a real *homo universalis?*

> *One tree, by being deeply wounded,*
> *Has been impressed as Witness Tree*
> *And made commit to memory*
> *My proof of being not unbounded.*

When Frost signed himself "The Moodie Forester" to this poem, he was recording something only comparatively recent in his knowledge, coming to his attention from a relative "down under." For fifteen years he had had a slight correspondence with this New Zealand distant kinsman of his mother, who had imparted the information that the proper way to spell the Orkney Island family name was "Moodie," not "Moody."

In 1943, when Frost was made George Ticknor Fellow in the Human-

[1] See Mertins, *Intervals of Robert Frost*, 16–18.

ities at his old freshman college, his letter of acceptance showed a feeling not often made public out of poetry.

"I am accepting your call back to Dartmouth," he wrote President Hopkins, "with pride and satisfaction. Let's make it mean all we can. The call back, I call it. In addition to what I do at Dartmouth, I shall belong to Dartmouth in what I do for my publishers and my public."

His office in the Baker Library Building was to him most lavishly furnished, and for this reason he referred to it as "The Golden Room." It was attractive and in good taste, measuring some fifteen feet by twenty, with two simply draped windows and a well-carpeted floor. For furniture there were certain Duncan Phyfe pieces, an attractive book-case-desk, more simple than Governor Winthrop's, with other articles in early nineteenth century. The desk was kept open with intent to deceive his visitors, hoping they would think it was used in writing.

When in his room during the brief spring or autumn sojourn at the college (his autumn visit was usually timed with the first falling of the leaves), there was always somebody in to talk with him, and as often as not somebody waiting to get in. He continued to talk with the one present regardless of who might be waiting outside. Frequently his callers were forced to wait an unconscionable time when they found he had not arrived; often he never showed up at all, having run into somebody along the road.

As he expressed it to Professor Earl Cranston (office next door), who often served as information officer in the poet's clientele: "The boys seem frequently to think that one conversation with me will open the way to making them acceptable writers."

Old grads have pleasant memories of a familiar figure with his dog coming through the trees toward Baker Library. This fine building, its heavenward-reaching, weathervane-tipped spire white against a brilliant blue background, was a fitting place for Robert Frost to haunt. He had no chronometrical excuse for being late, the clock—like so many college timepieces giving approximately correct time—always displayed its black hands on a dazzling white face.

Frost insisted on spending his weekends in Cambridge during these brief twice-yearly visits to the campus. He would come up on Monday, returning the 140 miles on Friday after school was out. The journey was a short one, three and one-half hours by train, sometimes shorter by automobile. By the former he came on the Boston and Maine Railroad, landing within one-half mile of the campus.

Underneath his false veneer of coldness, Robert Frost was a person of deep sentiment. His going to Dartmouth, where he had memories of freshman days with the spirit of Hovey still lingering about, gave much satisfaction to his soul. Whether or not he had had any influence in making the college at Hanover into the school of the outdoors, one thing was certain—"the great white cold" still walked abroad. Always in his days as a student he was an outdoor man—walking, hiking, strolling along the river through the woods to the Vale of Tempe and the Five Mile Round. Seventeen years after he left Hanover, Fred Harris of the class of '10 issued a call for the organization of the Dartmouth Outing Club. Fifty men responded to the first summons. By the time Frost got round to returning to Dartmouth a generation later, practically everybody belonged to the club.

From boyhood Frost was interested in athletics. But at Dartmouth in later years, though he may have been interested in baseball, football, basketball, track, and skiing, the interest was not sufficient to call him out on the sidelines or bleachers. He preferred to look on "Dartmouth Mountain" from the lower ground. "Hell's Highway" was a bit too strenuous for him to navigate.

When opportunity offered, he strolled along the old paths he knew as a freshman, "now sadly changed and altered," and, with companion or without, looked in on odd corners he had ferreted out in 1892.

In teaching, he tried to limit his seminars to a nominal fifteen members, but it came about in one way or another that the three or four sessions twice a year saw around twenty-five attending. When he gave public readings in the Tower Room, seating about 150, it was crowded by the earlier arrivals, so that those who came at the appointed time were left out.

His associations with the working faculty were always extremely pleasant. He was a universal favorite, all looked kindly upon him. There was visible none of the jealousy so evident at Derry, perhaps because of his nonacademic status in the school.

It was to be expected that the social experience of twenty-five years earlier at Michigan should be repeated at Dartmouth. He was in constant demand for dinners of the intimate type, for teas and all the other drains on one's time and energy. He declined gracefully wherever possible, only going when to decline would be rude and likely to give offense. Notoriety and fame costs more than money, but Frost tried to reduce the drain upon his strength to a minimum.

Publication in this period was slight—magazine appearances wellnigh negligible.

In 1943, Louis Untermeyer wrote the commentary and John O'Hara Cosgrave, II, did the art work for a book of selected poems called *Come In and Other Poems.* For the purpose in mind (giving a cheaper edition of the poet's best things, carefully selected), it was important. It served its purpose with repeated editions, growing eventually into a *Pocket Book* edition.

At Dartmouth, Frost's "manager" was Ray Nash, whose only sin, from the managed's viewpoint, was a penchant for collecting. Whatever movements were required of the George Ticknor Fellow during his weeks at Dartmouth each year had to be checked with Nash.

Nash brought out *Dartmouth in Portrait* for 1944 on a Frost theme. A new portrait of the poet was used (one of the best) and the first printing of "In the Long Night." A very early (1943) holograph of this is among our most precious possessions. When the poem appeared later in *Steeple Bush,* it had a note crediting Dr. F. A. Cook with discovering the North Pole. Frost was always taking the side of the underdog.

Beginning in mid-October of 1944, under the direction of Ray Nash, Dartmouth projected a celebration welcoming Frost back to the college. The purpose, as set forth in the brochure, was to demonstrate what "the George Ticknor Fellow in the Humanities has been doing since he left Hanover between two days in the middle of his freshman year."

In connecting with the celebration, an exhibition of Frost's books was held, together with certain magazines and manuscripts, in the Baker

Library. *Twilight* broke out of its prison for the time. There were certain early drafts of now famous poems showing changes in words and lines effected before final publication. For example, in a copy of *Mountain Interval,* loaned by Harold Rugg, there appeared an early draft of "The Runaway" on the back flyleaf, where the last three lines ran,

> *Whoever it is that leaves him out so late,*
> *When everything else is gone to stall and bin,*
> *Ought to be told to go and bring him in.*[2]

In a copy of the first edition of *A Witness Tree* in the exhibition, the poet added the word "out" and so corrected the ninth line of "The Gift Outright" to read:

> *Until we found out that it was ourselves.*

In the printed catalogue of the exhibit appears the eight-line poem (dated in MS June 14, 1943) beginning "Once down on my knees"—a first appearance.

The celebration, "Fifty Years of Robert Frost" (beginning with "My Butterfly," 1894), was calculated to enhance his standing no little. His place at Dartmouth seemed reasonably established. . . .

Sorrow and trouble shadowed him here, too, so that his visits to the old college campus were not always the happiest. Irma, who lived in Hanover, was suffering illness, mental and physical. This eventually led to divorce, in turn to aggravate the malady, the cause becoming the effect, the effect the cause.

Meanwhile there were grandchildren growing up. Lesley had two daughters. She accepted a post as librarian with the American Legation at Madrid, for which she was exceptionally well fitted. . . . William Prescott, III, was in the army, his education cut short for the duration. . . .

Occasionally, noted men dropped by Dartmouth for a visit with the Ticknor Fellow in the Humanities. There was Vilhjalmur Stefansson, one of the few men actually named in a poem by Frost. Long-time

---

[2] As printed in its first book appearance it read:
> *Whoever it is that leaves him out so late,*
> *When other creatures have gone to stall and bin,*
> *Ought to be told to come and take him in.*

friends, partly because of Frost's abiding interest in the ice zones, the two frequently got together—"two distinguished elderly gentlemen" at a table in The Inn, engaged in animated conversation. Both were Harvard men, both interested in exploration—one in books read by a warm fireside, the other in living off the country, getting lost and being given up for dead.

When Walter Hendricks, of Illinois Tech, dropped by to eat apple pie with the poet one day, the latter learned that Henricks planned to start a new college in a characteristic manner.

"I'm going to start a college, Bob," Hendricks is quoted as saying. "I'll be durned," Frost answered. "I've always wanted to myself."

This answer appears to have been followed by a promise on Frost's part to lecture for him if and when the college became a going concern.

Now it is more than likely that this promise was made on the gamble that the hazy venture would never materialize, though, as it turned out, it had much to do with enlisting Stefansson and Dorothy Canfield Fisher to help.

However, the matter actually came to fruition, Frost keeping his promise some years later. The college Hendricks started, became first president of, was Marlboro, "on a mountain in Vermont." Frost told about it at Amherst when he spoke at commencement.

> Charlie Cole and I, and George Whicher, are just back from having inaugurated the first president of a brand-new college. The extenuating circumstance is that it is a seedling from Amherst College. The chief event of the occasion for me was the history of the founding of Amherst College as told by Charlie Cole and the analogy he drew between the shoestring start of this new college on a mountain in Vermont and the shoestring start of Amherst College a hundred and so many years ago. My ear is always cocked for anything democratic these days, and the most democratic thing I know about America is shoestring starts.

During these Dartmouth days, Frost was thinking much of war and man's part in war. In a letter he wrote to a friend in 1943, he set forth the idea that he was working on his farms, raising all he could, which certainly was the least a patriotic farmer-poet could offer in help and to show his patriotism in wartime. His food raising, however, was limited to maple syrup in spring, his vegetable garden in summer at Ripton, and some scattered roots and fruits in winter at Coconut Grove.

In literature he was doing something in the way of the long-neglected drama. Having finished the manuscript late in 1943, writing on lined paper in a notebook bound in black cloth with fabricoid red corners, he sent *A Masque of Reason* to Holts. It was a venture which helped him forget his worries.

Earlier in 1943 he had received a pleasing telegram from Frank Fackenthal, of the Pulitzer Prize committee, telling him the trustees of Columbia University had awarded him the prize for the best book of poetry in 1942. This, of course, was *A Witness Tree.*

"Getting it for the fourth time rather stops me from saying anything against a fourth term for President," was his current thrust at the New Deal.

As he approached his Biblical threescore years and ten, Frost was still dissatisfied with the quality of his work, still following the will-o'-the-wisp of perfectionism, still correcting by omission, change, and interpolation lines which were good until the final adjective, the eventual adverb, made them perfect.

There is the poem, for example, in *A Witness Tree,* which underwent much revision, coming out of the operation an almost flawless piece—the poem "I Could Give All to Time." In the beginning he intended to title it "I Could Give All to Change." The substitution of "Time" was the touch of a master.

In the last stanza, the next-to-last line was improved by adding "have" so that it reads finally,

I have crossed to Safety with?

Originally there was an indefinite finish, jumbled in such a fashion as

But I am there
Making the most of it.

This he corrected to end with a knockout blow,

For I am There,
And what I would not part with I have kept.

Another poem in this volume he has strengthened by the omission of an entire stanza. It is "A Serious Step Lightly Taken." The stanza was to be number four. It followed originally the line,

And there today we are,

continuing the thought:

> *And mean to stay*
> *And make possession firm*
> *For ourselves and our descent*
> *For a long old-fashioned term.*

How pleasant it is to find the poet seeking to live up to his own standard of excellence. "I just want a book of hard little poems to go knocking down the years, so tight you can't stick a knife into them anywhere."

XXV. Meeting and Passing

Robert Frost was the recognized master of line-etching of character.

He arrived at perfection in this matter by making his characters talk. It is natural that a man who could make his characters talk and reveal themselves with Rembrandtesque vividness (unadulterated light and shade) would be without peer as a conversationalist. In talk he revealed the character of his friends—his own at the same time. Those conversational monologues of his, talk without reserve, limned many of the famous men of his generation, not to mention women, in lines of poetry (out of the realm) which Shakespeare might have signed.

At Ripton, as we walked among the boulders of the government land above his farm, he graphically described his last sight of his quondam friend, Hamlin Garland.

The last time I ever saw Ham Garland he had tottered all the way back East to make a speech before the American Academy. In the process of his talk he said that when *he* had been in revolt back in the nineties, he did all his rebellious acts, not for money, but from conviction; while the so-called rebels of this day and time are breaking away from convention only for filthy lucre, hard cash. There were a lot of old ladies present who applauded wildly, though noiselessly, with their white-gloved hands. When Ham came down from the platform and passed by where I was sitting, he tossed his Mark Twain mane as much as to say, "There, I've finished with Hemingway and the rest of that crowd." He never looked on me as much of a poet. Noyes, he thought, was the greatest poet writing in English.

Garland always laid claim to writing the constitution and bylaws of the American Academy, with Thomas's help. I wonder if the two did it. Robert Underwood I think tells quite a different story.

"Old Markham" he always called him. What is more to the point, he dismissed Edwin Markham's poetry with a wave of the hand, that is, excepting "The Man With the Hoe." Frost was never a poser (at least never an elocutionary poser), and it was Markham's posing which stirred him up whenever he was with Markham. He voiced his opinions.

"Old Markham" had the studied air and voice of the orator. He was never satisfied with giving his lines their proper value—he had to ad lib. and create a hit in saying them. His voice was high pitched and tremulous. He would get up before a crowd, dressed in his green turning coat, gravy spilled all over his flowing black Roycroft tie, and proceed to elocute. He was always a little Boy Blue, blowing his horn. One should forgive him so small a malfeasance, I suppose. He had grown quite childish about his own importance toward the end. The greatness was quite a load for him to carry. He was never very strong.

There was always affection and deep regard in his voice whenever Robert Frost had occasion to speak of Edwin Arlington Robinson. Though the two leading poets of the nation lived and wrote in two completely different worlds, they yet understood one another. One set down odd characters he had known in Tilbury Town—characters as erratic as High Tide and Gardner themselves—characters as bookish as his calling Gardner "Tilbury"; the other wrote of that which was not to be looked for in books—until he had put it into books—but his characterization of New England life had all the bleakness of the imaginary tragedy his friend set forth, with an occasional spice of humor to season it.

In our conversations he often reverted to the poetry of "Tilbury Town" in a manner revealing a high appraisal of it, as well as a fondness for Robinson himself; though he could never understand why his fellow poet, in his old days, should spend his time writing such "dreary, long-drawn-out poems" as he came at last to perpetrate. "Robinson," he once said, "at one time wrote good poetry—perhaps great poetry. This later stuff—I can't see how he can stay awake writing it." His discussion of Robinson reminds one of a surgeon with scalpel laying bare the tendons, muscles, and living organs of a man and fellow.

> Yes, he once wrote fine poetry, poetry that will live. I have liked him as a man and poet a long while. I have often visited him. Once he wrote under great stress as we have said of Housman. Now he is writing only because he is lonely and lacks something better to do. It seems to me he must set himself a stint, and rain or shine every day do just so much. They make a god of him at the MacDowell colony, which is, I take it, their right—maybe as it should be. They've sort of built it around him. Alec Meiklejohn goes up there and plays pool with him, to sort of save him from the female climbers. Alec is like that.

On that chill winter day when they carried Robinson to his grave, Robert Frost was one of the honorary pallbearers, other members of the Academy, including Markham, also serving. Long after, Frost referred to the closing scenes of Robinson's life.

> I never stopped admiring Robinson, nor did my regard for much of his poetry wane. It wasn't all great—I'll not grant that. But you'll have to admit he never quit. He just sawed wood to the last log. I wrote him a letter, a long letter for me, not a great while before he died and told him how I appreciated his work. He was a lonely soul and lived much inside himself. His poetry is proof of that, unmistakable proof. I have no way of knowing if my letter pleased him, but I'm glad I wrote it.
>
> Before I had published a book I was never conscious of the existence of any contemporary poet. But as soon as my first book came out I became jealous of all of them—all but Robinson. Somehow I never felt jealous of him at any time.

On another occasion our talk was of Hervey Allen, whose *Israfel* was no slight contribution to Poeana, but who at the moment was more famous for his behemothian *Anthony Adverse*. Frost knew him well as poet and instructor.

Again he talked of Vachel Lindsay, concerning whose genius he and Masters were in unbelievable accord. So well did he like Lindsay that he told us, as late as the forties, that he intended to get round to reading Master's biography of him. Of Vachel he had something to say.

> One of the saddest things in modern literary history is the way in which Vachel Lindsay lost his income in his last days. When his publishers suggested that in order for his poems to be made available to the children he should make the copyright over to them, the thing caught his fancy. It was with this in mind, the establishment of his name and fame with the rising generation, that he was willing to do it. The argument was too convincing for a mere poet to withstand. To know that the future would be secure, that in the years to come people would still be reading his verse —well, that would get nearly anybody who has written something he held in enough esteem to wish it might live. So, he signed over his best things for a consideration. Being improvident, he spent the consideration. Then came grinding poverty, which was more than he could stand up to. This undoubtedly brought about his death. He left this world thousands of dollars in debt. But then he was always a child as a manager. He told me once he had made $11,000 the year before—which I thought was a lot of money, lots for depression days. He used it all up as it came in, staying in the most expensive hotels, living like a lord. It soon went.

He now and again spoke also of Edna St. Vincent Millay, but his estimate of her literarily was firm: "I don't share the wild prophecy that Edna is immortal."

And so they passed before him. Not one of his contemporaries did he look on as uninteresting. Some he loved, some he hated. For a few he had downright antipathy. One remembers what Victor Hugo said somewhere, "A mountain must be accepted or left alone."

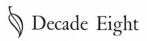 Decade Eight

XXVI. Not to Keep

NOTHING COULD have been more appropriate than for Frost, at the eighth decade's opening, to celebrate his seventieth birthday in the city where he was born. Conditions and Robert Frost (the immovable body and the irresistible force) intervened to make it impossible.

However, that seventieth year of his life did not go without proper celebration. Holts saw to it that his natal day had remembrance. The select crowd which gathered at their invitation included very few outsiders. It was a publisher's party for a publisher's poet. One reason for this celebration was the publication of Frost's first dramatic effort since *A Way Out.* The book, *A Masque of Reason,* was a notable one. It was shortly to be followed by *A Masque of Mercy.* Just what effect these two may have had on the then current revival of the poetic drama is not at issue. Frost expressed himself at the time that, like so many other things, poetry in the theater has always gone in cycles. In the early years of the century, he pointed out, Percy MacKaye and Stephen Phillips were cutting a wide swath with it. "Now," he added, "it may be coming back again with Shakespeare on the screen."

During these years his health had been variable. He was forced, he once wrote, to get out of the New England winter. It was not to California that he turned but to "feral Florida." The run down the coast was so much less time and energy consuming.

It was almost a decade after the first disastrous efforts to get him to come west that we made a second attempt.

With his promise made at Ripton (1941) that he would come out when proper arrangements were made for him, we started in at once upon our arrival in California to make such. After contacting a number of colleges, we forwarded some tentative dates to him, dates admittedly vague and indefinite. His reply to the letter urging him to correlate the dates was written from Cambridge, dated October 8, 1941.

DEAR MERTINS:

Say, before I start correlating the dates, you must correlate them a little more yourself. You mention times as far apart as February, March and April. Of course I can't be spread out over months and you wouldn't want me to be. Please begin with the most important date and try to pack as much money in around that as possible.

You don't even say when in March the founders' day at the University of California comes. One thing more, my dear friend. I must ask you not to press too hard for me in these and other matters. I should think some of them out there would be writing to me directly sooner or later if they wanted me very cordially. Please protect my feelings. I know you act only from enthusiasm for me, but don't let your enthusiasm run away with you. The world owes me nothing and my friends mustn't make me look as if I thought otherwise.

Always yours,
ROBERT FROST

This being our first glimpse of what his English publisher, Mrs. Nutt, may have seen in him when she called him a "dollar grabber," shocked us. We were prepared for the letter which came in answer to our setting forth what had been done.

DEAR MERTINS:

Now listen. You don't want me kicking round at my age for nothing. I can't run here and there for the sake of running. There must be some return proportionate to my expenditure of strength. Seven hundred dollars won't be enough to bring me to the coast. And there must be some warmth of assurance that somebody wants me besides you and Earle Bernheimer. I haven't had one word of invitation yet from anybody but you. Unless you make things look better—more inviting—right away, I'm afraid you'll have to give me up, and make up your mind to get along with only my ghostly presence at your conferences with Earle over my first editions.

I am in Florida for a week or so more, but the best place to address any further suggestions you may have to make would be to 35 Brewster st., Cambridge, Massachusetts, where I wish you could see how comfortably I have been provided for by the friendship of the lady who either writes my letters or forces me to write them myself.

Ever yours,
ROBERT FROST

ROUTE 2
DAVIS ROAD
COCONUT GROVE, FLORIDA   Till about Feb. 24, 1942

Definitely, this was the end. It did not need the telegram, slightly tinged with sarcasm, which he sent to the University of Redlands from Cambridge on March 25, declining the invitation.

Again we had to admit defeat, however unjust the suggestion in Frost's telegram that we had been altogether at fault. The poet was quibbling.

It all turned out happily, however, and culminated in a rare event at a more convenient season.

Toward the end of 1945 a suggestion of the poet's relenting came to us in a letter from Earl Cranston at Dartmouth, who had been talking with him. It set forth the opinion (based on chance remarks from R. F.) that should the invitation be renewed, the former Californian might be amenable. To such effect President Sproul, of the University of California, was written in January, 1946. This communication brought no reply. The whole matter, therefore, was dropped.

In late September we wrote Sproul again, this time concerning an exhibit of our Frostana to synchronize with Frost's birthday in March, 1947, and to coincide with the publication of our book *The Intervals of Robert Frost: A Critical Bibliography*, by the University of California Press.

Early in October the president replied that "through inexplicable circumstances" the letter of January 22 had just come to him. "I am," he went on, "immediately writing to renew my invitation to Robert Frost

to come to Berkeley to receive an honorary degree from the university.
I hope I shall have better luck with this than a number of previous occasions." In November he wrote again stating that "you will be delighted
to learn, if you have not already heard directly, that Mr. Frost has accepted our invitation and will be in Berkeley on March 23, next."

It had been a long wait since the first attempt had been made to bring
Robert Frost to California, back in 1935. In co-operation with President
Sproul, we were making arrangements to celebrate the seventy-second
anniversary of the poet's birth. When we wrote him of the plans for the
birthday party, he replied:

> 35 BREWSTER STREET
> CAMBRIDGE, MASS.
> January 20, 1947

DEAR MERTINS:

This celebration of my birthday sort of discombobulates my schedule.
I want to leave San Francisco on the 25 at least. Could we anticipate
it a few days and have the big blow-out on the evening of the twenty-
fourth? Now I want this done so there are no hurt feelings and I won't
suffer from the rivalries between my friends. You thought of it first but
I want you to go ahead and make Earle [Bernheimer] your co-manager
or whatever it is to be. Please speak to him at once and ask for his backing
and his name on the program if there is to be a program.

Now for the night of the twenty-eighth. [He had wired from Cambridge saying the twenty-eighth was the best lecture date for him and
asking us to wire confirmation.] No dinner party before the reading pos-
itively, anything you please after dinner. I'm always hungry and festive
then. I have to leave to get to Denver for a lecture on March 31. I suppose
that means leaving you early on the twenty-ninth.

I am having to cut everything short out there on account of my daughter
Irma who has come on my hands. She is a good deal upset mentally and
physically by a recent divorce.

I am sending "Neither Out Far Nor in Deep." You must have a complete set for the year: "A Young Birch."

> Ever yours
> R. F.

Robert was down in South Miami during February. Kathleen Morrison wrote on the twentieth that she had just been in Florida a week, trying to catch up on correspondence, and with the proofs of a "new book coming out the end of April." This book was *Steeple Bush*. She wrote that the schedule he had made for himself "is much too tight and crowded and he regrets it very much but I guess he has told you that family problems of a rather intense sort have been pressing him ever since last May and are by no means settled yet."

Frost also wrote Sproul a letter:

> Box 100 R.F.D. # 2
> SOUTH MIAMI, FLORIDA
> February 20, 1947

DEAR PRESIDENT SPROUL:

As far as I can think it out beforehand, my visit to California seems all provided for. I shall arrive there on March 21 probably so as to be in good time for the ceremony. I am counting on you to board and bed me. My friend, Mr. Mertins, tells me I am to be given a birthday party in San Francisco on Sunday March 23. On the twenty-fourth I should be setting out for Los Angeles on my way home. I shall be at your disposal while I am with you.

About the poem "Neither Out Far nor in Deep" in manuscript. Of course I should be only too proud to have you reproduce it in any form for the occasion. You may be sure I feel the warmth of all this. Don't judge me by the slowness of my responses. I began to feel afraid I shouldn't get out there till you had left being president there to become president of Columbia.

> Sincerely yours,
> ROBERT FROST

Back in Cambridge, Kathleen Morrison wrote again on March 12. In this letter she set us at rights about the first printing of the poem "In the Long Night." Robert had sent the prepublication manuscript of this fine poem at Christmas, 1943. We thought it had never been printed and wanted to use it for a place card at the dinner, printed on parchment. Kathleen wrote that if we wanted to use it, Robert gave consent, but that it had appeared in *Dartmouth in Portrait* for 1944. Later it was put into *Steeple Bush*. She added, appropos of the social activities and readings, that he "always wears a black tie for lecturing and will come with it in his bag." Then she said:

"The program sounds pretty stiff to me:—Friday 21st—Press, cyclotron. Please *nothing* more. Dinner with President Sproul. Press *must* be short. Saturday. Ceremony. Luncheon. Visit to old haunts. Gertrude Atherton call. Dinner for Charter Day. This is too much. An impossible day. Can you cut the dinner? He says he doesn't want to die in California—bad enough to be born there. Sunday—please *nothing* but the library and the dinner and a long rest between the library and party. By this I mean alone by 4:30.

"This sounds pretty dictatorial but it's only haste that makes it so. Robert has had a tough winter and although he is well, he is tired. He can do only so many things a day and needs solitude to recover himself."

On Friday, March 21, we drove out to the Durham home to take him to the press conference. On the way down we asked Garff Wilson, special assistant to the president for the occasion, if our guess had been pretty good concerning his height and weight. Fair, he told us, only a bit too heavy.

"I have never been heavy." Frost put in. "As a young man I was always light, sort of featherweight. I didn't start in to fill out till I was around forty or fifty years old. I never weighed as much as I thought I should. I used to slip weights in my pocket when weighing around people so I'd weigh what I thought I should."

He did a good job being interviewed. When asked the favorite poem of his own writing he replied, "I couldn't tell you if I would, and I wouldn't if I could. I'm parental in that. If I liked one of my poems better than another I'd never admit it any more than a parent would about his child."

"I vote in Vermont, but I've never been received there yet. It's a slow state. People who know of my various places ask, 'Where do you stay?' Well, I don't much stay."

The questioner persisted. "What one book would you take with you to a desert island?"

"Well, once I came out to Monrovia, California, and I brought along a single book you could never guess. It was a book of Lucretius' poems in Latin. I wanted to see what I could dig out without a dictionary from a language in which I once was proficient. When you've only one thing that way you have to depend on memory. Good experience. This question of which books are the world's best irritates me. I get mad thinking about the one hundred best books of St. John's College. I couldn't name a hundred best ones. While I'm waiting for the fall of the British Empire, I read Gibbon's *Fall of the Roman Empire*. It took four hundred years for it to fall, really fall. So, you can see how long we've got to wait on the British. Humpty Dumpty takes his time."

One of the reporters asked him how he ever took to writing. He said he supposed he just didn't take. Said he never lived a literary life. He only wrote occasionally, some half-dozen poems a year, counting all his life production. He said one of his daughter's said she was sixteen before she knew he was a writer.

The interview finished, he went to meet the students who were waiting to hear him talk and read his poetry.

Came the blustery, wild March day—Charter Day. The Berkeley skies were overcast. A wind blew in from the bay and chilled the marrow of the most seasoned. When the academic procession rounded the corner, we saw Frost walking with Douglas Southall Freeman, the South's noted editor, military historian, and biographer of Robert's namesake. Robert was holding his hand over his ear to keep out the chill of the stinging wind. He sat on the exposed platform of the open air theater, listened to Freeman's address, received his degree, and marched down again.

After the Charter Day luncheon at the president's house came the visit to the old haunts Frost had known as a San Francisco boy (described in the opening pages of this book) and to the home of Gertrude Atherton's daughter for a talk with the novelist.

The birthday party was set for Sunday. The invitation was signed by Robinson Jeffers, Gertrude Atherton, Robert G. Sproul, Louis Mertins, and Earle J. Bernheimer and read: "Friends of Robert Frost, the distinguished American poet, wish to honor him during his forthcoming visit to San Francisco, the city of his birth. Since Mr. Frost will be here during the week of his birthday, it is felt that a dinner party should be given to celebrate the first birthday the poet has spent in his native city for sixty-two years. You are therefore invited to meet with us in the Golden Room of the Hotel Mark Hopkins, San Francisco, at 7 P.M., on Sunday evening, March 23, 1947, to celebrate Mr. Frost's seventy-second birthday. Dress is informal.

The guest list included Sara Bard Field, and at Robert's suggestion, Stegner, Stewart, Schorer; his colleague at Breadloaf, Edith Marielles; and Alfred Harcourt, the editor who started Frost in America. Sunday night found the room filled.

Greetings from notables all over the world—telegrams, cablegrams, and air-mail letters—were read by Garff Wilson on the call of the toast-master. From Ireland, Lord Dunsany sent his verse of greeting written with his famous quill pen.

Very felicitously, President Sproul, absent at U.C.L.A. for the charter-day celebration there, sent his regrets for being unable to attend, quoting a notable line in "The Favour" by Frost. Addressing him as "a distinguished poet and a great American," the quoted line set forth that "his life and work 'have given the world a change of mood, and saved some part of an age we have rued.'" The only paraphrase he offered was the change of the word "day" to the word "age."

When the toastmaster announced that Robinson Jeffers could not be present, but that "from Tor House, the *Incestral* hall of the Jeffers tribe had come this greeting," the guest of honor snickered aloud.

Tor House, Carmel, Calif.
March, 1947

Dear Louis Mertins:

This is a note of admiration for Robert Frost, and of regret that I cannot be present at this birthday party in San Francisco. Will you show it to him, please? Or read it to him, and to the fortunate celebrants.

Certainly this party marks a memorable occasion. San Francisco and all California may be proud to have seen at least the inarticulate beginning of New England's poet; and though he went east—"against the course of heaven and doom," as Shelley says—and prefers the shrewd and kindly idiom that grows north of Boston, yet he belongs to the whole country and speaks for it, the east and the west. I think of Frost as a worthy successor of Emerson and Thoreau,—to name my most admired New Englanders,—and as a man who expresses the universal through the particular, a regional poet who is also universal, like Wordsworth for instance. I wish him many future years and poems, for his own sake and ours.

Good luck to you, Robert Frost.

Sincerely,
ROBINSON JEFFERS

Then, and often later, Frost expressed great admiration for Robinson Jeffers. Once he said:

"He never felt called by necessity to leave California and rush off to New York. He has just kept working his vein of poetry—good poetry. Stayed on in the west and succeeded. Good poetry isn't dependent on geography."

Walter de la Mare, whom Frost had always liked both as man and poet, sent his warm greetings from Beaconsfield, where Frost had spent his first exile winter in England.

"My love to Robert Frost; my gratitude and inexhaustible admiration for his poems and all my good wishes," he cabled.

Dorothy Canfield Fisher wired: "Greetings to Robert Frost from his neighbors in the Battenkill valley, to remind him that by our standards nobody is entitled to put on venerable airs at seventy-two. We consider Robert just comfortably ripe and mature and send him our affectionate and admiring certainty of fine things from him in the next twenty years."

The toastmaster introduced George Stewart. "This afternoon," he related, when Frost and Stewart got together, what do you suppose the subject of their animated conversation was? Not the technique of the drama, poetry or the novel. None of these things. They were spending their time talking about how 'swell' it was to each have a book in the twenty-five cent Pocket Book series."

Seldom does one listen to a more cleverly-conceived or felicitously worded talk than was delivered by the vice-president on behalf of President Sproul.

"In behalf of his recently-acquired alma mater," Deutsch said, "I express our pride in the newest and youngest member of our family. By a strange anachronism you who but yesterday became our son, are this night celebrating a birthday which has not yet arrived. This gives us the opportunity to greet you as our own on one day and boast of our infant son on the next."

Deutsch continued: "It is easy in our age of machines to boast of the inventions that have been made to make life easier, but which also furnish the singing advertisements of the radio and the equanimity-destroying as well as life-destroying motor cars which clog our highways and streets. But mankind is not made greater through machines alone. The great religious teacher, the great orator, and the great author—yes, the great poet—leave an impress that is far deeper than warrior or statesman.

"Dr. Frost, Horace's prayer for himself, I am sure, is realized by you:

> *'Give me but these, I ask no more, these and a mind entire—*
> *An old age not unhonored, nor unsolaced by the lyre.'"*

All we had hoped was a birthday dinner as distinguished as his fiftieth at the Brevoort. Whether it reached that high point of distinction would not be for any of the planners to say. Dorothy Canfield Fisher wrote after she had talked with Robert on his return east.

"It's wonderful to share a little in that Robert Frost birthday dinner. I am absolutely certain that Robert enjoyed it as he has few things for years."

When Frost said his little poems, and talked pleasingly, his speech was happy, full of kindly wit and good humor. In front of him was the remnant of his birthday cake, with a sleigh, a passenger, and a horse beside a stone wall, the dark trees as a background. His seventy-second birthday, not yet arrived, had been celebrated. Someone murmured:

> *But I have promises to keep,*
> *And miles to go before I sleep.*

XXVII. Beyond Words

ROBERT FROST'S VISIT to California in 1947 stirred memories in his heart. Those which moved him deepest were concerned with Carol and his life at Monrovia. Going about in places where the past surged over him —San Francisco, Los Angeles, and Monrovia—he talked of former days and opened his heart in a way he had never done before. Passing through Monrovia it came as a great surprise when he expressed a desire to see the house in which he had lived with Carol. Never having been one to admit a wish to go on any sort of pilgrimage, his willingness to see old homesites amazed us.

When we found the place, a great sadness came over him. He fell to musing about Carol:

> Carol was obsessed, even in those days, as we were later to learn from Lillian—obsessed with a desire to commit suicide. It was probably a feeling of the futility of his life, something he was seeking escape from. Sometimes he would talk about getting a gun. He may have been contemplating suicide even that far back. He had never kept a gun. I myself seldom. I have never hunted animals in my life, so I had no use for one, except for hawks after chickens. That was all I ever hated about keeping chickens— killing them for market, and all that blood and gore and butchery. As for Carol, nothing any of us could have done would have helped him. You did what you could. He was born under a crooked star.

One was never able to discover how far back into his early life Robert's apprehension went of having a mental break himself. He must have talked over his mother's incipient insanity with Blanche Eastman on the occasion of his visit in San Francisco with her. His reason for being glad his host wasn't there ("You'd have heard things I didn't want you to know") might well have been that. For all her seeming garrulousness Mrs. Eastman was too shrewd to do more than hint about the matter when we discussed Belle Moodie with her. "She was terribly queer," was her general summing up.

It may have been that the haunting dread he came to have went back a very long time in the past. The dreamy, absent expression which often came into his deep-set eyes, the haunted look that shadowed his face, observed long before there was even a hint of the reason, may have been caused by the unspoken terror. Many times he spoke in a veiled, hinting manner of these things to us, though he never came right out in so many words. Not till his western visit in 1947 did he speak freely of the spectre, and then to another. Was it his fate one day to follow the long, black road under a crooked star?

One thinks back over certain known crises in Frost's life. There were the two infants who died on the Derry farm, one of which happenings drew forth the tremendous lines of "Home Burial." One recalls paragraphs out of letters when he was passing through tragedy—the death of Marjorie—and wonders if perhaps it might not have been another than Elinor who "would never be the same again." Greater than all else was the eclipse under which he passed when his wife died. Wandering about Boston, scarcely knowing where he was, caring even less, all hope faded. Surely this experience added semblance to the horrible monster his mind had created and his fancy nurtured.

It was to be expected that the poet should have something to say concerning his birthday celebration just over, held at Bernheimer's at Brentwood on the real day of his birth. Coming so closely on the heels of the one in San Francisco, there was opportunity for comparisons.

The only person I was at all interested in meeting, not having seen him before, and having read his books, was Gene Fowler. He of course writes for the fast crowd such as Earle had invited to the party. He knows the gang and so can write about them. He lives with them. But he writes very well indeed, and one doesn't think somehow of him as a part of the bunch he writes about.

What surprised me most in that three-blind-mice affair at Bernheimer's was the almost total absence of college and university people—I mean those connected in any way with schools. With the exception of your wife and Mood [who flew down from the University of California], I don't know of another college person who was there. I had expected surely that he would have invited the English departments of U.C.L.A. or Occidental or U.S.C. or some of the other colleges near at hand. He said he did invite somebody at U.C.L.A. whose secretary (mind you this professor didn't even respond himself) replied that she wasn't sure if he could make it or not. Do you suppose it's from all this front-page scandal Earle goes through that makes college people stay away from his parties.

The crowd that came to the Mark Hopkins was more like what such a crowd should have been. Plenty of writers and no end of college and university people. Nothing wrong could be found with the grub at Bernheimer's party. Plenty of it and all of it good.

I wish you and Earle hadn't had that set-to about your taking me home right from the party instead of waiting till next morning. Your idea was good but ill placed. After you told me you had spoken to him, he came to me saying, "Louis's got ants in his pants about the long drive from Redlands" and that you didn't want to come back for me the next day. Then he added, "But if you want to go—" leaving it up in the air like that. I can't stand having my friends get mad about things like that, and fall out. So I went on up to bed and lay there waiting for hours and hours for Mood to show up. I wanted to talk. He was down refereeing the fight I suppose, after you left.

Not quite a fight, but as near one as you could come and not have it. Two of the guests got to holding a champagne-inspired argument, threatening blows. Earle told them to go outdoors and shed their blood if they had to fight. He didn't want to mess up the rugs. Verone, as you know, doesn't drink. Earle drinks a great deal—but he seems able to carry his liquor. He keeps inveighing against Hollywood, but he's never very far away from it. It was a strange crew he had at the party—Jews, gentiles, businessmen, actors, editors, insurance men—but no college men. I never cared for that sort of life he lives. I was never to a night spot in my life till once in New York Earle took me. They all seemed to know him and got him the best table money could corrupt. I can only stand so much of that sort of thing. I enjoyed being in his home all right, but it wouldn't take me long to get fed up on all that splendor.

I didn't make Earle too happy about his presents of the two pieces of luggage. Somehow I felt out of place with such fine bags. When the little boy came edging through the crowd trying to drag the presents for me (and the crowd) to see, I was flabbergasted. Next morning he kept wanting me to tell him how wonderful they were—*but* if they didn't suit, he'd exchange them—I told him one of them was all right but the other—well, I would like a different kind—he was a bit short. However, he exchanged them for me at no extra cost, I think.

I overheard a very interesting argument (egged on by stuff sold in bottles) between two lawyers, over how much Clarence Darrow shook down Loeb and Leopold in the famous murder case in Chicago. One said ten thousand, the other a hundred thousand dollars. The first one quoted Darrow's biography, the other said he knew a woman who had proof it was a hundred thousand, and she was right at the party. He went unsteadily and brought her. She was just as unsteady and to my mind just as reliable, dependable, as the others. She deposed it was a hundred thousand—no more—no less. Just then another called 'em all pikers and said it was a million. Nobody proved anything.

When you came to Beverly Hills to get me, while Earle and I were waiting for you to drive up I said, "Yonder he comes," for I knew your car, having ridden in it at Berkeley and San Francisco. He said no, "that's not his car." I can't say just what he must have been looking for—maybe your old Plymouth you drove from Redlands to Bread Loaf six years ago. I said it was, too, your car. "It's a new Chevrolet, isn't it?" he asked. "Yes," I told him, "at least it looks like a new one." "But, they want twice what a new one is worth to sell one. He wouldn't pay that much." I suppose what he really wanted to say was you *couldn't* pay that much.

As in the case of his poetry, so in each of his talks Robert Frost expresses for us the varied interests he has retained over the decades, interests as wide as the range of human thought and civilization. There was seldom any writing of which he had nothing to say.

How did this master teacher go about assembling his ideas into a coherent address? Frost might have paraphrased his often repeated saying and put it that any speech he made began in a cloud of all the conversations he had ever carried on. Conversation was his testing ground of ideas. Immediately preceding a public address he would suddenly seem far away, growling, "We won't talk now!"

For a consideration, he had finally made a promise to deliver an address before the annual meeting of the Western College Association on the campus of the University of Redlands. Having made the commitment by letter, through K. M., he tried to get out of it when it drew near, and he was on the ground. His sponsor was adamant. That morning (the thing was a luncheon speech) as time began running out to the inescapable, he mumbled himself out of the house and started walking up and down the road out front, under the magnolia and palms. We were watering irises, and as he went forth he scarcely noticed us. The listener could hear him stalking and talking to himself as if life depended on the outcome. It didn't last long, was soon over, and he condescended to say a word (a banal statement by way of question, "watering a little?") as he came by along the driveway to get into the house. He had satisfied himself that he was ready for any eventuality. He was running true to form.

Having prepared himself to "stand" another public speech, he greeted the presidents and professors in a way that made his friends realize that all was well. Again Pan had found his pipes.

I don't know what I am expected to say, unless I try to be obscure. That's always a good approach in educational circles, obscurantism. I haven't asked if I should merely talk on poems. I suppose you have all been talking to each other on education, so I might say a word about that. I'm a sort of ten o'clock scholar.

The war, or something, seems to have stirred up the college presidents I have encountered lately to see if they can't think of something to do about the present status of education. I've got a few cases I could mention without giving names. I could bring up a few who might lay claim to measurable good. Those appear to have hold of both ends.

But, let me say, the first thing the principles of education and pedagogy make me think of is that episode Bret Harte used in one of his poems, where the argument arises between Jones and Brown "That broke up the society upon the Stanislaus." Now it seems that Brown, digging around on his claim, had come upon some bones which he proceeded to reconstruct, claiming them to be the bones of some animal "That was extremely rare." Then, as Harte puts it:

"But Jones he asked the chair for a suspension of the rules,
Till he could prove that those same bones were one of his lost mules."

I'm afraid when we get all through with this matter of education, when all the dry bones we come upon have been stirred up in a cloud of atomic or cosmic or more mundane dust, we may find we've been trespassing on "Jones's family vault." But we must go warily here. This contains high explosives.

The congregation of college officials gave rapt attention to the master poet as he revealed a refreshing philosophy of education, touching upon broad horizons and the manifestations of both humor and wisdom. Moving into the realm of science, he went on:

Awhile ago I said something about science and that I looked kindly on it. I'll just make a little fun of it though, right here. It's all in one of my late evil poems, entitled "Why Wait for Science?" It's a sonnet of a sort. You see a sonnet is composed of 14 lines, no more, no less. It goes along for eight lines, and after the eighth line it takes a turn for the better—or the worse [and here he quoted the eight lines, and following them the remaining six].

After the science poem he said he'd say another "evil one." He chose the bitter, but perfectly true four lines, "U.S. 1946 King's X." Others were as apropos—"Etherializing," "One Step Backward Taken," followed by some older ones including "Mending Wall," "The Road not Taken," and ending with "Choose Something Like a Star," and "Departmental."

The luncheon over and the inevitable pictures taken, he turned to us and said, "Now, I'm hungry. Let's go home and have some of that cold turkey left from last night."

Meeting to chat with a group of students as he did that evening in President Armacost's home was quite different. What repartee went on! What understanding of the problems of youth! What free and easy talk that followed the questions.

The four Armacost children, ranging from five to eleven years of age, waited patiently until the crowd had reluctantly gone away and then each one of them brought out a Frost poem that had carefully been copied for his signature. And he was very pleased to sign them.

At a guild meeting in Pasadena just before Frost came west, we sat at a table with John Gould Fletcher. He told us about Harvard's asking Frost to write the tercentennial ode for the college, and how he tried to write it but found himself unable to produce on order. Fletcher told us how Frost worried and fretted over it till he broke out in a rash and had to go to bed, being genuinely sick. He gave it up, and Harvard got somebody else to produce the ode.

His knowledge of Frost and his apparent admiration prompted us to ask him and his wife to come to a little party we were having for the New Englander after his lecture in Redlands. When I told all this to Robert on our way out from Brentwood, he scolded.

"I wish you hadn't done that—hadn't asked him. He's one of my bitterest enemies. Has done me a lot of harm. But, now it's over, so we'll make the best of it, bad bargain as it is. We'll just pretend. But he'll be unhappy. He's a disappointed man. He can't stand seeing somebody else in the limelight.

For his part Fletcher had told us of being in London at the time of the first appearance of Frost's books—his two first books. He seemed well sure of his grounds when he related the story.

"During those days I was around London a great deal. I remember seeing a manuscript copy of 'The Death of the Hired Man' on Ezra Pound's desk. It is, as you say, certain this was between the reading of the proofs of *A Boy's Will* and its issuance. Or it was given to him shortly after. Pound wrote a review of *North of Boston* more than a year later, a year and a half perhaps, in which he told of showing 'The Death of a Hired Man' to an American publisher who would have none of it, giving as an excuse that he had printed a poem about a hired man two months before.

"I remember a very fulsome review that Edward Thomas wrote of Ezra Pound before Thomas went away to war. I also know that he came to regret this review, and wished he might recall it.

"Funny thing the way my path and Frost's keep crossing. We ran onto him in Florida in 1936 just before his wife died. He never seemed to be able to get over the shock of her passing. Again we saw him in 1942 in Florida. He was badly broken up then. His son Carol had just died.

"I saw Frost just after he had given up the writing of that Harvard ode I mentioned to you. He had taken a case of hives worrying over it, broke out all over, and gave the whole thing up. Harvard got Hermann Hagedorn to write the ode. I wonder why he, Frost, never thought to use the one beginning 'We have been three hundred years on our cisatlantic shore,' or the one about our being 'the land's before the land was ours.' "

Knowing his disappointment over the crowd gathered at Brentwood, we went to the other extreme, just to please him. There were two college presidents and a number of college professors invited. Fletcher was the only poet of world renown who was bidden, though Edward Weismiller, a youngster just gaining fair recognition for free verse, asked to be present. He wanted to talk with Frost about a chance he had to become a Rhodes scholar. He had studied under Frost someplace. He came and talked his problem over with the guest of honor who advised against his going to Oxford.

Nobody present ate with better appetite than our distinguished guest. Through with his "reading" in public, he lived up to his own assurance to us that after the lecture he would be "festive and hungry."

The former lion of the imagist movement sat glum and silent, dark as a thunder cloud, throughout the evening. He had driven directly to our home, skipping the lecture at the university. Frost did his best to be friendly with him. It was not to be. The "disappointed man" sat in the vortex of a happy, milling crowd of Frost admirers crowding around the man of the hour—and of the ages—looking for all the world like an inarticulate Buddha, cigarette ashes spilling down the front of his vest, choosing thus to wrap himself in a cloak of sphinxian gloom.

Frost was saddened as he remembered that evening, when in May, 1950, his quondam rival was drowned in a shallow pool, or millpond in his own yard.

XXVIII. To the Edge of the Woods

Moved by memories, some dismal, some gay, Frost found himself once again with an inclination to consider making his home in California. He was anxious for a look at our desert, curious about Lake Arrowhead and Big Bear, in a stew to get down to Palm Springs.

It was patently flattering that all this came to pass while he was our guest at "Far Hills." We even took credit for the change. Foolish thought! California might enthrall him, the climate might be what he desired most, but neither ourselves nor the weather had weight to swing his decision.

"I'm a wanderer," he blurted out. "Maybe one day I'll come out here to live." We could scarcely believe our ears. It was incredible that he could actually consider leaving New England.

Again in his mind he was hiding from something, or planning to. He was plainly, though vainly, seeking to leave trouble in the distant past or place miles between it and himself. Forever he came back to a wish to see Palm Springs, having heard and read so much about it. "I'd love to have a look at the place from curiosity," he said.

Now Palm Springs was but an easy hour's drive from our home. The day was pleasant, the ride exhilarating. Clouds hung about the bases of the three massive peaks—Gorgonio, Jacinto, and Bernardino. Above, as we saw from our lowland cloudlessness, the sky was greenish-blue. We could glimpse through rifts in the cloud banks snowy masses clinging to the mountain slopes.

He wanted to know all about the mountains—the names of the peaks, the location of the watersheds, how they were affected by forest fires, and how the water came through the mountains to irrigate our orange groves.

The deciduous orchards on the hill slopes made the terrain more after his knowledge than any so far encountered. He was never hesitant about the trees, about what each orchard consisted of.

"These are apricots—leaves all out," and so on. It was almost the same with the desert flora and fauna. We thought of Monrovia, Laguna, San Francisco, Bread Loaf, and Hanover, of all the places we had walked together. His keen eye took in everything, his observation was equal to his intellectual curiosity.

On the northern slopes of San Jacinto, desert sand had drifted in, forming long, undulating yellowish lines. He made us stop so he could see the spectacle at close range, and we clambered over the drifts, our shoes filling with sand. As we stood and looked, the phenomenon became a shifting, changing cinema, the desert winds swirling the soft sand into new lines.

Now, here. Who can tell. Maybe I'll come to California to live. I could winter in Palm Springs, spend my summers in Redlands. If I didn't care to go to the beach I could stay here on the sand and imagine water and wave. The only catch is the distance back east. I would want to go in March to my maple-sugar making. If I could only get used to flying. The time across the continent by rail is too great, though a lot less than it took me to make my first trip sixty-two years ago.

I've been feeling around, asking Mood and a lot of others to find a place for Morrison. If they could come out here to teach, then I could settle and be content. It oughtn't to be hard to get him a place. You've lots of colleges out here. Morrison knows Freshman English the way F.D.R. knew fireside chats. I shouldn't get homesick for a college with all you have in the SOUTHLAND. Maybe I ought to take a vacation from colleges.

From all I hear about Palm Springs, having lived so long around Miami, I would likely feel at home. They say Hollywood has invaded. Well, it has marched into Miami too. But we're not altogether dependent on the movie stars. We have an added attraction. We've the duke and duchess. We get mighty tired of reading what Wally wears to keep up her reputation as four of the ten best-dressed women. The two come over from the island occasionally to shove Hollywood back into its place. What she buys, whom they invite to parties, what everybody wears. Just as bad as Hollywood, and every bit as tiresome in print. Of course one doesn't have to read, only in self defense. Something might be slipped over on you if you didn't read. Bad news is better than no news.

Arriving at Palm Springs, he said we'd walk around and see the town and observe the people. Still seeking the ivory man Fletcher had given him when he was a little boy, he would have us go into every curio shop, every antique store, gaze into every window. His answer concerning what we were seeking was, "Old Indian things."

He wanted a keepsake to send Kay Morrison, but we never found just what he liked. He sent her a wire, we got a picture post card for her, and he sent her an air-mail letter. "I always draw a heavy line and make little doodles around these letters and mark them air mail," he told us. Getting a stamp for the air letter at the post-office window he was uneasy when the girl told him "Five cents." He made her weigh it. "Are all you New Englanders suspicious?" she laughed. "No, just cautious," was his answer.

"Why do they call it Palm Springs? Out here is only desert—no palms, no springs. I have always pictured it as a lovely tropical town, a great gurgling fountain in an oasis surrounded by date-bearing palms." I told him it was named from Palm Canyon, or else from the muddy springs of warm water in the town controlled by Indians. I said we'd drive out to the canyon later. There we found scraggly palms and some water. No Indians.

"Far Hills" stands at the edge of the woods that is Smiley Heights. We gave it that name because of ridge after ridge stretching away toward the sunset horizon.

Robert had scarcely arrived before he strolled out through the grove, comparing oranges with apples.

"We always tried to make a dollar clear on every tree," he said.

He asked endless questions. Oil, or chemicals, used in weed control fascinated him. His queries were all of a practical nature: Would it work in Florida? Was in costly? Would it increase the fire hazard?

He enjoyed looking down into the canyon where the blackberry bushes were climbing jungle fashion. When he sent his 1949 Christmas card, he remembered it all in his greetings scrawled across the top: "For the Mertinses in their grove by the deep ravine."

If you two had looked the world over, you'd never have found a place equal to this, not anywhere. It suits you perfectly. Such a home about tempts me to think of California again. Here you are, out of the world—almost out of the world. No neighbor crowding up against you. No traffic problem. And as quiet a place as could be.

Now I can stand just so much of city life. Not that I don't like cities. There are a number of great cities I like very much—feel very much at home in. But after all I'm a simple farmer. I can live just so many days in an atmosphere such as we found at Brentwood. Then I've got to get out —out like this. Somebody has talked about my seeking to probe the infinities for God, starting by probing the infinities of man, and from such a start go forward to probe the infinities of the universe. Well, a place like this is a good one to start it in, though I'm not one to play off seeing God in nature. I'm no pantheist.

I think one of the things that has stayed by me best in reading is the story of Evangelist in *Pilgrim's Progress* who asked Pilgrim, "Do you see yonder shining light?" and received the reply, "I think I do." To merely go on the assumption that he *thought* he saw the light was enough, no more needed. That answers everything for me. Just to *think* I see it. There's no room for dogmatism. I'm of such an opinion about God. Since you can't see him, how are you going to know him? Suppose we just continue with Pilgrim and *think* we see the shining light. Not much room for dogmatism in the world for us.

Fulmer Mood in his introduction to *The Intervals* described "Far Hills" as being "a ranch house which stands on the northern slope of Smiley Heights overlooking California's San Bernardino Valley. From the library window on the second story an amazing sunlit panorama opens out before the eye—rows of orange trees in the foreground, the broad sweep of the valley's floor in the middle distance, and beyond the massive brown bulwark of rocky crags beneath a brilliant sky."

It was to be expected that Robert Frost should like it, feel at home in and around it. "I always prefer a timber house," he said, and then added, "With natural beauty like this why do people spend time on formal gardens?"

Finished with speechmaking and social functions, there was now time to enjoy the hours in quiet contemplation, and we turned with him to the woods. Smiley Heights has been noted in the annals of California for decades as a place of pilgrimage. When the Smiley Brothers (whose portraits looking like cough-drop advertisements adorn the walls of the Redlands Smiley Library) were alive, they kept the many miles of winding roads, bordered with exotic trees, shrubs and plants, towering and flowering, open to the public. As time went on this became a financial strain on the heirs. The city refused to come to their aid, whereupon the gates were locked. Friends, however, still had permission to walk through the woods and enjoy the trees and vistas. These trees, imported from every part of the globe, grow in semitropic profusion.

The trees were lovely, the woods almost dusk, for the sun was westering. Ferns, palms, shrubs, and trees of every sort attracted our guest. Being a thorough botanist, and no mean horticulturalist, he shamed us for our ignorance. Below in San Timoteo Canyon the Southern Pacific wound its snakelike way southeastward. A hundred-car train struggled with two engines, one fore, one aft, up the long grade. The poet hurried to the clearing at the canyon's edge in fear he might miss it. He watched it until the last car was hidden among crawling foothills in the distance.

A broken water pipe attracted him, and we had trouble getting him past it. The water gushing out upon the ground seemed such a waste to him. Why didn't the people in the big house there come and fix it?

After walking a short distance, Robert suddenly broke out with the ballad:

> "O my father was the keeper of the Eddystone light,
> And he slept with a mermaid one fine night,
> And out of the union there came three,
> The porpoise and the Tortoise and the other was me."

He sang well, with a clear voice and a fine sense of sound and tone. After this one came "Go Tell Aunt Rhody." When I told him as children we sang it "Aunt Phoebe," he agreed that was just as good a name. He told us the lines, "Died in a millpond, standing on her head," were written thus because geese would dive for food in the pond and the turtles would catch hold of their heads and hold them under water till they were drowned.

At that moment the Little Willie quatrains were in general vogue. Frost started quoting some of the best.

> "Little Willie hanged his sister,
> She was dead before we missed her.
> Willie does such clever tricks.
> Ain't he cute—he's only six.

> "Little Willie wrote a book.
> Woman was the theme he took.
> Woman was his only text.
> Ain't he cute, he's over-sexed."

The piquancy of a great philosopher-poet saying this doggerel, rushing swiftly, as he always did, through the last line, was most refreshing.

At meal times his love for simple things was evidenced in his eating. For breakfast he only wanted a large glass of orange juice, in which he dropped a raw egg—and he insisted on squeezing the juice himself to try out a new gadget. For lunch he called for scrambled eggs, providing "I can come out and tell you when to take them off the stove. Most people cook them too long." And when we sat down to a supper of steak and mealy boiled potatoes he said, "This is just what I have been wanting."

Sitting in the twilight he is thinking of the long ago days on the Derry farm. He muses:

> On a farm one thinks clearly. There is time for ripened thought in a garden, in a hayfield. Out in the meadow, or the woods, or the orchard, there is nothing to distract. You are away from all the noise and bustle. We had a hard time on the farm at Derry; but it all turned out for our good. I have always been thankful that I took that road instead of going to New York as a youngster as they wanted me to do. I now look back with pleasure even upon the struggles and hardships we endured. It makes me understand what Vergil meant in his famous saying, "I remember with pleasure all these little things."

The time had come for the restless wanderer to move on. He packed his things in the new birthday bags. "If I have left anything, it's yours," he said. He had been interested in Ignatius Donnelly's *Atlantis,* found on the bookshelf in his room. We gave it to him to finish on the train as he traveled to Denver. As we climbed into the car, he looked up at the house for the last time and voiced one of his rare compliments: "The loveliest home I was ever in."

Trains were coming and going, for San Bernardino is on the main trunk lines of two great roads to Chicago and Kansas City. Luggage entrusted to a porter, we chatted until Robert's train was called. When he entered his compartment he could find no baggage. The porter, too late, had discovered he had put it on the wrong train! Robert was beside himself with anger. "The God damned fool, the God damned fool," he kept crying over and over as we ran after the departing train with a wild poet who had our assurance that we would see he got his baggage.

When he reached Boulder (his bags were put on the train sometime during the night), he was full of his experiences. Charlie Foster relayed his conversation, one sided.

I had a good time, but I don't think I'd ever care to go back to Berkeley, but I may change my mind. Things were pretty strenuous, what with Governor Warren, Historian Freeman and all the rest.

It was at the president's mansion on the occasion of the Charter Day luncheon that the governor tried to put me on the spot. He looked down on me (he being on a higher physical plane) with a sort of evil eye as a renegade son of California and wanted to know how I ever came to leave my native state anyway. I was on the spot.

"I went out very young," I apologized. "I was carried out screaming." I got out of that one.

Later Frost had a word to say about degrees in general.

You know that man Truman from Missouri started another new fashion in honorary degrees. He released the story of the doctor's degree from Cal before hand, when it is generally agreed that such things are kept secret until the victim appears on the platform—releasing the news is just not done. Somebody said that Harry called their hand while the thing was being talked over at the university. I don't know. One thing about Harry: he doesn't conform to the inconsequentialism of social and polite usage. That's why so many people swear by and at him, I take it.

Frost returned to Cambridge, Dartmouth, and the Homer Noble farm, but he kept thinking about certain things—little things but interesting. The broken water pipe, the glumness of John Gould Fletcher, the "Hollywood in the desert," as he called Palm Springs, the foolishness of his two collectors, and the stroll through Smiley Heights—invited.

In his busy running to and fro—Ripton to South Miami and back again with many stops—he paused long enough to write at least two of his infrequent letters. These still breathed of California.

The first came from Box 100, Route 2, South Miami, Florida.

DEAR MERTINS:

You will forgive me if I find myself a little tired of some of the incidentals of poetry. I have about decided to give myself a rest from collecting and autographing. After all it is better not to be made too self-conscious about reputation. Sproul told me frankly his only interest in sticking to me to get me out there lay in your *Intervals*. That should be gratification enough for you. I assume it was a good book, but I barely steal sidelong glances at books about myself. And as you may suppose I am more concerned with ideas about my poetry than with facts about my properties and publication dates. Oh well, I don't deny the innocence of your pleasure in these.

Your tributes to me of California oranges warm my heart. They would be like coal to Newcastle if sent to me here among these Florida oranges. It would be better not to send on any for a month or two. Wouldn't it be fine if you made the national broadcasting network? But we must always remember, I was going to say the flight of November—I mean the vanity of this world's glory. The walks about your house were more to me than most things in my travels.

Ever yours,

FROST

The second was written at Ripton, Vermont, dated June 16, 1947.

DEAR MERTINS:

Lets see, what were we saying or doing when interrupted? Was it anything connected with the big leak in the water pipe in the big estate where we three walked by permission that last evening? Was I saying that as a Yankee from Vermont I could hardly bear such a waste of water in what I looked on as a desert waste? I may have been saying something about the evil. Characteristically I was doing nothing. I should have marched right up to the big house and spoken up for action. Wait long enough and you may see me get elected to Congress on purpose to tell Truman about Russia. (Wait long enough.)

Or, was I thanking you in advance, American style, for the oranges you were going to send? You sent them and I am now thanking you in arrears. I've squeezed the last drop out of them and we've drunk your health and our own many times over the juice. Now I owe you a *Steeple Bush* if I didn't before.

I had a dazing time in California. I still feel somewhat knocked on the head. It's fun to be made of, but rather dubious to be made of for your age. It balances up on the bad side for the ego. I wish I were a lady so it wouldn't be polite to talk about how old I was. I mean it. We'll have no more of that please. Find something else to talk about. There should be plenty for a resourceful old Chataqua [*sic*] campaigner.

I have a book set aside for you till I get myself wrapping paper and string together to ship it. I'm home where I can get my letters written for me. (I shouldn't be writing this one by rights), but I'm too considerate a gentleman to let a lady perform the manual labor of doing up my parcels. But I grow lazier and lazier I sometimes think. I have always had a pretty bad conscience about my laziness.

My bag turned up late at night—at Barstow, perhaps. The Union Pacific took the best care I ever had taken of me be it of record. So did you and your wife, good 'cess to you.

R. F.

He never got himself "wrapping paper and string together," so we never had the special copy of *Steeple Bush* which he had promised. Meanwhile we managed to wangle one from the publishers, which later on he inscribed, having, which was unusual for him, evidently forgotten his promise of the one laid aside.

XXIX. WILFUL HOMING

IT HAS OFTEN COME TO US the propriety of Amherst as the capital of the Frost country—the seat of the Jones Library, whose presiding genius, Charles R. Green, so long and so faithfully, posterity in mind, looked after the bibliographical interests of the poet. Hereabout once lived and labored Lexicographer Noah Webster; here he accomplished the task of lifting the boys and girls of a far-flung frontier into literacy; here he vocabularized the American language for two future Amherst poets and one essayist, for use as a vehicle for thought. The first of the poets was Emily Dickinson, Frost the second. Nor does it seem unfitting that this should once have been the home of the author of "Little Boy Blue," an orphan knocking about in strange places.

Ancient buildings of brick and stone sprawl in the sunlight. The antiquated Amherst College chapel, suggesting a country school to which Robert might have gone to classes as a boy, the conglomerate architecture, the rolling hills of the countryside, the alternate spaces of grass and bare earth—all these things struggle together to make up Amherst College and Amherst village. Perhaps the thwarted spirit of Philosopher Meiklejohn walks abroad here, eased of his frustration for the moment, exulting and repeating the words which have greeted one in whatever place friends of Robert Frost have met together—"Frost is going back to Amherst!"

Under the historic elms of Princeton, a rival chronicler of Frost's life beamed the news. In his three-hundred-year-old house at Middletown, a former governor of Connecticut, poet, teacher, lifelong friend of Frost's blurted it out. At Hanover an early champion, still after forty-five years his enthusiastic apologist (the friend who wrote a blurb that became a classic), proudly proclaimed it. Echoes were heard in every conversation on poetry even in faraway William and Mary.

All the years of his exile from Amherst, Robert had chafed. It wasn't that he was not well cared for at Harvard, later at Dartmouth. The Cambridge interval may have seemed unstable in the oft-shifting of the poet in residence, but the Hanover interval was one of security, seeming and real. Still he always remembered Amherst. The year was 1949.

> I'm going back to Amherst. A lot of people have been stirred up over the way Stanley King treated me. They've been doing some good fifth-columning. They were all ready—Mrs. Dwight Morrow, George Whicher, and the rest—when Charlie Cole became president. Charlie knew me when he was a student at Amherst a long while back.
>
> It has never been much of a secret that I didn't get on well with King. He made a lot of attempts on my self-respect. He looked on me as an old skeezix who was just so much impedimenta. One winter when I was down in Florida he ran down and came over to see me at Gainesville. That was a case where the single word "now," properly emphasized, decided my fate, sealed it. I had been sick a good deal and was apologetic accordingly. "I'm afraid I've caused you a lot of worry and trouble, King," I said, before he had a chance to bring it up. I tried to beat him to the punch and led

with a left. "You see I've been sick and away from Amherst most of the time." He waved his hands with a sideways shoulder-shrug, and said, "We won't talk about that *now*!" His "now" in speech italics decided me. I resigned right away. I didn't wait to be fired. He couldn't fire me. I quit.

Going back to Amherst under Cole, with a job promised for as long as I live, is a vindication. When they offered me the job I said to a friend, "I believe I'll turn it down and not go back at all." I just said that. Right away I accepted quick before they could change their minds. I was like a girl with a ring in her eye. I said yes right off.

My roots sink pretty deep at Amherst. I've never quite cut them loose. I suppose no other place I've lived is more closely tied up with my life. My work there was more than just touch and go. Of course I don't know just what lasting impression I made there. None of us *know* that, just guess. Then, don't forget, I'm like an Indian at heart. I've a mean streak in me, and never forget a wrong. I take delight in winning out. My father in San Francisco was to blame. He used to egg me on to fight other boys, so that we would pummel one another till we were both knocked silly, half out. I still like to stick my tongue out at my opponent and say, "Yeah, yeah!" I still want the world to be perfect at last, if not a little before.

I don't own the house at Amherst where I lived during the thirties. Sold out to the college. They rent it to some professor in need of housing. I'm told there are a lot of people in that pickle these "Fair Deal" days. I always liked our home there, but I don't need a house in Amherst village. I can stay at the Lord Jeffery. Good hotel.

I don't know why I should worry about this college or that. Somebody the other day told me about a philanthropist who had given a good-sized sum to found a new college. It was money he had in some way, some un-disclosed manner, managed to salvage from the clutches of the New Dealers. He probably hadn't thought the whole thing through, and didn't realize what he was doing, giving money to start another college. Bad business. George Whicher said a good thing about my college connec-tions awhile ago. He said it was just like a bunch of monkeys with a basket in their cage containing a snake. The monkeys can't keep away from the basket to save their lives, but the minute they get close enough to it to endanger themselves, they run for dear life, only to come sneak-ing back.

The opportunity for Frost to return to Amherst came with the inauguration of his old friend and student, Charlie Cole, as president. In June of 1948, he was called back to the college where he and seven other distinguished Americans received doctor's degrees.

When Robert stood before the eleven hundred faculty members, alumni, seniors, and friends of Amherst that June day and talked on loyalties, he was establishing a new basis for loyalty. He had just returned from helping Cole and Whicher inaugurate an old Amherst grad, Walter Hendricks, president of a brand-new college—one he had encouraged with promises some years earlier. It was a shoestring venture, but Frost was always friendly toward the forlorn hope.

It was a promising thing that his return to Amherst should have seen him still in the role of Pan. He bantered Olympos in their loyalties, their attachments, and their attractions. He called himself "a bastard Vermonter." He poked fun at himself for a nonexistent loyalty to his native state of California and took a few digs at the governor who couldn't carry his own state in a vice-presidential race. He stormed at goings-on on Capital Hill, in a veiled sort of way. "Somebody said I didn't have to talk politics—they shone out of me."

In that talk Frost went back to the early days—his very early days— at Amherst, when Hendricks was Bond Prize winner in 1917. The philosopher was then president; George Whicher was considered new on the faculty; Stark Young was professor of English, associated with Whicher and Everett Glass. Frost, in that alumni address, recaptured some of the newness of things at the old college in the days when Meiklejohn was busying himself with building an unusual faculty. Now the philosopher was far away by the Pacific, his still small voice hushed or unheard in the clamor. Most of the old faculty were distant from the scene.

Frost later expressed it that on this special occasion he was taking the opportunity to kick up his heels a bit. It was the feeling of being vindicated—putting one over on Stanley King—which occasioned this heel kicking. There was a pardonable pride-taking in the simple, sincere citation for the degree given him.

Poet, philosopher and beloved teacher. Four times winner of the Pulitzer Prize for poetry and the recipient of other honors and distinctions without number, at three different periods for a total of eighteen years professor at Amherst college. Your works published over the last 35 years, from *A Boy's Will* to *A Masque of Mercy,* have made you America's foremost poet. But to us at Amherst you are more than that, for you have taught generations of Amherst students that for gaining an insight into life a metaphor is a sharper and brighter instrument than a syllogism.

He was preparing for a return to old scenes, for close association with old friends, and he could not properly associate with them if he wasn't informed on what they had been up to in his absence.

One gets a glimpse of Frost in the house of the president—the Coles out of town before time had come for the visitor to depart—listening avidly as the Negro "hired girl" tells what this and that family of both town and gown has been up to, the conversation going on into the night. Frost was always the undeniable democrat. To use his own phrase he was "more or less classless." Negro hired girl, important editor, fellow poet, great financier, Catholic Cardinal, world-renowned philosopher, profound pundit, or simple farmer—he was as much at home with one as with the other.

There were skeletons from Amherst closets amiably rattled in prexy's house that night, for there had been secrets in Amherst garrets since Emily Dickinson hid her own away from sight. The inquirer intended no evil to come of his knowledge. He just wanted to know.

This utter democracy which was Frost's greatest asset he himself perfectly expressed in his own doggerel,

> *High brow, low brow,*
> *Middle brow, no brow.*

"That's my poor middle-brow or low-brow notion of loyalty—not *no*-brow, I won't grant that," he once put it.

Memory recurs of another occasion where that utter democracy was so perfectly demonstrated.

A friend had taken him to lunch. While his host was paying the check, Robert went out the door, starting for the car. The friend hurried to catch him with the information that the waitress had asked if his guest were not Robert Frost, adding that she would like to meet him.

"Well, what the hell are we waiting for?" said Frost, and turned back to meet her.

XXX. Ah, When to the Heart of Man

Going back to Amherst to become Simpson Lecturer in Literature meant going away from Dartmouth. Friends, very old friends, must be left behind.

A Dartmouth picture comes to mind, where R. F. and Gillie were at stage center—the long lane southward from Hanover, the Connecticut rolling away on the right, the hills rising abruptly and humping away to the left. Yonder ahead, striding a purposeful giant down the country lane on the way to Ray Nash's, master and dog appear to romp together. We drew the car to the roadside to allow the home-hurrier time to get there and become domiciled. One doesn't fluster Robert Frost twice. A burnt child dreads the fire.

The old rambling Nash house (so often and so long the poet's seasonal hideout) stood on a hill slope to the left of the highway. Going up the side drive, we entered the house from the back porch. Gillie was finishing his supper in the old-fashioned kitchen, with its huge coal range, his master hulking above him to see if he had given him enough.

"Go in and sit by the fire. I won't be long. We'll be ready to go in a minute. I've got to do a little changing."

A single log lies graying in the wide-open fireplace in the sitting room. The afternoon sun streams through the west window, falling warmlessly across the floor. Through the window we see patches of snow on north hillsides, in secluded spots along steep banks, in little hollows among the trees, right down to the shores of the river for all the early spring.

Now Robert was dressed and ready to be on the way.

"We're going to Hartford, across the river a ways. The hotel there puts up a good meal. We'll have supper and come back here to talk."

The strange old Colonial town with its sidewalks of broad, thick boards, worn by innumerable feet through unnumbered years; the warm comfortable hotel dining-room—these set the stage for a satisfying meal of thick beefsteak.

Given proper setting, Robert Frost entered into eating with gusto. He seldom drank anything stronger than very weak tea. Now and then friends have known him to join in a glass of sherry, on other occasions even a cocktail. Before dinner he asked if we would have something to drink, and when we declined, grinned: "We had enough at Bernheimer's to last awhile."

Usually we found that Robert preferred hotels to restaurants. "They have better food, and I always go to one when I can."

In the kaleidoscopic pictures which come to mind of the last days at Dartmouth, one remembers the little Cranston girl alone in the house, the phone ringing. "I answered," she said, "and heard a voice saying, 'This is Robert Frost. Is Louis Mertins there?' I was petrified. It was Robert Frost talking. I couldn't open my mouth or say a word for a minute. It was Robert Frost!"

One remembers sitting in the living room at the Nash house, Ray and Mrs. Ray, Robert, ourselves, the conversation that went on into the night, until the poet showed how tired he was. Gillie was lying at his master's feet.

> I never thought I could become attached to any animal the way I have to Gillie. I started in once to teach him to talk, and got on pretty well. He got so he could say , "Eat, eat," quite plain. Over at the Hanover Inn on the same floor with us was a poodle in one of the apartments. Knowing he was there, when we passed Gillie would bark out, "Eat, eat," growing very excited because of the dog safe on the other side of the door. This stirred the poodle up.
>
> I've got so I lie about Gillie's cleverness the way parents lie about their children, grandchildren. It is a proof of the affection of the affectionate. I'm as much concerned over Gillie as I could be over a child.

When we were ready to leave, Robert said he believed he would go along and walk back with Gillie. This was a ritual he observed every night, taking the collie out for a long walk. Gillie, too, had become "one acquainted with the night," with "the doctrine of excursions" that went along with nocturnal prowling. When we arrived at the Cranston home,

Gillie piled out from between his master's legs, obedient as always, and after a muted goodnight we saw the two move off in the darkness— two black figures in a moonless midnight.

How very many classes Frost must have kidded into knowledge the way he did a certain group those closing days at Dartmouth. Sidney Cox was the teacher.

These two had slipped away the previous day, running over to Ripton to see if the Homer Noble farm still stood under the shadow of the Green Mountains. Frost and his partner, Stafford Dragon, had manufactured sixty gallons of Vermont maple sirup from the trees on his three-hundred-acre farm that year. Sidney left a note of excuse on his door which read:

> *Honorable Honors Group*
> Unexpectedly leaving town,
> we'll meet Monday and try to arrange a substitute
> meeting.
> Sidney Cox

In pencil across the face of the card a member of the "Honorable group" had scribbled the old Dartmouth Indian yell, "Wa-hoo!"

Later with a group of students we heard him discuss poetry.

With proper respect for, and due deference to our new Nobel Prize-winning poet I should say that poetry must concern itself with form. You may want to break out of bounds, feeling bound to be in bonds. But you'll come back to the norm which forever is form. Form is an essential, though sometimes it may be arrived at by accident. You take a piece of white paper and fling a drop of ink onto it. Nothing could be more without form and void than that drop of ink on the white space. If you will just bend the half sheet with its ink-splotch over onto the clean half and press it down while it is still wet and then open it, you will find you have produced a perfect symmetrical figure. The antiphonal lines make all the difference. Sidney has just muttered under his breath that this ink-flinging is used by psychologists, maybe by psychiatrists, as a test, and that it has a name— Rorschach blot. Well, maybe psychiatrists, of whom we have a great many too many, know what they're doing—maybe. When you do that sort of thing seriously, it proves *you* are crazy. I'm told Rorschach, its inventor, died in an asylum.

Going on, he expounded his opinions on "free verse" for those assembled, then shifted to a different tack.

I always think trueness better than truth. Trueness has a warmth about it. It's human. Stark truth is cold, frightening, unapproachable. It can be most inhuman.

> *We dance round in a ring and suppose,*
> *But the Secret sits in the middle and knows.*

I owe a lot to those who have made my road for me, who gave me my start in life, blazed my trees. But I won't have them telling me how I may walk on that road. If they're wise they'll go on and leave me be. I'll walk on it till I find another better, smoother or rougher. But that won't mean I don't owe them a debt, nor that I may not walk on it another day, even though I may be accused of imitating an imaginary earlier Robert Frost.

To hold students spellbound is not easy, not even possible for many, but there were no yawns that day at Dartmouth as the glow from the searchlight of his mind fell on poetry, philosophy, and science and ranged from Mother Goose to Bernard Shaw. His talk drew to a close:

Too many people are saying things and writing things when they've really nothing to say or write. I've found it a good plan when you know nothing about a certain thing to just keep still and say nothing.

So, we come down to this: Why write? Life and living are the things. I want life to go on living. Socrates never wrote anything. He had to depend on Plato and Xenophon who did good reporting jobs for him. Jesus never wrote a single paragraph that we know of, except a line with his fingers on the sand one day. So far as we know he never bothered to write anything down on skin or papyrus. He had to make his mark with a cross. After all—why write?

Outside, the sleepy old town of Hanover lay basking in the morning sun. Birds were singing in the trees that bordered the campus and climbed the slope toward the halls. In the Vale of Tempe the stillness was unbroken save by the chirp of sparrows and the occasional barking of a saucy red squirrel.

· 287

The poet was preparing to pull up stakes and move on; Amherst was calling. That college where he had been established so long was again to welcome him.

I plan to come back to Dartmouth every winter for a week or two. But my work from now on will be at Amherst. I'll no longer be George Ticknor Fellow in the Humanities at Hanover. I'll just be myself at Amherst, at least once in so often.

They've been nice to me at Dartmouth, couldn't ask anything better. They've been working me a great deal harder than usual since I've decided to call it quits. I've been willing to be used just because of leaving. I've always done just about as I pleased here in Hanover, never felt myself in logic bound to punch a clock—or watch a calendar. Once in awhile one of the professors would call me in to talk to his boys, maybe because he wasn't prepared for that day. I liked it. Sidney hasn't been the only one, nor English the only subject. Earl Cranston had me in a few times to talk to his religion classes, what there were of them. Rather dangerous, I should say, having a pagan like me to talk on religion, though some people, like Sidney, say I'm too religious to be a Christian. They mean, I suppose, that I'm no religionist according to either Catholic or Protestant patterns. I'm a free lance with God the way I am with college presidents, politicians. I've as many inconsistencies as a philosopher. For good measure I'll come back to Dartmouth this year [1949] for an extra week to gather up the thread ends. I've worked pretty hard here this spring, but I didn't mind it for these last few weeks.

A member of the faculty here at the college who runs a sort of three-ring circus wants me to talk to his class on my San Francisco boyhood. I'll have to think up all the wild west doings going on there seventy years ago, I guess. Maybe I'm supposed to bring along my two-guns. Two-gun Frost. Local color. Something like the way with people writing my biography, who sit round waiting for, and hoping for, me to do something like hold up a train or rob a bank so they can write it up.

XXXI. While the Customs Slept

WHEN WE FIRST MET FROST, collectors had not yet begun to pester him. There were requests now and then for signatures, for mere autographs, but so far as is known, except for the beginnings of the Jones Library (which never went in for inscriptions, but confined itself to first editions, magazine appearances, and manuscripts), there had been no major effort at amassing Frostana. In fact, not until *The Intervals of Robert Frost* came out in 1947 was the word "Frostana" used in a book as far as we know.

Very early (1932) Robert evinced a distaste for the entire pother of collecting, even before collectors started coming in platoons. It came up in conversation.

> You know this mail gets my goat. The teachers are largely at fault. They put the kids up to writing authors for autographs; and the kids, just at the age to misspell words (which some of them never outgrow) write: "We ben studing your poems and my projek is to get your signater." I despise to be insulted by having these dirty, misspelled letters, full of bad grammar, thrust under my nose by somebody who doesn't know poetry, never will know poetry, somebody who never can understand and love poetry. I'm a sort of raw convert to collecting, anyhow—if a convert. The Waterman people have egged the kids on to it, offering prizes and urging them to write brazenly and tell their victims they are working for a Waterman pen prize. Hard for me to cool off after just thinking about it. Nothing much more nettling.
>
> Of course when somebody writes me and shows he has read my things, and understood something about what I am driving at, if only a little understanding, I am always pleased and glad to sign for them. But there are limits to the thing. I feel about collectors and collections just as I feel about people interested in me and what I do and how I live. I want them to read and study my poetry, not myself. I'm transient—incidental. It's my poetry that counts. So I want people to buy and read my books, not just keep them for their dust-jackets. I had started to call them straightjackets, which wouldn't have been far wrong.

Encouraged by the many things he had sent out voluntarily (thus beginning for us a collection of his books and holographs), we went on from there until our collection had developed into one of the major amassments of Frostana. Then he had something to say about it.

> I don't mind signing things when you bring them to me in person,

so we can talk while I'm at it. It's being bothered by sitting down and signing a couple of hundred books, pictures, magazines, then finding corrugated pasteboard, paper and string, tying them up, addressing them, lugging them to the express office that worries me. It's the two-endedness of the thing that aggravates me, makes me a trifle grim.

I remember what a long time it took me to sign that cartload you sent me—was it in 1942? There must have been two hundred and so many of them. They lay on my study floor cluttering up the clutter. I'd give them a sidelong glance, and my heart would sink. Once when Bernheimer was there visiting me I said to him, "I've got to get after Mertins' things and get 'em signed and in the mail to him. I'll take a day off one of these times and have 'em over with." I wanted him to relay this information to you. I suppose I must have kept them on the floor gathering dust till around 1945 before I at last got at it. Even then some of 'em had got lost and you had to write a threatening letter and stir me up to get Kay Morrison to dig 'em out for me. I didn't get the last batch off till just before I went out to visit you in California in 1947. Was about time.

When Earl Cranston went to Dartmouth as Phillips Professor of Religion, we asked him to try to get some action by prodding R. F. into inscribing the hundreds of precious things already mentioned above as being in his possession at 35 Brewster. The two first met at a dinner party at the home of one of the professors. Frost showed the possession of psychic powers. He didn't wait for Earl to speak. "I suppose your friend Mertins has commissioned you to stir me up into signing the things he sent me. I've been thinking more and more about getting them signed. I have to get screwed up to do these things. They're all safe at Cambridge. Tell him not to worry. I'll get round to it in time. I've not forgotten."

In 1941, Frost started telling us about the Bernheimer Collection. His account whetted the appetite. Ordinarily one would have been content with something lesser had he not told of the greater.

When in 1937 the Jones Library at Amherst village brought out the book, *Robert Frost: A Bibliography,* by W. B. Shubrick Clymer and Charles R. Green, a change came over the poet in his attitude toward collectors and collections. The Jones Library (with which he was later to find himself at occasional loggerheads) set aside the Frost Room and gathered together one of the finest Frost collections. Now and then he mentioned various bibliographies, published and unpublished, usually with slight evaluation of their worth; but he always seemed proud of the Clymer-Green volume. When, in 1932, he went to the Huntington Library to see the various manuscripts of his poems lost in the vast and all-inclusive collections there, he said of the manuscript of his first published poem that it was a shame to have it preserved.

On this visit we discussed our William Jewell Collection in which he had always expressed interest. It was covered in the holograph will, in doggerel verse (one hoped in a humorous vein) which he signed as witness.

Again we found ourselves discussing collections. He said there was a man, a very rich man, who, like A. Edward Newton, collected Johnsoniana, but who also had a very extensive Frost collection.

This fellow invited us to see his collections, my own and old Sam's. The latter, of course, made up the larger design and the most expensive. He lived in a Chicago suburb. I found that he kept the things in a huge vault, underground, fireproof walls and ceiling. It was in the basement under his house. He had just about everything by and about Sam Johnson. After we had seen the things and were being driven to the station, his wife (much younger than her husband) kept telling me that Johnson was the greatest writer that ever lived. I kept denying and she kept affirming. Finally she gave as her last and clinching proof that her husband owned everything Johnson had ever written and everything that he had ever had written about him. I gave up. You can't meet manufactured evidence like that. We were just going round in a silly circle.

It was after the change of attitude toward collections had come that he told us the history of the Bernheimer Frostana.

It is common experience that most famous writers are careless about the disposal of their first-draft manuscripts. Up to a certain point in Frost's life, he thought little or nothing of what was to become of his written poems and prefaces. The change came when money matters pressed, occasioned, perhaps, by the crying needs of his immediate family. It all started, in the case of poet vs. collector, with a letter in which

Frost told Bernheimer that he would be glad to sell him the preface to E. A. Robinson's *King Jasper,* and other manuscripts. But he hastened to add, "I don't want to bother you with these matters."

Under date of November, 1938, he wrote the collector another letter. "I know all about your fine collection, and of course want to do anything I can to help you." Thus was opened the negotiation for the sale and purchase of rare books and manuscripts. A year later we find Frost suggesting to his admirer that he "might not be able to refuse serious money for *Twilight."* In January, 1940, the deal appears to have been consummated, one of the rarest of modern literary items passing into private hands.

Two and one-half years went by. On August 8, 1942, he wrote the collector: "I am enclosing the first draft of a prose preface I have written for a group of poems K. M. and I have selected for an anthology of American prose and verse made by Whit Burnett, editor of *Story Magazine*. There are very few of my absolutely first drafts in existance [*sic*], —as I suppose you know."

On October 1 of the same year he wrote Bernheimer that "Lesley has recovered the manuscript of *A Witness Tree* from the Library of Congress, and you shall have it very soon." On the manuscript he has written: "This becomes the property of Earle Bernheimer on the twentieth day of November, nineteen hundred and forty-two. Given under the hand of his November Guest, Robert Frost, New York City."

Two years later another book manuscript passed into the collector's possession. On May 26, 1944, a red and black notebook—cloth, fabricoid, red corners, pages lined, containing the play, *A Masque of Reason,* became Bernheimer's.

The collector confessed once that he had gone East prepared to pay just twice as much for *Twilight* as Frost asked. But, he said, he was making it up to him by sending him a subsidy of two or three hundred dollars a month for all the manuscripts Frost would send him.

"He has grown very canny and cagey with the years," the patron told us. "He nearly starved to death once in his life, and he has no intention of doing it again."

Years later Frost was to make denial of selling *Twilight,* or anything else, saying he had been given large gifts and was reciprocating. In whatever manner the book passed into new hands, the inscription on the fly appears in the form of a will.

"I had two copies of Twilight printed and bound by a job printer in Lawrence, Mass. in 1894 probably out of pride in what Bliss Carman and Maurice Thompson had said about the poem in it called My Butterfly. One copy I kept for myself and afterward destroyed. The other I gave away to a girl in St. Lawrence University to show to her friends. It had no success and deserved none. But it unaccountably survived and has lately leaped into prominence as my first first. A few scattered lines in it are as much mine as any I was ever to write. I deliver it into your custody my dear Bernheimer with the last request that you be not too fondly selfish with it, consent to lend it once in a long time to some important exhibition of my works as at the Jones Library in Amherst or the Baker Library at Dartmouth. Boston, February 1, 1940, Robert Frost."

Frost often said to Earl Cranston at Dartmouth, when that long-suffering colleague of his was seeking to have him sign dozens of items for a certain collector, that he could never understand why collectors of his stuff should go to such lengths to pick up every little item and then worry about having each one signed, when they all made up such a conglomeration of insignificances.

When in our home he asked if we had a book containing Bret Harte's poem "Truthful James." We went to the library passing first the section containing signed first editions. He flared up. "That's the trouble with you damned collectors. You think more of the signature than of the book. I want a book to get a quotation out of. Just where, if you own any, do you keep your usable books?" Later at the luncheon table he said to a guest, with malice prepense for our benefit:

> Collecting is the lowest form of literary appreciation. Very low. A fellow came to me with four copies of my earlier books, old but "in pristine condition," "mint copies," as it were. I cringe at the memory of it. These books all had their dust jackets on just like new—little kittens that hadn't lost their mittens. Those dust jackets were what caught this old duffer.

After I had signed the books he hesitated a minute and asked if I would mind doing more than just sign my name. I was in a liberal mood that day, so I told him to leave them and I would write something in addition to the signature. He started to go away but thought better of his property and came back saying, "I'll just take these dust wrappers with me. They might get soiled." You see, he wasn't a poetry lover, nor a book lover. He wasn't even a book collector. He was just a collector of dust jackets, and took the book because it held the jackets in place. He knew nothing about poetry, little about books—cared less. He would risk the books with me but not the dust jackets. After he was gone I wrote in one book, "Learn to enjoy what you do not approve of."

Once when his cabin floor was covered with things people had sent him to sign, he blew off considerable steam.

These things are all forgeries. Anybody with half an eye can tell the difference between a genuine collector's item and a faked or created rarity made to order. All these things on the floor! They are from people who sent books with requests for signatures, and with full instructions as to just *how* they wanted me to write *what* in them. It seems a form of rudeness to me; but I suppose I'm to blame for it by the way I have encouraged people in the past to such insignificances.

Following his western visit in 1947, he demonstrated his pride in having people troubling about his things to a friend at Boulder, Colorado.

"Don't let the old fraud fool you," Charlie Foster chuckled in relaying the conversation. "He's tickled pink having people go to such lengths to collect his books and things. It would be a big disappointment if you quit. He can rave on, making denial, but I know better.

"He told us his two principal collectors were in California. 'Between the two they have just about everything I have ever done. They're very jealous of one another. I like to stir 'em up,' he maliced.

"Originally his Boulder lecture was scheduled for the Little Theater, and we had enough tickets printed for the building. But the interest turned out so great that we had to move into a bigger auditorium. First and last we sold 3,000 tickets, of the second printing. Thus we had the original ones unused. Frost gave me two addresses and said, 'These unused tickets will make real collector's items, being for a lecture that was never given. Send Mertins and Bernheimer one each as an April Fool's joke. Each will think himself the only one getting one, and when they come together and compare notes, they'll hate one another more than ever.' That explains why I sent that mysterious ticket to you."

When Frost wrote on the fly of *Twilight* the phrase, "I deliver it into your hands, my dear Bernheimer," he fully believed that one fine day that rare copy would rest, with all its priceless companions, in some institution of learning for perpetual exhibition. In no conversation with us from 1941 until the day he landed in our home in California in 1947 did he express doubt. "A poor man," he probably reasoned, having us in mind, likely, "might be tempted to sell his collection for bread and butter. A rich man will hold onto it and pass it on to a college, and so build up his own conceit. Aside from conceit that would be to my liking." One often wonders what Frost thought when the famous sale of his things took place in 1950 when the Slide Mountain Press, Inc., issue of "The Cow's in the Corn" fetched fifty dollars. Originally he inscribed on its half-title, "Robert Frost to William Manthey-Zorn, November 21, 1936." Evidently its original owner gave or sold it to somebody so that it came to Bernheimer. On the same page with the original inscription the hopeful poet wrote, "Now transferred to kindlier keeping in the hands of Earl Bernheimer. R. F."

The two most interested in the sale of the Bernheimer Frostana by Parke-Bernet Galleries, Inc., that is, the donor and the owner, never told fully all that led up to the offering of the books, manuscripts, and magazines for purchase. Friends of Frost all over the nation were terribly shocked when the auctioneers sent out from 980 Madison Avenue, a carefully prepared, elegantly printed prospectus, which stated that "The Earle J. Bernheimer Collection of First Editions of American Authors, including his remarkable collection of the Writings of Robert Frost," would go on the block at that address December 11, 1950, 8 P.M. and December 12, at 1:45 P.M. The title page closed with the phrase, "Including the Unique Copy of Twilight."

Did a rift come between the two highly temperamental men? Was the collector again (as he often had been) miffed at something real or fancied, some slight on the collected's part? Did the visit to California in 1947 present a contribution of embarrassment to Bernheimer that precipitated the disposal of the precious tomes and manuscripts?[1]

We remembered what Robert had said to us as we drove him from Bernheimer's Brentwood house to our home in Redlands. "Don't have anything more to do with him. You'll be happier if you don't. I'd give anything on earth if I had never got mixed up with him."

Thus, an opening made for us, we told him what we said to Bernheimer when he first [1942] talked about *Twilight*. Bernheimer refused to tell what the consideration of the alleged sale had been, but he was told if he paid less than ten thousand dollars for it he stole it. Frost replied with bitterness, "If I had ten thousand I'd buy it and burn it to keep people from quarreling and bickering over it."

When in November, 1950, word reached us of the proposed auction we were stunned. We knew that what money we could bid on *Twilight* would be a waste of time on our part. However, in the hope the day might be stormy, or the sky might fall in, we made a token bid on the book. We also wrote three letters urging somebody, somewhere, to do something, somehow—one to Frost, one to Charles R. Green, and one to Charlie Cole. The first word that came to us regarding the outcome was from Green, who attending had made one small bid-in. He wrote that Captain Cohn had bid *Twilight* in at thirty-five hundred. All told the Frostana brought sixteen thousand dollars.

"I still have hope that someday *Twilight* will come to Amherst," President Cole wrote. Alas, in slightly more than a decade *Twilight* saw its final sale to a collector who passed his Frostana on to the University of Virginia. It sold at the last for ten thousand dollars!

XXXII. Puritan Yankee Through and Through

Kirkland 7–1820!

The dial on the phone might have been a prayer wheel, we the devout Tibetan dialers.

[1] On the occasion of his eightieth birthday, R. F. assured us that such was the case.

If we should finger that number might our god answer with a voice? Why not? He himself gave it to us; and after all, was it not here at Boston in Boston University that Alexander Graham Bell had perfected the telephone?

It had been an experience often repeated that seeking to contact Robert Frost was like praying to a god. You went on time after time and nothing happened. Then, just when you were giving up, deity made answer, vastly astonishing the votary.

This, he told us, was his telephone number at 34 Brewster, Cambridge, and when we got to Boston on such and such a date, dial that number—he'd be there.

Of course there was always the chance he had changed his mind and was in Coconut Grove, Florida, or on the Homer Noble farm looking after his sugar crop, or just somewhere. If he had held to his purpose he was at home, and we had the open sesame—Kirkland 7–1820.

Presumably it was a blind number (though we never investigated) and given only to a choice circle—a very limited circle—of close friends. To hold such thought was a morale builder. Not everybody had R. F.'s blind telephone number. So, in our quarters at the house of a friend in Boston, Mount Vernon Street (facing toward the Esplanade but seeing nothing), we made as if to dial the telephone.

Suddenly a world-smashing realization came to our communal mind. "What," we cried, just to make assurance doubly sure, "What is this house number?"

Right! Eighty-eight Mount Vernon, the very house in which, during those nerve-wracking days succeeding Elinor's death, he was not sure he could live out each day as the morning called him to face it. It was from this very house that he went to live at 35 Brewster across the Charles. It was unbelievable. Yet, we should have known that merely to associate with Robert Frost was to never experience what ordinary people experience. A memory flashed of an inscription he had written in a book about a visit his friend had paid to this very house number.

To enter 88 Mount Vernon, since it was a modern-modern apartment house, one needed only to press a button, presumably connected with a door bell. Then, a message through the tube, in a split second the door opened, and in another split second closed behind you as you entered. You found yourself no longer facing the Esplanade, only a blank wall ending in a pleasant waiting room. Perhaps it was this understandable sense of imprisonment in any sort of apartment that made the place a house of despair for Robert during his despairing days.

The poet had invited us to Cambridge. Kay Morrison would be there, we would have tea, and then we could go out to dinner and talk—"not about me," he growled—"just talk and have a good time."

When we arrived Kay was there, and so were Robert and Gillie. But Robert had caught a cold; Lesley, just returned from her library work at the American Embassy in Madrid, was coming up from Washington with plans already divulged to us in advance by Dorothy Canfield Fisher. So, our mission must be performed with dispatch. Dinner was out of the question.

Robert Frost's Cambridge house was a two-story frame, unprepossessing on the exterior, handsome and comfortable inside. Books lined the walls of the living room, with an occasional picture by some famous artist, some etchings, woodcuts and certain portraits of the poet. Kay's hand was seen in the entire ensemble and arrangements. Robert came down from his upstairs study, a book-lined, four-wall hide-out.

Our host sat on the sofa, his unruly locks of hair white as might be. His broad shoulders were stooped, his hearing dulled. His face was swollen; but still a twinkle, lit by a flitting smile, brightened it. Yet, somehow, that smile was not as convincing as it once had been.

Gillie was demanding attention. Robert insisted on feeding him on the floor, unmindful of deleterious results. Kay was solicitous for the rug's welfare. When, to divert attention, I told him about visiting at 88 Mount Vernon, he smiled.

> Strange how these things work out that way. Your coming over here from the same address at which I lived after my wife's death. With my bucolic inclination—country, outdoor life—I found that place most confining, being penned up on the floor in a small apartment. It seemed absurd. There I sat like Little Miss Muffet eating my curds and whey. Kay said I was more like a caged lion, walking the floor, not knowing what to do with myself. I had been sick and heartsick and needed to be

out. I haven't any too clear idea of all that went on during those months, seemed years. I know, however, that Kay decided it would not do for me to continue there. So we began to look around for a suitable place. That, I take it, is about it—the whole thing.

In those days real-estate prices had not yet started to follow the New Deal into astronomical proportions—which, I should say, is very much like my old counterfeiting friend who believed in free coinage in a free country. After looking around awhile we just happened to learn that 35 Brewster could be had. We got it for a ridiculously low price, so I moved in. My boldness, coming just at that time, was startling. It's just exactly what I need. I can keep my eye on Conant; it's near enough for Kay to see that I don't pile it up too much; I can get most anywhere from here on a train; and as much as anything else it is comfortable. Gillie and I find it much to our liking. Once in so often I find it a convenient place to come back to.

I've never been much of a hand to gather up things, but I like a few.

About everything is belonging and belongings, your concern and your concerns. A long time ago in Dublin Æ gave me a painting in blue which he had done. Chapin gave me a few things. I have a lot of cuts Lankes made and gave me. Kay has fixed all these things up in fine taste as you can see. This sort of accumulation of the years makes up the essence of a thing.

It was in times of free forgetfulness that one heard from Robert Frost the purest clearest conversation. When he was troubled, his themes changed more often, though the tones remained more nearly invariable. The Puritan Yankee was perturbed when we told him that a Boston woman had said his New England characters were just made up or been seen by him through his own special eyeglasses.

I don't invent characters. I'm not writing about entire strangers. I put them down as I see them, more often than not, reminiscent of something. I see only one part of them—that which is interesting to me. I'm human. This woman sees only a part interesting to her. Somebody else probably sees another part. I'm not making snapshots of people. I'm trying to stress the side that I see. What seems important and interesting to me, faults so glaring they can't be overlooked. This woman must be ignorant to say these things about my poetry. She's probably never read more than one or two of my poems and these didn't strike her just right. She's likely a religious crank, or an educational crank. But—that's enough of her.

The voice had a metallic sound, as of talking through an iron pipe, not pleasant to hear. It didn't stay, though—at once he was on another trail, mollified by our telling him some fine compliment made by an English professor at Northeastern University, Boston, who had given a course in Frost's poetry. College turned his thoughts to another matter left over from a former visit.

Your old Jewell friend was greatly disappointed when he was not renamed to the World Court. He had every reason to believe he would be; but politics entered in and Roosevelt [sic] didn't appoint him. I understand that he made a good record during his term which began in 1936. Even his enemies grant him that. They admit that Manley Hudson knows international law—who better? Of course there's a lot of proper prejudice at Harvard. Very naturally when the Bemis Professor of law got named to a court which judges nations, there were other professors who knew more, to hear them tell it, and were better qualified to sit and judge than he. They sneered at him for a quisling. It's an old story, one I know backward and forward. The ultimate goal of every lawyer has been The Hague. You'll not go higher. His pride got a jolt.

We can pretty much divide mankind by assortment into schemers and dreamers. I suppose Hudson would be classed about fifty-fifty. His dreams got him there, but his schemes couldn't keep him there. You'll have to admit Judge Hudson isn't likely to win any medals for modesty.

I must be getting old. I go round quoting myself for want of something better. One time I said something about being tender to our dreamers. But I didn't have Hudson in mind. I was thinking of young poets. I said they might seem like picketeers, or a committee on rules for the moment; but we shan't mind what they seem so long as they produce good poems. I believe in these young people of ours, however much I get out of sorts with them, aggravated. Some of the old ones aggravate me too. I visited with Ezra Pound's son awhile back. Poor old Ezra. He stands in need of being redefined. They've accused him of treason. Maybe he did foolish things under the spell of the New Rome of Mussolini. I can't say. He was always capable of doing foolish things as well as saying wise ones. I take it, though, this was his first real blunder.

I've read a story of a French ship which had a huge cannon on deck. This cannon had not been properly anchored, bolted down. It swung about from side to side, nearly capsizing the ship. The man in charge of it worked hard to get it fastened down securely, which he at length succeeded in doing. Having secured it, the day was saved. Then the commanding officer commended him, read a citation, decorated him for bravery and his skill in saving the ship. Then he pinned a medal on him, kissed him on both cheeks and ordered him shot for permitting the cannon to get loose in the first place.

Ted Morrison says that's what ought to be done with Pound—only he says he should be shot first for treason, decorated afterwards for his poetry.

I don't look at it that way. How are you going to differentiate between Pound and the poet and critic, and Pound the traitor. Which *is* Pound? Which one do you intend to shoot—poet or traitor?

The first time I ever sat down with a known poet and talked poetry was with Pound. We talked of several poets in the limelight at that time, but mainly about E. A. Robinson. I remember what a good time we had with "Miniver Cheevy," and how we laughed over it—a laugh was something for Ezra—especially how we laughed over the four "thoughts" in the poem. The first three—

Miniver thought, and thought, and thought,

were all right. But when Robinson dragged in the fourth

And thought about it,

it was a sort of intolerable poetic touch.

There can never be a successful doubt established concerning the old Pound I knew in England, knew well, and the critical genius he possessed. Here is one small sign of it. Once I sat in a room with him and William Butler Yeats and listened while Pound took the Irishman apart. This was how it happened. On that occasion Pound said to Yeats: "You're too full of adjectives and expletives. Let's wring you dry." He then proceeded to take some of Yeats's poems and, as he put it, wring them dry. It is my opinion that any discriminating reader will readily see the effect of Pound's criticism on the later verse of the Irishman. He advised T. S. Eliot toward the Nobel Prize, also.

Poor old Pound, he's still working away with relative unsuccess. He's not in prison, as such, neither is he officially in a psychopathic ward. They've never tried him for treason nor committed him for insanity. Just for what he once was, suppose we give him the crowning mercy. I asked his son if his father could read Chinese. He said no, that he took the best translations he could find and made his own synthetic paraphrases from them. He always gives them a special turn, expressing them in his own way, something he always did very well.

Parenthetically, somewhat later, Frost discussed the same noted poet. We had met Pound's daughter in Venice at the International Poetry Society, where she was busy trying to win friends and influence people to get the former Fascist out of the hospital for the insane. Frost took the long way round her brother to her.

> Once I asked T. S. Eliot what he thought about Pound. "Do you think he's crazy?" "Well," Eliot hesitated, coming finally to the point. "Well, you know how it is." Just like that. I talked to Pound's son about him. "Do you think your father is crazy?" "Well—you know how it is." As much as to say, "You know him. Why ask me?"
>
> This was the son Pound left in an institution in England. Ezra couldn't see himself pushing a baby buggy all over London. The son never knew his father in all his unhappy childhood. Now that Ezra is notorious he enjoys being in his reflected (dimly reflected) glory.
>
> Back in 1914 when my wife and I went with the kids down into the West Midlands with Gibson and Abercrombie, Pound by contrarities furnished the reason. When I first met Gibson I had grown sick and tired of being round with Ezra in London. You see, Lascelles was first to go to Dymock, followed shortly by Wilfrid. Then we came and Rupert Brooke and Edward Thomas last of all. Gibson looked down on Edward and his "hack" writing. He didn't have much to brag about himself—all that horrible stuff he calls poetry. If, as he told you, he is forgotten, that's the reason.

R. F. had said quite a piece regarding Pound, but the book on their relationship was far from closed. Frequently "Poor old Ezra" cropped up in our conversations. Though unknown at this time, another chapter was yet to be written wherein Robert would go out of his way in displaying the quality of mercy.

The original conversation—one-sided—went on:

Pound was always pretty good at saying one thing and meaning two very different things. A poet has that right and privilege. The custom existed a long way back. Lately I've been reading up on it, and thinking up on it. I came onto one of the old critics, a contemporary of Vergil and Horace, who was writing of a poet's concept of a ship where he used veiled allegory, if you can tie that. This old Roman critic said the poet was using double talk. It was in such a way, that far back, that the concept of the Ship of State came into use. I take it that my greatest debt is to the Greeks and the Romans. Lucretius not only had the atomic theory well in hand, he also, in an altogether unbelievable way, saw the possibility of splitting the atom, and foresaw what might happen if any when it split. It had to wait a long while for Millikan, Oppenheimer, Lawrence, and the rest—for Nagasaki, Hiroshima, and Bikini. Nobody will ever know how many of our concepts sprang from the classic writers. After all, what do we know that Lucretius didn't? We're still a part of the human race, pretty much what the pre-Augustan Romans were. There's something indestructible in us which will save us from annihilation, even with the A-bomb, or whatever other bombs they say they're going to cook up, a thousand times more destructive. These annihilative tendencies in mankind are all apt to bump into and counteract one another. Maybe the race has a manifest destiny; maybe it's pure cussedness.

I had some fun last year [1948] when I went back to speak at Amherst. To show there can be no proper rule that covered I quoted what I had read out of the *Columbia Encyclopedia*. I told 'em I was looking up "potato" and stumbled onto "poetry." This was what I found under poetry—good high-brow stuff. I don't know who wrote it, and I don't think I want to just now. It went like this: "Poetry is largely a matter of rhythm and diction. Meaning is not essential and by many is considered detrimental." That's because they can't see into it, through it, or even under it. A poet, I maintain, if he wants to, has a right to say one thing and mean another. I've done it in a lot of poems. I'm not going to name the poems. That's for you to figure out.

His old formula.

About this same time he was encountered by a pseudo-poet and anthologist who kept pestering him about what he meant when he wrote a certain line in the poem "Stopping by Woods on a Snowy Evening." Frost relayed it.

He wanted to know what I intended to imply when I wrote

The woods are lovely, dark and deep,
But I have promises to keep,
And miles to go before I sleep,
And miles to go before I sleep.

I told him I meant that it was time to go home. "Yes, but what did you have in mind when you made that statement?" "I had in mind that it was getting late and I should be moving on." "Yes," he pestered, "but what hidden—symbolic—meaning did you intend to record?" "Well," and I was about fed up, "I thought it was about time I was getting to hell out of there."

Bret Harte came next into his thoughts.

Bret wrote two good poems—one was the "Heathen Chinee"; the other I used in a speech you'll remember in California when I borrowed the book long enough to get the verse fixed in my mind, the lines about one of Jones's lost mules, and the ensuing argument which "broke up the society upon the Stanislaus." He never wrote anything else. That, I take it, is a personal opinion. Every man should be allowed at least one such. His famous "Dickens in Camp" is a lot of sentimental slush. I can stand just so much literary sentimentality. I remember once being in a theater in London when I came very nearly being thrown out. The play was a slushy hodge-podge, and I got to expressing myself about it out loud. A fellow in front turned round and said, "If you don't like this play, why don't you get up and go home?" "I don't like it," I told him, "but I'm not going home. I'm going to a vaudeville show." So, up I got and stomped out and went to a vaudeville as I said. At another time I was in a playhouse over there where Barrie was being acted. I noticed a fellow in front of me all slouched back in his seat, gripping his hands together and mumbling to himself. Finally he couldn't hold it in, and blurted out, "Barrie, you sentimental old fool." Both Barrie and Harte could be sentimental without half trying.

One never dared take pity on, or feel sorry for, Robert Frost. Yet, in the last analysis there was something sorrowful about him. Sitting there before us he somehow seemed very old and very frail. A little more than two years were to pass before he went under the surgeon's knife. Perhaps the great scourge of the human race was already insidiously at work. Few people had even an inkling of it.

What were the burdens he carried which deepened the furrows in his corrugated face? One felt on looking into his eyes that a vast tension was imprisoned behind them, tearing his mind, likely to burst bonds at any moment. A man of iron must give way at last. That which beats from the outside may be withstood. That which throbs within, beating against the inner wall, must have an outlet. So we mused to ourselves.

Added to the cares of memory, the stresses of his own life, and the lives of his children, Robert at this time had taken on the cares of his grandchildren. To further burden his soul, great-grandchildren began to arrive on the scene. Thus, he found himself at mid-twentieth century as close to the first of the New Hampshire Frosts as he was to the farthest removed of his lineal descendents born 155 years later. Concerning the first of these great-grandchildren, Lesley's granddaughter, a mite of an incubator baby, he quipped when asked what it seemed like to be a great-grandfather: "Well, this one is so small it really doesn't count."

Prescott, out of the army, had gone to Miami University to get out of the cold of the Massachusetts winters. There he had met and married Phyllis Marie, daughter of Mr. and Mrs. Donald Precourt Gordon. Finishing at M.I.T. after getting his bachelor's degree in Florida, he lived awhile in Virginia, having a job as Navy small-craft architect. Later on he bought a home for himself, his wife, little Carol Marie, and Elinor Gordon, two more great-grandchildren, on the Maryland side of the District of Columbia, at Garrett Park, Maryland, in easy driving distance of his work in the Pentagon. Still, though he had two daughters (one born in 1949, one in 1951), there was no son to carry on the name. This was remedied one year later. The man child was given his grandfather's name, becoming the second Robert Frost.

Knowing the two enemies unceasingly besieging the family, Robert must forever have been the more harrassed as the descendents continued to multiply. He shook his head as he pictured the Frosts to come. A composite photograph.

I suppose I should stop worrying about my children, my children's children, and my children's children's children. (Sounds like Major Bowes, and where it stops, nobody knows.) I came onto one of my granddaughters reading Henry Miller in my home. I didn't tell her she mustn't. I suppose she'd learn all that Henry had to tell in some other way—but, I take it, not so fast as by reading him.

Prescott turned geographical "Copperhead," trying to live up to his family reputation. He's running true to form in another matter, also—married into a teaching family. A lot of fuss has been raised among the kinfolks about his perpetuating the name. I've said nothing, which I take it is better than saying too much. He was the only chance the name had in our line, anyway, and there've been times when scrawny little Prescott, sick all the time, didn't seem very promising for posterity. Until lately. Now the matter's been straightened out with another Robert Frost. Prescott's been living at Falls Church, Virginia, in the woods, battling his way back and forth to Washington among the bureaucrats every workday. His mother thinks he's in a job he likes and that he'll about keep his raises up with inflation. Somebody's got to win. First and last we've all had pulmonary trouble. Maybe it's for our good. Keeps us guessing. We fight it when we're young so we can work up enough resistance to live an old age in peace.

Prescott's got a civil service job, something I'm told is above politics. (Nowadays, what can be above politics, I ask you.) So he doesn't have to be either for or against Truman—"Harry, the Miracle Man," according to Wilbert Snow, pulling rabbits out of a hat. He'll probably pull one too many rabbits out of a hat one of these days and —pouff!

XXXIII. An Old Man's Winter Night

ROBERT FROST was one of the first men in America to try to do something about getting our native literature into colleges. An American through and through, he not only scorned aping the letters of other lands but wanted recognition according to genuine American productions.

Looking back over more than one-half century of unending, unrelenting battling for American recognition of his own poetry, as well as the true native letters of all American writers, the author of *North of Boston* could well be proud of what had been accomplished.

When I was at Harvard in the nineties there wasn't a genuine course given in American literature. Our poets and essayists and novelists weren't considered worth a whole course. The old slur, "Who reads an American book?" though fifty years old, was still in vogue.

About the time I went to teach at Pinkerton some few professors were making a beginning of courses in long-neglected American Lit. But it took time. Of course before this somehow Longfellow and Emerson had been dragged into literary studies, but entire courses in our own American literature, risen out of our own ground, were not considered earlier. The heavy hand of English Lit was on our schools, just as classicism had continued to be for better, for worser. Our native professors just didn't think our native writers had anything worth passing on to our native students. Who reads an American book?

In all his teaching—Pinkerton, Plymouth, Amherst, Ann Arbor, Harvard, and Dartmouth—during the years from 1905 on, American writers had a champion in Frost. He not only was a genuine native American, he was the protagonist of a native American literature.

By the time he reached his Diamond Jubilee year (old style) in 1950, the voice of Robert Frost ("flung out from the crags") was more American than the Voice of America could ever become. And what acclaim had come to him from sources high and low!

So many honors had been given him, in fact, that one which sought him out on the eve of his seventy-fifth birthday might be passed by as of little moment, did it not contain the seeds of immortality.

When the gold medal, given "to the American author of that book, published in the specified years preceding the award, which is considered more likely to attain the stature of a classic," by the George Macy Limited Editions Club, was awarded to the poet upon the appearance of the *Complete Poems,* the recipient dragged himself down to the Starlight Room of the Waldorf Astoria. Date, November 15, 1949.

A Vermont breakfast was given in his honor. The breakfast was in its cuisine much to his taste: baked red apple, johnnycakes and Vermont syrup (which might have been boiled in his own pans on the Homer Noble farm), huckleberries, and a fresh Green Mountain trout. "Johnnycake and huckleberry flummery," somebody called it.

The Starlight Room was packed with subscribers to the Macy Book Club and a few invited guests. There was more than a little speechmaking. Flanking Macy were a number of men whose long service in the field of American letters distinguished them. In addition to the honoree and the two Van Dorens were Frederic Melcher, Henry Seidel Canby, Burton Rascoe, W. G. Rogers, and Harry Hansen.

Mark Van Doren presented the medal, his speech being as simple as one of Frost's own eclogues. "Robert Frost is the only living poet I should be willing to call great." He had no cause to amplify that statement. It said all that was needed. Some of the former rivals of the poet might have felt that it said more than was true.

Another Van Doren, this time Carl, a member of the committee, in speaking of why *Complete Poems* had attained the status of classicism, declared that "a classic is a book that has no reason on earth to be written again."

It was not the intention of the honored guest to speak. The planners knew he would say he would keep still and let others do the talking. They also knew he would break over when the talk had gone on long enough. At a certain point nothing could keep the Vermonter in his chair. After he had listened to all the praise that came in such unstinted streams from the hearts of his friends—after he had found himself pictured as a mountain of genius, a range of greatness—he warmed up. His theme had to do with the poet's intentions.

"I don't know what to say," he grinned. "Too much already has been said. After hearing the Van Dorens and all the rest of you it seems that about all that remains of me is greatness."

In the list of diners at the Waldorf Astoria that November morning were some who had been in Frost's classes—some at Amherst, such as Will Rogers, of the Associated Press; some at the New School of Social Research, such as Harry Hansen—and trains of thought and muffled conversations were started as reminiscences were stirred.

In light of the fact that this was only the fifth time since 1935 that a supposed yearly medal had been awarded, the ovation given the Vermont farmer was tremendous. "Just like Toscannini's when he takes the baton," somebody put in.

Not the least remembrable thing of the breakfast was the saying of his poems by the author. First he read "the poem I am asked oftenest to say, 'Departmental.'" This poem he had said so often he usually knew it forward and backward. His train of thinking somehow went askew so that the opening lines wouldn't come to his tongue. For a moment three hundred diners wondered. He stood silent, scratching his head. Then the thing clicked, and he went forward to the eventual lines,

> *It couldn't be called ungentle.*
> *But how thoroughly departmental.*

Then the medal winner went on back up to New England carrying his trophy and his intentions with him.

It was to be expected that the jubilee should come in and go out in a series of events, each succeeding one eclipsing the other. Friends all over the world remembered the twenty-sixth of March, 1950—many did something about it.

In some of their manifestations of affection, Robert acquiesced gracefully, bowing to the feelings which prompted the acts. Upon some he looked askance.

One recognition from a high, and unexpected, source certainly came without warning. He had word from the United States Senate wishing him well on his seventy-fifth birthday. This august body is not given to greeting poets, however distinguished, on their birth or any other day. The resolution adopted by the Solons was to the effect that his poems had "helped to guide American thought with humor and wisdom." This, it would appear, was the highest form of wisdom displayed by the Senate in many a decade. He had not always been kindly in his remarks about the lawmakers—even the biennial Congress, the Senate of which had passed the resolution. Continuing, the official pronouncement said: "Setting forth to our minds a reliable representation of ourselves and of all men, his work through the past decades enhanced for many their understanding of the United States and their love of country. Therefore, be it resolved that the Senate of the United States extend to him the felicitations of the nation which he has served so well."

As the celebration of his seventy-fifth birthday approached the poet came from Florida to Cambridge, anticipating (not altogether ungrudgingly) the fuss about to be made over him on account of his age. Relaxing in his book-lined study, he took time out to spoof the representatives of the press and others, giving forth some rare bits of wisdom in his somewhat mischievous manner of speaking.

Somebody once asked me why I believed in this wasteful democratic system of government we call a republic. I told 'em it was because it was full of checks and balances. Maybe we've got too many checks in it sometimes—we can't have too many balances. It's a system of power divided against itself, so that nobody can get more than is good of power—I mean more than's good for the rest of us.

What do I want for my birthday? I want prowess for my country, and by prowess I mean native ability to help in everything its people attempt.

I'll not grant you the whole human race is bad—just foolish. How would I cure the ills our flesh seems to have fallen heir to? Just as I cured my own ill about fifty years ago. I got my grandfather to finagle me a farm of thirty acres or less—really it was twenty-nine acres, and not very fertile. There's not left so much land to go round now, though my own acreage has continued to increase. I lived on that twenty-nine or so acres ten years and made enough money selling it to take my wife and kids abroad for two and a half years. Now there are so many farms in my family I have to stop and count 'em up the way I do my children, my grandchildren and my great-grandchildren. My main farm, where I spend much of my time, is up in Vermont. I'll look to the people of Vermont to accept me as a neighbor and citizen and resident there in another twenty-five years. No trouble getting 'em to accept me as a taxpayer, Republican as they are. I'd solve all those problems of our American lacklands by giving each family twenty acres, just as my grandfather gave me twenty-nine acres. That size farm would show them all their burdens and all their responsibilities and all their privileges. I know it will work—I've proved it. I go over into the Green Mountains on my farm and putter around every late spring and early summer. Puttering on my farm's my refuge. Wise old Vergil says in one of his Georgics, "Praise large farms, stick to small ones." Twenty acres are just about enough.

First and last I'm a farmer, and I am always embarrassed when people call me a poet. On my income-tax report I put myself down as a teacher. Next year I'm going to put down the explanation "Resigned." When they ask me what I'm resigned from I'll say, "I'm not resigned *from* anything, I'm just resigned *to* everything."

At my age I suppose I ought really to be reading the book of Job. I don't know where you're likely to find a better. I've been thinking about another great literature lately. For vigor of expression where can you look for anything to equal the old Icelandic sagas? Where will you find adjectives, coupled with nouns, such as "bloody eagles and pale adders," or, "far and wide the dusky ways"? Where can you come onto a figure like the image of the king in his warm, lighted hall, a swallow entering by one door, going out the other, winging its way from winter to summer, back to winter? Where is there a truer picture of eternity—time-eternity? I sort of grew up on that kind of stuff and haven't fully outgrown it.

Not having the poet with us, we of the west had to content ourselves with celebrating the Diamond Jubilee with what we had of his works. Four colleges and universities, widely separated, joined forces and, during the time following March 26, held exhibitions of Frostana and gatherings for the discussion of Frost and his place in letters.

The University of California, Los Angeles campus; William Jewell College, Liberty, Missouri; Scripps College for Women, Claremont, California; and the University of Redlands—all these synchronized their schedules for the series of modest events.

From his Florida hide-out, R. F. wrote giving his blessings to the things being planned.

> Box 100—Route 2
> South Miami, Florida
> Feb. 10, 1950

Dear Louis:

There you go again with your attempts to make as much of a Californian of me as circumstances permit. Surely I should have no objection to having my birthday celebrated if I don't have to show up for the rites. All I can say is you are an irrepressible friend—and an incorrigible. You refuse to get it through your head that not everybody is as interested in me as you are. Your president up in Berkeley told me that. He may have told you. Word comes to me that you have a biography of me on the market. I thought it was sort of understood that you would spare me until I was in one of the other worlds. But I suppose I can't expect too much compassion in my exposed position. I am farming for a few weeks among

the loquats and avocadoes of California's rival climate. Good wishes to
you and Esther.

Ever yours,
ROBERT

Nor had he forgotten on the day of the big celebration what we were
attempting in the West, sending warm telegram greetings from Cambridge, dated March 26.

> Your spreading my books out to celebrate my birthday is some com-
> pensation for my age. I'm always proud to be thought of as a Californian.
> Here's thinking of you in requittal.

ROBERT FROST

On a copy of *The Manchester Guardian* for August 17, 1950, coincid-
ing with the old-style observance of the poet's seventy-fifth anniversary
(in the cards to be corrected at no great distance in time), Frost wag-
gishly wrote an inscription for us.

This inscription was pieced out by utilizing, in lazy-man fashion, the
"by Louis Mertins" under the title of the piece called "Robert Frost in
England." To this the poet added his name, "Robert Frost with thanks."
He then struck out the "by" in the by-line, and added "to" instead, with
the printed Louis Mertins to finish the inscription. It then read "Robert
Frost with thanks to Louis Mertins."

The same year, 1950, saw *Hard Not to be King* dressed in blue buckram with gold lettering come out under the colophon of House of Books
Ltd. With thrones toppling all over the world, the poem was not without
modern implications, however much it dealt with ancient Persia. The
inscription, "To Louis Mertins who should have heard me read it on
television at the Academy, Robert Frost" was in itself a bit of history
recording, as well as prophecy. The poet was just entering his career as
a television artist.

XXXIV. And Even Above the Brim

ROBERT FROST had climbed far up his birch toward heaven before the
coming of his diamond jubilee year, but his friends had reason to believe

that he was all the while looking from his deserved eminence to the green earth below, longing to go swishing and "kicking his way down through the air to the ground."

In all the years that went before he had appeared to live in two worlds. It was a combination of accepting the universe, and, while remaining on friendly terms with this world, looking toward another. He always wanted to climb right up "to get away from earth awhile," tired of life as it was, "weary of considerations," of pathless woods and cumbering obstructions. But he was in no hurry to be quit of the present sphere. "Earth's the place for love," he said feelingly many times, quoting himself, "I don't know where it's likely to go better." So he was never anxious for a willful fate to half grant his wish, take him up and not bring him back. He merely wished to "climb black branches up a snow white trunk *toward* heaven," and then be set down again. He wanted life to go on living. His was a restatement of the old, old philosophy of becoming.

From such an attained height he could survey all creation, peacefully. His "call back" to Amherst at the very opening of his diamond jubilee had all the appearance of the true essence of permanence. The others may have seemed so—this was under contract. It was more: He belonged in spirit to Amherst, and Amherst was at last, and finally, convinced.

It was not that his order of living was to be revolutionized, or even changed in any measurable degree. He still intended to spend much of his year at Cambridge, with a winter flight to Florida and a spring return to the Homer Noble farm. It was just that he had his old terminal back again. Home once more would be at Amherst, though a room at the Lord Jeffery was hardly equal to the home on Sunset, facing into Hadley Meadows.

Students at the college were little different from the ones he and Stark Young and George Whicher wrestled with a full generation earlier. The teacher, however, had attained to the stature of an elder statesman, whose philosophy had fermented into a Socratic vintage. These students of a later generation appeared wise enough to sense this. They were dealing now with a philosopher-poet who had a philosophy of his own, not a poet who merely *knew* philosophy. Perhaps it was to fall to one of this generation to systematize his philosophy through a lifetime of work.

It takes long—long—to arrive at the perfection attained in Frost's incomparable conversation set forth in his philosophy given out from his armchair, especially about his own life experiences. Once we told him he had had a most interesting life. He countered:

> Your life has probably been just as interesting. Seen through your eyes of memory it has turned out commonplace. No man sees his own life quite as interesting as the other fellow's. That's why we like to read fairy tales.
>
> If everybody's life was interesting to himself, then there'd be no books read—only written. Then what would become of our Boswell's, our Plutarchs? Have to balance things somehow.

First of all it seems that Frost accepted the universe. When told on one talking occasion that he did, he grinned grimly, quoting, "One jolly well better." To him accepting the universe included a passion for all created things, even the simplest—more than all else the simplest one should say. What could be less complex than going out to clean the pasture spring, the little calf standing by its mother, the longing for companionship: "I won't be gone long, you come too."

Just as he accepted the universe, so Frost accepted God. With God he accepted people. It is very likely he didn't realize what a good choice he had made for a poem to read when his first teaching job after Methuen depended on it. That lovely, haunted poem, "The Tuft of Flowers," in which he tells with startling poignancy of one who has grown weary working alone. The one who mowed the grass went before the sun. But he left his aura behind for that one who came to turn the grass after him —the whetstone on the breeze, the leaping tongue of bloom the scythe had bared. These things made possible brotherly speech under the shade of noon. Before was only an accepted universe, after was companionship.

But even in an accepted universe he knew very well "there were roughly zones." Some things must stop this side of the Arctic—peach trees among them. Man comes to this knowledge slowly, reluctantly. He wants to change things—even the universe. He would like to believe there is design in all things (but speaking of the spider he questions "if design govern in a thing so small"); however it may be he would still like to change things.

He accepted the universe in people as well. God put them here, and with him or not they were a part of the accepted universe. "We live in all kinds of a world, which explains the all kinds of people who are here with us," he might have said, having the Lorens and the Starks in mind.

One may accept the universe and still want, however futilely, to do something about it. Frost first and last had a lover's quarrel with the world—if not the universe. "It's knowing what to do with things that counts," he has written. Then he has added, "All the fun's in how you say a thing." Such thoughts show an intention of continuing to do something about the universe, which may be one indication of the direction he pursued in his philosophy.

There was, to use a further example, the little girl who hadn't yet learned to let go with her hands and so was not deterred from being run off with by birch trees into space. Such a thing offered a fine foil for Frost's philosophy of holding onto things with the heart. The hands are different; we must learn to let go with them. Most important, he philosophizes, is to turn loose with the mind—"of cares at night to sleep." But nothing requires us to turn loose with our hearts.

"To "exchange troubled glances over life" would seem to be what the human family is doing at its best all the time. This is a touch of good psychology. Long before Freud's dream analysis was popular, Frost was giving psychological analysis in his verse. With a keen insight into the workings of the human mind, he began, even at Pinkerton and Plymouth, to set down quirks which serve as a soul index. Out of these studies came "Home Burial," "The Witch of Coös," "The Code," "The Fear"—excellent analyses.

Once in Whitehead's apartment in Cambridge, Frost shared talk with the philosopher. The listeners could scarcely distinguish between poet and philosopher. In fact it seems for the moment that they had exchanged roles—Frost talked philosophy, Whitehead poetry, demonstrating the basic element of philosophy in the former's work.

Life must all come down to a phrase we meet now and then among plain people. Apple-pie order. I suppose most of you remember how your mother used to make apple pies. You should. She would lay the ingredients all out, place them within reach, all in apple-pie order. Thereafter it was easy to assemble them into a pie. When you start a thing hold back till preparations are in apple-pie order. By this I don't mean you've got to know what you're going to do at every step—not that cut and dried. Those things come as you go forward.

Once up at my New Hampshire farm—one of my New Hampshire farms—a little birch had fallen across the road and been run over by a wagon wheel. Finding it crushed and half-broken off and lying on the ground, I wasn't sure anything could be done to save it, but I started in to do the best I was able. I lifted it up just as far as possible without breaking it sheer. Then I bound it with splints, drove in some stobs, and tied it up. I was dubious about it, but made a stagger.

I didn't see my little birch for some time. Then I found that nature had reasserted herself, helped me out. The tree was taking on new life. The sap was running up, the leaves coming out. That little tree never quite straightened up, but it grew tall, sturdy and strong. I've just about come to the conclusion that nothing is irredeemable, least of all the human race. We may be broke, but we're not broken. . . .

One spring we had a little calf we were trying to wean. It was past the tottering stage and old enough to give up sucking and drink out of a pail. With four hungry kids of our own we needed the milk worse than the old cow needed it for hers, so we started in. All this came back to me the other day when I got to thinking over so-called progress, human progress. I'm not so sure all this gadget civilization of ours is the best. Maybe modern technology hasn't accomplished all we have attributed to it. Perhaps the old tried paths, the old established ways, were best after all. But about that calf.

Now so long as we held a finger in the milk for the calf to use his imagination on, he would suck in enough milk to fill up. The minute we removed the finger he would jerk his head out and bawl. At last we made up our mind he was just afraid of the shiny new pail; substituted an old battered, unshiny one, and soon he was drinking milk without benefit of finger. Maybe we should go back to pails that are battered and worn. Now, there I go, living two or three fashions back. . . .

Often I have remembered a letter Elbert Hubbard (the hero of a boy not long a man) wrote to me in which he advised to always remember that on every thing he said there was the rubber stamp, "Good for this day and date only."

When I come to think of the philosophy of Robert Frost, jelled and unjelled over the years of our friendship, I more clearly see what the Fra meant. Just when you get Frost pinned down to a set of rules, he eels out of them.

Is the world trembling toward progressive education—he is stressing rules of hard learning. Do university professors look askance at Long-fellow—he sees his truly great little poems (perfect in their structure) and shows their greatness. "He is a pretty good poet after all," he said.

It seems that, in a book that purports to set forth a great man's exist-ence in this planet, there should be a place devoted to his thinking. I especially have in mind in this case educational theories and processes.

Just here we come head-on against a series of contradictions and in-consistencies. Frost wanted, always, for himself and for his students, complete freedom of thinking and acting. But when you had him in a corner, you encountered all sorts of hedging and countering. He wanted the student to be a free agent, untrammeled by the teacher or the system. But he went against the "new" theories that "readin', writin', and 'rith-metic" were expendables and unimportant. How many times he has excoriated some lazy pupil for handing in a dirty school "projeck" full of horrible spelling and impossible grammar! How many times he has exploded when one such would ask how they could learn to spell, or what case to use of "lay and lie and sit and set." For the slovenly teachers who said case didn't matter, he had many scornful words.

I should say that Frost, while willing to teach the unwilling, was im-patient in the task, more willing to be sun to shine on the sprout (be it grain, or tree or what not) that responded to his warmth and poked an inquisitive head out of the soil to look and see how to become a stalk of corn, or bean vine or tree, than any other task.

He liked people who couldn't help thinking to the highest reaches. This explains why he forever inspired those who sensed what it was all about, and why he held forth to them the light which they, like Pilgrim in "The Progress," *thought* they saw. But he wanted students who had not been completely dehydrated of ideas and principles.

"They've got to have *something* and *some things* to hang on to," he often said. He refused steadfastly to cast his pearls before those who were apt to trample them underfoot and then turn and rend the caster. He had to know there was somebody out there ready to absorb his ideas. He would never bat a ball out into space. Somebody had to be there to toss it back to him, whatever the game—old cat, tennis, baseball, or ideas.

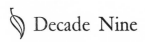 Decade Nine

XXXV. The Time Table

AMERICA'S NUMBER-ONE POET was about to be eighty. Gown and town of Amherst decided to note it with due recognition of exactly threescore years of national publication.

Looking back over the five years leading in reverse to the Macy "classic" award for the publication of that which was looked on as Frost's "final" collection, the infrequency of publication during that period well-nigh equaled the lean years at Derry. There were a few magazine offerings, the annual Christmas cards, *Complete Poems,* and *Hard Not to be King.* This told his story of publication, though the poem "New Hampshire" in its first appearance by itself as the entire content of a book was scheduled.

Early in February, 1954, the committee sent out invitations to fewer than one hundred friends of the poet—friends in the main who had some claim upon him. Charlie Cole's letter to the Californian told the whole story.

AMHERST COLLEGE

AMHERST, MASSACHUSETTS

OFFICE OF THE PRESIDENT

February 12, 1954

DEAR PROFESSOR MERTINS:

Robert Frost's 80th birthday (his real one) falls on March 26, 1954. On that date, Amherst College and a Sponsoring Committee of his friends (Frederick Adams, Joseph Blumenthal, Huntington Cairns, Edward Hyde

Cox, Archibald MacLeish, Stearns Morse, Mark Van Doren, George Whicher, Louis Untermeyer and myself) are planning a birthday party for him here at Amherst, at the Lord Jeffery Inn at 6 P.M. At the dinner, Archibald MacLeish will be toastmaster and there will be a few speeches and perhaps we can persuade Mr. Frost to say some of his poems.

On behalf of the College and the Sponsoring Committee, I would like very much to invite you to attend the dinner (black tie). Please let me know if you can come and whether you would like us to reserve you a room at the Inn. If you can come, I will send you further information about transportation.

> Most Sincerely,
> CHARLES W. COLE

For a long while it had been a struggle for some of Frost's informed friends to keep from disclosing the fact that he had been born in 1874, and not, as set down in all works of biography, in 1875. It was a temptation to us when we received a carbon copy of the biographical sketch of the poet from the editor of *The Columbia Encyclopedia* in 1948 for our criticism and suggestions before it was put into type to proceed to set the record straight. But we resisted. However, when Macmillan's brought out a new edition of Miriam Huber's encyclopedic work on Children's literature in 1955 (Miriam two years earlier had sent us the Frost sketch in advance for our approval) we made the suggestion that inasmuch as R. F. was born in 1874, she might as well be the first to record the correct date in a standard work.

Though we thus had somewhat secretly known the truth since 1947, a surprise came to us while we were at Dymock, England, in 1953, visiting the haunts of the poets, when in 1914–15 Frost had lived there at "Little Iddens." During our Dymock "interval" the genial vicar-historian gave us his book, *Dymock Down the Ages.* In it we found the birthdate of the visiting American set down correctly as 1874!

Was Frost playing fast and loose all the years succeeding 1915 with his true birthday? His first entry in *Who's Who in America,* (1916–17), stated that he was born in 1875, which biographical sketch, of course, had to be visaed by the biographee. Only Frost could have given the right answer to what he was about. If he had been asked, his answer likely would have been, "That's for you to figure out."

"What proof have you that I was born in 1874?" he growled as we sat together in his front room at 35 Brewster the night after the Amherst dinner.

"Your Aunt Blanche told us in 1947 in San Francisco that you were a year older than you claimed."

"Huh! Can't believe anything she tells you. What else?"

"Well, your father wrote a letter to his class reunion at Harvard in 1874 saying he had named his son after Robert E. Lee."

"Is that letter still in existence?" He continued to hedge.

We assured him that it was.

He studied a minute before shaking his head and grumbling: "That settles it. You can't go behind a properly dated letter. I don't think he could have made a mistake about the year, March is too far along for him to still write 1874 instead of '75. January would be different. I wouldn't take it as final if it had been January. I suppose the letter has a postmark? Anyway, that settles it. This was one time we celebrated the right birthday in the right year. Eighteen-seventy-four and not seventy-five. I'm aging fast—two years at a time."

He grinned sheepishly.

"We never celebrated birthdays at our home in San Francisco," he mused, still seeking an excuse. "The kids I played with invited me to their houses when they celebrated. I suppose that was how I got mixed up on my birthdate. It was pointless and got me nothing. Jeanie was a Centennial baby—born late in seventy-five—so I probably got to saying I was born early in that year so I could be a Centennial child too. Later on all the records were destroyed by the San Francisco fire. Oh, well. When a man gets my age, one year, more or less, can't matter much. Nothing else matters much, either. It's the way you look at it."

In the light of this conversation, it is interesting that an Amherst spokesman gave the information previously that March 26, 1954, had been established by the poet himself as his *real* eightieth birthday. Perhaps it was just a little game the inveterate prankster had been squeezing the last bit of fun out of, not the least significant his calling 1875 the Centennial year.

Frost himself once put it that the history of a nation might well be set down in the tab-names of certain great men.

One might paraphrase him by saying that his life could as properly be tabbed by noting the celebration of his major birthdays. The noting of these events, major or minor, may have been long in coming—in the light of what he said about never having known such celebrations when he was a child—but when they started with, say, his fiftieth at the Brevoort in New York City, they were on their way to becoming as much a fixture as the national debt.

When his many friends and well-wishers gathered at the Lord Jeffery in Amherst on the evening of March 26, 1954, they found themselves made up of diners from far places and near. One flew in from California, another from Florida. One had come up from North Carolina, and a fourth had journeyed from Iowa. But New England made up the bulk of the guests, New York being satisfied with a premature celebration the night before at the Waldorf.

"Charlie didn't much expect you to come," Frost said to the Californian. "Not that he just sent you a perfunctory invitation, not that. But California is so far, and we knew you had just got back from abroad. To turn right round and fly back over the whole United States —that was something beyond the line of duty. I thought maybe you'd send a telegram. There was a poet out in the Middle West whose book I got Holts to take on. He's making $8,000 a year, and all his children out from under. He wrote he couldn't afford to come. Takes money to keep up with the new Cadillacs these days."

Frost admitted making some suggestions concerning certain people who should be asked to come. "They'd never have thought of Foster out in Iowa or Robertson down in Florida if I hadn't."

A vacant chair was eloquent, its missing occupant seeming to be present. The soul of George Whicher was felt almost poignantly by many friends who missed his kindly face, his sparse white hair, and his genial spirit. If one were asked to define the role played by Robert's close friend and associate for nearly forty years on this famous occasion (the only Amherstian who spanned Frost's entire career in the college), the answer well might be that of "oversoul of friendship." Whicher was present in more than merely the written word read by F. Curtis Canfield—the manuscript Whicher had completed as his last task of a long and useful life. He would have given it himself had he not died before the great occasion.

His words came back out of the void where he was still pursuing the great adventure. Not from Istanbul, where he had taught in the University in 1952–53, and where, of all unlikely places, he had the year before been shown a letter written a dozen years earlier by an Amherst senior about what Frost had meant to a little group of "learners" at the old college. It was a clear-cut picture of the poet and a small group of boys on the Inn porch, in the moonlight, talking all evening, and far into the small hours about "Capitalism, which he calls 'the struggle for existence with the dollar sign just a little ways ahead,' and Communism; Walter Lippmann; selling on the market, and any number of interrelated and unrelated things."

The letter said that not one of the eleven boys who walked back from the Inn to the campus that morning was able to say a word. There were diners at the Lord Jeffery that celebration night who understood the lack of speech shown by the boys who had been moved by a great soul.

Frost's friends were thankful for a paragraph in Whicher's posthumous address which set forth a matter of history, something the poet himself had corroborated more than once.

"It was at Frost's suggestion that a course in American literature was added to the curriculum in the fall of 1917. I was to share it with him as a sort of assistant and reader of papers, I supposed; but as it turned out I gave most of the course as best I could with Frost appearing as lecturer perhaps eight or ten times. Then and there I was committed to the main work of my professional life. Out of the course there came in time a combined major in American studies. So the grain of mustard seed dropped by Frost has shot up and ramified into a substantial tree with many birds singing in its branches.

"I find my mind dwelling most on smaller matters; casual encounters on the corner which almost invariably turned into times to talk, walking along village streets and country roads, occasional quiet lunches together, firelit evenings which might be described as Amherst nights' entertainments rivaling the fabulous Arabian ones, and times of seeing each other home, back and forth through falling snow, with last words reluctantly spoken under an arc light exactly midway between Amherst and Pelham. Always incomparable conversation about every subject under the sun but always recurring to poetry. Frost constantly brought to our introverted academic community news of a larger world. To our everlasting benefit he ventilated the faculty."

A silence that could be felt came over all who had listened to the posthumous account of what Frost had meant to Amherst College. It fell to Charlie Cole to tell his own findings and what they had meant over the years, first as student under, then as friend of, the poet, and finally as president of Amherst with Frost as semiannual visitor. Such a talk was well prefaced by the suave, kindly words and gentle manner of Archibald MacLeish, who said:

"Robert Frost is a mountain, and nobody talks back to a mountain in Massachusetts, or even to hills in New Hampshire and Vermont. When a voice speaks truly, nothing can stop it."

Eighty-odd diners sat at thirteen tables looking toward the fourteenth, where three members of the American Academy sat, with a message from a fourth, Mark Van Doren, who could not be there. These speakers were Charlie Cole, Thornton Wilder, Robert Frost, Archibald MacLeish, Louis Untermeyer, Hyde Cox (reading Van Doren's message), and Curtis Canfield (reading Whicher's manuscript).

To every guest Holt's had presented their latest selection of Frost's poems. It was a creditable book inside and out and was titled *Aforesaid*. As Cole suggested, it was so named because the poems in it had been said many times "afore." Noting that all the localites which had put forward a claim to the poet were represented at the dinner, Cole said:

"Robert Frost is very like Homer, being a much-claimed poet. There are many sections which have staked out a claim, all of them justly. California, Massachusetts, New Hampshire, Vermont, Florida are states claiming him. Then there is Cambridge, which is a state of mind. Amherst had him as early as 1916. In fact, Alexander Meiklejohn's great contribution to Amherst was Robert Frost. After all these years of semiannual contact, our poet has become a legend among the students of Amherst, Holyoke, Smith, and the University of Massachusetts."

Then followed rare recollections with a Frosty tang.

"I remember a time when Robert was giving an examination. My roommate was a senior, and he needed the grade to get his diploma. But he took a chance. Instead of putting up a series of questions, more or less banal, Frost wrote one sentence on the board. 'In the light of what you know of me, write something that will please me.' My roommate simply signed his bluebook and handed it in blank. That night he got uneasy and told me he was afraid he had made a mistake. 'What if he doesn't like it? Why, I can't graduate.' But Frost must have liked it. He was graduated.

"On a chill, dark, winter afternoon back in my undergraduate days Robert was teaching a class, if his method may be called such a common thing as teaching. Night came on, and the room grew dark. He talked on and on, past the supper hour, and we all sat there in the darkness listening until seven o'clock, and nobody offered to leave. He was talking about the syllogism. This talk gave me an entirely different outlook, not on the syllogism, but on the metaphor. Robert Frost has shown us what the life of the mind is.

"This afternoon our Amherst students working in the laboratory detected a bit of atomic dust which had wafted over the Pacific, then across the U.S.A., and had settled here in Massachusetts. I got to thinking that atomic dust is a little like the thought of a poet, though the latter drops on us, not from half round the world, but from all round the world."

As the evening wore on, Robert's dinner grew cold on his untouched plate. It was no surprise to most of his eighty-odd friends to see him shamble out into a room back of the place of dining. He was following an almost unbroken precedent of ritual. He had to be alone with his thought before being called on to "say" some of his poems.

The speaking over, the Andrew Wyeth portrait presented to the subject, Frost stood at the end of the dining hall, away from the speakers' table, his *Complete Poems* in hand, and relieved himself of memories of "yesterday's agonizing."

The agony had started the morning before at nine at the Waldorf where he faced a formidable battery of television cameras under glaring lights for hours on end. There were questions put to him on every conceivable subject. But this was only the beginning of horrors. Twenty-five newspapermen made up the inquisitorial composite—Torquemada succeeding the morning's grueling. After noon he stood on his feet the whole time—"backed against the wall"—and answered questions without number. All this was followed by the first of his two celebrations where a vast audience of heterogeneous diners gathered twenty-four hours before he was eighty. Came the calendar-conforming, chronology-agreeing March 26, 1954.

"The old saying is that poet's die young," he grinned standing to "say" his poems at the Lord Jeffery. "So, a lot of people seeing me still kicking around say, 'What's he doing here, then?' Poets die in very different ways, not just in the grave—into businessmen, into critics, into philosophers, perhaps one of the noblest ways to die."

I don't read much about myself, but I hear about it. People tell me. Then I lie awake all night wondering if it's so. I've heard a lot tonight to think over, and it makes me look back, think about my poems and why I wrote them. Sometimes I hear praise of my wisdom. I've threatened to think about that a little. I have always thought that what begins in delight ends in wisdom.

Lately I've been collecting absolutes—ever hear of them? Some say there aren't any, you know. An absolute was to me always a more or less light, funny thing, a thought; but it grows more interesting to me. I'll tell you some I've collected—as far as I've got. One, with my compliments to Mr. Einstein is this: You can cover a given space with no more than three kinds of tile—equilateral triangles, hexagons (the bees know about that), and squares. Then there is another absolute I give you with my compliments for Mr. Einstein. It is expanse. That's what the universe is—expanse, nothing else. Just expanse. And while on this scientific absolute I might put in that after all these years my favorite magazine remains the *Scientific American.*

Getting off of absolutes: A fellow the other day said his favorite poet was Joyce Kilmer. "I never saw much in him," I told him. "I like him, and that's that," he answered. I held it. I didn't answer—I just held it.

I had a talk with some Greeks at a corner fruit stand a while back. They got between me and the fruit, so I couldn't touch it, I guess.

"Do you read Service?" one of them asked.

"Not much," I answered.

"He's not thought of much along with this poet Robert Frost, I guess," he said.

"Well, you know how things go, stock up and down," I countered.

"I suppose Amy Lowell's not even on the curb any more," the fruit seller put in.

"Could be," I answered.

Nearly a quarter-century earlier the poet expressed a wish for poetic immortality to the Californian. As he began this Amherst night to read his "little poems," leaving so many of his friends at their tables with lumps of sadness and nostalgia in their throats, he said almost exactly the same thing once more.

"You know people say you're this and you're that and you sometimes wonder if you're anything. Words are strange, aren't they. Hard to get out. Perfection is a great thing. All I've wanted is to write a few little poems it'd be hard to get rid of. That's all I ask."

Then he read some of his poems which all who heard knew belonged in that category—read with the same natural, vibrant voice that so long ago one had called the perfect organ of a perfectly uncowed human being. They included a new one called "One More Brevity," three months later to come out in *The Atlantic*. But there were old favorites, too—"West-running Brook," "Spring Pools," "The Need of Being Versed in Country Things," "Reluctance," and George Whicher's favorite, "Choose Something Like a Star."

If there had been even a little lingering doubt in any listening heart that night, it surely was forever dispelled. Somebody said softly, "This—*this* is the star to stay our minds on and be stayed."

Having been farthest to journey for the birthday dinner, the Californian was invited to come over to Cambridge, the night following. Frost was very, very tired, limply sprawled on the sofa in his front room, but talking on and on through the late afternoon until darkness succeeded twilight. Seeing it suddenly pitch dark, he asked the time. The spurt of a match disclosed the fact it was seven o'clock.

The poet's three strenuous days showed on his face when the lights were switched on. His eyes looked tired, and dark bags surrounded them. The visitor felt qualms of conscience when the host suggested walking ten blocks to his favorite eating place, but there appeared no alternative.

It was a delightful dining room under European-trained management, and a dinner of duckling, preceded by a dash of rum (he had not touched a drop of the unlimited and excellent wines and stronger drink at the hotel the night before) was all the heart could ask. The noble "talks-eating" equaled the "talks-walking" of a quarter-century of friendship. After dinner, going home by the way of Brattle Street, the conversation went back a long way into the storied past of Colonialism. The Brattle Street mansions lie very near the poet's hide-out. It was a happy turn which caused the New Englander to go out of his way to show the Californian how rich and opulent and lavish the "Tories" were who built that portion of Cambridge in pre-Revolutionary America. From these magnificent houses reaching back to 1660, the Loyalists had run away from danger and sought refuge in Canada when the tide turned against them. Their homes stood in the soft street light of evening as full of grace, dignity, and charm as they had stood when their owners arrogantly promised to hang all the Warrens, Frosts, Hancocks, and Adamses from the lower branches of the nearest trees when the "rebellion" had been properly put down. These mansions, built in royal style, the northern replicas of southern Williamsburg, today remain in perfect state of repair, with broad, deep, well-kept lawns, tall stone-and-iron fences, with false wooden urns over arched gateways.

"You'll scarcely find sturdier, better looking homes anywhere, I suppose," Frost said.

Brattle Street was left behind and the more down-to-earth Brewster come upon. The Californian had brought along a copy of an immediate post-Revolution Boston newspaper which contained an article on the

Constitution written by John Adams. This copy had been addressed to William Frost, Robert's Colonial officer ancestor, whose name was written legibly in ink on the space above the masthead. R.F. was pleased to see it, having just come by the old Tory mansions. He said he would read it and return by mail. His visitor, realizing that he was actually touched by it in an unusual manner, said for him to keep it. He seemed pleased. Thereafter, uninterrupted, conversation went on. There were many things suggested by the party and the old-timers who were there.

Whicher was a good friend, but I'm not much for talking about a man who is gone. Doesn't the Bible say "Let the dead bury their dead"? You ought to know. I think I've had enough birthday parties for one incarnation. Let's call it quits. Better not start planning to have me out in California on my ninetieth. I won't be *there*.

What pleased me most last night was the long-time friends who were there. I've known you a long time, but others longer. I gave a sidelong glance over the tables and was pleased to see so many I've been close to all these years. Joe Blumenthal, who's been royal printer so long, Louis Untermeyer, and Bob Hillyer. Certainly I was glad to have Archie MacLeish beside me, as well as Ray Nash out front. Been close to them both in and out of season. And there was Bill Snow and Elizabeth Sergeant. She wrote a most flattering piece about me back when everybody was asking, when they heard my name, "Frost? who's he?"

You know it's funny about my being a native son of California. I stayed away a long while. Now I've been back three times. Whenever I tell people I was in California for the Olympics, some of them ask, innocent as anything, if I participated.

Since you stirred up my memories and shook up the old bones for me with the addresses my parents had, I've thought a lot about them. There are some you didn't get from the State California Library that I half-remembered. These were probably left out of the occasional directories of San Francisco because my parents moved between printings. There must be two, maybe three, such not in your list. I suppose I get my wandering habits from my folks. We moved often. I once said I had as many addresses as a crook has aliases. I was always a wanderer. When I was a kid I went on a tramping trip down south. It was a wonder I ever got out with a whole skin. I got in with a bunch of bargemen, rough, but of a good, respectable sort. We went into the waterways that skirt the seacoast on down to Florida. It was a good experience toward toughening me, I suppose, and didn't hurt me much. I think maybe Prescott, having to take responsibility as he has, has benefitted from the experience. It never helped Carol, though. You saw Prescott last night. He's grown up tall and handsome. Nearly died when he was a kid. But he's licked into it as a family man. He's a good boy. Robin was there last night, Marjorie's daughter; she's at Smith College. She and Prescott's boy are the only ones named after me. Now we have a Robert Frost, II. He must be three by now. I can't keep track. His [Prescott's] two girls are growing up pretty fast. If I hang on long enough I'll be a grandfather twice removed. I remember out in California when we visited Gertrude Atherton we found she had made it. Pretty spry, too, I remember.

Down in New York the other day a reporter asked me what I thought about juvenile delinquency. Maybe I should take a refresher course in order to be able to advise my children's grandchildren. I asked him what I *should* think, since I was a juvenile delinquent once myself. I very nearly was made acquainted with whores—though without experiential knowledge. It was when we lived on Grace Terrace in San Francisco—the neighborhood where we had our talks about Conant as we climbed the long, steep hill back in '47. I would walk down through whore town to a drug store. Of course I didn't know what a prostitute was. Their houses were flush on the street, one door and one window. In the doorway would be a little bench and on it a whore with a white and tan lap dog. That's my memory of it.

In those days, like most San Franciscans, my father always kept a loaded pistol about. With other newspapermen he'd go out and shoot into the water. One day a bullet went wild and somebody, a bystander, was killed. Nobody knew who fired the shot, so nobody was hanged. When my mother brought us kids back east to visit my grandfather, my father wrote her that the stock exchange in San Francisco was going to open fire on the newspapers. They had barracaded the doors and windows to repel the attack. However, nobody actually started any fight.

I should have written my Aunt Blanche after I had found her in 1947, but I didn't—procrastinated as usual. When I went back to San Francisco in 1953, I visited George Stewart. I tried to get in touch with her at her old address, but they said she had gone to a nursing home. She probably died in the home. She had every right to die. She would have been over a hundred, maybe a hundred and three at the time.

You know you've plagued me no end over the years with your collection. I never mind signing some major things, but signing a piece of toilet paper is going too far.

So, you might just as well open that suitcase. I know it isn't filled up with clothes. You don't own that many suits and shirts.

I take it you were largely to blame for Earle Bernheimer's selling his collection. I'm not blaming you too much. Maybe you were tempted above your power to talk back. I know just how it all came about. You had once shown him a manuscript I had given you. He told me he had a right to expect everything like that I disposed of. He quit sending me a check which he had been accustomed to sending. He was very peeved. I had been happy with my arrangement with him. It was comfortable to feel that I had established myself with a liberal patron—a modern Macaenas. He was generous and made large gifts. I returned his generosity with similar large gifts—in a different coinage.

You weren't to blame, though, for the final straw, except indirectly. Circumstances brought it about and the camel's back was broken. I mean the way he was treated at Berkeley in 1947. He didn't like playing second or third fiddle. Just being in the string section wasn't enough. So, the thing grew and grew on him. I knew I had made a big mistake when I was at his home after the shouting and the tumult. He told me he wasn't interested in any college for the collection. He only wanted it as an estate for his son. So, I was prepared for the shock when Parke-Bernet advertised everything I had passed on to him, including *Twilight*. I thought it pretty cheap to sell it that way.

A twinge of conscience beset the Californian. But the harassed poet had said, "Let's get it over with," so the suitcase was opened, the many items laid out. Unperturbed Frost proceeded with the disagreeable task.

For an hour or more, unmindful of the hundreds and hundreds of items he had signed under protest in bygone years, he sat patiently inscribing book after book, picture after picture, and magazine after magazine. His cracks were priceless.

The previous night in the Lord Jeffery basement, for convivial conversation, little groups had gathered. The Californian, Robertson from

Florida and Blumenthal gravitated together. The printer was in full bibliographical form. He told how Robert signed special editions.

"When the printing was all done, vast quantities of half-titles were sent to the poet, the entire fold being forwarded to him special delivery. Though they were shipped 'special' these folds were pretty badly messed and crumpled.

" 'I don't think these things can stand special handling,' Frost said, 'so I'll just mail 'em back regular mail.'

"He would sit in his armchair, the well-advertised board across the arms of it, calling out a new name each time he signed—'Smedley Butler,' 'Lydia Pinkham,' and so on to the last signing. But each signature was always perfect."

We remembered Blumenthal's word picture as the poet signed for us, talking about each thing to be inscribed. We had always looked on his picture on the cover of *The Atlantic* as a monstrosity and were surprised when he passed that for attack and centered his fire on one we had always liked exceedingly, Chaliapin's cover picture on *Time*. He signed it without demurrer. He only said it looked more like Sandburg than himself. Then he was off again.

Once Old Carl came to speak at the "poor man's university," the University of Massachusetts. He stayed at our house because he said "all the swells did."

I knew how the audience and chairman worry when a speaker is late. I told Sandburg he should call up and explain that he was already in town and would be on time for the lecture, just to relieve the chairman's strain. He had his banjo along and strummed away on it. I got more and more uneasy, for I was afraid they would blame me when they learned he was at our house. Certainly I didn't want to steal him from them. I at last told him I was going to call and explain that he was there, for fear they'd think I had kept him. He went on strummin' on his banjo, but I go the chairman an the phone and explained that they should come for him. They came just before he was to speak. I told him to bring the committee back with him to my house.

I don't know how he feels about the present state of the nation. Quite a change from "The people—yes" of the New and Fair Deal days. Eisenhower seems to me to be pretty colorless. Somehow, watching him vacillate in the White House—he wouldn't say yes and he wouldn't say no—I can't believe he was ever very much of a commander, except to follow a schedule handed to him. Sort of push-botton general. Funny thing, isn't it, the Republicans getting into a lather over states' rights—the thing they fought the Civil War over. Now they're on the other side. . . .

I'd have to be more cantankerous even than Old Carl not to think well of last night's celebration. Charlie and his committee did a good job. I kept expecting Wilder to hit somebody on the head with all his gesticulations as he orated. It was as good a night as an octogenarian has any right to expect.

Maybe the least said about the Waldorf shindig the better, though. Last night we had writers and college people. They were my friends. Down in New York they were businessmen, and professional men, and publishers, and booksellers—even collectors. Just what a federal judge was doing there you needn't ask *me*. There seemed to be plenty of liquor in the pre-prandial room last night. No place for a prohibitionist. I didn't taste any of it. I'll take your word it was good stuff. Haven't seen as much since the Bernheimer party back in forty-seven. Some of my birthday parties seem to have featured the strong drink which is raging, San Francisco was an exception. Nobody got pie-eyed last night. In the Waldorf the night before— well, some did.

I've had enough birthday parties for one lifetime. After the eightieth there ought to be a law—no more for another hundred years. That'd excuse me. I'll not be here in 2054.

All things come to an end—even the signing of books. The poet was very, very tired, but he would not consent to our leaving, declaring that we would never find a room at that late hour. So, in spite of our protest, he wearily made up a bed in the spare bedroom upstairs and asked only that we leave quietly when we got up next morning, allowing the door of the house to lock inside without slamming it as we went out. Then he said goodnight and good-by and went to his room.

The bedroom was filled with books, the larger proportion being history, with Mexico paramount. The Californian crawled into bed and with the journal of one of the old *Conquistadores* for a nightcap slipped away to sleep, to dream of a stubborn little boy in Lawrence grammar school being moved, as he read the story of Cortes and Montezuma for the first time, to write his very first piece of literature as he wandered up and down the nearby woods. To that embryonic poet his many-stanzaed verse was a shining glory, as all poems must be to the author. He called it "La Noche Triste,"[1] and it had for a final stanza,

> *The Montezumas are no more,*
> *Gone is their regal throne,*
> *And freemen live, and rule, and die,*
> *Where they have ruled alone.*

Fifty-seven years after the boy Frost published "La Noche Triste," the man Frost brought out another poem on kings. It was a satirical verse, the whole content of a little book published in 1951. Place these lines beside the four above. The king's son speaks:

> *. . . Consider me,*
> *How totally ignored I seem to be.*
> *No one is nominating me for king.*

There it is for all the world to ponder. All the rhetoric and bombast gone that one-half century before, in fact more than one-half century before, appeared in "La Noche Triste." Age has mellowed content, philosophy, language, and form. The poet has reached a place where he dares a pun. Now he can laugh at the world and at himself. Mostly at himself.

On the pillow that night, the poet's inscription still fresh on the publisher's page, lay *Aforesaid,* No. 215 of 600 numbered copies. The author had written these feeling words:

"Robert Frost to Louis (as he may as well be called after all these years of friendship.)" The author had drawn his pen through the "Frost," making it "from Robert to Louis."

XXXVI. An Equalizer

No HINT WAS GIVEN his visitor following the eightieth birthday celebration at Amherst of an impending good-will visit to South America, via

[1] See Appendix.

air. Frost had always avoided air flights, but the trip to São Paulo, Brazil, in any other way was out of the question for him.

Good Democrat that he was by inheritance, he was not averse to flirting with G.O.P. Washington. How much his friend, Sherman Adams, fellow New Hampshirer, had to do with the arrangements is dim. But one suspects.

Junkets and good-neighbor tours about this time, to put it mildly, were becoming epidemic. It was looked on as imperative that we keep friends down Equator way. The four-hundredth anniversary of the founding of the metropolis of the Great Plateau about to be celebrated in 1954, Washington chose the poet for its ambassador of good will. He flew down to deliver the message from the Great White Father in the national capital to the friendly São Pauloans. Later in California the globe-flying poet was full of memories—mostly pleasant.

I never deny that we are a materialistic nation. Why stick your neck out? The highways and freeways tell it, just as the poor old railways used to proclaim it. Not now—not any more. We have more automobiles per square highway than anybody else. More sky scrapers, more airplanes and jets. Sometimes they're so thick in the sky we imagine they're swarming.

Yes sir, we are materialistic. I know because the people in São Paulo told me so. I had suspected it before. They'd always hurry up to add, "But we don't mean *you*," just like that. "We don't mean *you*." They didn't want me to think them personal about it. They just kept telling me how much we of the north loved money—how commercial we were. Almost as bad in this as the English—they were. Now, all this was happening in São Paulo, the most materialistic city in the entire western hemisphere. São Paulo was founded by the S. J.'s (members of the Society of Jesus). I've got a lot of S. J.'s for friends. I enjoy talking with 'em. But, somehow, the trend that was started very early by the Catholics to get away from materialism—pillar saints, monasteries, nunneries—didn't exactly turn the trick. These things didn't take 'em out of the material world—except in their minds. I asked a good Catholic in São Paulo if they had many cardinals in Brazil. His squeaked answer was revealing. "Too many."

But don't get me wrong. I had a good time in the most materialistic city, let us say, in Brazil. It lies just six [*sic*] degrees south of the Equator. I flew over the Andes getting there. I went there to woo the São Pauloans.

· 335

I kidded 'em instead. I think I did some good. Can't all make a *faux pas* in Latin America you know. Somebody's got to win. The altitude of São Paulo is 2,700 feet above sea level. That may have had something to do with prices. I can't say. *Something* did. It's the commercial and industrial city of Brazil. That helps, too.

And thus he dismissed his good-will tour with a good-will laugh.

It was in the nature of things that new Frosts should be discovered by varied individual explorers with the passing years. Fame and notoriety began to seek him out. That radio and television waited so long to give him a lift was in keeping with the other media of public hearing and seeing and judging over the years.

One remembers the incisive manner of his replies to questions. The answers rarely were the ones expected, but Frost was there in every response. His voice, still the perfect organ of an uncowed human being, continued to send little shivers up and down the spines of listeners.

There were occasional changes of lines when he said his little poems, either because he did it through design or because he had a lapse of memory and had to say the poems *ad lib*. Such tamperings with established lines spoken on radio or television (not to mention personal appearances on the platform) gave the person who knew the poem by heart an accelerated pulse. Sometimes the heart missed a beat. But the sense was always there, and the poet went forward with power.

It must have come as a shock to some teachers of English to hear the moderator for "Meet the Press" on N.B.C. declare that this man (referred to by some critics as "a good period poet") "in the opinion of many, both here and abroad, has probably written more poems that will endure than any other writer of our generation." Nor could there be serious denial of his added words: "He is still young in hope and in dreams, free from despair and pessimism."

Both sides of his octogenerian year, the poet's mind turned by constant prodding and reminding to the long struggle from his Lawrence days in the beginning of his poetry to the day he stood on the mountain top and surveyed a world that lay far below at his feet, well within his grasp. From many conversations of memory, thoughts prevail.

I have sometimes pointed out that the forty—first forty years of writing I made just two hundred dollars out of my verse. I can't say that was a living. I've done better since. I'm making a living now. I suppose it's explainable in this way: more people reading my poetry. They've found me. I should say there are more people reading poetry in America than in any other country. There are more people reading poetry today, or as many, as ever read it in any other age or land. Take Homer. Nobody read poetry in his time, except a few people at court.

Wherever I go I find what I call the best audiences on earth—the town and gown crowds—coming out to hear me. I have the big crowds, and I have the understanding—all I ask. I musn't be too important about it.

I believe the poet has a better chance today than Homer ever had. I like to say the lines often quoted about him:

> *Seven cities claimed the Homer dead*
> *Through which the living Homer begged his bread.*

In the period of the Renaissance, and before, poets and artists and troubadours had patrons who let 'em eat below the salt. I have a better audience —a better multiple patron—other men have 'em too. But I'm concerned with what they do, and have done, for me. I refer to the American colleges —fifteen hundred of them. These have taken the place of the nobility and the royalty of the middle ages and the rebirth of letters—and the artist sits on the elevation *above,* not below, the salt.

A poet, patron or no patron, must find an audience. And he must get a publisher before he finds a patron. Cost of publishing is so great that one poet can sometimes break a publisher. But there's an answer to this. My publishers have found it—cheap books. It can be done—will be done. We learned it from Europe.

People ask me sometimes why there are so many poets. Well, it's just in the nature of things—the nature of us all. We all started out with Mother Goose—and it's a good start she gave us. I suppose poetry has been written in one form or another for many thousands of years, so that rhythm and meter have become a part of our existence. So, when you throw meter away, how do you know you have anything left! That's the danger of modern poetry. Throwing the meter, the beat, away. Poetry, I like to think, and say, is the seasoned extravagance of the spirit.

If I say something to a student in the first semester in prose, then I have to take all of the second semester to explain it to him. If I tell him in poetry he ought to be able to tell by the tone and everything how I mean it to be taken. A long time ago I called this the sense of sound, or the sound of sense. I've never yielded an inch. I've said many times that a poem should begin in delight and end in wisdom like a love affair.

We're a great people to talk. I suppose we're like children whispering in the dark to keep the "fraid" away. Down in South America on that good-neighbor junket awhile ago I found 'em looking on us as an over-anxious country. That's a nice way to look at it. We want to be decent. It gets us into a lot of trouble, but we worm out of it somehow.

Memory recurs of conversations in long night vigils with truth, or in public appearances when the poet was playing cat-and-mouse with inquisitors.

There has been too much talk about—too much emphasis on—my chance remark away back in 1932, out in Pasadena with atom-splitter Millikan—the one I made in answering a woman who wanted to know if I were a conservative or a radical—whether I was about to embrace the era of F. D. R. (He hadn't yet been elected.) I didn't take much time to think about a reply. I just snapped right back with "I never dared be radical when young for fear it would make me conservative when old." She didn't have a come-back. It's like being in a cell, or dungeon, or buried in a tomb you can look out of.

I may be conservative in politics. I'm radical in education. We're all radical about something, conservative about something else. It makes the world.

Somehow I covet a new boundary in education. We need to map out new horizons beyond Lucretius even. As for poetry, I've said somewhere that poetry is a way to take life by the throat. I'll stand by that.

I was in Harvard while the old education, unaffected by Madison Avenue, was in full swing. There wasn't too much difference between the way I was taught there and the way my father was.

Got to thinking the other day about how good it was for my father's literary—newspaper—career to have had to learn all that Caesar by heart. He had those Latin sentences right in his head. You see, he was permitted to offer those two books of memorized Latin of Caesar for the whole course. Good sentences. Not poetry. If you want to be a reader of Latin—

Birch tree at the Derry farmhouse, New Hampshire.

Present for the dedication of the Robert Frost Room in the Jones Library in Amherst, Massachusetts. *Left to Right:* Frank Prentice Rand, author; Robert Frost; Roy P. Basler, of the Library of Congress; and Charles R. Green, curator of the Frost Collection.

Robert Frost and his dog Gillie at the farm in Bread Loaf.

The apple orchard at the Derry farm, Derry, New Hampshire.

The old pump at the farmhouse in Derry, New Hampshire.

Robert Frost's cabin at Bread Loaf.

Robert Frost's garden at Bread Loaf. Shown is the electrically controlled wire to keep the deer away.

The Chapel at Amherst College on the Morning of the Frost Memorial
Service, February, 1963.

speaker of Latin, you oughta do somp'n like that. Wouldn't that idea kill the progressives in education, though.

This matter of genuinely learning your subject in school—no foolin'— is important. You've got to get familiar with it—so familiar with it you can throw it away, and in the elation of the moment call it back—get what you want.

The first time I got to thinking about these things was when I first read *Middlemarch,* George Eliot. I must have read it by myself—never had it in school. But I got the great light there in that book. One's got to know the thing. Notes don't count. Card cases won't do it. It's got to be in you— part of you.

Homer nodded—I don't know how much he nodded. Maybe you can figure out by comparing his *Iliad* and his *Odyssey.* One is much more the gift. Baseball, tennis, poetry, art—it's all there. You have to have the thing in you if you want to get anywhere.

Another comment at another long night vigil explored the "range-finding" in education:

In and out of education my interest in young people has always been more in their convictions than in their performances. They are like the coming out of stars at nightfall—the slow outshining of stars—at twilight as night and darkness come on. One by one, one here, one there. Maybe they'll constellate by midnight. I've watched 'em gather, each a separate star against a blue arch, separate even in constellation. I love stars. I've been steering and being stayed by stars all my life.

When we come to remember the old education we were all exposed to, and compare it with the present, we usually start out with the thought that the main difference lies in too much memorizing in the old, too little in the new. Social living can't take the place of hard and fast knowledge, nor can etiquette.

We just simply aim too low in our school program. Maybe the old system aimed too high, but it didn't aim to teach all creation the ablative case— nor even the accusative. The new education seems bent on teaching the genitive.

And so, with starry night turning into morning the poet-philosopher betook himself to bed. There would be other, perhaps more distant, ranges to explore tomorrow.

XXXVII. But We Were England's

Nearly a generation had passed since Frost had gone back to England for a visit in 1928. Tremendous changes in world opinion had taken place. The old friendship so natural between blood brothers, between peoples of the same cultural heritage, was beginning to creak at the joints. The great task of bringing the two nations possessing a cognate literature—a bond of cultural inheritance—into better understanding of one another might well be undertaken by a poet.

It had been forty-five years since an unknown poet had landed in the British Isles, making his way to London. Now that poet was to go back to the land which had sired his ancestors, back to visit a kindly people who had given him his first and his second chance with published books, Such a junket had possibilities for untold good.

Early in 1957 it began to leak out that the poet was about to undertake a good-will tour. He first let it out (the offer having just come) on his way north from Florida, when he stopped at Chapel Hill for his annual lecture and reading. The State Department wanted him to go to Britain. Brazil was one thing, England altogether something else. It was more than language and blood. In England, for Frost, was the basis of all inherited things—culture, letters, and outlook. He might quarrel with the English—kinfolks are notorious for quarreling amongst themselves. He could make it all up when it was over with.

It eventually developed that he would not go alone. His long-time friend and former pupil, Larry Thompson, of Princeton, not altogether altruistically, offered his services as general factotum, baggage smasher, travel agent, and manager. Who better than his long-time friend and biographer! As Larry summed it up in historical perspective, briefly:

"The result of the matter was—I went."

As was to be expected, Frost began early to play the whole affair down. He shouldn't have come. It was all a waste of time. And so on, as none could do more than he. There were the poets in London, the hangers-on, and the ones who counted. He would have to see all these. Even Masefield? He was never too kind to the laureate, but his quip at the time about him was kindly, if barbed.

"Who is Masefield that he should not write a bad poem for Queen and country?"

Right off, following a breathing spell in London, he went down to Cambridge where later he was to receive a degree. On the preliminary trip he read his little poems to the boys and their tutors and had a genuinely good time. But when he found himself placed in "an hotel" he exploded.

"I'm only just a country cousin, am I?" Or (on second thought) "are the English manners different from ours?"

Wherever he traveled he liked to be housed with people in their own homes. He liked to eat with them, to loll in an easy chair after dinner and talk. Here he found himself islanded in a common hotel, apart from anybody English. But, being Frost, he got over his peeve and rationalized, accepting the situation as it turned out.

Previously the poet had been given a doctor's degree in absentia by Durham University. He happily accepted an invitation to visit the old school perched high on its hill above the River Wear, which river wellnigh made an island of town, cathedral, and college.

As the train moved swiftly northward and his companion took in the scenery, alternating between lush meadows and green pastures where sleek cattle grazed contentedly and industrialized communities with smoke-stack trademarks of a manufacturing country, Frost began to take stock, aloud to Thompson:

"Whatever did I come over here for, anyway? I should by rights be in Ripton at this minute. Just before I came away I set out a little orchard —apple trees—below the cabin. Stafford Dragon won't water those trees as they should be watered. Little new trees have to be kept soaked if they are to come on well. I ought to have stayed home and looked after them. I wish I were in Ripton right now carrying pails of water to those trees."

But when the train reached Durham station, he forgot the apple trees for a while. Here was friendship, hospitality. He was housed in the swankiest, plushest suite of rooms in the Bishop's own quarters in the old castle, there on the cathedral grounds beside the ancient Norman pile. His companion agreed with the poet that the college gave him an elegant stay in Durham. In fact, Frost spoke of the whole period there as one of the pleasantest. He even remembered the beauty of the rose-medallion window with the sun softly falling through in the vast sweep of the Norman cathedral roof.

This 1957 experiment was proving the best of the three visits he had paid to the British Isles.

It was back in London that he discovered how famous he was—how famous he really was—in England. Word soon got round, and there came to be one unending stream of visitors. If he hadn't already known the plague of photographers, the manner in which they descended upon him in the metropolis would have taught him. "I came to wish for a camera-man's holiday," he quipped back home.

But, there was more than newspapermen and photographers. Invitations poured in from all sorts of groups and individuals—luncheons, dinners, and evenings with groups of friends. Such a bedlam gave him a sharp feeling of regret that he had come at all. To escape he even considered packing up and going home.

But such an ending to the great adventure would not do, and he knew it. "After all," he reasoned, "I came over here to represent the good-will of the 'colonies turned states' for the mother country now about childless. It was my own ancestral home. I owe something to the past, the present, the future. I'll have to suffer it out."

Perhaps he thought of the honors to be given by England's two great universities, perhaps also one of Ireland's. No American literary figure had ever been given honorary degrees by four great faculties such as Durham, Oxford, Cambridge, and University College, at Dublin. It may have been that he remembered the hard days and insults he suffered when seeking a place in the college world back home, or his agonizing days in 1912–15 in England seeking a place in the literary sun. At any rate he dismissed the idea of running back home and decided to stick it out. Out in California it passed before him in racy review.

The main trouble with the whole shebang was the long wait between events. The Irish degree was almost a surprise. Its offer came late. And if I must I will admit that at last I came to the conclusion that the end was worth the long wait between. So many of my friends of my first trip were gone. But there was a young radical—who'd been a young radical when I first met him in London—a young fellow I tutored somewhat—a lot younger than I. We stayed more or less friends. The last time before last summer when I was over there, 1928, he was the head of the London School of Economics. Very radical. I saw him that time, too. He is now Lord Beveridge, not talking at all any more about radicalism, economics. He's won his victory, created the Welfare State in England. We had a nice time together—didn't conflict at all. I teased him a little bit. I said, "What're you doing in the House of Lords, you old radical. Are you going to bore from within to destroy the House of Lords?" "Me destroy the House of Lords?" he scoffed. "I never thought of such a thing. It's just that Labor crowd," like that, "just that Labor crowd." He'd forgotten what I'd remembered. No, I suppose he's remembered all right. He's a fine person, full of ideas, and bright. We had a good time. He said he didn't mind my talk. It's all talk, he thinks.

Here's an odd happening in connection with Beveridge—goes back a long way. Happened that night at Monro's I told you about when I first met you in 1932, the night I met Flint on the stairs. Well, that night there was a woman sitting by me, Flint on the next step up. Very handsome woman, pleasant. She told me her husband was an archaeologist. Her name was Gardiner. She asked if I were a poet, and we got to talking. It was through her I first met Beveridge, whose career I was to follow and whose friendship I treasured to the last paragraph—at least up to now in the chapter. He was a red-eyed radical. Got over it when he was ennobled. Most of 'em do. I'm glad she brought us together. He's turned out to be somebody—even without Attlee's help, which didn't do him any harm. Big man he is, with lots of space in the International and British *Who's Whos* —Space he's never got just being Lord Beveridge—first or even tenth Baron Beveridge. He's written and published and worked and planned. Good fun, too. Little changed from the young man I knew in London in 1912. Just matured, that's all.

Good talk I had on B.B.C., later to be broadcast. Day Lewis queried me. I took a fall out of a great many things, such as the way I started quitting the use of such ornate words as "fain" and "list," which I used when I started out, as every one does. It's the effect of the great poems on young poets. I remember we talked about "Mowing" which I told him was straight goods—all mine.

I've always been interested in folk talk of the new country and the old.

I told Lewis I remembered a dialect below any I had ever used in poetry—little cruder, I mean. But that I had never known anything in the American country speech of the rustic sort—cruder sort—that didn't come originally from some quarter of England. We discussed one word "clide" used instead of "cloyed." Keats wrote about something "that leaves the heart high sorrowful and cloy'd." It's a word—cloyed—that would never be used in connection with cows overeating. The English though, country livers, say cows get "clide"—when foundered—bloated.

I found a great deal of misunderstanding this time in England concerning my publication and the friends I made there, way back in 1912–13, in London. I told Lewis how that it was at Monro's Poetry Bookshop that I first met—that I got to know—Pound and Gibson and Abercrombie, though not especially any one of them till my first book came out in 1913. Then my second book, and all that; but that I had not gone over for that, but only to be poor and write some more where I wouldn't distress my relatives.

I told Lewis that to me a poem was a way out of something—a clearing up of something; that I could call up twenty-five or more poems that answered to something somebody had left me dissatisfied with—some argument—maybe a year after the argument. A poet never takes notes—you never takes notes in a love affair. One's mind is full of nebulous things. These lie around, and one day we see the way through and a poem comes out. We never use all the stuff. But a little idea—theme—comes out.

Funny thing about narrative poems. All my poems are sort of like that. Anything I read I want talk in it—novels have to have. There's somebody talking in every one of my poems, as you'll see by looking them over. Talking all the time. Talk, talk. You know there are three great things in the world—there's religion and science. Then there's gossip. The biggest is the last—just good gossip.

One could not but wonder whether this B.B.C. broadcast could have possibly been as good as—up to the standard, quality of—the manner in which he retold the tale.

Observers who knew Frost, who had watched him perform under ordinary circumstances and under extraordinary conditions, testify that his performance at Oxford on this trip was his supreme achievement. The Sheldonian, which the year before had greeted another great American, Harry Truman, with an overflowing house, was crowded for the poet, packed like sardines in a tin, listening to him for one and one-half hours in what his companion looked on as the triumph of a lifetime.

There seems little doubt that here was the ultimate reach of his academic and literary career. He had a word about it.

Yes, I must confess it was a good trip—hard but good. Sometimes the English can stir me up. Then, again, they couldn't be better. Maybe I stir *them* up, too.

A great experience—one of my greatest—more than that. Probably, all things considered, it *was* the greatest experience of my whole life. That's saying a lot. I've been accused of saying this same thing before about this same trip. I don't regret it. I don't ever hold the agonies I had to suffer against the planners.

If I were to put into words what the whole thing meant to me, I should have to call it a rounding out which brought my career to a full circle. Always before there was something lacking. Now the circle is complete. No vacant rim. No flattening at the poles—just a complete circle.

I don't know if I created any goodwill between us and the British. Maybe I was so busy I never even tried. But if the invitations to dinners and gatherings and a general good feeling between them and me were indications, then it did something for hands across the sea. We've been a bit askew with the British now and again. I think we'd best try to understand 'em hereafter.

And those Oxford robes! I might have been taken for a Cardinal at the very least. You should have seen me. Larry says I was a gorgeous sight —an academic spectacle. When it comes to pomp and circumstance who can outshine the English universities? They've been at it, though, since Chaucer. We in this country only go back to Tom Jefferson. There's a difference.

With time available (urged on by *Life* operatives), he went down into the West Midlands, to his old haunts of forty-five years ago, into Gloucestershire. *Life* was at Dymock in full force to follow and photograph the poet where once there had been companion poets. While he was in London, he made an effort to contact one of those poets, Wilfrid Gibson, down at nearby West Byfleet. But news concerning his old Dymock-Nailshop friend and companion poet was extremely disconcerting. Three years previous to this we had visited Gibson and found his memory fleeting. Now he remembered practically nothing.

"No sense, I'm afraid, of torturing him and myself uselessly and fruitlessly," was his summing up.

Other things than pictures for *Life* or a sight of the old oven at Little Iddens and the house where he had lived "under thatch" beneath the Ryton Firs, written about in "Thatch," drew him. It is to the eternal credit of the poet that his visit to the old community was to pay a visit to the Haineses, down Gloucester way, for it was John Haines who wrote early and with discernment and understanding of Robert's life at the Triangle.

What thoughts, perhaps long unthought, passed through his mind as the old scenes passed before him. He might decry it as sentimentality, but the ghosts of men—Thomas, Abercrombie, Haines, and Brooke—must have passed before his face, their voices coming back in the still of English nights, perhaps even in the noises of London streets.

There was still Dublin, University College, another degree. He was frank to hint that he was more especially interested in getting it because of his playful Eire connections, and because it was from a Catholic college in the Auld Sod, than for its intrinsic worth. Already having three doctorates in England, he actually *wanted* the Irish one. No time for day dreams.

His traveling companion summed it all up in a few words describing his arrival, stay, and departure.

"From the time someone at the Dublin airport shouted down from the parapet above the field, 'O, Frost!' until we'd weathered the next two days, Ireland was tremendous to and for him. Everything was handled beautifully. The whole pace was changed. Now he was staying with a private family, that of the president of University College, and was being taken rides, rides out into the country. He was almost persuaded to be a Catholic because the children in that Catholic home were so fine.

"But the hitch was that too much space had been scheduled between his giving a talk-and-reading in Dublin, and his being given the degree by the University College. All of a sudden he collapsed into a kind of dark fury of disgust with himself for being there. He felt he could scarcely bear to stay even long enough to get the diploma. Part of it was plain fatigue. He had taken a tremendous beating—taken it like the great trooper he was then and always. The strain of it all was beginning to make him ugly. And all who know him know how dangerous he might get in that state. So it was necessary for him to have a part of each day to himself, being turned out to pasture and left alone. It worked. But the day after he got his degree we took off for Shannon airport to catch the first possible plane.

"Once on the plane and headed home his whole attitude changed. He had run the gamut from despair, gloom, disgust to the full circle which made the trip a fitting climax to his career."

An incident at the airport was related in later days:

> Just as we were boarding a plane at the Shannon airport here came a messenger with a package. The charges were five dollars. I paid, and off we flew. When I investigated, after so long, what should this precious package contain but a damned cast-off suit of Larry's. He might have thrown it in the wastepaper basket, not left it hanging in his closet in the hotel.

But safe back home he could laugh at many things, as he did laugh when we told him that on our first visit to Dymock—1953—we had talked with the only living person, an ancient housewife, who was there in 1914–15 and remembered something of his life at Little Iddens in those days.

She told us that the Frost children, keen gardeners, did all the gardening in the mornings while the poet slept, something he never denied, or even shrugged off. Then she went into some detail about why they thought him a German spy. Word got round that the Little Iddens house was full of books. Everybody said nobody but a German spy would have that many books.

"Faulty logic," was his only reply to that bit of unwritten history.

It was no displeasure which caused him to say it.

There was another anecdote of the same visit that we made to Dymock which brought a corrugated grin to his face. We told him we had tried to get into the Gallows but were ordered away in a peremptory tone by a woman's voice from the depth of vine and shrub and tree which completely hid the house. We went on to a house a quarter-mile down the lane, where we enquired of the householder and got the double-jointed reply: "She's not responsible. A clergyman's daughter has always to be careful of whom she lets in."

Vermont and Ripton and the little apple trees were calling. The prodigal poet was home with a cargo of high and unprecedented honors. It wasn't too late to save those little saplings. He'd start watering them before noon tomorrow. Wonder what Stafford Dragon had been up to while he had been away.

XXXVIII. A Masque of Mercy

For years friends, admirers, and kindly disposed people in general had been trying to get Ezra Pound out of St. Elizabeth's—released from the hospitalization which saved his life, confinement with others not accused of treason.

The actual truth of the whole matter was that if he had been guilty of overt acts of treason, death was the prescribed punishment. In which case, what was he doing in a hospital for the insane? How could he be guilty of treason if he were insane? On the other hand if he were guilty of treason—? These were questions which had no reply.

Held in St. Elizabeth's, he owed his life to the humanitarian feelings and kind offices of Archibald MacLeish and others. However irregular the proceedings, he was held to be a victim of paranoia—declared insane but harmless.

When release had finally been accomplished in the spring of 1958, Robert Frost related the course of the proceedings in some detail. The old chronicler was infallible, precise, and encyclopedic, if a bit rambly. Yet, a new voice was speaking. The hands were Esau's, but the voice—could it be that the constant needling by Pound had put a saw file into his voice—his usually tolerant speech?

Ernest Hemingway, T. S. Eliot, and Archie MacLeish were all in some way involved in the case. Years went by. Nothing happened. Ezra, right or wrong, stayed in confinement. You see, Hemingway was an old-time friend—Paris, left bank, you know—and Ernest was certain Ezra was the greatest living poet. For that matter I suspect Archie felt the same way about him. Hemingway wrote me a long letter concerning the case. I never have known Hemingway personally, but he had heard I was getting anxious about Ezra's being held, and he had offered to give Pound a home—wanted to endow him that way with a comfortable house someplace. Ezra's royalties would keep him very well, Hemingway figured. Even in the asylum his books brought him around a hundred dollars a week income. He could pretty much count on that.

Pound has always wanted a doctor's degree—an honorary one from some college. He of course isn't what even the most prejudiced of his disciples would call a scholar. But a doctor's degree, he figured, would help with certain readers who take his cantos for translations from the Chinese—and all that—something you and I know enough to know isn't so. He knows little Latin, and what he knows he knows illy. He was innocent of Greek, and certainly of Chinese.

I'm in a notion (nothing'll probably ever come of it) a notion of writing him a letter like the ones he writes Eliot, with a tiny little "e.p." (lower case) as a salutation, and a big inch-high "R. F." (upper case) as a subscription. I'm in a notion of telling him now that he's out he should go ahead and show his appreciation of the American people and government and what has been done for him—his life, home, protection, royalties on his books, friends—by staying here.

Eliot's been anxious about Pound's status. On the other hand, Pound has been very nasty to him. He writes scurrilous letters, putting Eliot's name in small characters, as I said. Eliot burns them as fast as he gets them, and completely ignores the writer. Eliot told me about it last summer. Well, he got released from the charge of treason by reason of a charge of insanity.

I've never particularly cared for—liked—Pound. He was always what we used to call a self-boomer. He was a sort of fake with it all. I should say of his poetry that he wasn't as good a poet as Santayana. Maybe that isn't just what I mean. I'm no professional critic. I'll leave that for my friend Eliot.

I never visited Pound in St. Elizabeth's. Been forty-five years since I saw him last—over in England. I seldom go close to a mental hospital. Have had to go too often out of duty to be visiting for the sake of visiting.

The sorrows of past and present days clouded his mind and thought and saddened his voice. But the shadow swiftly lifted. The cloud passed.

His face cleared, and there was Puckish humor in his voice once more. Pan again with us!

There have been a lot of people working over the years in a magnanimous fashion trying to get Ezra out of St. Elizabeth's. Magnanimity is what such acts are called. Mercy, compassion would do as well. Some call it meddling in other people's business—affairs. These people have been well meaning. They kept writing letters to lawyers, government officials. They organized groups to help and to expound. Some of them bought his books, a lot of them did that, and that was good. The ones who hollered the loudest bought the fewest books, I guess.

Archie MacLeish was one of the earliest, and he stayed right up to the last—almost the last. He didn't get it done. He and his wife gave up and went off to their island, discouraged. So, you see, I was not the first to try. But I was the last. You'll have to grant me that.

All along everybody's been talking about it. People writing letters about it. I have a little bit of pity for him, but don't like him very much. I've known him since—I haven't seen him since 1915. On general principles, because everything's been talked about him, and because he's a poet—just roughly speaking—something of a poet in the American story—and because one person and another kept talking about getting him out—and went off and left it, you know—and did nothing definite about it—I went down to Washington and got him out in a week. That was all. I just went down to the Department of Justice and said I wanted to know what mood they were in in the department. "We're in the same mood you're in," they said. "Go ahead and get Pound a lawyer. It's got to go into court. There won't be any dispute—any trial—there can't be. It'll all have to go through the form of going to court. The judge'll have to pass. So, go out and get him a lawyer."

I did. I got Thurman Arnold. I talked with Arnold, and he said he'd handle it without a fee. Rogers, head of the justice department, is a straight Republican. I got the two on the phone, and they decided to end it that week. And that's all I did, except write out the statement that I was speaking by permission for Hemingway, Eliot, and MacLeish, as well as for myself. Hemingway had sent me a long letter. He heard I was interested in the case. I'd never had much communication with Hemingway before. Been a long while I've shown this interest—inactive interest—in

Ezra. Humanitarian interest. Maybe we were lucky and picked the right week. Somebody said, "Better do it this week."

The trouble all along has been they were making too much fuss about it—writing letters to everybody—boring everybody with it. You can't do anything when everybody's in on it. Just three people of importance in the case. One was Overholser, head of St. Elizabeth's, Attorney General Rogers, and Thurman Arnold, the defense lawyer. A lawyer by pressing could get a day in court. I wouldn't know how to do that. He got the day in court, and it was all done in a week—everything settled properly and legally. I don't suppose such a case was ever settled, all settled and finished, in a week before. I may procrastinate on my own affairs, but I'm a natural expediter where other men's affairs are concerned.

I should have been there in court for my own good that day, but I couldn't make it. I had to lecture way off someplace that day. Ezra was in court—not to speak at all—just there. His wife was there. His son was there. Ezra was all dressed up for it—dressed like a troubadour. They took pictures of him, a handsome old man he's become—always was handsome—handsomer than ever with all that rig on—thin whiskers, big hat, flashy scarf, white shirt, no tie.

He talks all the time about usury now. He gets it somehow into all his letters. He's been saying that Eliot's a mistake—no poet at all. I've felt this a long while about Ezra—that this thing ought to be off of us and everybody. All clear now.

We're all glad Ezra's free. It's so much better. It's a matter of high magnanimity. I'm glad I had something to do with it—a little something.

Amuses me, though, when people say the only reason I helped get him out was to ease my conscience—that he'd made me what I am and I had a debt to pay. They said I owed all my success to him. He reviewed my book, *A Boy's Will*, in 1913, and my *North of Boston* the next year—reviewed 'em in Harriett Monroe's *Poetry*, Chicago. I was in England at the time. These two reviews made up the sum total of the making of me by him. Really, neither one of the reviews could have done me too much good. They couldn't in reason have sold more than a few hundred copies of the second book which sold fifty thousand copies. They mainly consisted of Ezra's opinions about poetry, not much about the books under review. He called, if I remember, my *North of Boston* things "Modern

Georgics." They weren't "Georgics." They *were* modern, though; so he was half-right.

But suppose my willingness to go to Washington to get him out of the custody of the *hospitaliers* should be traced to gratitude. You know if you're ever searching your mind for a simile, a figure of speech to represent the lowest common denominator, just try this little word "gratitude," —benefits forgot as Shakespeare puts it.

You forget the cantankerousness that has so long bothered you. You remember benefits forgot. Poor Ezra.

Been times, you know, when it was hard for me to say something good about Ezra. That ought to be over with now. He's paid his debt—on installment plan. He did more for me than just read and review my first book. He gave me copies of his own, though when I said they were good he almost got mad, saying to me, "Oh, well, if you like 'em." Then going on self-satisfiedly, "they're passé now." I suppose his cantos are more to his liking.

But, that's all over and done with now. Ezra couldn't resist a dirty dig at me after it was finished. I couldn't be in court, as I said before, being speaking off someplace. So, as he came forth a free man, resplendent in scarf and flapping hat, he looked round and asked where Frost was. Then he added to Overholser:

"Frost got me out, but he's not here, you see. He couldn't face me."

Came June, 1958. Robert had expressed himself to us in California a month after the trial, about Pound's desire to go to Italy. The first week in June, the newspapers announced the freed man's decision to make a trip to the country where he had spent his days under Mussolini. The State Department announced they would speed the parting guest.

Once again Frost was full of commiseration for the man who first and last caused him so much trouble and anxiety.

He had talked with Flint in London the year before; he had sought out Gibson at the same time; now the third still left alive of all his poetic confreres of English days was on his way to his former Italian haunts and familiars.

Could it have been sadness remembering the old friends he did not, could not, see in England? Might it have been continued thoughts of the ingratitude of Ezra Pound for whose welfare he had gone so far out of his way? Whatever the cause he became morose, and his whole conversation became tinged with melancholia.

You have achieved if you can be successful and not be made proud, or a failure without being defeated and vanquished. If you can come through both success and failure unchanged, you've really arrived. There's Eliot (he's a success—great success—I'm not gainsaying it), but I'm placing him relatively. He's a pessimistic Christian; I'm an optimistic pagan.

Somebody said, "what about walls—wouldn't you like to get rid of walls?" No, we always have walls—have always had them. While some are being torn down, others are being built up. Whether you want 'em or not you'll always have 'em.

One danger in the United States is that we have reached the point where we can make everybody happy and comfortable. Sad state. A rich woman asked me, "What hardship," she asked, "can I give my children to toughen them?" I didn't see anything much to offer under the circumstances. She might, I told her, make 'em go barefoot on the thick carpets, but that wouldn't be like stubbing their toes on hard stones. More like the monk who was given penance by having to walk five miles with beans in his shoes, but who took pains to boil the beans before he put them in his shoes.

Poetry is a still small voice in a tempest and tumult. But it sometimes deals with gore—killing the thing we hate—or love—or are indifferent toward. Now, killing of itself may not be bad, at least for millenniums men have thought that way. The hunter, the soldier are proud and respected. On the other hand the butcher in some countries, not our own, is not to be associated with. The same is true of the hangman, or the headsman, or the *guillotinier*. In medieval days to protect his life the man with the executioner's head-ax wore a mask. The thing I hated about the farm I lived on at Derry fifty or more years back was killing the chickens for market, or to eat at home—all the blood connected with the whole business. Something revolting about it.

People are scared stiff we are going to destroy the world with the big bomb. I remember how we worried after the first world war—poison, mustard, and lewisite gasses were all ready to be used by and against us. When World War II came, we didn't attempt to use any of these on either side. The same'll be true of the Bomb. We're a lunatic race, but we'll stop short of extermination, which nuclear war certainly would guarantee.

I like to talk with S.J.'s I meet up with now and again. Awhile ago I was talking with a couple, arguing and being argued with. I told 'em I might look like a convertible, but I was a hard top. Beyond theology is the true religion you can't talk about. I like to argue with people who have decided opinions. S.J's have.

About the time Santayana died, I sat down on a train beside an Irish priest. He must have known I was a literary man. He began right off: "Have you remarked the death of the philosopher Santayana?" and I said, "Yes, I have." He said, "There was a confused mon." And I said, "He was my *teacher*." He said, "I trust he didn't confuse you." I said to the priest, "What's the matter with him now—what are you complaining of?" He said, "The old carcass is lying around over there and they don't know where to bury him. They don't know where he has a right to be buried."

"The old carcass," he called him. He didn't know whether Santayana believed in the Greek or the Roman mythology.

I was told just awhile ago that Santayana wrote a letter sometime before he died, saying he didn't remember me as a student in his classes. His were big classes, and I was never one of the well-known boys in college. I never had studied English. Of course Santayana and I got to know each other later. He was more than a confused man—he was a lost soul.

This matter of Santayana's not remembering me shows the trouble with thinking backward to when I was in his class. I never went visiting my professors. I puzzled over Santayana's meaning. He distressed me a great deal. He wouldn't be my kind at all. He was a very beautiful speaker— very deliberate. Somewhere in his prose Santayana talks about the Greek gods and metaphors—very pretty. When I was in his class I had no place— I had nothing. Just because I am somebody now doesn't mean I was somebody then. I had no money. I wasn't one of the important boys. I had my own thinking about these things. Santayana finally said one day in his lecture, and I caught him up on it—he said, "All is illusion of two kinds— the false and the true." That's where I got him. Two negatives make a positive—affirmative—so a false illusion would be a truth. Just playing with words, he was.

After this the train conversation got going. I told the Irish priest that the Great Reformation produced as a by-product the Congregational church movement, and this movement had given mankind Milton and Cromwell and the new world starting with New England; but that now (having done its work) Congregationalism had relapsed into Unitarianism. I remember when I got my degree in Eire, there stood Eamon de Valera towering above me as a symbol. I felt tyrannized over.

Santayana did monkeyshines in poetry. He just played with words. But he did have his inspirations. Poets are like baseball pitchers. They have their moments.

And so the talk went on. One set it down as history that you needn't agree or disagree with Robert Frost. You only needed hearing and a mind to record. The hours with him might never be forgotten. Always, just when a vast depth had been plumbed, a new phase of argument came to mind. Was it writing, teaching, farming, or politicking—there was always that which the Greeks introduced to man.

Take a bit of athletics along with this. A pitcher on a team has to know and understand the coach. The pitcher may go in one or two times a week. He can't have a moment every day. He may be conscientious and laborious, and it doesn't count at all. It's skill that does it. That's the danger of the critical approach to poetry. It doesn't recognize this. Take Browning— any part of Browning. One part's as good, or as bad, as any other, and most of it is no good at all. He never knew when he had it. He got so facile he couldn't stop writing. A Browning specialist never realizes this. I've known 'em on the faculty. Moments. The matter of a poem has to do with some- thing about the moment. Sometimes a pitcher goes in and looks toward the dugout to be invited to quit—'tisn't one of his days. No moment has arrived. What that is is just the same as poetry. Top moments. The rest is just writing. Should be doing something else. A little teaching is all right, a little agriculture, gardening. Something to get away from other people's papers. They're very hard to take. You can do it—just so much of it— almost with sympathy—too much sympathy. You've been through it your- self. It's a regret to you. You see they haven't got it, but they're trying. They may be better than you are. Hard to hunt for that.

That's what I usually say to begin with—these moments. Shelley speaks of 'em, various poets have spoken of 'em. Poe also. Shelley writes of "spirit of delight—rarely, rarely comest thou."

On one side athletics—on the other religion. The lapse is called absidia. It's almost existentialism. A lapse of the spirit. One of the seven deadly sins, you know. Chaucer describes it. You've got to get away from it. If you're a saint or a monk you gotta go out and do something—dig, carry dirt and move a mountain in baskets. Shovel it into baskets and move it—carry it—to another place, just for something to do.

That starts you off where poems come from. You get in and out and have doubts. Wait for the spirit of delight. Now the novelist has a better life, easier time, than the poet. Homer would nod some of the time. But he keeps going. Then you have a spurt. There have been novels written all on this high plane—short novels. And the greatest novel ever written was that way—Homer's *Odyssey*. The whole structure of it that way. Magnificent thing. People always praise the *Iliad* more; but it's not as good as a whole poem. Parts of it beat the *Odyssey,* but the *Odyssey* has a better structure. I had the *Odyssey* in school for the love of it. Had it twice in Greek, once in high school, once in college. Like a portrait painter who can't command the sitter whenever he needs him—he can't do that— so he loses what he's after and wants to start all over again. You can see his desire to be swift about it—catch something he sees. Can't get it on the bounce. He has the fear of losing it if he stays with it too long, works it too hard. They always say, "I lost it at this point."

You can work anything—you can work poems—till you've lost what you were after. I'm talking about spurts. You can't always stay on a high plane. Wait for the spirit of delight. Poe was like that. You can take any long thing, he said, and cut out all but the poetry. That's the way he would work. Some people keep going and wait for the spurts.

The novelist who works every day may have the best of it. He may get better when he just keeps going dutifully along. Mark Twain caught it in "The Jumping Frog." "O, just a newspaper piece he dashed off," some said. Not that. It has high felicity. He did those things all through life. High points of writing. Take the early chapters of *Connecticut Yankee in King Arthur's Court.* Far from having it in the last part of the book. Sump'n all gone out of it. That's the trouble with graduate studies—graduate school. They think you command what is in your notebook. You can't command it. You've got to be so familiar with it you can throw the notes away. George Eliot in *Middlemarch* has such a character. He has card cases full, but he can't get anything out of 'em. A lady said to me the other day: "Don't you think," she said, "that this character represents George Eliot herself—unable to get things out of her card case?" Whether George Eliot could command what she had in her card case for the purpose of great art is the question. Lost in great scholarship.

Theses from graduate school are hard to sell. I have a friend who wrote a thesis on the early—young—Longfellow. It was so good a regular publisher took it. He has gone on from there publishing. David Nutt, London publisher of forty-five years ago, made a business of publishing American graduate theses. Never got very far in the world.

Yet it was David Nutt's firm and colophon that gave the world the poetry of Robert Frost.

XXXIX. IN THE HOME STRETCH

THE FACT that Robert Frost had been named honorary president of the California Writer's Guild in 1932 was the starting point for his visit to California in 1958. The silver anniversary of the Guild called for a celebration. The Board decided that of all years 1957 was the one the Guild logically should observe and celebrate, and the secretary was instructed to write a letter of invitation to Frost urging him to turn Golden Stateward as soon as possible.

Months passed. Nineteen-fifty-seven turned nineteen-fifty-eight. January was nearly half finished. Then came his letter, all properly typed on handsomely-printed stationary which proclaimed the address as 35 Brewster Street, Cambridge, Massachusetts. The date was January 13, 1958.

DEAR LOUIS:

You started something that seems to have gone quite a way with your friends and mine at Stanford and Berkeley. I don't know how much you have got into communication but I feel your part in arrangements about my coming out are a little vague. It grows on me that I want to come to the Coast again the more I think of it. It's of course somewhat personal. I want to see you and Esther and I want to see the Wallie Stegners and the George Stewarts. It's about time to get more definite about dates and I suppose money. I think it would be fine if I restricted myself to three big engagements reasonably close together at one thousand dollars apiece and I pay my own expenses going and coming. I don't know who started putting it this way. I hope you like it. I am almost too full of things for a person of my laziness but I think I must carry out this idea of seeing my native state again under good and great auspices, don't you think so? I've already talked about it a little openly with stray Californians I have run into here. I seem committed. I begin to look forward with a sense of pleasure. I mustn't spoil it all by letting myself get scattered all around. The visit mustn't be a trial of my toughness. I expect you to understand and protect me. Many years have gone over me since you took me out to ride in your well-aged car at Monrovia. I'm no longer the child I was then. K. will help you about this. I hand it over to you two.

Ever yours,
ROBERT

The good news of the imminent advent of the poet galvanized his western friends into action. He was immediately written that we wished to take advantage of his presence at the University of California at Berkeley to present the collection he had helped to build up, that it might for all foreseeable ages to come be safe from the tooth of time, ready to be exhibited frequently in Cal's vast library. We assured him we were making every effort to arrange matters. There was a delay of a few weeks, then came Kay Morrison's letter from South Miami, date, February 14, 1958, assuring us of Frost's interest in the presentation of our collection to Berkeley and telling of his agreement to speak at the University of California at Berkeley, Stanford, and in Southern California.

The air thus cleared, the whole matter was then resolved quickly. We of the west made ready to celebrate the coming of our recalcitrant native son to his native state.

Frost admitted that the three good-will tours (Brazil, Britain, and California) were all more or less surprises. He had long since resolved to stay on the Eastern seaboard and go wandering no farther. But such a decision on his part had been made many times before, only to be countermanded later. One would remember past times when he would murmur, "I'm a wanderer." Indeed, his life scheme proved him to be. If Belle Moodie spent her energies wandering from house to apartment to hotel and back to house again, her illustrious son devoted himself, with ever-widening frontiers, to wandering from county to county, from state to state, coming in the end to wander from continent to continent, almost

from hemisphere to hemisphere, hinting that if Cape Canaveral succeeded in the rocket field sufficiently, he might track his own poetry to
make his travels interplanetary, or at least follow the lead of his boyhood
hero, Jules Verne, and commute between earth and moon, or another
hero of his adolescence, Edward Everett Hale, and go up in a moon of
his own making and circle the earth. But he always voided his theories
by playfully adding:

> "*It takes a lot of in and outdoor schoolin',*
> *To get adapted to my kind of foolin'."*

At this time the poet's mind and conversation turned consistently to
science and the opening of new oceans of ether, some of it in fun, some
in deadly earnest. It is historically and critically true that, for a dozen
years previous to his 1958 visit west, his poetry touched lightly and deli-
cately on space travel, and that long before any serious attempts had
been made he had predicted the coming of the space age. Since science
was his pet study, and *The Scientific American* admittedly his favorite
magazine, the venture into space verse was a foregone conclusion.

This caused him, as he drew near his eighty-fifth year to turn his conversations and public utterances toward science, scientists, and kindred
themes, looked on as being far removed from poetry. In the very midst
of revisiting his old haunts, giving addresses to seventy-five hundred
students in the Greek Theatre at Berkeley, where eleven years before
he had received a doctorate; five thousand at Stanford; and to the largest
audience ever assembled in the Memorial Chapel at the University of
Redlands; these thoughts came back. They began as hanks of unspun
yarn; they ended as tapestries unrivaled in perfect sequence. He had a
word.

The "sarcastic science" poem was written a long while before "Sputnik
I" showed up. I take this attitude in connection with our space travel. The
Russians won the first quarter. The game's early yet. This poem's not
hostile to science. I like science. The poem had to do with these some time
before the fact. I feel kinda cross with people looking on the skies to see
the sputniks, when they don't know one star from another. Never looked
at the skies in their life before. Now they break their necks looking up.

I've walked with professors in country colleges out into the country at night. I'd say, "See, northern lights." They'd say, "Where?" They'd never seen the aurora borealis—didn't know where to look for the lights. When my father died and my mother and sister and I went east, I salvaged one book which I still have—one of my favorite books. It is *Our Place Among the Infinities,* a book of astronomical essays, written in the seventies. One of the first books I ever read. I read it as a child. I've always owned a telescope till my grandson talked me out of it. I've got to get another, what with this being the tag end of the geophysical year. Russians might put one over on me.

Up at the U.N. they have a meditation room. You'll have to go in pairs as they have only two chairs in the room. In the room, beside the chairs, is a lump of iron. The King of Sweden sent it to the U.N., and it's supposed to mean something. I take it that's why they had me down to see if I could tell 'em a metaphor for it. I've inquired into the matter with iron-mongers and people like that, and here's the metaphor:

> "Nature within her inmost self divides
> To trouble men with having to take sides."

That lump of iron is the basis of both tools and weapons. I'm on the weapon side. I sent that couplet to them. One very fine friend, he's a Pakastani, president of a university and all—he's the one most anxious about it. He didn't say, but I know what he's hanging around for. He wants a poem, so I sent him that couplet, and when I met him again he said, "Oh, you've written better poems than that." I don't know that I have. I've written a lot of couplets.

Now that telescope of mine my grandson has—I've only looked at real planets with it—things like that. I like to tease about politics, and I like to tease about science and education. I talk as if there were no such thing as education.

> "What're you back here for? I'm an adult.
> I went to school young without result."

I was going to write more on education, but I got lost in the couplet.

There was a finesse about the luncheon at the home of President-elect and Mrs. Kerr. The occasion was the presentation of the Frost collection, with the collector making the presentation. Later on Frost growled that the donor's wife had had as much to do with the collection as the donor.

Librarian Coney responded to the presentation, accepting the Frostana on behalf of the board of regents.

"This is a wonderful occasion. It is wonderful to have together in one place a distinguished, beloved author, the able and amiable collectors of his works, and a librarian. Herbert Putnam, long the Librarian of Congress, once said that in his earlier days he had thought a librarian's job a simple one—that you put a citizen and a book together in a room— and after a while the book is inside the citizen. Librarians love book-collectors and never more than when they have given books to a library.

"When I first heard of the Mertins Collection, I was pleased not only for the distinction and worth of the collection, but because Robert Frost was one of the few poets I had seen and heard. He was poet-in-residence at the University of Michigan in the twenties when I was an undergraduate, and I still remember how a friend and I called on Mr. and Mrs. Frost and their family soon after they arrived in Ann Arbor. I remember this with some embarrassment, because we called so soon that all of their possessions had not yet been put away in their newly-rented house. While my friend, who is an artist, drew Mr. Frost's portrait, I interviewed him for a student publication. His kindness and graciousness to two undergraduates are well remembered.

"If I may be excused for another personal reference, I should like to remind you that in 1912 Mr. Frost published a poem in the *Youth's Companion*. I was reading the *Youth's Companion* in those days, waiting for the Wednesday postman through the long, hot Michigan summer. I wish I could say I had been struck, as a perceptive youth, by the lyric beauty of that poem, but I was following intensely an adventure story—continued story—and I had no time or thought for poetry. Some of you will remember the poem that I might have read:

> *"O hushed October morning mild,*
> *Begin the hours of this day slow.*
> *Make the day seem to us less brief."*

"In the years after we had seen at Berkeley a sample of the Mertins collection, I used to wish that the collectors would beguile me—to quote two further lines from the poem in my childhood's *Companion*—'*release one leaf at break of day / at noon release another leaf*'—and let us have the collection by installments. But Mr. Mertins, like a true collector, treasured his collection, and it remained at his ranch home in the South. However, in 1954, an episode happened that should be a lesson to all book-collectors; a brush fire threatened his house to such an extent that he grew worried for the safety of his books, and now, thanks to the generosity of the collectors—and to the accidental nudging of near-catastrophe—a very important part of the collection has come to the Library of the University of California.

"Because of the personal annotations for Mr. Mertins from Mr. Frost, in books and periodicals beginning with the first 'professional' poem the poet ever published—'My Butterfly' in the *Independent* for November 8, 1894, sold to the editor for fifteen dollars—this is a collection of an intimate and personal character like no other. Here at Berkeley it will be well kept, and, if I know the Berkeley faculty and their graduate students, well used; and if I know the Library staff, carefully used."

President-elect Kerr spoke a word and with a happy thought turned the tables on the poet and suggested that he might have a word to say in rebuttal. One—all who knew Frost's attitude toward collectors—stopped breathing a moment. Frost did have a word to offer, speaking at some length, and not in an unkind manner, though he continued to express disgust at collections and collectors in asides. The only way he had been mollified on the occasion of presentation was by the donor's statement that the poet always called collections and collecting the lowest form of literary appreciation.

"That's better," he grumbled.

He tried manfully not to appear impressed. But those who knew him best realized how happy he was to see the almost definitive collection housed in a permanent home. . . .

Across the Golden Gate, beyond the bridge that spanned the bay, one could see the snaggle-toothed skyline of the city where the poet spent a childhood which he remembered with an astounding clarity. . . .

Then followed the happy aftermath.

His work in the Bay Area over, the poet shuffled along the corridors

of the Cal Library, pausing to look at the books, magazines, and manuscripts and to read his own handwritten inscriptions on pages and fly-
leaves of his own published works set down over the decades. There
were all the landmark poems going back, as Coney had pointed out, to
1894, and "My Butterfly," He was especially interested in the little volume of sermons by the Reverend John Doughty, his mother's San Francisco pastor when the poet was a child and also in the separate photograph of the doughty Mr. Doughty, who was alleged to have failed to
keep his word given to Robert's father to vote for Cleveland in 1884.
Having perhaps once been informed, but forgetting, Frost wanted to
know how on earth this little book reached the collector's hands at so
late a date, how come upon and how acquired. The photo was even more
of a puzzle to him.

Reading the inscription he had written on the fly of the books years
before, he asked:

"Did you ever find out about the scar on Doughty's head from the
wound made, according to report, by the Indians as he crossed the
Great Plains? Or was it all a legend? The Indians were supposed to have
done something to his scalp when his wagon train was attacked."

The case contained the "career" of the poem "Neither Out Far Nor
In Deep," from the photograph of the author standing under the shale
cliff at Laguna Beach long years before (which cliff and which occasion
he had remembered perfectly for twenty-six years, and commented upon)
to an early draft manuscript of the poem, greatly changed on its first
appearance in *The Yale Review;* the pirated first printing of the poem
in its earliest draft form in *The Citizen;* then its successive inclusions in
A Further Range, Collected Poems (Halcyon House); Collected Poems;
and on to its final fossilization in a text book. He exhibited more than
interest, almost amazement, over the display.

But that which he found hardest to grasp was the large number of
magazines containing his poems, inscribed by him, which space would
not permit of being placed in the many display cases. These were ar-
rayed on a room-length table in the Rare Book Department, not open
to the public, but privately shown to the poet.

"If I didn't see all these laid out here," he explained, "I'd never believe I had signed that many for you over the years."

It was pleasing to him, also, that at every exhibition table and case students were pouring over the collection of books and magazines, photos and manuscripts. Some students he paused to speak pleasantly with, even to point out something of interest, after which he passed smilingly on.

The oracle propounded:

"Well, maybe some rich patron of the arts will buy *Twilight* and send it out to this collection. Anyway, some of these books, while first printings, are not really first bindings. I'll send first printings, first bindings when I get back home. I have some left."

One who had been needled by the poet's "sneering" over first editions could not but recall his words to Day Lewis on the B.B.C. from London, where Frost, of all people, admitted owning two first editions of Crabbe's poems!

Later, when signing time came again after he had become domiciled at "Far Hills" in Redlands, he snorted over the interview by Arthur Harris in the magazine *Think* for March, 1958. He merely scribbled "F." His spleen was vented on the phrase in the magazine referring to him as "Cracker-barrel Socrates." He savagely crossed that out, rasping, "None of that!"

Other signings, refusals to sign, provide a composite insight into Frost's acquired phobias. But not one is to be explained on any proper basis.

As an example, later on as collector and collected sat in the library at "Far Hills" before the large open glass case in which the residue of the collection rested, awaiting recognition from his pen, accompanied by spleen, petulance, and plain cussedness, patience and understanding, the gamut was run.

Because we had known the poet and his original armor-bearer together, and shared friendship with both, it was taken for granted he would at least visa with initials, if not tribute in writing, the one book which seemed to be indispensable. But when the posthumously-printed-published *Swinger of Birches* was handed to him for such written tribute, he only growled an indistinct something and brushed it aside. We could not but wonder at his refusal at least to initial his own foreword in the book. After all, whoever understood Robert Frost? Two and one-half years later visiting "Far Hills," he signed it!

He made a statement the night following the orgy of signing a huge pile of books, papers, magazines, and photos, that when he gave a book or something *to* somebody, he signed it "To So-and-So"; but when they brought one of their own to him to sign, not having given it, he wrote "for," not "to." Yet on a number of books and magazines that very day he did not keep to this, but signed "to" on items he had by no means given the collector. One such turned out to be the copy of *Saturday Review* containing the controversial Ciardi article about Frost, which was at the moment still a bone of contention among literary people. Then there was the photograph made from a negative which inadvertently came into our possession from some unknown source, with R. F. standing in an unmistakable New England meadow, with woods on the border, dressed in rumpled shirt and gawky suit, beside a nattily attired man.

He told us that the man was somebody he didn't know—some stranger who probably passed by and had his picture taken with him. He remembered his own suit, however, as one he had bought in England around 1914–15. Oddly enough he signed it "Robert Frost in British clothes, for Louis Mertins to treasure."

In so many ways one could not but note changes in Robert Frost which had come gradually over him, almost unnoted, as years passed. Nothing basic. A certain sad preoccupation with his own thought. Yet on occasion the old Frost came sweetly to the fore, as when we first greeted him at the door of the preparation room at the Greek Theatre at Berkeley. His face lit up, his eyes gleamed. His voice was soft and full of affection—no hard-file in it—no knotted timber under the saw as he smilingly extended his hand saying:

"Louis Mertins!"

That was all. But enough—more than was to be expected.

It was our wish that our grandchildren, living in Berkeley, should meet Mr. Frost. He was the essence of kindness with them, and it was to be expected that they should be deeply moved by the experience.

It turned out that they took but a moment to catch his genuine interest. It was plain that here was a man who had not been worn down by veneration, one who could well-nigh meet a child on the child's own grounds.

On the way home from the visitation, the little boy and girl remained very thoughtful. He especially seemed in deep study, almost troubled. His mother offered him the proverbial penny for his thoughts and got the answer:

"I was just thinking that when Mr. Frost talks, he *talks* poetry."

XL. FAR IN THE PILLARED DARK

"I'M BACK IN CALIFORNIA WHERE I STARTED FROM."

So simply, so like his Athenian master, did the returning wanderer express himself at the silver anniversary dinner of the California Writer's Guild Board.

Gathered in the living room following dinner, our guests sat bound by the spell of the great conversationalist. A modest lady board member was seated on the divan beside the poet. After a time she became uneasy and suggested she give her place to someone else. "You sit right here beside me," he replied. "I can understand every word you say. It will be easier for *me*."

And so the talk went on and on—rich talk on whatever theme came to the poet's voice and utterance. How many times have his close friends marveled at the depth and breadth, and length, even, of his tremendous conversations. The quarter-century guild celebration was no exception.

English and Irish authors came under discussion. Holling C. Holling, holding Irish pretense, asked Frost what he thought of Lord Dunsany. The Irishman had died in a nursing home in Dublin a few months before. This query sent the poet forth on a discussion of Ireland and Irish authors.

I didn't know Dunsany as well as Louis—Louis Mertins. I knew him somewhat—Louis knew him well. He was a fine man, and he didn't deserve the ill-treatment given him, by Yeats, for example. He was a good—certainly a prolific writer. Published no end.

You see there was a lot of jealousy in Irish literary and theatrical circles around the turn of the 1900's. When Lady Gregory started the Abbey Theatre every Irish playwright wanted his plays acted. For some reason Yeats was determined to keep Dunsany's plays from being produced there—and succeeded. He did more than this. He tried to talk down the literary merits of Dunsany, while he built up his own. I know of few such things in the literary circles of our day, though I have had to suffer something like them. He kept Dunsany down for a long while—did him great harm with the publishers and producers.

Æ and Yeats were believers in reincarnation and spirit travel. They were the early ballistic-missile travelers, I take it. There was a difference, though, in the extent, or size, of their beliefs—between what each one saw of the little folk or the big folk. Yeats, being of coarser fiber, only saw the little people. Æ didn't stop at these. He saw also kings and queens—mainly these. But there was never a doubt but that each one believed, in an Irish sort of way, in what he *thought* he saw.

Yeats put on a lot of airs. He was very different from Æ. The latter was an artist, brush and canvas for painting, pen and ink for poem and play. Good artist. Somebody asked Æ if, during the Irish rebellion, he was ever shot at. He said a bullet once came through the window of a room in which he sat. That was all. He was ill treated by fate. Had to eke out a miserable Irish existence editing an agricultural journal—hack work—in a stuffy office, all day every day.

Again Frost's "ripe and rich philosophy":

I've never paid much note to Dylan Thomas. I haven't studied him. I'm waiting for the women's clubs to get over being scandalized over him —about him. I'll decide then whether I like his poetry or not. Somebody asked me at the advanced studies class at the University this afternoon what I thought of him—whether I thought he had reached peak before or after he came to America. I know a scattering bit of his poetry, but I don't know about when he reached his peak—what his peak was. I never saw him. He was at Amherst once or twice when I happened not to be there. He always talked against colleges, but he always wanted a job in one. He drank very hard and cried very hard. They didn't mind the drinking as much as the crying.

Modest, unassuming Umbach, etymological editor of Webster's New World Dictionary and professor in the University of Redlands, had been included in the list of guests for the after-dinner conversation. Perhaps his soft-spoken exchange of ideas with the great one had more to do with the emphasis Frost placed on what he always called "the nicety of words" than any other one thing of the occasion. The two talked rather briefly together, but Frost was impressed. It was one of those slight things which catch the imagination of persons involved.

This proposition of the nicety of words is always with us, whether we will or no. Words are pliable. They are rigid too. The Greeks mainly had, or are reputed to have had, a single word for each meaning—each idea. That made it both easier and harder to speak and write. In our language we have a variety of choices deriving as we do from Greek, Latin, Celtic, Saxon, Danish, and Norman-French. But there's only one word that will fit perfectly the idea we have to convey. That makes a choice obligatory. The nicety of words.

Robin, one of my two grand-namesakes (Robin, Marjorie's daughter, and Bobby, Prescott's son, both named after me)—Robin used an expression once, "do good." She was corrected and told to say, "do well." Her answer was pretty sharp. "Can't you do good, well?"

Fine distinction. There's my long-time friend, Dorothy Canfield Fisher. She has spent her whole life going about doing good. She has given her life for others—doing good. Then there's Willa Cather. She has done well. In the end I'm not sure but I care more for the doing of the latter. Do well. Do good. The nicety of words.

Poets and scientists have in common the biggest thing of all—their metaphors. The poet and the scientist think by metaphor. In the same way I meet with—at the other end with—the etymologist, like Mr. Umbach here. He's a scientist too—in languages, and we have in common the nicety of words. Both science and poetry are exact. And especially in the nicety of words. And now that everybody is thinking about one world, where all would speak one language, if we came to that all the poetry of the different nations would be wiped out. That would be good-bye to all the poetry in the world.

The man who had much to do with the Scrolls—discovery of the Scrolls—awhile back, told me he spoke eight languages. Our language about as I do, offhand, I should say. I have one language, I told him. He said, "If you had more you couldn't write poetry." It blurs the idiom. It dulls the nicety of words, phrases and all that. Now he didn't mean a casual knowledge of a little French, a little Latin, and such—such as I had. I didn't know enough of 'em to be hurt. He knew that he had been so far in he had lost the nicety of words.

Up in New York I have visited the tower—tall tower—probably taller than the Tower of Babel. It hasn't been named yet—it ought to be named the Tower of Anti-Babel. It's to undo what the Tower of Babel did. Babel gave us all these languages that poetry's made out of. My friends up there don't know what they're doing—wipe out languages and with them poetry. We'd all have to start all over again. Been three or four languages in my lifetime—Esperanto and the rest—designed to be the language of all the world. If they wiped out all these languages, out of which poetry is made, there'd be a new world of poetry. You might ask what nation ought to have the right to supply the universal language. If we could only tell what nation had the best poetry and let all the rest submit to that—it might take a bomb or sump'n to accomplish that. Have to throw a bomb at 'em. That's the kind of thing I like to begin with. That rouses me. Never occurred to me until lately.

Returning to a subject he never was far away from, that of education, he made this comment before going into the reading of a number of everyone's favorites of his poems:

The matter of giving a pupil an A or a B whether he deserves it—has earned it—or not, made me say awhile ago to some of my New Deal friends that they are trying to homogenize things so that the cream never will rise to the top again.

Frost recalled the high plateau of ancient Gilead in troubled Jordan as we climbed up and up, through the welcoming gateway toward Smiley Heights—his favorite walking woods on former visits. We had only to hike three minutes uphill before losing ourselves in the depth of a forest whose plants and trees had been gathered from all parts of the world. Sometimes we walked three times a day, but always we

walked nightly after the day's agony of speaking and being photographed and interviewed was over. Through more than a quarter-century of friendship we had come to understand a vast number of things—
things which had puzzled men's minds—learned them through such
talks-walking.

There was the matter of his love of solitude afforded by the deep
forest, his passion for horizons beyond, reaching out far from his vision.
The valley lay before and below, and the Southern Pacific and the Rock
Island, using the same tracks, nearly always provided a train for his view.
Though the roadway was clear for long distances, one of the trains furnished him on a certain walk was invisible at both engine-end and
caboose-end for a space. That which held his thought on the rim of the
"woods, lovely, dark and deep" was that on the west the forest ended
with an almost sheer suicidal drop of one thousand feet into a series of
cactus-fringed canyons. That nobody ever lost his life by falling over
the rim to almost certain death was not altogether reassuring on a cloudy,
moonless night.

It was inescapable that we should remember vividly the woods known
to us—woods at Monrovia, Berkeley, San Francisco, Lawrence, Hanover,
Derry, Amherst, Ripton, and Dymock. Then there were his walks,
1914-15, with John Haines and Edward Thomas, through the woods,
along the streams of the Malvern Hills. Here in our own setting, in a
wood and terrain far different, far removed, we thought of the months
he spent at Little Iddens. We recalled certain lines from a poem in his
noblest collection, from the group, "The Outlands—the Andes, the Himalayas, and the Malverns." ("But these are only hills.")

> One misty evening, one another's guide,
> We two were groping down a Malvern side
> The last wet fields and dripping hedges home.

Nor was it strange that these lines should rush to memory along with
others from his rememberable verse said aloud—poems surcharged with
the lure of tree and flower. In fancy we sought the purple-fringed of
long ago. We came upon a weed-grown garden path, to pick again the

faded blue of the last lone aster. For us there were a thousand orchises, with resting place of yesterday's delight, and withering witch hazel.

Woods, flowers, memories, and talk. No, not just talk. More than mere conversation. Unprinted literature! These indeed were talks-walking. Like all conversation they treated of things ephemeral, things soon to be forgotten, and things eternal as the hills we looked on through long vistas far away.

This, then, was our setting for talks-walking on poetry. Sometimes the poet's words took us back to a recent public conversation. Sometimes they anticipated tomorrow's.

I wonder at times how much of my poetry is understood. One thing. You have to know the difference between a rake and a hoe to understand it. As to what I mean by some of it, let me say, I have the first and second reason for writing it—either one or both of them—after which the critics proceed to add from a third to a seventh reason. They have more reasons, more meanings, than I ever thought of for my verse.

Some people ask me how I find time to write poetry—that's one of the great questions, you know. I have said sometimes to those asking: "Like a sneak I stole some of it, like a man I seized some of it, and I had some of it in my tin cup." I haven't begged much—but a little.

I suppose people think I lie awake nights worrying about what people like Ciardi of the *Saturday Review* write and publish about me. They ask me what I think about the criticism. Well, I haven't read it—any of them. But I hear about 'em, know all about 'em from my friends who tell me. I know about it. Now Ciardi is a nice fellow—one of those bold, brassy fellows who go ahead and say all sorts of things. He makes my "Stopping by Woods" out a death poem. Well, it would be like this if it were. I'd say, "This is all very lovely, but I must be getting on to heaven." There'd be no absurdity in that. That's all right, but it's hardly a death poem. Just as if I should say here tonight, "This is all very well, but I must be getting on to Phoenix, Arizona, to lecture there." Or, after an evening with friends, reading and talking. "This is all very well, very cozy and nice, but I've got to be getting on. Got to teach a class tomorrow morning."

It's becoming sickening in school. Students get tired of being told that a piece of literature means something like this, or something like that. If you feel it, let's just exchange glances and not say anything about it. There are a lot of things between best friends that're never said, and if you—if they're brought out, right out, too baldly, something's lost.

The joke on Ciardi—he's current, not specially important, just a symbol —Ciardi and other critics, has always been that they think that a man must have a long night's struggle with a poem. I used to struggle like that, as I've told you long ago, in geometry when I found something I couldn't solve. I'd study and study. Then I'd take a little nap and it'd all come clear.

Now, some poets like obscurity. It gets people talking about their verse. These critics like to swim way out beyond the danger signal and stick their necks out. "Stopping by Woods" is a perfectly natural poem. No mystery about it. There doesn't seem to be any way to keep people from making up meanings and creating mysteries and interpolating ciphers when it comes to poetry. They're always breaking into—about to break into—Kit Marlowe's, or Ben Jonson's tomb to dig up a cipher. What we'd do with 'em if they found one is a question. These people can't seem to get it through their heads that the obvious meaning of a poem is the right one. That's too easy. They've always done these things to Blake and Browning—even to Aristophanes and Sappho—what there is of Sappho. Maybe they're right. Most poets are clear and intend to be understood just as they write. Critics have to do what readers expect of them. So they fog it all up.

I'm going to get up a children's book of my poetry pretty soon. "Stopping by Woods" will be in it. Short poems to see who can learn 'em at one hearing. Always girls first. A teacher tried these out to see how many could get them memorized by hearing 'em once. One little girl remembered "Stopping by Woods" at one hearing. She went home and said it to her mother. The mother said,

"Why, dear, I knew that before you were born."

She spoke right up: "Then, why didn't you tell me!"

That was a nice adventure.

That poem's on my mind lately, I suppose because of the fuss it has stirred up.

We gave our visitor what was tantamount to a suite of rooms—the library, an adjoining bedroom, and a farther adjoining bath. Knowing his habits, we were certain that when all others were sleeping from sheer exhaustion, he could feel free to wander among the books and read to his heart's content.

"I never read the *New Yorker*," he growled when we showed him to his "suite" and handed him the current number.

One morning it was required that I get something from the library. I crept silently into the room, thinking him asleep in his bedroom. I had got what I was after and was just slipping noiselessly out, at least I thought it was noiselessly, when he growled from his bedroom door, half ajar:

"Get out of my library."

Returning to the woodland conversation—one-sided conversation—part of which grew out of books he had opened:

> Anybody who knows even a kindergarten course in my poetry knows that I've been interested in flying ever since Kitty Hawk gave us success under the Wright brothers—you ought to know about it. You were there with me when I began writing about it back in Monrovia in 1932. Well, last night I just happened onto and took two books from your shelves and read 'em—books I'd never seen before. One was about Orville and Wilbur Wright, written by Fred C. Kelly. The other was Hoover's *American Road*. Good books. I've been trying to do my little stint for the Wrights in deeds and verse a long time. It's an old story, now, going back thirty years—maybe more. I always remember the die-hards who said nobody could ever fly—there'd be no Darius Green and his flying machine. The newspapers, whose editors always know everything, back at the century's turn said no use to send a man down—reporter down—to Kitty Hawk. You *can't* cover what *can't* happen. So, the biggest event of the century, up to then, had nobody on hand to write it up, so the public was never informed.
>
> We're doing it in the opposite fashion nowadays. We write big about rockets going to the moon tomorrow. Cape Canaveral sees and hears the explosion. Nothing goes up. We talk too much and do too little. The Wright boys talked and did. The papers fizzled.
>
> There's one thing I'm sure of about space travel: Whenever men travel into outer ether they'll have to take along a lunch pail and a can of air.

Who better than the poet who said it first could appreciate the meaning—

> *Earth's the right place for love:*
> *I don't know where it's likely to go better.*

Another book he had at least looked into, judging solely from the place he had left it the night before. This was Edith Hamilton's *Greek Way to Western Civilization,* paperback edition. We did not discover it until we had returned from taking him to the plane. The night had been cold for early May, and though we soft natives slept under an electric blanket, Frost had asked that we give him no covers, only two sheets. This we did, wonderingly. On our return from the airport we found the book lying on his pillow, the two sheets folded carefully back. On the pillow, Edith Hamilton's book!

It was odd that, without knowledge of the book on his pillow, on our way to the airport I had mentioned Edith Hamilton's two books on Greek and Roman contribution to the West and asked him if he had read them. He answered cryptically, with no answer. He only said: "I know Edith Hamilton."

Of course this might be taken any number of ways. Yet, classic Greek scholar that he undoubtedly was, reading her books on Greece and Rome concerning the contribution of the two civilizations to western culture would have provided faggots to his already burning backlog to make a crackling fire.

Once again we had come to the parting. No more lectures, no more soirees, no more woodland strolls by starlight, with a mockingbird trilling in the exotic trees shrouded by nightfall and shade.

The long planning, the carrying out of the project, the happy talk— all these were over and done. The Homer Noble farm was calling.

Few literary figures in the American story had won and continued to hold the affection of the common people, the literati, the intelligentsia and government officialdom up to the head of state, in the way Robert Frost had. None had done so with such complete unconcern. If he were aware of its importance he concealed such awareness perfectly.

His simple breakfast—a raw egg in a glass of orange juice and a few drops of coffee in a cup of hot water—nothing more—had been ritualed. He was off with his host for a morning walk in Smiley forest. Now he had come back to meet the last barrage of questions—the last grueling battery of flashlight bulbs. The big town had sent its best man for the story.

Frost had kept his word. He had fulfilled his every promise. Now he was turning homeward. His steps were reluctant. He was loath to go. But there remained tasks to perform elsewhere—other promises to keep. More than kept promises was his written permission for us to use for publication the letters he had sent us over the years.

The old fear of missing a train—changed now to missing a plane—was still with him.

"Let's get started. I mustn't miss that plane!"

It was a mere sixty miles over a great freeway to the international airport by the sea. The plane was not to leave by schedule for nearly four hours.

The current "well-used" car moved out into the road.

XLI. To Flourish—Not for Us

What had a quarter-century and one year done for Robert Frost? What notable changes had come over him?

In so many ways he had remained unchanged—the same sardonic humor given to be taken or left, the same rare smile that crept silently and slowly across his disfigured right cheek, the same volcanic anger which erupted so unexpectedly. These remained, but not unchanged.

There was the new facet revealed in his tacit admission that he was not unproud of fame—wide fame. He was happy with his television appearances. He took pride in being called the greatest living poet—in being summoned to the nation's capital—of his new post as consultant in poetry for the Library of Congress. He had become less gossipy about his contemporaries, less talkative about his children, his children's children, and his children's children's children. At one time he was addicted to much talk concerning the continuance of the line, speaking often and long about them.

Perhaps the greatest of all changes was his showing of fatigue. His eighty-four years were evident in this area. It was not physical tiredness, except that fatigue of mind and spirit passed for him into the realm of the third part of man's existence. His former-day eyes of sparkling brightness rarely shone. From out their inscrutable depth came instead dullness and lackluster. Only when his steel struck flint was a sparkle to be seen.

He still remained a careful epicure, an avid talker, a student of daily events which he chronicled after the Socratic fashion inside the yard of the lapidary. But when it was all said and done he felt called on to say ruefully:

"Let the dead past bury its dead."

Looking back over the crowding events of the preceding days prior to his departure, his conversation turned naturally to public talks and politics. He paraphrased his own poem and called himself a "politician at odd-seasons." He talked of things he had touched on first and last for nearly a generation, always with new and unexpected facets. This was especially the case with a familiar topic of his—how he helped elect Grover Cleveland as president in 1884.

> What makes a good president? So many people want to know—think they want to know. We've had all kinds. I started politics when I was about ten. I've been a backslider ever since.
>
> Well, a president needn't count much on patience. It's no good. You need brains—and I suppose courage—you need—everybody has to have—courage for all they seek to accomplish. Sometimes the game turns out one of endurance—of courage. Then you've got to have faith. Faith in what? What do I mean by faith? You've got to figure that out. The game of politics isn't as simple as it sounds.
>
> On the Democratic side I've been thinking lately of the Stevensons. I know both Adlai and his wife—who was. I should say that, taken both together, they'd make a good president.
>
> Of our leading Democrats I've come to regard Henry Wallace way up at the top in quality. He has had money—still has—plenty of money—so he doesn't lend himself to corruption. Of course I don't mean a rich man has so much he can't be corrupted. He can be. The fact he is rich is a good proof he'd like to be richer. Henry is a good man. His father pioneered the hybridization of corn in Iowa—got rich at it, I'm told. I remember once

being at a gathering where likes meet likes—or unlikes. Henry and I were standing off having a little chat by ourselves when I noticed Norman Thomas standing alone, being snubbed by the snobs. Henry saw him and asked to be excused and left me to go and speak to Norman. I saw what was up and joined 'em. The three of us stood all arm in arm and were photographed together. I suppose, now they're throwing rocks (and less solid matter) at Nixon down in Central America, I should have my picture taken with him. He'd probably balk at Henry Agard and Thomas, though—maybe me.

I was talking with Eisenhower in the White House awhile ago. He got confidential—no secret, I take it—and told me he supposed he was a Jeffersonian Democrat—not a Jacksonian. I told him I was a Democrat (upper case) by training, a democrat (lower case) by birth. Snobbery isn't in my line.

I didn't go into my dark political past with the President—didn't want to corrupt him unnecessarily. I didn't tell him I helped the machine in San Francisco to corrupt the politics of the most corrupt city politically in America in my day—when I was still in grammar school—barely ten—out here in California.

Having followed him about from place to place to hear him lecture and talk about his poetry, we were very interested in what he had to say concerning his method of gathering ideas and giving them out.

Moreover, there was the study of how he had changed these poems over the years—or how he had left them as they were. In the old days he was still uneasy about his place, his standing. Now, after the years had hurried after one another, all the doubts and fears were gone. He knew what he knew. If people didn't, too bad for people.

I get invitations to be made president of the International P.E.N. Club. If I had known this would happen to me—all this frightening recognition —I probably never would have written a poem. I suppose I'm more at home in the middle of a crowd of students who feel their lack and want to learn than anywhere else. The other day in Redlands at the advanced studies group, the kids peppered me with questions—mostly pretty good—nothing trivial. One of 'em wanted to hear me read "Home Burial." I said no, but I explained.

This is a poem I never like to read in the afternoon. Then one of the girls asked me why I didn't like to read it in the afternoon—too much passion in it for afternoon reading? She wanted to know. I had never put it before that way. Just thought of it at the moment. But I said it then. Best time for passion's in the evening. Who can get all worked up at a matinee performance. Evening's the time for the opera—the play. Afternoon's not the time for such.

People are always asking what I stand for. I never hold tenets on anything—just tentatives. I'm not much of an absolutist. People—shallow listeners—call me dogmatic. I may sound like a man who never changes his mind. Maybe I'm one who never makes it up, but never the other. It all comes down to this—my idea of a poem's shape—the meaning of a poem as I see it—can be compared to the meaning of life, which is to force matter to a point. I often think of the leper—self-made leper—Damien as an example. He was strong and well. He chose to go among the lepers, contract the disease, and work with 'em for their—or his—soul's sake. Doing this, he died a leper. Now, was his death beautiful—was it horrible—which? He really committed suicide, you know, by doing what he did. Was that suicide (deliberate suicide on his part) a sin, an act of penance, or an act of beauty and benevolence? Here we come right up against a blank wall. Solving such mysteries is one of man's impossible tasks. Sophistry alone can show the way around—sophistry and double talk—Thomism.

A note of sadness (somehow such came oftener as the years swiftly winged their way)—came to his voice. It may have been no more than a moment of nostalgia. But there it was.

You know I miss—sorter miss—maple-syrup time on the Homer Noble farm. When you used to see me there we made it. The government got too exacting. Too many rules—bureaus—bureaucrats. It was just a century ago—I think a century ago—that Fisk—Perrin Fisk—wrote the verse about sugar making. Went as I remember like this:

> "When you see the vapor pillars
> Link the forest with the sky
> You may know the days of sugar—
> Making—

(odd division of words there, "sugar" on one line at the end, "making" on next at start)

"Making then are drawing nigh.

Frosty night" (no reference to me)

"Frosty night and thawy day
Make the maple pulses play
Till congested with its sweetness
It delights to bleed away."

Dragon and I hated to see sugar days—syrup days—syrup season come to its destined end. There was usually a depth of snow in the timber—maple woods—when we'd get round to start tapping. We'd cut a gash around the tree and fix a spile—spigot—into the trunk. The gash would lead the maple juice into the spile and thus into the pails. Then nature looked after things, and we carried the full pails to the kettle which was fixed on a pole and made easy to swing onto and off of the fire. This went on and on, and we would go from tree to tree for the raw materials.

When a kettle-full was ready, it was strained off and put into containers. Hot cakes and maple syrup—nothin' better. Now all that's over with. No more maple syrup. No more spring woods full of the smell of burning fagots and the boiling maple juice turning into sugar and syrup. I must say we lost something when all this passed. Too much progress—too much regulation. I'm still a States'-rights rebel.

It was but a verbal step from sugar making to poetry—a step our distinguished departing guest made with such ease.

Never understood my own shyness. Queer the way I've held back but somehow gone ahead. I've been a perfectionist. Now, don't misunderstand me. I'm not an advocate for the non-perfectionist. Shakespeare was a perfectionist. So was Milton. But perfectionism does one thing that's hard to take. Makes you wonder in the face of all precedent whether you've got it—holds you back. But I've always said I was satisfied with a fistful of little poems so hard you couldn't get a knife blade into 'em anywhere. On that I rest my case. I've got 'em or I haven't. Fatalism again.

Some say it was shyness on my part. Maybe. I just kept on plugging even when I didn't sell a clam. Kept on. But rejection slips are hard to take. Maybe I said—I don't say I said—maybe, I said, "one day I'll show 'em." I gave up college—two colleges. I gave up farming. I ran away to England and buried myself to get away. But that's an old song. No regrets about running away. Running away from, you're bound to run into—something. It all depends on where you run. I was lucky. Ran away to England, and you know the rest. Old story. I learned the hard way. But the friends I made there helped.

You know the old bards—troubadours—of medieval times weren't very far different from the poets we've known. They went about saying their verses—singin' 'em, maybe—to the nobles in the great halls—always having to sit below the salt. Some of those old houses still stand with the great open fireplace, the dais and the level floor where the above salt and below salt were easy to see—and live up to. The poet was below with the preacher and teacher.

You've been a bard on the old Chautauqua circuits back yonder, going about saying your poems. You ought to understand these matters better'n most. I didn't do it that way. Every man does what he's permitted—able—to do. And you may believe it or not. Discouraged, turned away, held back, I never doubted. That's how all poets worth their salt got there. You've got to know what you know and hold it fast.

So the poet talked as the "well-used" car moved into the International Airport. Arizona was waiting. We waved good-by as he climbed the steps, turning to wave us a reciprocal good-by.

The purr of the engines . . . the slow turning toward the runway . . . gathered speed . . . the roar, the lifting, the great bird swiftly winging toward the sky . . . the poet had twitched his mantles once again for pastures new.

XLII. On Our Cis-Atlantic Shore

Robert Frost had been so long a part of Amherst College and Amherst village that nobody thought of the town without linking his career with town and gown.

How—one would like to know—how could you celebrate the bicentennial of the village and leave the poet out? Lord Amherst had accepted the invitation and would be there from England. Thus the poet who was *sui generis* and the current nobleman would be present. And we, being invited, would ourselves be there. ("We didn't know whether you would or wouldn't come. But we took a chance and asked you. Nothing to lose, you know." So the poet said with a grin when we showed up.)

The occasion for the invitation was the dedication of the Frost Memorial Room in the Jones Library. Here, since the inception of the library in 1921, Charlie Green had been the tireless, steady, and efficient wheel horse. As a part of the future-seeing task, he had very early started the home-town Frost collection. Amherst appeared to us to be altogether unaware of the genuine greatness and importance of the Frost Library, now the monument to the quiet man who did so much to establish the standing of the poet. Of one thing we were very sure. When Charlie Green finished the task set for himself, all future historians of literature would have to take the beaten path to the door of the Jones Library to visit and study in the Frost Room.

Regardless of the fact that Roy Basler, representing the Library of Congress, was present to make the dedication address, nobody doubted the pre-eminence of another present. Seated on the stage at the right, his white hair rumpled (just as his dark hair had been when he first came to Amherst as the poet-in-residence) was Robert Frost.

When in 1916 the poet came first to the college, the man from Washington was still in grammar school!

When the principal address was finished and Frank Rand had presented the poet with the golden key to the Frost Room, Robert came up talking, but not before the capacity audience had thundered its appreciation:

> I'm bowed down with recipience. But I've been thinking as I sat here how American this whole affair is. You know, I'm still a believer in nationalism. I still like to meet somebody from some other country who is very national. I don't know what to do with the one-worlders.
>
> One of my poems is a fitting thing for such a gathering as this. It is called "The Gift Outright." There was somebody in England not long ago who took some of the lines of it and used 'em as they thought against us.
>
> > *"She was our land more than a hundred years. . . .*
> > *But we were England's, still colonials. . . .*
> > *Possessed by what we now no more possessed"*

The person I mentioned in England said these three lines and added one of his own: "Yes, Australia, Canada, New Zealand ripened off. Your's fell off green."

Following the poet's acceptance talk, the whole body went to the library and to the Frost Room upstairs, where on the third floor, the hundreds, if not thousands, of Frost items were stored or displayed. The poet was modest as could be in the presence of friendly hero-worship.

There was the display of the so-called "favorite books" of the poet. These showed a commingling of the classic with the common, just as Frost did in his own life.

Now it doesn't necessarily follow that the mere fact of these books being in the Frost Library at Amherst meant that they were his favorite books. But there is other evidence to show them in that light—at least to place them among his favorites. The English sojourn represented about one-half the total. It was our conviction that as time went on he had more and more come to feel the importance in his life's work of the Dymock Interval. As this idea grew on him, he mellowed toward the principal actors and gave them due credit. The list of titles is comprehensive.[1]

In the midst of a celebration of the bicentennial of the founding of this typically New England village (named for a great general who refused to fight for England against the colonials), it was in keeping that the noble descendant of the first Lord Amherst should spend the week in the town that bore his name and that he should listen to the speeches of dedication and take part in the opening of the Frost Room. Frost casually called the whole thing, Amherst village, Lord Amherst, and all the rest, "A confirmation of the reaffirmation."

[1] *Modern American and British Poetry; Oxford Book of English Verse;* Emerson's *Works;* Kipling's *Jungle Book;* Poe's *Works; Robinson Crusoe; Walden Pond; The Odyssey; Kensington Gardens,* Humphrey Wolfe; *Letter From a Distant Land; Letter from Robert Browning; Poems,* John Haines; *Collected Poems,* Edward Thomas; *Happy Go-Lucky Morgan; The South Country; Glass Case; Rest and Unrest; Light and Twilight; Edward Thomas,* Coombes; *Life and Letters of Edward T.; Edward Thomas—Last Four Years,* Farjeon; *World Without End,* Helen Thomas; *The Heart of England; E. T., Looking Back,* Norman Douglas; *For Remembrance; A. St. John Adcock; American Decade; Golden Treasury; Longfellow,* complete.

An Interfaith Convocation was held in the afternoon of the Sabbath preceding the dedication in the Regional High School Auditorium. It played to a crowded house, with Robert Frost sitting in the midst of a vast audience which filled every seat. The music was the production of Randall Thompson, sung by men's and women's mixed and separate choruses. The lines were from the poems of Robert Frost.

It was inevitable that a call should come from the vast crowd for the poet to take the stage. In due course he stumbled and scrambled out of the middle of the row in the center of the auditorium and went on stage to receive the prolonged applause that followed the close of the performance and to hold up the hand and baton of the composer-con-ductor.

Seven poems had been set to music by Thompson. One was a master-piece of collaboration in the opinion of listeners and music critics—"A Girl's Garden." It skipped out across the footlights in a manner seldom heard. The words fitted the music, the music the words. Not often do poet and composer achieve such unity. Lesley should have been proud. She had been the subject of the poem.

Because of the press of circumstances, Robert had been forced to hold us at arm's length, something we well understood. We asked ourselves, after all, what rights had we above all the others to his time. But this was not to continue.

On our second day in Amherst we ran into him in the self-serve mar-ket where he was provisioning—prunes, Pepsi Cola, candy, grapes, and peanut butter—for his larder. On our way down to the Lord Jeffery, he said:

"Now, you two go into the lobby while I take these groceries in the back way. They don't mind my taking things into my room to snack on, but I don't like to be too open about it. Secretive—you know. Then I'll be right in to see you. We'll get all this matter straightened out."

In five minutes he was in the lobby full of a new idea. We were to have dinner that evening together, the three of us, in the dining room of the Lord Jeffery. In this way we could talk while we ate.

"Been talking to the football team," he said, with his sly athletic smile covering his face. "I've got to rest before supper. You come back at six-thirty. I have an appointment with a man I must see at nine o'clock. We'll get our visit partly out by that time."

Now there was time and opportunity for him to talk, for us to listen. A full year had passed, so many things had happened. This seemed the time of summing up and taking stock. The poet had become a fixture at the Library of Congress—first in poetry, next in the humanities. He had often dined with President Eisenhower and the first lady. He affectionately called the President "the Old Man"—a term of friendship and respect. One remembered the way in which Calvin Coolidge, when president, dismissed the suggestion made by Dwight Morrow that he do something for poetry by having Frost at the White House to dine. The future was to reveal Robert as close friend of two presidents—a Republican and a Democrat. The day had arrived when taking a President in his stride, regardless of party or person was his forte. The 1960 campaign was to clinch this.

About the happy board, listening to the rapid thought-propelled talk covering such wide divergence of fields, one forgot the world and its problems. This was cosmic, conversation at its best!

Characteristically he took up where we left off on a walk of the three of us into the shadows of Smiley Heights, overlooking the long stretch of Southern Pacific road bed below us.

Say, did that big orange grower out on the hill—Smiley Heights— ever fix that hydrant and water pipe that was leaking all the water in California where we walked together last year? No water to waste in a land where you're forever on the dividing line between desert and sown.

Then he was off still wearing that infrequent smile which played impishly about the corners of his mouth. Said he rarely heard from his great-grandson, Robert Frost, II.

President Cole told me he had given me to the town for the bicentennial. The Jones Library belongs to the town, you know. Charlie Green's been here so long, done such a good job, people think it belongs to him. This town's grown so. I remember when we referred to the *village* of Amherst. In connection with the bicentennial, the college is featuring Emily Dickinson. I wasn't asked to be on the panel of discussion. Now some who *are* on the panel don't know too much about Emily—Archie doesn't, I know. Louise Bogan doesn't know as much as she thinks she does. The other fellow, a college man here, Richard Wilbur, isn't interested in Emily at all. If you want my opinion, she is the best of all the women poets who ever wrote, from Sappho on down. As for the other women poets—Mrs. Browning and the rest—they can't touch Emily. Really, Mrs. Browning wasn't much—greatly overrated. Emily wrote fine lines—right from the soul.

You know, Archie has always been derivative. Did you catch the end of *J. B.* People think everything is solved by love. Maybe just as many things are solved by hate. Some of it may be traced to his inheritance. His folks—big merchants in Chicago. So, he's always had money—lots of money. Has an island down in the West Indies to run off to when needed. Not all settled yet, but there's talk about starting a new college, down in the middle of all these colleges now here.

So, you didn't hear Old Carl when he spoke at your college. Can't tell me then if he's still the same Sandburg we all three used to know. Hair comber. Disdained him, did you! You know, if I had a few more friends as loyal as you two! Sentimental Sandburg. You know, Charlie Green's the same sort of friend as the two of you—good friend. Never had a finer.

If you read the papers I guess you know I've been having quite a time in Washington. Last year was there a full week out of each four. . . . Cole's leaving Amherst. It may be I won't be back—invited back—any more after he's gone. Don't know who'll be president here. I remember I was afraid of my tenure at Amherst when I first met you in California in '32. I was afraid to face Stanley King when I got back. Remember? Maybe things will be changed here after Charlie becomes vice-president of the Rockefeller Foundation.

About this time of the year my friends start telling me I am going to capture the Nobel Prize for literature. But I never do. I'm too American—think too much of my own country—think too much *about* it, too. The Danes are against me—your country—you know. [This was a dig at my wife in fine fun.]

People ask me who's President in Washington with the Old Man down in Georgia, out at Palm Springs, at Gettysburg. He's not done so bad. He knows when to rest, when to work. Now that he's going to retire there are a lot of big firms, you know—could be.

People have talked a lot about my "call to Washington"—to the Library of Congress. They have thought of me as a Democrat and wondered some. After all, it's the Library of Congress—and Congress is bi-partisan. As a States'-rights Democrat I fit in pretty good.

Recognition of my poetry, as a sort of national affair, seems implied here, and as consultant in poetry for the Library of Congress I could well consult about my own poetry and read it too. Some of it to children. You see, I have just acted myself. Nice, too, for me to be sort of neighbors with members of what I look on as the most interesting body in government— any government—the Supreme Court. Three of 'em are among my best and closest friends. One of them is Warren. You know it was sort of you who got me together with Chief Justice Warren, must have been in 1947. Warren and Freeman were with us at the Charter Day luncheon at Sproul's house.

So now Warren is in Washington, and I see him occasionally. We have good talks. Then there's Douglas. He's retiring. And Frankfurter. You can't beat a court with justices of this caliber. Now, since Mumford has named me consultant in the humanities for a three-year term, I'm likely to say a lot of things, consulted or not. No law against it, I usually don't need to be consulted to start me off. Self-starter.

Lapsing into a reminiscence of Ezra Pound, as he frequently did, he continued his conversation with the comment:

There's a postscript to Ezra's goings on. I got him out of St. Elizabeth's with the understanding that he would be looked after—looked out for financially. I talked with the top people of *New Directions,* who agreed to the gathering up of his things—all his things—into a book—new things as well as old—and to pay him royalties and in this way care for his needs. And you know, a man in Italy needs some little, quite a little, money. All this was agreed to, so I suppose—I haven't audited the directors of *New Directions* yet, but give them—and me—time.

That's enough about Pound for awhile. He was always a controversial figure—troubler of men's souls.

Nowadays I'm a consultant without much consulting. Poet-in-waiting, I suppose. But hope deferred, you know. Some of these newspapermen call me a chain talker. That's better than being a chain smoker, isn't it? Enough of that.

After some comments on Alex Meiklejohn, he switched to a local incident which had recently occurred:

> I was talking with some Greek friends here in Amherst who own a market—run it themselves—make a lot of money. Good businessmen. The nephew of the main owners—young man—broke in and said something about literature. "That wouldn't mean anything to a man like Robert Frost, would it?" (I knew he knew who I was.) He turned to poetry and said he liked Longfellow. He quoted one poem he said he liked and asked me what I thought of it. I said it was nice but it got involved toward the end.
>
> One of the main owners—older man—was away, and I asked about him—where he was.
>
> "Oh, he's gone to Greece to take twenty thousand dollars to operate a school in his home town."
>
> I asked him where the town was; he said in Sparta.
>
> I wish we could match that with another twenty thousand dollars that would go right straight to the people for a school, and not through the government.

Nothing could have been more appropriate than our carrying the rare item of roguish malfeasance, *The Memoirs of the Notorious Stephen Burroughs,* with us on the day Frost invited us to go out across the wildwood countryside to find the haunts of this fabulous counterfeiter, preacher, and rapscallion.

Our host had gone casually into the life of crime which New England's picturesque criminal had lived—counterfeiting being his most important crime—and had introduced us (ex post facto) to his fellow Pelhamite. So, we went prepared to see Pelham and its surrounding forests—the latter, alas, on the way to complete extinction.

Robert having hired a car and chauffeur, we set off to see and visit the neighboring villages and the timber surrounding the villages. We hoped to equal Robert's own achievement of seeing three ghosts instead of only one—Burroughs, Shays, and Lysander. Furthermore, we were very happy at having provided Robert with a good reason not to sit through the Dickinson panel. To us a live poet was preferable. The dead Pelham rogue provided sauce.

As we ducked out of his room at the Lord Jeffery, Robert locked his door at the hotel remarking:

"You see, I have to have bolts and bars to keep collectors from coming in and stealing my manuscripts. Of course the ones in the lobby on the walls (they're other peoples' manuscripts) are never stolen. But—you know—"

Thus it came that ahead of us were uninterrupted hours of conversation in the busiest week Amherst village had seen during the two centuries of her existence—the bicentennial she had gathered her children together to celebrate. All this we owed to the notoriety of a colonial François. This was the meat of the visit far above the shouting and the tumult. The conversation started right off.

The trees—woods—around here are second-growth timber. Poor land. Better land to work elsewhere. Must have been poor land back there in the time of Shays' Rebellion. Iowa farmers seeing us with our land having no more than five inches of good—tolerably good—soil, say they farm land with five feet of soil. They wonder how we can make a living. We tell 'em, "Oh, we make out. We live off our produce, sell some, and buy first mortgages on Iowa farms. We live all right." Iowa farmers are such good farmers they keep one home out in California—Long Beach—and one on their Iowa farm.

You know, things are getting bad for wild animals, wild plants, and trees around here. All the foxes in New England are getting the mange. Elm trees all dying out. In fifty years there won't be an elm left in the forests around here, or even along the lanes if it keeps up. Maybe won't be a fox, but I wouldn't gamble on it.

I've given Farmer Dragon a freehold of his own—you've been at the Homer Noble farm—given him one out there by way of notifying him that someday he'll have his own land to look after. This is to be his life insurance from me. *My* life'll pay for it. You know his ancestors way back were French. Name comes from the French word dragoon. Dragon is something else again.

I read very little in the newspapers. Mainly I read about sports. Favorite is baseball. Here's the way I read the papers: Front page, sports, editorial, stock market. In that order, if I get as far as the stock market—I don't own any stocks—I just try to keep up with things. I like to see a chart of the way they are going.

I like to come now and then out to California—not to rest. Prefer to rest here in New England—around Amherst—around my farms up in the hills—Homer Noble farm. Ripton, you know, is halfway between Hancock and Middlebury. Thermometer drops pretty low there. Known it to fall to fifty below, fahrenheit. Farmers don't much like to work when it drops so far. The sugar maples were valued for their syrup once—now only for their red leaves. There was a time when it was a horse of a different color.

And so went the pleasant one-sided conversation. It was this very thing, more than anything else, that brought us to the week of celebration. A dead man and a rascal gave spice to our pudding.

Passing through these happy lanes, we saw the house in which Robert once lived. A house of brown shingles on a deserted street-car line—interurban—now overgrown with weeds and underbrush. Happy memories, listening to his talk of things past and present—sometimes future. Informing talk. So it was we came at last to Mill Valley, beside the ancient millrace where water power once turned the mill wheels. So we sat for an hour or so at our midday meal of good solid beef and fixin's (new England style) as we listened to golden conversation on many themes.

There were pumpkins in the windows everywhere, and my wife mentioned them, calling them the way the word was spelled. He shot back with a broad smile: "Now I know you didn't grow up around here. If you had you would 'a called 'em punkins. *Some* punkins! See what a difference that exclamation makes. Only educated people who've read about 'em, didn't raise 'em in a field or garden—read about 'em in books and places call 'em pumpkins."

Then he was off on the man we had come ghost-seeking for.

I shall always be glad it was W. R. Brown who put me onto the notorious Stephen Burroughs. Brown and Whicher stand for Amherst to me. If I hadn't met up with this not-too-innocent rogue through my real-estate friend I might have missed him—missed knowing about him.

I was a sort of uncalendared fellow townsman of Burroughs out here in Pelham off and on, and later we both were Dartmouthians—a bit separated of course—Dartmouth where I took turns studying, rough housing, running away, coming back to teach later—sort of teach—the discrepancy of Chronos in placing us together a century and a half apart is beside the point. We once breathed the same air. So I knew him.

Lincoln MacVeigh and I were talking one day, not too many years after I got back from England. I called his attention to Burroughs as one who could do something about keeping his candle of crime burning. You see the first edition (printed in Burroughs' lifetime) was almost extinct. When MacVeigh read one of the few remaining copies of the first edition of the memoir of Burroughs (very scarce) he being editor of the Dial Press asked me to write a sort of introduction—preface—for a new edition. It was done.

Burroughs had a way of gathering friends from the world of necromancy —notably Glazier Wheeler, a coiner of money on his own. Good business if you can keep it a secret. But his other friend, Daniel Shays, organizer of a rebellion that failed, deserved our sympathy. Big historical character— Shays. Better be careful what you say about him to Pelhamites (and Amherstians, too, for that matter). Some of the best families around here were represented in his rag-tag-and-bobtail army. Back there in 1786 they figured if the Colonials could fight an unjust government overseas, they'd a right to fight one over here in Amherst and suburbs. It's anybody's good reasoning, too. Not much came of it. Just a name now.

Remember how the histories—school books of our childhood—talked about Shays' Rebellion—made much of it—scarcely mentioned any more I suppose, I'd not likely lend money to any one of the three. But when a man has a sneaking affection for François Villon, hiding in the gutters of Paris or rotting in jail, he's likely to have a sneaking feeling for Stephen Burroughs.

I suppose we might as well stop worrying about the country being swallowed up by towns. Pelham's a reassurance. The town comes in and seems permanent. Some few have lasted some thousands of years—Babylon, Ur, Rome—maybe Damascus doesn't need mention—for a lesser period Carthage, Athens—Athens really some thousands of years. Then there's a tell, and archaeologists start digging.

Nation the size of the United States usually lasts about a thousand years. But there's lots of trouble between now and the end of our millennium.

Take Cuba, causing us to lie awake nights. This fellow Castro seems a dedicated man. Where we made our mistake was leaving Cuba free to go about her own business. Should have kept her as we did Puerto Rico. Interesting comparing England's colonialism with Spain and Portugal. England did the most—gave the world the U.S.A. and Australia, Canada and New Zealand. Now these can carry her in her declining years. Strange cycle—very strange.

Then he was off on his favorite topic, the youth of the country. He never came to doubt that everything would turn out well for them.

I don't think our young people are all on the way to ruin, any more 'n I was when I stole that pig in San Francisco—helped steal it. We were a gang. Anyway, I'm pretty thick with our young people—gotta believe in 'em.

We're so prosperous we're like a rich father who would like to give his children the hardships which he thinks made him into the man he became. *Thinks.* Some American families have come down for three centuries— still going strong. Mine did. It's courage—courage that makes art, business. But to me the greatest thing in life is not courage, it's magnanimity. Love, justice, learning, faith, works. Hard to tell which is greatest—all important. To me the greatest thing in life is magnanimity with all these things. But I don't want to sound as if I believed in the perfectability of man.

People always asking me if I'm happier, or as happy, in my eighties as in my fifties and sixties. Funny thing—I've always been happy—unhappy. You know the song—when you drink it makes you happy—it makes you sad. We Americans are always supposed to be a rather merry people. Humor itself's a funny thing. Lawrence Spivak, of "Meet the Press" told me he once started a humor magazine—American humor magazine. It didn't go over. Maybe American humor isn't funny enough.

We're really a sad crowd, sometimes. I often think of the Wright Brothers—one of 'em became a close friend of mine in the few years before he died. They never thought of—seriously thought of—all the harm that would come out of the plane and flying. What did they do when they succeeded down there at Kitty Hawk? Went right straight to the army to sell the idea. Talk about bombs for peace—sewing machines for peace is what I want.

XLIII. This Man's Art and That Man's Scope

"Gettin' so I think I belong here. Mr. and Mrs. Mertins, particularly—they're my long-time friends. We met at the Olympic Games in 1932—when the Olympics were here at Los Angeles. And we were really successful. I remember a fellow near me in the seats, every time the flag went up the fellow—a stout fellow with a nice red neck—you know—he stood up and said: 'That's us. Look us over.'

"Really American. All American."

These were the opening remarks made to a group of admirers on his last visit to his native state. The year was 1960—November. The preceding ten months had been busy ones for the poet. Adviser at the Congressional Library, he turned to advising Congress. With what success we never were informed. Only we know they had listened as he made his appeal for a National Academy of Culture. An award of $2,500 and a gold medal had been pending for the poet. The bill was fathered by Senator Saltonstall, of Massachusetts. Robert had come west to us following the prearrangements made in Amherst—Lord Jeffery looking on—the rogue Stephen Burroughs smirking nearby.

He continued:

It's funny how I go round with whatever native wit I have, you know—I go round—I've been teacher as much as anything—teacher more than farmer—farmer more than editor—and so on down. And I go round talking to young people about what I want of them—what I expect of them. And I think tonight, I just thought of a word—I expect—I expect scope—scope. Now I came on that years ago in Shakespeare. It says "desiring this man's art and that man's scope." And these are the two things that make it all. Some people have art—enough art to make a very little scope go quite a long way. That's all right—that's called finessing, I think. But the great thing to me—the thing I always envied most was scope.

The point is, when I talk about anything at all I like to show scope. I try to be so comprehensive, I get the whole U.S. history in a few minutes. "That's us" as the fellow said at the game—"That's us. Look us over." Now the way I approach that in my teaching is to wait for something like that—say something—my way of puttin' it once on a time, I remember, was to say, "Say sump'n as in 'sump'n.' " I don't care whether you spell it right, or punctuate it right, if it is sump'n, if it is one of these things that show scope.

Former students who had seen firsthand his reactions to poor spelling might have taken issue with part of this statement, though content was no doubt the measure of their actual success or failure in his classes. He went on to treat comparisons of types of leadership and the extent of the leadership of youth before expanding to a further field:

What's the most inclusive thing I can say about the universe? I've been through that lately. Most comprehensive thing I can say? Just for the fun of it. I've been with some of these scientists, who are saying their say. And so I say this:

> *The Universe is but the thing of Things—*
>
> *(capital T for the last.) the thing of Things,*
>
> *The things but balls all going round in rings.*
> *Some of them mighty huge, some mighty tiny,*
>
> *(these balls, you know.)*
>
> *Some of them mighty huge, some mighty tiny,*
> *All of them radiant and mighty shiny.*

That's the universe. I haven't left anything out, have I? Only one line is all you need to describe the universe: just balls going round in rings. That gets us clear down to Adam. I haven't left anything out, far as I can see. The only thing left out, I might say is purpose. You see, that's another verse. Materially I have covered its purpose in another verse. I won't go into that. It's another attempt at being inclusive. Wasn't Shakespeare wonderfully inclusive in that line—"desiring this man's art and that man's scope"? That's all there is to all our thinking and talking—art and scope. Wonderful line. Goes unnoticed a lot because it's in a love poem. A kind of a love poem—they're all love poems of his.

I've a mind to linger over another line of his. He says somewhere of the North star:

> *Whose worth's unknown,*
> *Although its height be taken—*

(It is the star to every wandering bard.)

Whose worth's unknown
Although its height be taken.

Now that means two things—science and the humanities. And that's one of our controversies today. I hear of a college founded right now—just now —all going to be devoted entirely to the humanities. Just as if that had to be attended to with science running away with the show—stealing the show, you know. Got to do sump'n about the humanities. But the quoted line covers them both—the star—North Star—who's worth's unknown— the humanities—of untold worth. It brings home these things that should come home—and those that shouldn't—nobody knows—although its height is exactly taken with the sextant. Science is the exact part of it— the other, the humanities, part of it. Wonderful lines. Two things there you've got to think of all the time. Scope for all of us. Let's be free and easy for a moment or so. That's all too serious. I had a notion one night—these talks too difficult. Don't think I've been too difficult tonight. One night I tried to distinguish between being elected and being one of the elect. I thought my audience wasn't brought up right. You couldn't tell 'em about that. So, all night long—I'm making up a lie—want to hear one? All night long I dreamed—I'd had such a hard time—I thought I was eating a twenty-pound marshmallow. And in the morning I couldn't find my pillow.

As I said, the month was November, and we had just elected a president of the United States.

We had met Robert's plane in Los Angeles ten days before this talk and had taken him to his first lecture date to be given at Occidental College.

One of the first words after he deplaned on what ten years before would have been called "his last visit to his native California," was a quip:

I was talking to my friend Warren—you know, Chief Justice. I said to him—asked him—"Do you know Nixon?" He shook his head. "No, I don't know him." So, I said, I'll vote for Kennedy. Before I asked Warren I was planning to write in Matthew Arnold, or Benedict Arnold. Couldn't make up my mind.

Two days after the poet touched down at the airport, we heard him speak and "say his poems" at Occidental College. In Berkeley the following week he liked neither his building nor his sponsors, nor his crowd at the Berkeley Community Theater. The billing read, "The Dana Attractions Inc. presents in person, America's poet laureate, Robert Frost," to Frost's vast disgust. By this date Robert Frost had become a profitable item of verbal, mobile merchandise. He was vastly stirred up.

> They got me under false pretenses. And they had Schorer to introduce me. Others knew me better—and had currently a better right to do it—my friends of long standing. But, let that pass. It's over. The main thing was the nonacademic angle. I don't like these outside affairs. I like college appearances—not the Ivy League only—colleges everywhere—east—west—British Isles—everywhere. College crowds understand me. These outsiders advertise me as a sort of polite Edgar Guest, which certainly I am not—I'm neither polite nor Eddie Guest.

Again he was the same old "politician at odd seasons." Yet, when the shouting was over in the Bay Area and he came to us by Santa Fe train, he never wore a sweeter smile. But there had been ameliorating circumstances. The George Stewarts had brought in (as always) a few of the elect, and the poet had scintillated. After one and one-half years of absence from each other, coming together uninhibited, there was much to occupy in conversation—relevant and irrelevant—politics (being election year, and perhaps not a safe subject for discussion), poetry uninhibited. It was talk not possible except in one's own home, walking through the woods or sitting about the fireplace.

Ellery Sedgwick, one of the leading editors in America, the eighty-eight-year-old editorial director of *The Atlantic Monthly* for a good generation, had died early that year of a heart attack. Sedgwick had "discovered" many brilliant youngsters. Perhaps his greatest prize was Hemingway. But there was one youngster he had *not* discovered, as we have already seen. This he would have given much to forget. That youngster was Robert Frost. Sedgwick had threaded the magazine he piloted through troubled waters, up from 10,000 to 120,000 subscribers. He was a stormy petrel in the field of editorship.

So when "a time to talk" came to us, it was natural that old sores should be opened when we got round to gossiping about the feud of the twenties. It was still fresh in our guest's memory when we met for talking.

I never mind a little such—but Sedgwick was too good—expert—at it to suit me. I remember the letter he wrote you about his help to me. To hear him talk always *he* was the one who found and encouraged Frost when nobody else would. The same old story. When you're down they keep you down. When you climb out of the mud, in spite of their interference or neglect, they tell how early they gave you recognition.

I suppose in all reason I shouldn't talk about it any more. But, I'm an Indian. Not a dead one, either—live one. I scalp 'em, talk about it later on. But, now he's gone, we'll let the dead past alone.

As we looked retrospectively back over the months of 1960, there were things that made us laugh. There was the great *faux paus* of a French magazine remembered. In April *McCall's* devoted the front cover to Marilyn Monroe, where her name was followed by that of Robert Frost, same type, same size. A Parisian magazine, mistaking the juxtaposition and position of the two names on the cover, featured as author of the Marilyn blurb "The famous American poet, Robert Frost." The fine article about Frost in the same issue was unmentioned. The poet little more than growled over this journalistic *mésalliance*. But it started him off:

That's the trouble with translations. You gotta know both languages—from—to—so's the sense carries across. Maybe I oughta be proud they made the mistake and put me in her class—made me her press agent without portfolio. I can bask in her glory—might take on my youth again. You know we—come right down to it—we could not have had all these translations—exchange of permanent ideas from the earliest days, without the alphabet—the one we inherited, or some other. You might call 'em inevitable. Our ABC's are wonderful, but we didn't invent 'em, anymore than we invented babies. They sorta grew up. The best survived. Most democratic thing we possess is the alphabet. You seem to hold that it went back two peoples ahead of the Phoenicians who adopted it. Somebody on Sinai peninsula, copper mines, or sump'n, left carbon-datable writing showing similar letters in the mines' environs to have been the beginning of our own ABC's. Anyway, it's democratic—among the people—no high-brow stuff. The alphabet is our path—our cinder path on which we have run our course—our two thousand—three thousand—years of history—like a bill of fare. Been a growth like our diet. Marx caught it and gave us the prescription. All Marxism is—a prescription—medicine. Doctors tell us that vitamins are all we need for a week running. I prefer a little roughage.

Sump'n else been with us, all these centuries back, besides the alphabet—yes and long before the ABC's. I'm talking about wars. They've been with man ever since the Stone Age. Look at the neolithic weapons man used against man. Once in every so often we've got to establish our nationalism with ourselves. You know I'm not friendly toward things like the U.N. I was the same way with Wilson's League of Nations. A country's got to stand or fall on its own. I remember I once said to somebody long time ago that Wilson came not to bring peace but a League of Nations. Well, can you trust a nation in the U.N. any better than out?

I don't know what's going to come of all this expansion of our prowess into space. When you find the answer, wire me collect, will you? On second thought, just write me. Maybe your theory won't be worth more than the four-cent stamp we're gettin' used to—maybe not even the three-cent stamp we used to mail letters with. Most ideas I've been exposed to haven't been.

I've never been a pacifist. Civilization has never come by that method. We won't hold it by that method either. Just trace it from the Stone Age—tribal wars—national wars—international wars—all man's history has been a survival effort. Man is a lazy cuss—hard to stir him up. But, with or without reason, he's been stirred somehow to climb out of the swamps, and it's been wars that stirred him. The crusades, the knightly days, the Norse sea fighters—on back to the earliest rise of civilization in Meso-potamia and Egypt—everything turned on war. It was the explosion inside the man who had a vision—big vision—that made war—war in all ages—and that has clarified the atmosphere, just as it clarified man's thinking. It's a lot more than Darwin's survival of the fittest. It comes down at last to a definition of what's fit—fitter—fittest. Who's to judge? I don't want anybody to think I'm a warmonger. Wars ain't everything. The arts—you know—the arts. Ever stop to think what has come down to us in America—of the great American past of which the white race had no part? Indian, Aztecs, Toltecs? You've picked up Indian arrows—arrowheads—maybe a stone ax or two. Not much else of Indian artifacts left here in the United States. That's because, aside from a few ruins north of the Rio Grande, the only civilizations the white invaders found under Cortez in Mexico (my first poem was about it) was that of the Aztecs and Toltecs. Their ruins are grand. They show a moving spirit of somebody great. Wars come and go. Civilization leaves tracks. You can follow these tracks from Cambodia to Delphi, from northern Africa to England. All of the past to be looked for in the ruins.

But just make up your mind, from now on we've got to live with science, art or no art. It's here to stay. One of my science poems is about living with (even getting along out there somewhere with) science. I recall that you've got that poem in all its changes from sump'n on to sump'n else. We've got to live with science. Gone too far. No way out.

It's got us in a mess of trouble—science. Ever think of it? You and I— a lot of us—have practically watched the Indian arrow warfare turned into atomic war of infinite dimensions. All in a lifetime. My ancestor—Major Charles Frost—fought the Indians with simple weapons. And you tell me your uncle stopped some Indian arrows that made great scars on his back.

About time we quit seeing the world go to pieces ever' time somebody in Europe or Africa—started doing it down there lately—or Asia—gets her multiple back up about sump'n. We're a hard crowd to down. Forever somebody stirrin' up trouble. Man's always been a turmoil-stirrer. Just made that way. If we only have a few leaders keepin' on an even keel, we won't quite explode.

From war and destruction the poet naturally turned to poetry, with a word about its ways and means.

People always askin' me how I write poetry. Might as well ask a frog how he jumps. How do I know? I feel somp'n here—in my breast—and pretty soon I'm sweatin' over an unborn thought. Birth pains for poetry are the worst of all pains. Worse than real childbirth, I should say. I've said before that the poems of mine that are delivered the easiest are the ones I like to think about—say to people—like my "Stopping by Woods."

No, I just can't say how they are conceived—where or how. Some like Topsy just grow up. You see, I go up to my farm in Vermont—Ripton— three hundred acres—and plod around, making out I'm farming. I let my manager of agriculture, name Dragon, do most of the planning, and *all* the work. Have a team to pull the machinery, so I can truthfully say I farm with two horses and a dragon. And here, on occasions, few and far between, I get an idea for a poem. Then I begin to sweat—always have done it that way—started that way with Cortez and my kinsman's *Conquest of Mexico*.

The great danger of all poetry is facility. Now facility has no connection, except in the opposite direction, with felicity. They are poles apart. Poetry can't be produced to order. Nothing more deadly than that. It can't be poetry and be spun off like yarn. I've written a lot of farm poetry—country poetry—mainly because I lived in the country, knew and loved the country and farm life. My first two books had a lot of farm poetry in them, one kind and another. But I have never said to myself: go to, I will write farm poetry. Eddie Guest, for I don't know how many years, would say every morning, "Time to write a poem," and would dash one off. Other rimesters, too. They were well paid, all that ilk, in good U.S. currency. In my case when a poem idea hits me in the solar plexus, I'm not good for anything till it's on the way to finishing. Didn't get there for a long while, usually, but was on the way. Horrible how you feel when you're poem-possessed. I think that's the word—possessed like the man in the Bible who was possessed of a demon, I've been poem-possessed. You can't get away from it till the thing's done. Terrible! Somebody asked me about this the other day, where a poem comes from. I told 'em that was the danger to be reckoned with—that and facility. In "The Gift Outright" I tried to say in fourteen lines the whole history of the Revolutionary War. Maybe I should have left it in one line—one line there tells it all, "The land was ours before we were the land's."

I never pay any mind to what the critics say. I don't have to. My friends read them and come right to me with the doleful news—and how *they* defended me. They say I ought to stick to tools. I know all about rakes and hoes.

Then suddenly he turned to the stars—forever a favorite subject for him.

I've always had a telescope. But I refuse to look at anything unimportant. I only look at real planets and things like that. I have always got on with scientists—but I've been teasy with 'em. I've been close to men like Niels Bohr. Had great talks with him. Words and science come close together. Etymologists at one end—scientists at the other. No conflict. Sometimes I think there's no such thing as education. What are you doing back here—what did you come back here for? "I'm a young adult. I went to school once without result."

After verbal excursions into areas from T. S. Eliot to the Wright brothers, and from Pasternak to the Peloponnesian War, he came to say:

> Just for fun I think I'd enjoy being a statesman on a temporary basis. I'm still waiting to be consulted. I went up to Washington as consultant at the Library of Congress. I thought I'd be consulted by all departments of government. So far I've been consulted three times by the Executive, once by the Supreme Court, not at all by the Congress. I just wait till they come along. If I were in power I'd take advice if they'd let me take credit when it succeeded. The trouble with us Americans is we're afraid of intellect—afraid of intellectuals. That's why we wouldn't elect Adlai Stevenson—egg head!
>
> People always asking me if I think there should be a poet laureate in the United States scene. Well it'd be a recognition—if I were the one it'd be better than being a consultant never consulted.

One sees the poet far from being weaned from the woods he loved for so many years. At every opportunity in hours of rest and respite he would say, "Let's walk." There were many sunsets to love—vast acres of brightly colored clouds above the hills that humped themselves westward. As he looked with eyes of wonder upon the setting sun, he remembered other days when he laughed at the "sundowners" he was associated with at Derry and the doggerel he wrote. But this was another day, and he was an old man. Yet, despite his eighty-six years, he outwalked and outtalked us all. So much of the accepted and understood gruffness and shoulder chips had gone from him. Friendship that so often was present in reserve had become transmuted into gentle sweetness. If there were a new feud somewhere in the background, it was not revealed.

During the many years there had been half-scorn for the books and magazines he had been asked to sign wherever we came upon him. Often it seemed he resented the efforts we had made for perpetuating his writings in every form. Sometimes he signed with a subdued growl. But when age had touched his head with snowy, unruly locks, when his ninetieth birthday lacked but three and one-half years of arrival, a change came over him—more notable in 1960 than at any previous time either in California or New England. A touching incident occurred on this current visit. My wife was in the kitchen one day, and Robert came in holding in his hand some tell-tale manuscripts.

"Where is he?" (Meaning myself.)

Being told I was upstairs in the library, the poet showed my wife what he wanted me for—a sheaf of precious manuscripts. Then he sought me out, secretively. He held the manuscripts out to me with:

"Here are some pieces I brought out for you. I tried to find a whole composition book, but couldn't. These are first drafts, and there are very few of my first-draft manuscripts existing."

Then he was gone from the room, leaving me rich in soul, with five manuscripts, including the holograph of his introduction to Sidney Cox's book *A Swinger of Birches*. In addition were four first-draft holograph poems (along with one unnamed), "Of a Winter Evening," "A Next to Nothing Song," and "Spacious Thoughts." The gift of the holograph introduction he had written for Sidney's book stirred me. I had often wondered why it took him so long to sign his own introduction to the Cox book. All the more strange was the fact that Sidney had died his oldest friend. At the time of his death, we had spoken of Frost's last appearance at Dartmouth with Sidney's class of "Wah-hooers." The two had now and then disagreed but always made up. I should say they probably understood and appreciated and believed in one another for more years than either was willing to admit. The forthcoming book of his verse was to be, very properly, dedicated to Untermeyer, Bartlett, and Sidney Cox.

The evening before he was to leave, we were seated at the supper table when the phone rang. Answering, we were told that Congressman Udall, in Tucson, Arizona, wanted to speak with Mr. Frost. We had notified Udall that Frost would be coming to Tucson on the Southern Pacific arriving the following morning. The call confirmed all this, and in due course the trip was made.

In the *Complete Poems* volume for the grandson, Christopher, age twelve, our noted visitor wrote, "From his grandfather's friend, Robert Frost, Far Hills, Redlands, Calif., November 1, 1960." In the copy for the little granddaughter, Lori, he set down, "From Robert Frost, old friend of the family."

So, again he had come to us, said his say, eaten our bread and salt. Each time he came and went away we wondered, "Will there be another day? Another visit?" Hope forever was on our side. Our evidence concerning things not seen was the poet's happy spirit and firm resolve.

On the evening of his departure by train for Arizona, accompanied by Bill Meredith, I had to meet a class. I promised to cut it short to have a bit longer with the two, who would be brought over by my wife to Colton, some miles from Redlands, to catch the train.

All connections were made; the travelers were awaiting my advent and the appearance of the train. The de luxe locomotive whistled in the distance. We began our good-byes, thinking of past joys and expectations for tomorrow.

Congressman Udall was to entertain the visitors at Tucson. We had not heard much politics before this hour. He gave us a parting word. The train was whistling a mile or so away.

> You know, I inherited my status as a States'-rights Democrat from my father—maybe my grandfather. I've never outgrown it. The electoral system we have worked under politically for so long's got to be preserved, basically unchanged, only modified somewhat.

In due course we came to see how all things political were shaping up for our poet. It was only a matter of a few weeks until plans became performances, and only a matter of as few weeks until arrangements were made for Robert Frost to read a poem at the inauguration. The President-elect stated his reasons for the innovation in a news release. Nor was this the last important collaboration between poet and President, the poet and the Arizonian.

"Mr. Frost was chosen," said the President-elect, "because he is a great New England poet whose poems I have long admired and read."

Moreover, he might have added, he is a Harvard man.

When the telegram from Washington, D.C., reached 35 Brewster, Cambridge, Massachusetts, informing Frost what was desired of him, his reply was as Frostian as "Stopping by Woods on a Snowy Evening."

"If you can bear at your age the honor of being President of the United States, I ought to be able at my age to bear the honor of taking some part in your inauguration. This would have pleased inordinately the kind of Grover Cleveland Democrats I had for parents."

In addition the poet decided to do what he had never done in his whole life (at least not since high school graduation), that is to write a poem of introduction to the one chosen by the incoming President. There he made his abysmal mistake. Trying to read in blinding sunlight a poem that was new and with which he was completely unfamiliar, his sight paralyzed by the glare, he threw the new verses away in anger, and in a voice clear as a bell read from memory "The Gift Outright."

How true to form his handling of the problem. He long before had, for our education, shown his own mistake. The poem he had written had neither facility nor felicity, that which he read had both. One's mind returns to a statement he made in California with us, "Never," he said, "Never read a new and untried poem before an audience." He failed to take his own advice.

On the train platform, leaving for Arizona, he had said:

The only thing that worries me about Kennedy's election—victory—is the Old Man—Ike, you know. After he got rid of Adams, Eisenhower came out and did things. He thought of Nixon's going to Russia first. That trip to Russia was what caused MacMillan's victory in the British elections —made him the head of government. The Democrats over here haven't done much but talk so far. Labor in England has already gone too far. Looks as if Labor in the U.S.A. is going to do the same—make the same mistake. Men like Hoffa don't help. But, you know, there's still a lot of us not yet organized—not likely to be.

I feel pretty sorry for Ike. Good man.

As the half-mile-long train rolled to a stop, my wife finished her tale of how we found the Jutlanders in Denmark shipping the small fish to Continental Europe, the big ones to the U.S.A. He chuckled, one foot on the coach step, and shot back his parting dart:

"You know, I had guessed that a priori."

From the coach window the departing guests were waving. The East was about to take her genius from his native land once again. The diesel-propelled engines started pulling the multi-numbered coaches, full, half-full, empty—they turned the bend, leaving only darkness behind—and us.

XLIV. The Last Mowing

When in February, 1961, the President of the United States in a television appearance, more or less in Frost's honor, spoke of the greatness of the poet, he compared politics and poetry and showed their cognation. The rash of television eulogies which followed left Frost, now in his eighty-seventh year, in a dazed state of being. One who didn't know him would have been led to think that it was all objectionable. His friends knew better. He was still the little boy on the sandy beach at Cliff House playing with the long seaweed, fearing of being forgotten and left behind.

When he, on a time, said to me, "I never go anywhere on purpose, I just happen by," he was not speaking of the inauguration of a president in the year 1961.

Few might realize what the election of fellow-Harvardite Jack Kennedy to the highest post in the nation within the gift of the American voter meant in the poet's career, and, one might add, for the arts as well.

Occasionally in pre-election weeks, Frost mentioned his hopes that one day we might have a president who appreciated the arts. In fact, he more than once suggested in private conversation his belief that a cabinet member for that department, along with state, war, and commerce, if not even alongside labor, was a desirable thing.

Poetry has never been a favorite of American politicians. Been looked down on before and since Cal Coolidge. What they held tops used to be big business—now its big labor. Always poetry and the other arts ranked down at the bottom next to zero. Very bottom. Maybe one day we'll get recognized. I've been harping on it in my capacity as consultant to the

Congress. Been wondering if I've made any progress. Still wondering. Maybe the road'll turn a ways down.

My grandfather was of the practical school. Poetry was a bad word to him. Business "more than usual" was his aim. He tried to do something with his son, my father. This drove the son to California, made a politician out of him. Then when I was under my grandfather's thumb in Lawrence, he was sure he was going to make me respectable. But he failed. I was not made for respectability.

This leveling process I've been watching a long while. Maybe I'll get two or three to fix it up the way I want it, so I'll be able to sleep nights. You gotta' do sump'n, I suppose. I've encountered in my time a great wave of free verse. Goes along with all this socialism. I've always written regular verse. Some of my friends write free verse. I say sonnets for 'em. And I go to sports for expression. First one is from cars. I got it from cars. Now I don't know one car from another. Don't know much about 'em. Not the way young people do. I know very little about 'em. I come, in speaking free verse and regular verse, such as I write, to have another metaphor. I'd as soon play tennis with the net down as to write free verse. Now that goes a long ways into the problem of form. Myself, when I used to play tennis, I was always distressed when I was doing too well because the net was down an inch or two, when I discovered it had been down, spoiled the whole thing. Not hard as it ought to be, tight and clear. That carries over into all the arts. Carries into painting, music, poetry—all the arts. Take the metronome. It has a lot to do with it, too. That makes form. In poetry you have to keep within the beat, and yet not be doggerel—beat, beat—nothing but beat. Not that way.

It's all right for them to dream about anti-Babel, all right. But it'll have a hard time coming true just because the poets are such stinkers. Got to think about a lot of things before we go too far. Poetry must be kept poetry. Been a lot of good poets ruined by this method of refusal to recognize the high place the arts should have—occupy—in a great nation like ours. We keep waiting for the flowering time—new renaissance. It never comes. And all because the politicians look down on it. Now whether recognition of the arts as an integral part of our national life along with science and business will bring poetry to the fore—give it a place—I'll not say. Worth a try, anyway. If it fails we're no worse off than before—poetry couldn't be. But I want to say right here—I want to stand up for my country and my people. It's all bosh saying we are behind Europe in the arts. There isn't a writer in Europe but would give a lot—all he had—to have his work published in America. We've become a nation of readers. Paperbacks, you know they helped.

Now in poetry you can have something suggestive or not, as you like. I'm aware of this, sometimes, though I'm not aware—I wouldn't want to be asked to put it into prose under the poem. I just assume that people are getting it out of the poem. Everything doesn't have to be right out. Don't say it out too boldly, sump'n's lost if you do. That's what's called diffidence.

Word came early in 1961 that a one-man invasion of Israel was on the agenda. Frost had been invited to deliver a series of lectures before the faculty and students of the Hebrew University at Jerusalem. It was the new Israel's thirteenth anniversary. Anything might happen—much did. Most naturally this visit was to develop into more than a week of non-stop activities—enough to tire out a man of one-fourth his years. The grueling seven days was to be followed—and was followed—by his lectures at the University of Athens, climaxed with another "farewell tour" of the British Isles. With him on all these jaunts went his "Man Friday," Larry Thompson.

"What're you trying to do—make a prima donna out-a me?"

Such a growl from the poet was not unexpected. The unexpected thing about it was that he was enjoying it all.

Friends familiar with Frost's vagaries could understand what happened on the plane as it eagled its way over the shimmering, tideless sea. The manager of the El Al line had prevailed on the poet to go along with the newsmen and passengers en route to the New Jerusalem for the opening of the new Sheraton hotel. On the plane the visiting lecturer was surrounded by big-time columnists.

Now, if one such had been deliberately planned to stir Frost up to white heat, it couldn't have succeeded better than the ad lib remark ricocheted across the aisle by one of the newsmen. Above the purr of the big jet, a prickly statement came to the ears of the poet. The gist of it was that Frost had hair like Sandburg's. It was just that simple. It appeared that the author of the once-shocking poem "Chicago" was the last person and/or thing Frost wanted to talk about.

En route to the scene of one of his most important and romantic lecture series, the poet had been rather happy up to that moment. Came a rumble as of bees disturbed in a hive. The rumble was almost audible. The explosion was warded off, though the governor belt slipped a bit.

Why're they always talking about my hair and Sandburg's? Carl has a complete hair-do every once in a while. I've not gone to a barber shop for twenty-five years. Cut my own hair. Barbers always talkin' you to death—worse'n newsmen. Most of their talk is that your hair's falling out. I couldn't take it."

The poet kept mumbling along under his breath, turning from pompadour to poetry.

I don't write poetry the way Sandburg does, I say it takes form to perform. Not alike at all. He's against form, like Bible creation, he's without form and void, with darkness reigning on the face of the deep. Carl's out there in Hollywood now making a three-million-dollar picture. Big-shot cinematologist—name on a brass door plate, he told me, and all that. His verse is all right—if you like that kind of verse.

What I'm interested in is a little extension of government help to struggling artists. I was a struggler for forty years before I pulled out of the woods, sorta by accident. We've a lot of anxious youngsters—beatniks, some of 'em—who need encouragement. Give it to 'em and they might even shave off their beards.

But these things were all forgotten when the airplane dipped down from over the Mediterranean and taxied across the runway at the Lydda airport twenty-odd miles from Jerusalem. Stony Israel lay all about. Soon he was to hold the land and all its people in the palm of his chubby hand. Certainly if the claim his friends made for him as the rightful holder of the belt (worn so long, so well, by Leonardo) needed added proof before touching down, Israel, from the kibbutzim of Esdraelon to the Byzantine beach at Askelon, provided it.

"I feel perfectly at home here," he quipped to the director of the cultural relations division of the foreign ministry of Israel and to the cultural attache of the American Embassy who met him at the landing field. "After all," he went on, "Israel is one of the American colonies. Never been here before. Took the first invitation I got. My mother'd be pleased to see me here. She was a faithful Swedenborgian—believed in the Bible. This to her would have been holy ground—Dan to Beersheba, she always called it. Got a lot to see and do here, the little time I'm here. The 'New Jerusalem' you call your city. She'd a liked that."

Thoughts of his childhood in the Church of the New Jerusalem came drifting back to the visitor. He remembered Pastor John Doughty in San Francisco, who had preached sermons concerning a city "with foundations whose builder and maker was God." This, he thought, was different. It was built by a brave, strong, and clever people. His mother had talked and sung about "the gathering of the faithful in the New Jerusalem." Here he found the place, a city of refuge for a harried, suppressed, and persecuted people, a continuous possession, however in absentia, over the millenniums. He once called it the oldest deed of possession in the world, the abstract being in the Bible.

Now, such thoughts might not be unthought in the poet's mind; for one thing was clear: He had flown to the New Jerusalem on wings of light, and the men and women, the youth, and the children in school took him to their hearts. Nobel Prize or no, the Israelis were certain that a supreme poet was a current visitor to the coasts of Israel.

Thus he came to see and found that he had conquered.

From the moment the poet touched down at Lydda air terminal to the hour he lifted on his flight to Greece, observers noted that he was as much in his element as though he were in either the Old or the New England, both of which he knew so well. His heritage from his Scottish mother was English, which heritage had been buttressed by the King James version of the Bible. In Israel he found need for both.

But his task was more than learning. Almost immediately the poet stepped into that work for which he had flown the Atlantic and the Mediterranean: lecturing to the students of the Hebrew University, where he was honored as plowman to open the first furrow in a field which had never known a plow. He had been called from afar to be the first Samuel Paley lecturer in American culture and civilization. None questioned his fitness for such an important post.

The Israelis marveled at the strength and stamina he displayed. They had been told that his eighty-seventh birthday was on March 26, 1961— that very month and year. And here he was saying his poems for an excited, overflow crowd of students, carrying out his part next at a closed student seminar, followed by a series of talks on philosophy, art, and people, given at various places in the capital city, the audience being the cultural elite of Jerusalem. He had conversed at length with top officials of Israel on agriculture, absorbing the history of what the new nation had accomplished on the rich soil which absolutism and absentee landlordism had permitted to become more like a desert. Then he visited a sick friend, thereafter going through a grueling experience for one and one-half hours with the newsmen and cameramen. All these things were beyond the power of most Israelis to understand. How could eighty-seven years of a busy life stand up under them?

There were things to see as well as things to do. His friendship for Sukenik who, as he expressed it, "had so much to do with" the Dead Sea Scrolls, crystallized his conviction that the "endless chain" dramatically connecting the ancient past with the present was best seen here. Perhaps nothing in his long life had more vividly linked his entire career with the beginnings of history than this visit. Here, safe in the vaults underground, the Ain Feshkha scrolls, via New York, were existing documents to see, even to touch. For a decade he had often referred to the scrolls in our conversations together. Now he was here not only where the scrolls, more especially the "Isaiah" document—perhaps the greatest find in all the history of ancient lore—was kept in its cement vault far underground, but also the results of the 1960 year of "digs" in the caves of Israel alongside the Dead Sea.

Indeed, the poet had come to the new land of Israel to leave behind, when he lifted, facing west, a legacy of rare wisdom and vast good will. All sorts of people and places were objects of interest. Perhaps none were more interesting (always excepting the university youth) than the Essenes, the Balm in Gilead, and the practitioners of the Aesculapian art. The site of the new hospital, Kiryat Hadassah, high on the Hill of Healing (above Ain Karem, now a suburb of Jerusalem) may have been the heights of historic Beit Hakerem. Near the top, in ancient days, signal fires were lit to be seen as warning signs many miles away. For here the Hadassah, Hebrew University's Medical Center, was on the visitor's "must" agenda. Israelis said of this great hospital that it couldn't be come upon by accident. You had to seek it out by way of the modern road winding up and up, and at the end of the highway you would come to the buildings. When you had reached the summit you remembered Galen and the Apollonian hospitals of antiquity—Corinth and Pergamum and the rest. On the day Frost paid his respects to Galen, the wind was wild. The hills of Judea are deceiving. The car climbed steadily until at last on the eminence the Israeli Medical Center (one of the world's greatest) was found all but finished to receive the poet. Aside from its elevation, this hill might have been selected by the Greek followers of Aesculapius themselves. The poet was provided with a bit of history concerning the past and present of the scene. He was told of the days of Jeremiah when the leaders set a sign of fire upon the hills overlooking Ain Karem, anciently Beit Hakerem. Now in modern times, they told the poet, it is not a sign of fire that Hadassah has set on the hill, but a sign of healing.

The anxious, waiting doctors were certain the day was too chilly for the poet to show. The wind howled and wailed. Then, of a sudden, the car arrived, and out of it clambered the visitor, dauntlessly facing an angry March wind.

Certain it is that two Israeli physicians (having been doubters) had a new insight into poets and poetry when the lithe-limbed, vigorous-minded lover of the arts stood upon their eminence. There he was, bare headed and quizzically smiling, taking in the hospital and its surrounding mountainscope in true Frostian fashion. Somebody said that for looks he might have been one of the old prophets.

His Galenic hosts were solicitous for his comfort. Truth is, he looked chilled to the bone. But he smiled it off with a quip when they wanted to get him into a warm place, out of the wind, so he could talk.

It's not cold, only it sort of blows you to pieces—that's all. You ought to try to use this wasted wind for energy, or sump'n.

I'm goin' to tell the world about this—all this. I've seen the waifs you've brought in from everywhere—given 'em a home and a hope. I've had a chance to look at the Israelis you've pledged asylum to. They're the most touching thing of all. All this noise of building—people hammering, put-

ting in plumbing, laying tiles—all this here to heal the sick. This is everybody's concern—yours, mine—everybody's.

I'm glad you told me it was the Jewish women of America, the Hadassah,
who put up much of the money to build all this. And I'm glad too that
you planned all this to safeguard the people, below, underground—and
made it a modern city of refuge. American money everywhere, most people despise us for it, but you people are not fools. I'm glad our people are
concerned with a good and important place like this.

The visitor never stopped asking questions as they gave him a conducted tour through the vast buildings. He wanted to know how many
doctors would operate here—where they were coming from—the number of patients that could be cared for—where the marble was quarried.
He was from marble states—New Hampshire and Vermont. Good
marble.

Frost's knowledge of the Old Testament amazed the doctors. When
they had gone through the doorway out on the veranda to "spy out the
land," they pointed out the place where John the Baptist had secluded
himself. This was when he wore a garment with leathern girdle and sub-
sisted on locusts and wild honey in the wilderness. At once he wanted
to know in which direction the forerunner had started from the spot
pointed out. The questions kept up. Only a man with knowledge of
the Bible could have asked them.

He was intrigued by a wizened old man sitting cross-legged on the
floor, working on a fixture of some sort. He addressed him with his
magic shibboleth—a word on the tongue of every man and child, heard
at every turn—"Shalom!" This expression was the sesame. The man
smiled and answered "Shalom!" The visitor asked where he came from
and was told, "Morocco." He said "Morocco" over to himself and "Shalom."

"Beautiful words," he said softly.

They took the elevator to the top of the vast building, there to view
the land. From this unequaled vantage, the learned medics (authorities
on the Bible as well as medicine) pointed out the historic sites in view
round about. It was to the surrounding slopes on the north, timber lands
in Saul's day, that the exiled David, on advice of counsel, came out of

Moab to secrete himself from King Saul. The hospitable Israeli doctors were good enough to point out to the man from Vermont, who now and then referred to himself as "an Old Testament Christian," the spot among the vineyards where Mary came to visit her cousin Elizabeth as set forth in the Gospels.

As the visitor looked over all the land from the vantage point afforded by the height of the Medical Center, he mused on his own New England countryside, so like this in topography and prudence. He spoke of Vermont, "a place of stones and flowers," and marveled over all he saw, shaking his head:

"When I get away from contact with it, I'll have all this homogenized in mind and heart."

Then as they announced that departing time had come, he reluctantly turned away.

Once in the car, he had his last vision of the vast buildings. Looking back, he called out above the roar of the wind with a sweep of his hairy hand: "A darn good building."

The car turned and headed back toward Jerusalem.

It was one who had spent much time in Israel (one almost a birth-claimer) who told of things which made Frost's visit memorable. For it appears to have been just that—memorable to the Israelis in the little land bordering on the tideless sea.

"I can't remember any visitor who so quickly held the whole country in the palm of his hand. Why did so many Israelis catch the meaning of Frost's philosophy? It was because they, as well as he, had known sadness and suffering. The poet had walked through the valley of the shadow to write lines which the Israelis so well knew and understood. How clearly they probed his heart when he summed it all up in the lines of a poem,

> ". . . Earth's the right place for love:
> I don't know where it's likely to go better."

In the same way, he enthralled the youth of the country. University students at Jerusalem stood in hushed silence listening to him recite his poems or converse with the audience as he did. They fell in love with him as a person—a poet—which was proved by the incredible respect and admiration they showed him as such. It was almost unbelievable to listeners who heard the youngsters talking of him and his poetry as though they were his age, he theirs, and as though they were partaking of his thoughts and of his art as a part of their natural heritage. It is in this simple approach to youth that his greatness was so apparent.[1]

Frost forgot weariness brought on by constant interviews, lectures, readings, on his occasional visits to places to be seen in Israel. He rode south to look at the country below Askelon which borders on Israel by a historic fluke—Egypt's Gaza Strip. And as he rode south, looking upon "the Coasts of the Philistines," he shook his bare head, his white, unruly locks blowing in the wind.

"I've never seen so many stones in all my life," he mumbled, "I always thought we had more stones in Vermont than anywhere else. This country's made out of 'em."

For some reason the poet was in his element at storied Askelon. He had left his hat in the car. His mussed-up hair blew in the wind that came in from the placid surface of the sea. He was truly experiencing at Askelon his first feel of Israel out of Jerusalem. There had been a grueling five days of lecturing, interviewing, and city life. Once, as the broken Corinthian column witnessed, this had been a place of consequence. It was the proud gem of the five cities of the lords of the Philistines. Looking at marbles dexterously finished, the visitor asked about clues to prove whether the coastal settlers were from disaster-plagued Crete or not. The savants of the Hebrew University joined in the wish to know the truth of the unsolved mystery.

The one disappointment of the poet's visit to Israel was that he was unable to disappoint anybody. He went everywhere, did everything, talked to everyone, faced all kinds of audiences. He seemed to be living in two or more worlds all the time. One world was the changeless world of the land of Israel, a tiny spot of earth exploited over the millenniums by Hittites, Egyptians, Assyrians, Philistines, Romans, Turks, and British down through nearly four thousand years. Then the restoration

[1] Told by Faigel Broude, Tel Aviv, Israel.

of the land to its former state as "a good land, a land of brooks of water, of fountains and deeps, that spring out of valleys and hills."

"I'm not here to talk about American civilization," he quipped on the day he came to the Hebrew University to lecture. "I *am* American civilization. Just now I'm working on a poem covering everything from the Mediterranean sea to the coasts of California. Plenty of latitude and longitude. Big undertaking."

Characteristically he wrote in a copy of a first edition of *North of Boston* presented to the Hebrew University Library by Charles E. Feinberg, of Detroit, Michigan, the simple inscription: "To the Library, from Robert Frost in friendship forever."

Again he had a word:

> You know, when I left New York before getting on a plane to fly me here, almost the last thing before we started I told the reporters that I was coming over here to rumple the students' brains fondly—*fondly*. That's the important word in the phrase—"fondly." And I couldn't help thinking of a Bible verse my mother used to quote—something about somebody "taking the wings of the morning and flying to the uttermost parts of the earth." That's just what I have done—flown here. That would have pleased her if she had known.

In this fashion the visitor paid tribute to his hosts and to the country that had long existed in his memories out of a turbulent childhood.

Just here the poet combined admiration, regard, and love for a language and literature in the wise words:

> Yes, this country was worth fighting for if you will only keep your language—your ancient tongue that made the poetry of the Old Testament—so you can write new poetry in it. I said yesterday to your president that Israel must keep Jerusalem as a city so it may be founded over and over again.
>
> For you must have poetry—your own poetry—to match—nearly match —the poetry of the Old Israel. Somebody a little while ago asked me why I was the only major poet whose verse could be understood. I came back at him by asking why I should write obscure poetry. Your poetry in the new-old language must be indigenous—must be Israeli—just as the Song of Songs was for its day and time.

It was at historic and beautifully situated Askelon, Israel's seaside resort, ancient Askelon, that the poet felt a kindred wind that transported him back to his early days in California. The blue Mediterranean, lying in the spring sunshine, shimmered below the new resort city being built on the sands of the seashore. Corinthian columns were scattered hereabout. A few capitals remained not yet transferred to the museums. A new city was rising on every hand. But nature was still here—surviving. A bevy of quail rose and, frightened by the sound of men's voices, drummed away across the sandy shoreline.

> These quail are the direct lineal descendants of the birds which the refugees out of Egypt had to eat along with their morning manna. The old land and the new have proved the eternity of time.

But leaving time approached. The American Old Testament Christian had seen and experienced much. He might not remember all, but there were pictures of memory that the poet's photographic mind would hold forever: a small boy sawing steel with a modern saw; a handsome be-whiskered Israeli with a slouch hat and wrinkled half-smile; a boy and a girl doing school work in a laboratory each with a compound microscope; an Israeli youth of twenty or so, dressed in uniform taking observations with a sextant; a tiny, happy, smiling three-year-old girl with shiny black hair; a nurse in uniform holding a baby up for inspection, both wreathed in happiness; a youthful housewife with wind-disarranged hair, hanging clothes on a line; a ten-year-old boy eagerly doing his written work; a Jewish kibbutz farmer, refugee from half-slavery, driving a tractor, cap on head, unkempt hair, sparse black wind-blown whiskers and heavy eyebrows, intent upon his task; a fourteen-year-old girl piping to her goats on a reed pipe, the reclaimed desert stretching to the horizon; a woman garbed in heavy winter weather head-dress of black, weaving a basket; a thin-faced Jewish girl putting the finishing touches to her ceramics with paint brush; two tool-surrounded architects going over the plans of a building. All, from the tiny baby wreathed in smiles, to the ancient woman with her basket weaving, merged to show the proof of Israel renascent.

Israel, one of earth's newest-oldest countries, can never blot out the impact of Robert Frost's visit. Those with him on his sallies over the tiny country saw with what unqualified respect he was listened to. Here was a tapestry woven from a kindly-faced man reading poetry new as tomorrow, old as ancient Job; a vibrant soul, a winning personality, forming a saga of something forever to be a part and parcel of Israel.

One of its true builders said of this visit in, and concerning, Israel:

"In the future, so great was Frost's impact on the land and people, two men will forever be associated in the minds of the Israelis, both wearing a crown of snow white hair, both men of vision, hope, faith in the future. These men looked much alike—solid as granite, pliable as hope, full of faith. Ben Gurion and Robert Frost will stand as eternal signal fires from the heights of Ain Karem—Beit Hakerem."

But Athens called, America beckoned. The departing guest remembered what Luke said of the people who had heard St. Paul speaking on Mars Hill, that Athenians and strangers spent their time in nothing but to tell or hear some new thing. Without his knowledge, all arrangements were in the making for his visit as ambassador of good will to Moscow.

Might there have been a connection between the 1962 issue of Frost's new book of verse, which he named *In the Clearing,* and the poet's stormy visit to Russia to read his poetry to the Muscovite intelligentsia? The question, however relevant, is likely to remain unanswered.

The striking title to the new venture in poetry stood out along with *A Boy's Will, North of Boston,* and the rest for strength and beauty. *In the Clearing* followed the patterns set decades before and links his poetry with those dark trees that stretched away into the edge of doom. One may feel sure that the poet was not to be withheld but that some day into their vastness he should steal away—fearless. For when he talked with the Russian head of state, looking him in the eye without fear for self or country, he asked questions to which there is no reply. Very appropriately, the man who visited Moscow in company with him was none other than the Arizonian who had opened the way for the poet in Washington—Udall.

The poet was looking forward. His words to friends and reporters seemed portents of a troubled tomorrow:

> We never can quite know how to act with Russia. Sometimes I take one tack, then I trim sail and take another. But being a mariner where Russia is concerned is not easy. Khrushchev came over here and went everywhere. Maybe we can do the same over there.
>
> What am I going to do in Moscow? For one thing I'm going to see if Khrushchev means trouble or peace. That ought to be enough if I manage it. We can't go on forever the way we've been going. We've gotta get down to cases. Two great countries border one another in the Aleutians—between their last and first island of the chain is only fifty miles—here we are bordering one another actually from any one of the boundaries—over the pole—across the Pacific—across the Atlantic—back door to one another. Close as Alaska once was—or Mexico—close.
>
> But the thing I am scheduled to do is to see about some cultural exchanges. We've got things—cultural things—they need. They've got things we need. Oughta get together and swap a little. One thing is sure. If we are going to—if we keep on going on and on with brinksmanship till we all go together over the brink into mass destruction, there won't be anything left, or anybody, to swap—there won't be enough left to swap what we don't have.

So he went to Moscow and somehow found himself on arrival a sick man—stomach upheaval—and was sent by the officials on suggestion of Khrushchev to Gagra on the Black Sea. Thus it happened against all protocol that he was called on by the head of state. There in the delightful seaside resort the American received the Muscovite, and the two talked things over. Safe home, he was willing to tell his story.

> Well, we looked things and people over and formed opinions. Maybe good'll come out of it. We didn't get down to burying the hatchet. We had good talk together—good as people can have in languages so widely separated as ours. They may both have come from the Caucasus as some say. They got a long ways apart. But he was nice to me—blustery, yes, but not too bad. Nothing would do him but I must fly down to his place on the Black Sea. He came down and we had a long talk. I got a stomach

upset and a cold. That was why he came down to see me, how I was doing and all that. Really I've nothing evil to report on him. We got along. There I was, weak as a cat and sitting on the edge of my bed talking to him. He sort of laid the law down—sort of. I should pass on to Kennedy some things we shouldn't do. Reasonable things they were.

I couldn't very well fight back. I was on the bed, sort of sitting up, weak you know, and he was standing and sitting by turns, talking a lot. We kept it all on a high level. No partisanship, no low level. He's a giant of a fellow, short but full of fire. All ready for a fight. I went to Russia to talk the head of state into a stand against us—not war—in strife and magnanimity. Rivals in art and rivals in business. He's no fool. He knows war isn't the solution, only the dissolution of everything we are and have. I told him God would have us take sides and contend with one another peacefully. He never said anything about God. I told him what I went over to tell him, that the only purpose in conflict—no war—peaceful conflict—was competition. No dirty play—no blackguarding. You know, when I talked with Khrushchev my mind went back seventy and more years ago to the little Swedenborgian church of my mother's religion in San Francisco—her belief in God. Couldn't help it. I thought of something she used to tell me.—"Be a witness," she'd say. Here I was far from America, far from San Francisco, and I was talking about God to a godless country and to a godless ruler. Be a witness, she would say, and I remembered. Funny thing, the way life goes along and turns out. I was a poor witness, but I talked about God to godless rulers. It was all as natural to me as though I had been in my mother's Swedenborgian meeting house in California, back in the nineteenth century.

I told him the world was to be in the hands of Russia and the United States for a good hundred years to come. How were we to handle the situation? Fight it out along this line in rivalry in sports, in art, and science. No more blackguarding. That was my point of departure. We ought to get together somehow. But he said that would be difficult—not impossible—difficult. He didn't say he wouldn't try.

He came quite far when he said we should consider these things, maybe we could find a solution. But he clammed up when I brought up Pasternak as the great Russian writer.

Well, people say I gave in to Khrushchev. I didn't give in—I gave out. I told him we must find a manner of getting on together. Two great powers like the U.S.A. and the U.S.S.R. have no call to plunge the world into a war of extermination.

I gave Mr. K. a book of my poems and wrote in it, I believe, the words, "From a rival in friendship."

What did we accomplish? Too early to say. But a good talk such as we had certainly won't plunge us into war. We are dealing with a powerful man—powerful in character—powerful in brain—powerful in statesmanship.

Whatever was accomplished or not accomplished, I got on with my fellow writers. You see, when they called me a poet I sort of soft pedaled. I told them I was a verse writer, not a poet. These Russians are an epic race. They think a poet has to be another Homer. I thought I was keeping up with the basic patterns. I was on an exchange program, and there I met my alter ego—Alexander Tvardovsky. I met a young poet—friendly sort—named Yevtushenko. He smiled at me, and I said to this poet called the angry young man, that, being poets we should laugh in the same language.

I suppose that as much as anything else the reason I never got much out of the poets they brought to talk with me was lack of communication between us. I knew no Russian, they knew practically no American. I made 'em laugh once, though, when I told them my ideas of poetry and countries—localizing the muse.

I tried to start conversation with them about men of great nations admiring one another regardless of patriotism. No response. I went on about great nations doing the same. Not a word. It may be they just didn't understand what I said well enough to answer with any definite opinion on the matter. They just kept a stony face, held a still tongue.

But I got a rise out of 'em—got a rise out of all who stood around— when I told the poets that if Russia beat my country in everything—art, literature, agriculture, manufacturing, high standard of living, then I'd turn Russian. But nothing I said did more than bring a smile to the faces of the receiving poets sent to meet me on my touching down. We knew that one of them could talk English, but he didn't do it. Maybe was afraid he'd say the wrong thing by some use of a word of two meanings. He listened, grinned, and the interview was over.

Poetry or no poetry, my visit to Russia convinced me—my talks with Khrushchev, especially—convinced me that they want peace. They think we have drawn a wall of camps and warlike preparation all about. And

I agree that was too bad. You know my inadvertence in calling Khrushchev a ruffian was a mistake. What I really meant was a rough and ready
character. Maybe I meant it to be a compliment. But it backfired.

But, however you may sum it all up, I have to say, no matter what may
or may not take place, I had the time of my life with Khrushchev and with
the Russian people, high and low. They asked me if I planned to come
back. I told 'em I'd some day be back when I got older and wiser.

But it was with the reporters and editors that I had my fun. Hard for a
Russian newsman, very serious, you know, to take the joking you want
to belabor him with. They all marched into my apartment to get a story.
Just like American newsmen—after a story. Nice boys—intelligent—good
writers, I imagine. They're an important cog in the Soviet machinery—
vital cog. We went to the literature department of the Moscow library,
and they gathered around me with questions. I finally got round to reading
my wall poem to 'em. Never found out whether I did or didn't get off
on the right foot, or stirred 'em up by walling out or walling in, with ideas
about which wall I meant, whether a real New England wall on a farm
such as the one at Derry, or a prison wall, or a wall keepin' us out, or
them out, tariff wall, or what. Language is a funny thing. Really, though,
I think we understood one another without anything but ourselves to get
across the language barrier.

Lot of talk over here about my reading that poem. Always a lot of talk
by people who like to talk about something they don't know the facts
about. Mainly American criticism. I usually read this poem to new audiences. But some took it I meant a wall all around Russia. None of the
Russians, so far as I know, took it that way—wall east, west, north, south—
all around Russia. Strange, wherever I go that is the poem always asked
for. It's local New England, of course, but universal everywhere at the
same time. Anyway, I'm back, and I love America.

How strange his final prophetic words of afterthought turned out
to be.

"But I'll be dead when the show-down comes."

In just four months he had come to the end of the way. The Russo-
American situation had not changed. And more true to what he so long
before had written,

They would not find me changed from him they knew—
Only more sure of all I thought was true.

XLV. A FURTHER FURTHER RANGE

WHAT WERE THE MAPLE TREES saying at Ripton and Bread Loaf? It was deep winter, and the brooks were covered over with a dim glass of ice instead of free singing waters.

All was quiet at the Homer Noble farm. All was quiet at Amherst. Likely Stafford Dragon was considering his sugar proceedings on the acres which had been his pension at the hands of our poet. But this year there would more than likely be very scant sugar or maple syrup— of that syrup guaranteed to please a prince of the blood—or even please a native Vermonter.

Robert Frost was gone.

His poor, tired body had worn itself out trying to keep pace with the lightning speed of his mind and the agony of life's burdens. In youth his mother had moved from house to house, from apartment to apartment, with her little brood. The poet had moved from farm to village, from state to state, and latterly from expanding nation to expanding nation on junkets for the man in Washington—the Harvard man—to see how things went on in the Near East and Europe, and finally to discover the truth about Mr. Khrushchev, face to face.

Hereafter, there would be no more junkets. The tired world would have to look out for itself. Had the poet quitted life ten years earlier, it likely would have been no different. No age in which he might possibly have lived could have parted with him without deep grief, even though the circle of friends would have grown day by day to become a multitude.

It was in December, 1962, R. F. having just returned from a trip to Detroit in November, that the wires reported Robert Frost hospitalized with surgery. Then followed a heart attack and blood clots, but at Christmas time word came from his son's widow, Lillian, that the attack had caused no permanent heart damage. Guests were permitted to talk with him in the hospital. In mid-January, 1963, the belated 1962 Christmas card arrived implying that all was well with our friend.

Then, in the early hours of the morning, January 29, 1963, the transistor radio which was clocking away the hours announced that Robert Frost had slipped into Infinity. One could only respond—Robert Frost may leave us, but he cannot die.

Word came to us that a service was to be conducted at Amherst in the little college chapel (forever reminiscent of Colonial Massachusetts) and that we were among the invited. We at once accepted and prepared for the nation-wide journey. Distance from Amherst was for his friends no deterrent.

Amherst College and Amherst village were plagued by the cold that settled down through the moaning trees. The bitterness of zero-degree temperatures froze the streets and cut our faces and ears like a cold knife. Amherst was a miniature glacier. But inside the Lord Jeffery was warmth with logs blazing in the open fireplace. And there were friends of the poet and low-spoken words of calm, subdued conversation. Somehow there was nothing beside the poet one cared to talk about.

The crowd of town and gown friends of Amherst and the poet was forming. Amherst, the college which took him in for life when he came —at the beginning of the First World War—back from England, back to Massachusetts, and in end, and to the end, to Amherst village and college. They were gathering, some at the Lord Jeffery along with ourselves, some in homes of Amherstians. Many would motor in from local and even distant places. The President of the United States was unable to be present. In his place, to represent the head of state, he sent Udall, the friend who had gone on junkets with the poet in missions abroad, themselves representing the head of the nation and its people.

The snowy-haired chief justice of the Supreme Court of the United States walked through the crowd. Here Mr. Warren was, after all the passing years, paying tribute and last respects to one who all his life had held the Supreme Court of the United States to be the most interesting department of the national government. Robert Frost had continued to hold a close personal friendship with the members of this court until the day of his death.

Nothing said at the final rites cut deeper than one line of a sentence uttered by Amherst's president, Calvin Plimpton, in his address of recognition in the chapel.

"Robert Frost's poetry is with us. What we shall miss is the man."

To resolve the intricate problem of the faith held by this poet was to the end an impossible task even for a thinking man, his friends or others. The bishop made the attempt, lifting the veil, however slightly.

"Robert Frost believed that the source of all truth was God, so that the passing of his life was an opportunity to discover more truth on his part. To him religion was a mystery beyond complete solution."

So long our poet had spoken for himself. Now he was silent. Others must speak for him, haltingly, to be sure, not with full knowledge. They must speak the little they knew. We had known the poet in his moments of tenderness. We had known him when anger swept him like a furnace blast. Action was over. The time had come to evaluate. Robert Frost as a citizen was gone. Robert Frost as an influence would live on. Now he indeed belonged to the ages, just as the ages belonged to him. The bishop outlined it well when he said:

"In the same fashion it is for us to realize that Frost, the man belongs to us. One never felt he knew him all, the part he gave was of such intensity. He was forever being afraid of being afraid."

These thoughts were uppermost, doubtless, in the minds of all his close friends. The panorama of the poet's life, to the knowing, moved across the decades. To some it outstripped a full generation of time, to others a few years, to many a few short months, perhaps to some no more than a negligible day of knowledge. But, however short or long the time, the impress of Robert Frost was as strong as the memory that he had held of looking upon the Great Stone Face as a child.

There was a phrase often quoted by the poet that so well fitted himself, his times, and his living:

> *Ten cities claimed blind Homer dead.*
> *Through which the living Homer begged his bread.*

There are other lines, far from epic, which so well express the scope

of his life work, lines covering poverty and prosperity, sadness and joy—
lines like winter leaves drifting to a resting place somewhere nearby.

So much you knew of earth which men have lost—
Dark winter woods and new-ploughed fields of spring—
May we not find you where the thrushes sing
Above their nests by April breezes tossed?
And when you answer may there be soft words
Of gentle, lasting friendship, smiles and tears—
Our friendly answer to the singing birds.

And when you come to walk with us again,
Up to the heights which touch a pale green sky,
Let us be gay, with never tear nor sigh,
Counting the coaches of a mile long train.
Let us touch hands and hearts, dear, poet friend,
With new horizons which shall know no end.

 Epilogue

ALWAYS THERE COME BACK other, almost forgotten, memories. The diary is laid aside. Notes are filed away. Only sweet and tender remembrances remain stored in the mind.

We stand together at the edge of the wood, looking far away down into San Timoteo Canyon, where it merges and becomes one with the San Bernardino Valley—an indistinct blur on the horizon. The walk into Smiley Heights is over and done with. The shade of those mighty trees will enfold us no more.

Standing thus, his voice, that perfect organ of an altogether untrammeled thinker, soft and low, but perfectly clear, quotes a line out of Vergil. It is a line which every reader has encountered, which many have at the tip of the tongue.

"Forsan et haec olim meminisse juvabit."

Yes, we shall forever remember all these things.

Down the hill we came, listening as he sang song after song. Reluctance was in his steps, nostalgia in his voice. We had come by the highway home, and, lo, it was ended. So long ago it was that Sidney Cox remembered his singing "Blow the Man Down."

For the last glimpse backward we paused at the northern edge of the woods. There was the locked gate which had not prevented our entry. It no more could prevent our exit. We slipped through the fence and turned our faces resolutely homeward.

Our friend was going away, far away. But we would see him again. . . .

Today we stand at the edge of another wood. He has entered in as we have lingered at the gate, loathe to follow. Who shall say which it was, prescience or prophecy, he owned when he wished that those dark trees were not as 't were the merest mask of gloom, but stretched away into the edge of doom?

Has he discovered—what he so often wished to do here on earth—the secret of Lucretian infinity out there among the infinities? Is it, we wonder, infinity of extent though not of content? That something called Robert Frost who never loved a wall—has he reached the ultimate freedom where no walls are?

From his place of permanence we should like to fancy him looking back upon us and quoting himself in a final line:

> *I could give all to Time except—except*
> *What I myself have held. But why declare*
> *The things forbidden that while the Customs slept*
> *I have crossed to Safety with? For I am There*
> *And what I would not part with I have kept.*

 Appendix

Tinochtitlan

Changed is the scene; the peace
And regal splendor which
Once that city knew are gone,
And war now reigns upon
That throng, who but
A week ago were all
Intent on joy supreme.
Cries of the wounded break
The stillness of the night,
Or challenge of the guard.
The Spaniard many days
Besieged within the place,
Where kings did rule of old,
Now pressed by hunger by
The all-relentless foe
Looks for some channel of
Escape. The night is dark;
Black clouds obscure the sky—
A dead calm lies o'er all.

The heart of one is firm,
His mind is constant still,
To all, his word is law.
Cortes his plan hath made,
The time hath come. Each one
His chosen place now takes,
There waits the signal, that
Will start the long retreat.

The Flight

Anon the cry comes down the line,
The portals wide are swung,
A long dark line moves out the gate,
And now the flight's begun.

Aye, cautiously it moves at first,
As ship steered o'er the reef,
Looking for danger all unseen,
But which may bring to grief.

Straight for the causeway now they make,
The bridge is borne before.
'T is ta'en and placed across the flood,
And all go trooping o'er.

Yet ere the other side is reached,
Wafted along the wind,
The roaring of the snake-skin drum
Comes floating from behind.

And scarcely has its rolling ceased
Than out upon the lake,
Where all was silence just before,
A conch the calm doth break.

What terror to each heart it bears,
The sound of ill portent,

Each gunner to escape now looks,
On safety all are bent.

Forward they press in wild despair,
On to the next canal,
Held on all sides by foe and sea,
Like deer within corral.

Now surging this way, now in that,
The mass sways to and fro,
The infidel around it sweeps—
Slowly the night doth go.

A war cry soundeth through the night,
The 'tsin!' the 'tzin!' is there,
His plume nods wildly o'er the scene,
O, Spaniard, now beware!

With gaping jaws the cannon stands
Points it among the horde;
The valiant Leon waits beside,
Ready with match and sword.

The 'tzin' quick springeth to his side,
His mace he hurls on high,
It crasheth through the Spanish steel,
And Leon prone doth lie.

Falling he died beneath his gun—
He died at duty's call,
And many falling on that night,
Dying, so died they all.

The faithful guarders at the bridge,
Have worked with might and main,
Nor can they move it from its place,
Swollen by damp of rain.

On through the darkness comes the cry,

The cry that all is lost;
Then e'en Cortes takes up the shout,
And o'er the host 't is tossed.

Some place their safety in the stream,
But sink beneath the tide,
E'en others crossing on the dead,
Thus reach the other side.

Surrounded and alone he sits,
Upon his faithful steed;
Here Alvarado clears a space,
But none might share the deed—

For darkness of that murky night
Hides deeds of brightest fame,
Which in the ages yet to come,
Would light the hero's name.

His faithful charger now hath fall'n
Pierced to the very heart,
Quick steps he back, his war cry shouts
Then onward doth he dart.

Runs he, and leaping high in air,
Fixed doth he seem a space,
One instant and the deed is done,
He standeth face to face—

With those who on the other side
Their safety now have found.
The thirst for vengeance satisfied,
The Aztec wheels around.

So, as the sun climbs up the sky,
And shoots his dawning rays,
The foe, as parted by his dart,
Each go their sep'rate ways.

Upon the ground the dead men lie,
Trampled midst gold and gore,
The Aztec toward his temple goes,
And now the fight is o'er.

Follow we not the Spaniard more,
Wending o'er hill and plain,
Suffice to say he reached the coast,
Lost fortune to regain.

The flame shines brightest e'er goes out,
Thus with the Aztec throne,
On that dark night before the end,
So, o'er the fight it shone.

The Montezumas are no more,
Gone is their regal throne,
And freemen live, and rule, and die,
Where they have ruled alone.

'92

Lawrence High School *Bulletin*
April, 1890, pp. 1–2

Index